Ricardo's Macroeconomics

The outline of modern macroeconomics took shape in Britain in the early nineteenth century thanks, in part, to David Ricardo, the most influential economist of the time. Britain was challenged by monetary inflation, industrial unemployment, and the loss of jobs abroad. Ricardo pointed the way forward. As a financier and Member of Parliament, he was well versed in politics and commercial affairs. His expertise is seen in the practicality of his proposals, including the resumption of the gold standard, which was essential given the destabilizing policy of the Bank of England. Ricardo's expertise appears also in his debate with T. R. Malthus about whether an industrial economy can suffer a prolonged depression. Say's law of markets and the quantity theory of money figure prominently in his works, but not in an extreme form. He was instead a subtle theorist, recognizing, among other phenomena, the nonneutrality of money, trade depressions, and unemployment.

Timothy Davis has a Ph.D. in economics from the University of Toronto and a law degree from Oxford University. He is a practicing attorney and a member of the New York State Bar.

HISTORICAL PERSPECTIVES ON MODERN ECONOMICS

General Editor: Professor Craufurd D. Goodwin, Duke University

This series contains original works that challenge and enlighten historians of economics. For the profession as a whole, it promotes better understanding of the origin and content of modern economics.

Other books in the series:

Ricardo's Macroeconomics

Money, Trade Cycles, and Growth

TIMOTHY DAVIS

CAMBRIDGE
UNIVERSITY PRESS

CAMBRIDGE UNIVERSITY PRESS
Cambridge, New York, Melbourne, Madrid, Cape Town, Singapore,
São Paulo, Delhi, Dubai, Tokyo, Mexico City

Cambridge University Press
The Edinburgh Building, Cambridge CB2 8RU, UK

Published in the United States of America by Cambridge University Press, New York

www.cambridge.org
Information on this title: www.cambridge.org/9780521169271

First published 2005
First paperback edition 2010

A catalogue record for this publication is available from the British Library

Library of Congress Cataloguing in Publication Data

Davis, Timothy S., 1969–
Ricardo's macroeconomics : money, trade cycles and growth / Timothy S. Davis.
p. cm.
Includes bibliographical references and index.
ISBN 0-521-84474-6 (hardback)
1. Macroeconomics. 2. Ricardo, David, 1772–1823. I. Title.
HB172.5.D38   2005
339′.092 – dc22   2004020558

ISBN 978-0-521-84474-1 Hardback
ISBN 978-0-521-16927-1 Paperback

Contents

Appendices

A   The Bank of England

Acknowledgments

I am indebted to Sam and Perlette Hollander for the abundant hospitality they have shown me, first in Toronto and more recently in Israel. I must also thank Sam for reading the twelve drafts of my doctoral dissertation and for answering, over the past ten years, a stream of questions, both temporal and spiritual.

David Laidler has been wonderful. I took his course in the history of economics years ago. He later served as the external reader on my doctoral committee. As I finished this book, he provided valuable direction on points where I might otherwise have become mired. His help and good cheer have been encouraging throughout.

I extend thanks also to the three anonymous readers at Cambridge University Press who spent long hours reviewing multiple drafts of this book. They saved me from mistakes that had wholly eluded my attention.

Some paragraphs and tables in this book appeared in earlier publications. I appreciate the permission from Thomson Publishing Services to use excerpts from Timothy Davis (1999) "Ricardo's Use of Say's Law: The Case of the Post–Napoleonic War Depression," Chapter 16 in *Reflections on the Classical Cannon*, edited by Evelyn Forget. My thanks also go to the Taylor & Francis Group for permission to use excerpts from Timothy Davis (2002) "David Ricardo, Financier and Empirical Economist," *European Journal of the History of Economic Thought*, Vol. 9, No. 1, pages 1–16. The journal can be found on the Web at <http://www.tandf.co.uk>. I am grateful again to my friend Steven Kates and to Edward Elgar Publishing Ltd. for permission to use excerpts from Timothy Davis (2003) "The Historical Context of the General Glut Controversy," Chapter 8 in *Two Hundred Years of Say's Law: Essays on Economic Theory's Most Controversial Principle*, edited by Steven Kates.

In the Appendices are eleven tables that include data drawn from Brian Mitchell's book, *British Historical Statistics*, published in 1988 by Cambridge University Press. The data are used with permission.

ONE

Introduction

The desire of power in excess caused the angels to fall.[1] It has cast down a host of their creatures as well. With the Treaties of Tilsit in 1807, the Emperor of France gained dominion over Europe. The ancient monarchs became his servants, their treasures his treasures, and their armies subjugated to his command. One check remained to end of his ambition – the British navy – and behind it, the burgeoning commerce and institutions of law and government of a free and sanguine people. To these and to their annihilation, the emperor's thoughts turned. He intensified the campaign to undermine Britain's commerce and thus her means of financing the war effort, and sought to build a comparable fleet. If the strategy succeeded, invasion was inevitable. On the opposite side, Britain fought to maintain her trade with the Continent while funding resistance in Portugal, Spain, Austria, Russia, and the Mediterranean, which sapped the emperor's resources.

The Napoleonic Wars proved a watershed in the development of economic theory because of the extreme conditions created by the conflict. Under the Continental System, Britain was cut off, partly, from foreign supplies and British farmers resorted to land of poorer quality to feed the country's growing population.[2] The rise in production costs associated with the extension of cultivation led to the discovery of the law of diminishing returns to variable inputs (labor and capital) given a fixed input (land). Similarly, after the Continental System collapsed, economists

---

[1] From Francis Bacon's essay "Of Goodness and Goodness of Nature."

[2] My comments about the Continental System and Britain's response to that system are based on Heckscher (1922).

1

noticed an inverse relationship between imports and prices that suggested a downward-sloping demand schedule. With respect to macroeconomic theory, Britain's war finance – which required the suspension of the gold standard during the war and its resumption afterward – proved crucial to the progress of monetary theory. Also, the periodic crises of the post-war years prompted much study of the law of markets and of the fiscal response to unemployment and stagnation. I begin with a discussion of monetary theory and policy.

At the height of the Napoleonic Wars, Parliament was spending £100 million annually – one-third of national income. The government at first tried to fund the war through taxes, but that proved impossible. In the end, the campaign was financed by several hundred million in long-term bonds, with sales of Exchequer bills and advances from the Bank of England smoothing cash flows over short periods. The Bank played a central role in the war effort. This required the sacrifice of its financial interests more than once to Brittania's cause.

Extending credit to the government interfered with the Bank's ability to manage the circulation of its notes. Loans to the government early in the war prevented the Bank from checking the inflation of the 1790s; this led to the loss of its treasure and to the suspension of cash payments.[3] The directors of the Bank protested but could not refuse ministers who granted the Bank's charter and who protected its monopoly powers. After the initial bout of wartime inflation, prices receded and the gold standard came again within reach. But, just as events favored a return to cash payments, the Spanish uprising triggered a second round of inflation.

Spain's revolt against Bonaparte opened the Iberian peninsula to British soldiers and the markets of South America to British trade. The Bank was active in what followed on both fronts. The annual average of discounts given by the Bank to merchants, manufactures, and traders increased by £2 million in 1809, then surged another £5 million in 1810,

---

[3] Notes of the Bank of England were convertible into gold and/or silver prior to 1797. This meant that a person holding a banknote had the right to exchange it for gold or silver at the Bank at a fixed rate. During the inflation of the 1790s the market price of gold surpassed the price at which the Bank was obliged to sell gold. It became profitable for anyone holding a banknote to trade it for gold at the Bank and to immediately resell the gold in the market. Millions in notes returned to the Bank, depleting its hoard. To avoid default, the Bank appealed to Parliament for the right to stop cash payments – that is, for the right to stop exchanging its notes for gold or silver. In 1797, by an Order in Council, the government allowed the Bank to suspend cash payments. From 1797 to 1820, the Bank was not legally obliged to exchange its notes for gold; this interval is termed the "Restriction period."

reaching £20 million.[4] At the same time, the British government looked to the Bank to finance the Peninsular campaign. This set off a fiscal moil in London because the campaign was expensive,[5] the limits of taxation had been reached,[6] and ministers feared that further loans would depress bond prices. The government's official position, stated at the annual presentation of the national budget, was that public finances were robust and the supply of funds for the war effort was abundant (12 May 1809, *Hansard* 1s 14:531–535; 16 May 1810, *Hansard* 1s 16:1044–1048). However, private correspondence between Spencer Perceval, Chancellor of the Exchequer, and the Bank reveals that the government urgently needed assistance.[7] The Bank upheld its duty: it provided the government direct loans and purchased securities in the market.[8] Its directors never refused the Chancellor, but only because they feared what would happen if the nation's finances collapsed. On 7 March 1811, the Bank informed Perceval that further advances to the government would be conditioned on the government's repurchasing large sums of Exchequer bills. To this, Perceval replied:

I regret that I have not found it in my power to reduce the amount of Exchequer Bills in the hands of the Bank. . . . The urgency of the public service [make it

---

[4] The discounts of 1810 were not as inflationary as they appear. The South American trade collapsed in the spring of 1810. The *Minutes* of the Bank Court for that year are filled with pleas from merchants asking for extensions of time to pay. An average delay of two weeks by the Bank's clients in repaying their debts accounted for the increase in the volume of discounts.

[5] The initial phases of the campaign caused the army's budget to rise from £24 million to £29 million annually. At the end of the war the army's budget swelled to £50 million (Mitchell 1988, 587). The navy incurred increasing costs to protect merchant ships from French, Danish, and, later, American privateers.

[6] See the comments by the Chancellor of the Exchequer and by William Huskisson in the debate in Parliament on the Budget of 1810 (16 May 1810, *Hansard* 1s, 16:1052–1054). According to Huskisson, "What he had said was, that it would be difficult to find new taxes which would not be extremely objectionable – that there was a limit to taxation – and that we had nearly reached that limit."

[7] The Chancellor of the Exchequer asked the Bank to purchase public securities in the market – £2 million at a time – on 29 June 1809, 28 Sept. 1809, 21 Dec. 1809 and 29 Mar. 1810. On 15 Feb. 1810, the government obtained also an advance from the Bank of £3 million (Bank of England, *Minutes of the Court of Directors*, G4/33, 66–67, 128–129, 181–182, 217–218, 254).

[8] The Bank's assistance to the government began to increase in 1807. The combined value of public securities held by the Bank and advances to the government stood at £13,665,339 in Aug. 1807; £15,677,539 in Aug. 1808; £16,009,339 in Aug. 1809; and £17,689,739 in Aug. 1810. By the end of the war, the Bank held £35 million in government securities (House of Commons, *Second Report from the Secret Committee on the Expediency of the Bank Resuming Cash Payments*, 1819, App. 3, House of Commons, *Report from the Committee of Secrecy on the Bank of England Charter*, 1832, App. 5).

impossible].... I will endeavor as much as the circumstances of the public service may permit to diminish or keep down the advances of the Bank; and I trust that with this assurance, the Court of Directors will waive any express condition and consent in the usual manner to accommodate the public (Bank of England, *Minutes of the Court of Directors*, 23 May 1811, Document G4/34, 63–65).

The Court of Directors agreed, granting the government an additional £2 million, but with the demur that "were it not from an apprehension that the public service would be seriously impeded, the application could not be acceded to" (Bank of England, *Minutes of the Court of Directors*, 23 May 1811, Document G4/34, 66).

A sustained rise in the circulation of banknotes began in the fall of 1808.[9] Signs of inflation soon appeared: a rise in the market price of gold and a fall of the pound sterling on the foreign exchange. Gold was selling close to its Mint price early in 1808.[10] But toward the end of the year its price suddenly advanced and by April 1809, gold was selling at £4 12s. per ounce.[11] The change represented a fall of sterling by about 19 percent, vis-à-vis its former standard. The pound fell similarly against foreign currencies. There was no true par of the exchange given that the relative price of gold to silver fluctuated. But, based on the amounts of gold and silver in English and foreign coins, the pound should have traded in the range of £1 to 25 francs in Paris and £1 to 35 Flemish shillings in Hamburg. By the summer of 1809, however, the pound traded at £1 to 20 francs in Paris and £1 to 28 Flemish shillings in Hamburg[12] – a fall of 20 percent.

Hundreds of pamphlets and articles appeared, purporting to identify the causes of these events and advising Parliament how to respond. In retrospect, the episode has been termed the "Bullion Controversy." At the height of the controversy, an anonymous letter restating arguments critical of the Bank of England appeared in the *Morning Chronicle*.[13] It

---

[9] The Bank's circulation increased from £17,365,266 in Aug. 1808 to £24,446,175 in Aug. 1810 (House of Commons, *Second Report from the Secret Committee on the Expediency of the Bank Resuming Cash Payments*, 1819, App. 10).

[10] After the Bank restriction began in 1797, the market price of gold remained at the Mint price (£3 17s. 10$^{1/2}$d.) for two years. From 1799 to 1801 the market price of gold increased about 10%; it then gradually declined toward the Mint price.

[11] House of Commons, *Report from the Select Committee on the High Price of Gold Bullion*, 1810, p. 1.

[12] House of Commons, *Report from the Select Committee on the High Price of Gold Bullion*, 1810, App. 58, 59, and 60.

[13] An article titled "The Price of Gold," published in the *Morning Chronicle* on 29 Aug. 1809.

was followed by two more letters to the *Chronicle* and then by a pamphlet, *The High Price of Bullion*, published under the author's name: David Ricardo. The pamphlet was an immediate success and sold four editions. It marked the beginning of Ricardo's career as a public figure and of his contribution to economics.

Ricardo was not an academic. He was a financier and politician. His preoccupation with the business and politics of London is reflected in that his published works deal almost exclusively with immediate national concerns: the monetary policy of the Bank of England, the causes of unemployment and depressions in trade, and the effect of the corn laws on economic growth and on the distribution of income. Within his analyses of macro issues Ricardo applied a number of theories for which he is now famous in undergraduate textbooks: the idea that comparative advantage is the basis for international trade; the labor theory of value; the quantity theory of money; some form of Say's law; the concept of diminishing returns; and "Ricardian equivalence," which is the conjecture that public debt and taxes have equivalent effects on consumer behavior. For pedagogic purposes, textbooks address these theories separately and in the abstract. But Ricardo did not develop his theories as isolated, abstract concepts. They were instead components of larger models he applied to contemporary debates about monetary, fiscal, and agricultural policy.

Monetary Theory and Policy

The Bullion Controversy, during the course of which Ricardo came to prominence, concerned the extent to which the Bank of England was responsible for wartime inflation. Bullionists interpreted the premium on gold and the fall of sterling on the foreign exchange as evidence that the notes of the Bank of England were depreciated. Subject to minor qualifications, the premium on gold was also interpreted to measure the extent to which banknotes had been issued in excess. Thus, when the market price of gold was £4 12s. per ounce, Bullionists anticipated that the Bank would have to curb its circulation 20 percent to restore the currency to par. Because of their concern with inflation, Bullionists endorsed the gold standard. Tying banknotes to gold, they believed, would prevent the Bank from issuing its notes in excess, and that would put a stop to inflation.

Antibullionists defended the Bank. They attributed the premium on gold and the fall of sterling to causes beyond the Bank's control, among these that sterling had fallen because of subsidies paid to Britain's allies and because of the costs of foreign military operations; that sterling had fallen because of large importations of foreign corn; and that the rise in gold and the fall of sterling resulted from too great a circulation of country-bank notes. Antibullionists based their position on the Real Bills Doctrine. The doctrine arose from a misinterpretation of a passage in Adam Smith's *Wealth of Nations*.[14] The passage says nothing about the management of an inconvertible currency. Smith merely observed that prudent bankers discounted bills of exchange backed by collateral such as actual goods in process. Smith understood that without the check of convertibility, an excess issue of banknotes was possible (Smith 1776, 354–356). For, whenever the market rate of profit surpassed the rate of interest – then a maximum 5 percent under the usury laws – the demand for discounts was potentially unlimited. If the Bank indulged this demand, spiraling inflation was inevitable inasmuch as inflation would raise the nominal rate of profit, leading to ever greater demands for discounts, which, in turn, would expand the money supply, causing further inflation.

Despite the difficulties of the Real Bills Doctrine,[15] it was central to the position of the Antibullionists. The doctrine implied that the Bank of England could never overextend its circulation so long as it only discounted bills of exchange that represented actual commodities or goods in process. It thus lent credibility to the Bank's management of the money supply and became for that body a sort of mantra until the 1820s.[16]

Bullionists relied on the quantity theory of money. The quantity theory describes the relationship between the supply of money (M) and the level

[14] "When a bank discounts to a merchant a real bill of exchange drawn by a real creditor upon a real debtor, and which, as soon as it becomes due, is really paid by that debtor; it only advances to him a part of the value which he would otherwise be obliged to keep by him unemployed and in ready money for answering occasional demands" (Smith 1776, 331).

[15] The Real Bills Doctrine relied on a number of fallacies. The first, just mentioned, was the failure to recognize that there would be an unlimited demand for bills whenever the market rate of profit exceeded the discount rate. Second, the doctrine did not distinguish between credit and credit instruments and so failed to account for credit instruments forming part of the circulating medium. Finally, the distinction between real and fictitious bills was spurious because the length of time a bill was discounted did not correspond to the time that goods were in process (Laidler 1987, 4:635).

[16] Not all directors of the Bank were Antibullionists. However, the Bank's official position, both toward the Select Committee on the High Price of Gold Bullion (1810) and toward the House of Commons Secret Committee on the Expediency of the Bank Resuming Cash Payments (1819), was that the price of gold and the value of sterling on the foreign exchanges fluctuated independently of the Bank's control (Horsefield 1949, 442–448).

of prices (P). Given the volume of trade (T) and the velocity of money (V), this relationship is summarized by the following equations of exchange:

$$M \times V = P \times T \quad \text{or} \quad P = (V/T) \times M$$

The right-hand equation shows that the price level, at any given time, is proportionate to the supply of money. This much was not controversial. What concerned classical economists was whether inflation was always and everywhere a monetary phenomenon.[17] In other words, was there a stable proportionate relationship between money and prices such that fluctuations in the money supply were the key determinant of changes in prices? A subordinate point of contention concerned how the price level, and thus inflation, should be measured.

For Bullionists, the market prices of gold and silver and the value of sterling on the foreign exchange served as proxies for the price level. They interpreted a premium on gold or silver or a fall of sterling on the exchange as signs of inflation (Viner 1937, 125–128). The extent of the premium was also assumed to measure – approximately – the extent to which the Bank of England issued its notes in excess. The measure was only approximate because, as the more subtle theorists understood, the velocity of money was likely to rise in an inflationary boom. And this rise would contribute to a rise in prices more than proportionate to the increase of the money supply. Thus the standard measures of inflation would overstate the excess circulation of the Bank's notes.[18] There was a second qualification: the price of gold and the foreign exchange were affected by the activities of country banks. Country-bank notes were convertible into notes of the Bank of England so there was ultimately some check to their value. However, country banks were not constrained by a fixed reserve requirement. They were thus vested with the ability to cause inflation by expanding credit too rapidly; or, in a financial panic, the country banks were likely to cause deflation by suddenly withdrawing credit. The variations of the country circulation, which were often extreme, affected prices independently of the policies of the Bank of England.[19] A third qualification was that gold and silver were commodities that fluctuated in value for reasons

---

[17] Friedman 1987, 3–20; see also Laidler 1991b.

[18] Ricardo knew velocity is not constant: the value of the money supply as compared with the commodities which it circulates "depends upon the rapidity of circulation, upon the degree of confidence and credit existing between traders, and above all, on the judicious operations of banking" (Ricardo, 3:90).

[19] In the long term, Ricardo thought that the country circulation was rigidly proportionate to the circulation of the Bank of England (3:88) but this did not preclude short-term

not connected with the money supply. Wars, the discovery of mines, and the policies of foreign governments all affected the value of metals. Lastly, wartime remittances or sudden changes in the level of international trade were likely to affect the foreign exchange. The investigation of this final point proved of lasting significance to monetary theory.

At the outset of the Bullion Controversy, there was no coherent analysis of how the balance of international trade adjusted to certain disturbing factors; the principal disturbances were (1) subsidies to foreign powers, (2) the importation of grain upon a failure of the domestic harvest, and (3) an excessive rise in the circulation of Bank of England notes. David Hume described how an increase in the domestic money supply – comprised wholly of specie – would trigger inflation in the home market. With inflation, imported goods would seem relatively cheaper at home and British exports would seem exorbitant abroad. He reasoned that the disparity in prices between the home and foreign markets would cause a trade deficit that would be funded by an outflow of specie, the international movement of which would gradually raise prices abroad while lowering prices domestically (Hume 1752, 3:333). Hume did not explain why gold – a commodity also rising in price – would be exported in preference to other commodities. He also provided no analysis of the effects of inflation when the money supply consisted of inconvertible paper.

Adam Smith did not improve on the specie-flow theory. In fact, experts debate whether he even accepted it.[20] His formal analysis of an exogenous increase in paper money was less sophisticated than Hume's, being only a physical analogy to water overfilling a channel: when paper money circulates in excess, coin leaves the country till the excess is eliminated.[21] His thoughts were more subtle elsewhere. He allowed that the international movement of bullion is regulated by its supply, relative

---

variations (3:86–88, 231). For a discussion of the role of country banknotes in the currency, see Fetter 1965, 48–51.

[20] Hollander (1973, 205) reviews the debate about whether Smith used the specie-flow theory.

[21] "The channel of circulation, if I may be allowed such an expression, will remain precisely the same as before. One million we have supposed sufficient to fill that channel. Whatever, therefore, is poured into it beyond this sum, cannot run in it, but must overflow. . . . But though this sum cannot be employed at home, it is too valuable to be allowed to lie idle. It will, therefore, be sent abroad, in order to seek that profitable employment which it cannot find at home. . . . But though so great a quantity of gold and silver is thus sent abroad, we must not imagine that it is sent abroad for nothing, or that its proprietors make a present of it to foreign nations. They will exchange it for foreign goods of some kind or another" (Smith 1776, 318–319).

to the effectual demand, at home and abroad.[22] He also understood that variations in foreign exchange rates affect the balance of trade and thus the international movement of gold and silver.[23]

Ricardo's contribution to the study of the balance of international indebtedness lay in describing how inflation would lead to the export of bullion when the money supply in the home market consisted of specie and/or convertible paper. Ricardo described the mechanism of international debt adjustment and other aspects of the Bullionists' position in the *High Price of Bullion* (1810) and the *Reply to Bosanquet* (1811). Both works attribute the rise in the domestic price of gold and the fall of sterling on the foreign exchange to the wartime monetary policy of the Bank of England. Consonant with the quantity theory,[24] the pamphlets show an inversely proportionate relationship between the circulation of banknotes and the value of sterling on the foreign exchange, and a proportionate relationship between the circulation of banknotes and the price of gold.

Ricardo's account of the mechanism of international debt adjustment begins with Hume's theory of a commodity money system (*High Price*, Ricardo, 3:54). The account proceeds to consider the mechanism when the circulation consists of (1) specie and convertible paper, (2) specie and inconvertible paper, and (3) convertible paper alone. Under each monetary arrangement, an excessive issue of coin or banknotes leads to an unfavorable balance of trade and to the export of bullion. Ricardo envisioned the process as follows. An expansion of the money supply lowers the rate of interest. The fall of interest stimulates demand in all markets and thereby raises prices. As prices rise, the demand for loanable funds increases until such time as interest rates return to normal levels.

---

[22] "When the quantity of gold and silver imported into any country exceeds the effectual demand, no vigilance of government can prevent its exportation ... If, on the contrary, in any particular country their quantity fell short of the effectual demand, so as to raise their price above that of the neighbouring countries, the government would have no occasion to take any pains to import them" (Smith 1776, 463).

[23] Smith described the consequences of a fall of sterling on the foreign exchange: "The high price of exchange ... must necessarily have operated as a tax, in raising the price of foreign goods, and thereby diminishing their consumption. It would tend, therefore, not to increase, but to diminish, what they called, the unfavourable balance of trade, and consequently the exportation of gold and silver" (Smith 1776, 461).

[24] Ricardo was acquainted with the quantity theory in the form $M \times V = P \times T$. In the *Notes on Bentham* he wrote: "May we not as before put the mass of commodities of all sorts on one side of the line, – and the amount of money multiplied by the rapidity of its circulation on the other. Is not this in all cases the regulator of prices?" (3:311).

[I]f the Bank were to bring a large additional sum of notes into the market, and offer them on loan ... they would for a time affect the rate of interest. ... If the amount were large, the Bank ... might not be able to lend the notes or the money at four, nor perhaps, above three per cent.; but having done so, neither the notes, nor the money, would be retained unemployed by the borrowers; they would be sent into every market, and would every where raise the prices of commodities, till they were absorbed in the general circulation. It is only during the interval of the issues of the Bank, and their effect on prices, that we should be sensible of an abundance of money; interest would, during that interval, be under its natural level; but as soon as the additional sum of notes or of money became absorbed in the general circulation, the rate of interest would be as high, and new loans would be demanded with as much eagerness as before the additional issue (*High Price*, Ricardo, 3:91).

To the extent that monetary inflation raises the market price of gold above the face value of coins, it becomes profitable to melt coins and to sell the bullion.[25] A similar result obtains if the currency consists of convertible paper alone; a rise in the market price of gold provides the incentive to return notes to the Bank in exchange for bullion, which is then sold.[26] The end result under a system of either commodity money or convertible paper is that the market supply of bullion increases. The rise in the supply of bullion reduces its value relative to all other commodities, making it the least expensive commodity to export in exchange for foreign goods.[27] The fall in the relative value of bullion thus leads to a trade deficit:

The effect of an increased issue of paper would be to throw out of circulation an equal amount of specie; but this could not be done without adding to the quantity of bullion in the market, and thereby lowering its value, or in other words, increasing the bullion price of commodities. It is only in consequence of this fall in the value of the metallic currency, and of bullion, that the temptation to export them

[25] "Would not the coin be melted and sold as bullion at home, till the value of bullion had so much diminished in its relative value to the bullion of other countries, and therefore to the relative value of commodities here, as to pay the expenses of transportation" (*Reply to Bosanquet*, Ricardo, 3:212).

[26] "The excess [notes] would be immediately returned to them for specie; because our currency, being thereby diminished in value, could be advantageously exported, and could not be retained in our circulation ... but if the Bank ... continued to re-issue the returned notes, the stimulus which a redundant currency first gave to the exportation of coin would be again renewed with similar effects" (3:57–59).

[27] Marcuzzo and Rosselli (1994) represent the condition for the export of bullion by this expression: $P_{\text{gold}}(1 + T_{\text{gold}})/P_{\text{gold}}^* \leq P_i(1 + T_i)/P_i^*$ for all tradeable commodities $i = 1, \ldots, n$; where P_{gold} is the domestic price of gold; T_{gold} is the transportation cost of shipping gold abroad as a percentage of the price; P_{gold}^* is the foreign price of gold; P_i is the domestic price of commodity (i); T_i is the transportation cost of shipping commodity (i) abroad as a percentage of the price; and P_i^* is the foreign price of commodity (i).

arises.... But exporting of bullion is synonymous with an unfavourable balance of trade (*High Price*, Ricardo, 3:64).

The process of melting coins, converting notes to bullion, and exporting bullion continues until the money supply contracts sufficiently to bring the market price of bullion to par. Once the price of bullion returns to par, there is no longer an incentive to melt coins or to convert notes. Thus there are no further additions of bullion to the market that act to depress its value relative to other commodities.

The consequences of an excess circulation are markedly different when the money supply consists only of inconvertible paper. In this situation, an increase in the money supply raises the prices of all commodities – including bullion – but there are no coins to melt and gold cannot be withdrawn from the Bank. The supply of bullion remains unchanged. Its price relative to other commodities does not fall, so there is no incentive to export gold in preference to other commodities.[28] Instead, the value of sterling falls on the foreign exchange, which brings about an equilibrium in the demand for and supply of foreign bills.

A natural extension of the study of international debt adjustment would be to distinguish a fall in the value of sterling on the foreign exchange that results from an excess circulation of paper money from that resulting from nonmonetary causes such as foreign remittances or corn imports. Ricardo never undertook the study. From his point of view, it did not matter, because he defined "excessive" and "redundant" in circular terms – any fall of the foreign exchange regardless of the cause was evidence of an "excessive" and "redundant" currency.

Mr. Thornton[29] ... supposes that a very unfavourable balance of trade may be occasioned to this country by a bad harvest, and the consequent importation of corn; and that there may be at the same time an unwillingness in the country, to which we are indebted, to receive our goods in payment; the balance due to the foreign country must therefore be paid [in gold coin].... If we consent to give coin in exchange for goods, it must be from choice, not necessity. We should not import

---

[28] "When the circulation consists wholly of paper, any increase in its quantity will raise the money price of bullion without lowering its value" because the money prices of other commodities rise in the same proportion (*High Price*, 3:64).

[29] Henry Thornton was among the foremost monetary theorists of the nineteenth century, famous for *The Paper Credit of Great Britain* (1802). Along with his brothers, and their cousins the Wilberforces, Thornton is also renowned for winning the abolition of the slave trade in 1809, for promoting popular literacy – to which end they established Sunday Schools – and for financing Christian missionary endeavors including the British and Foreign Bible Society.

more goods than we export, unless we had a redundancy of currency (*High Price*, Ricardo, 3:59–61).

If, which is a much stronger case, we agreed to pay a subsidy to a foreign power, money would not be exported whilst there were any goods which could more cheaply discharge the payment... Thus then specie will be sent abroad to discharge a debt only when it is superabundant; only when it is the cheapest exportable commodity (3:63).

Ricardo disagreed with Thornton's analysis of foreign exchange markets as expressed in *The Paper Credit of Great Britain* (1802). Thornton attributed the fall of sterling in 1802 to high wartime expenditures, high taxes, and the failure of successive harvests, which necessitated vast importations of corn. His analysis coincided with actual conditions. The harvests of 1799 and 1800 failed, driving wheat prices to more than 150 s. per quarter. There were also sharp increases in taxes as Prime Minister Pitt, convinced of the necessity of financing the war through taxes, proposed a triple assessment – a trebling of sales taxes on common articles of consumption. Ricardo never disputed that nonmonetary factors altered exchange rates over short periods. He allowed that a deficient harvest, foreign subsidies, the foreign expenditures of the British government, and even "a change of taste in one country for the commodities of the other" could, for a time, cause an unfavorable exchange (6:39, 73–74, 89).[30] What Ricardo rejected in *High Price* was the notion that sterling could fall 20 percent on the foreign exchange because of nonmonetary causes: "Mr. Thornton has told us that an unfavourable trade will account for an unfavourable exchange.... That limit is probably four or 5 percent. This will not account for a depreciation of fifteen or 20 percent" (3:83).

By 1811, sterling traded 20 percent below par. The foreign exchange had been falling for three years coincident with a well-documented and dramatic increase in the money supply. There was no famine; there had been no change in taxes; and foreign remittances were stable. Ricardo thought the fall of sterling could "be accounted for only by the depreciation of the circulating medium" (3:83). Accordingly, *High Price* proposes "two unerring tests" by which to identify monetary inflation: the

---

[30] Another statement of his position appears in a letter to John Broadley: "by exchange we always mean the price of the currency of one country estimated in the currency of another.... What may be the cause of a high or low exchange is another question. Subsidies, bad crops, unprosperous commerce may disturb the equilibrium of exports and imports, and produce powerful effects on the exchange, within its natural limits, but they do so only by affecting the relative value, or price of currency" (Ricardo, 7:43).

"rate of exchange and the price of bullion" (3:75).[31] Given the circumstances of 1811, Thornton agreed that the foreign exchange could not be depressed for a long period apart from monetary forces. He described before Parliament "that dangerous doctrine" according to which an unfavorable foreign exchange "was no indication of an excess of paper or of a depreciation of it, but was simply an evidence of an unfavourable balance of trade. . . . It was an error to which he himself had once inclined, but he had stood corrected after a fuller consideration of the subject" (13 May 1811, *Hansard* 1s, 20:84).

Ricardo and Thornton agreed on other monetary topics, the most important of which was the need for discretionary management of the money supply. Ricardo's pamphlets *Economical and Secure Currency* (1816) and *Plan for a National Bank* (1824) are much concerned with the effects of monetary policy on economic activity. As a financier, he understood intimately the short-term effects of monetary policy on interest rates and thus on Britain's merchants and manufactures. Too restricted a circulation of banknotes might cause "considerable distress and difficulty to the mercantile classes."[32] Interest rates and the supply of credit would eventually return to normal levels, but during the adjustment process "the prices of commodities would fall, and great distress would be suffered."[33] Because he recognized the real effects of monetary policy, Ricardo did not want the central bank fettered in its management of the currency. He considered and rejected the system adopted by the banks of Amsterdam and Hamburg, whereby the variations of a paper currency mimicked the fluctuations of a fully metallic circulation. The security of the Amsterdam system could be acquired by restoring convertibility, but it was not necessary to impose a 100 percent marginal bullion reserve:

The plan here proposed appears to me to unite all the advantages of every system of banking which has been hitherto adopted in Europe. It is in some of its features similar to the banks of deposit of Amsterdam and Hamburgh . . . but in the foreign banks of deposit, they have actually in their coffers, as much bullion, as there are credits for bank money in their books; accordingly there is an inactive capital as great as the whole amount of the commercial circulation. In our Bank, however, there would be an amount of bank money, under the name of bank-notes, as great as the demands of commerce could require. . . . The amount of the circulation

---

[31] The price of bullion is the better measure of inflation. Ricardo describes the foreign exchange as "a tolerably accurate criterion by which we may judge of the debasement of the currency" (3:72).

[32] Letter from Ricardo to Tierney dated 11 Dec. 1811 (6:67).

[33] Parliamentary speech by Ricardo on 12 June 1822 (5:199–200).

would be adjusted to the wants of commerce with the greatest precision (*High Price*, Ricardo, 3:126–127).

The austere policies of the banks of Amsterdam and Hamburg contrasted with the free-wheeling trade of the Bank of England. The Old Lady of Threadneedle was a private institution having a monopoly on the right to issue banknotes in the City of London and within a 60-mile radius. With an eye always to profits, and unfettered by convertibility, the Bank conducted a procyclical policy; that is, its policies made the fluctuations of the business cycle more extreme. The Bank extended credit liberally in prosperous times, causing inflation. Yet during financial crises, it did just the opposite. The Bank reduced its trade bills and notes under discount from £19.1 million to £6.5 million during the depression of 1816. In the panic of 1793, and again in 1825, the Bank refused all credit. When pressed by members of Parliament, the Bank's directors rejected outright and repeatedly a role for the Bank as lender of last resort, and instead looked to the Exchequer for support.

In *Secure Currency* and *National Bank*, Ricardo recommended policies to limit the harm caused by the Bank's management of the money supply. *Secure Currency* argued for the superiority of a paper currency, convertible into gold or silver, over other monetary arrangements. The message resonated among opponents of the Bank and won for Ricardo entrance to the inner circle of the Whig Party where he was instrumental in shaping the debate that led to the Resumption Act of 1819. The act largely followed his recommendations. It required the Bank to pay its notes in gold ingots at the ancient par, but gave the Bank two years to effect the change, sufficient time to amass a hoard of bullion and to raise the value of its notes (through deflation) by about 4 percent. Some authors infer that Ricardo disregarded the real effects of monetary policy because he endorsed resumption during the year 1819, a year which saw the collapse of Britain's foreign trade and manufactures brought to a standstill.[34] The criticism assumes that Britain was in the midst of a long-term depression at the time resumption passed the House, that the Act of 1819 required immediate deflation, and that the alternative to the gold standard was the continued, prudent management of inconvertible paper by the Bank of England. In actual fact, the crises of 1819 were not part of a long-term

---

[34] "Ricardo seemed oblivious to the influence of monetary policy and of price changes on economic conditions" and testified before the Commons Committee on Resumption that monetary deflation of 5 percent was "not very formidable" (Fetter 1964, xiii–xiv).

depression, resumption did not require immediate deflation, and there were no tolerable alternatives to the gold standard.

Ricardo began his last pamphlet, *Plan for a National Bank*, in 1823. By this point the Bank had returned to gold, but there was lingering resentment in Parliament and in the City against that body because it so badly handled the process. Ricardo concluded that the directors of the Bank were unfit to manage the currency. Thus, not surprisingly, the central theme of *National Bank* is that issuing banknotes and providing credit are distinct and separable functions, and that the first of these would be managed better by national commissioners than by the Bank. As it turned out, no national commissioners were appointed; but following the concepts put forth in *National Bank*, the Bank Charter Act of 1844 split the Bank of England into an Issue Department, which supplied banknotes, and a Banking Department, which accepted deposits and extended loans.

The Bank Charter Act was the culmination of a controversy known as the Currency School/Banking School debate. The central issue of the debate was whether the Bank of England should have discretionary management of the money supply. (By 1844, the contentious point of the Bullion Controversy – convertibility – was no longer at issue.) The Currency School rejected discretion; they advocated a paper currency the variations of which would mimic the fluctuations of a fully metallic circulation. The Currency position appealed to the Bank because it was eager to divest itself of the duty of managing the money supply. In January 1844, the Governor and Deputy Governor of the Bank, William Cotton and J. B. Heath, submitted to Prime Minister Peel the terms that would become the 1844 Bank Charter Act (Horsefield 1944, 180–189). From the Bank's perspective, it was essential that the Issue Department maintain a 100-percent marginal bullion reserve because this stripped the Bank of all scope for discretion. Its circulation could only increase (or decrease) if private citizens brought gold to the Bank (or demanded its withdrawal), thus permitting the Issue Department to be completely passive. The split between the Issue and Banking Departments ultimately proved untenable as the Banking Department was pushed to the verge of collapse with every financial panic, while the bullion reserve at the Issue Department remained untouched.[35] But that is beside the point. What matters is the

---

[35] For example, in the crisis of 1847, the reserves of the Banking Department, measured in notes and coin, fell to £1,606,124 against deposits of £13,607,474. At the same time, the Issue Department had £8,121,695 in gold and silver locked up and inaccessible because

assumption, frequently made in the secondary literature, that because the 1844 Bank Charter Act adopted the distinction between issuing bank-notes and extending credit outlined in *National Bank* that the Act of 1844 incorporated all aspects of Ricardo's monetary policy. It did not.

Depending on an author's interpretation of *High Price, Secure Currency*, the Resumption Act, and *National Bank*, Ricardo is usually assigned to one of two categories. Either he is an extreme Bullionist, a doctrinal father of the Currency School and an opponent of discretionary monetary policy, or he is a moderate Bullionist who – unlike the Currency School – recognized the need for discretion. In précis of the history of economics, Ricardo usually winds up in the first category, whereas his friend Henry Thornton lands in the second.

The literature identifies an extreme Bullionist theory according to which the price level – as measured by the price of gold and the foreign exchange – is rigidly proportionate to changes in the circulation of Bank of England notes. The proposition implies a simplistic version of the quantity theory characterized by a constant velocity of circulation and the neutrality of money (Schumpeter 1954, 703, 724). No independent role is accorded the country banks. Moreover, the effects of foreign remittances and the importations of corn on the foreign exchange are ignored (Viner 1937, 139).[36] Because *Paper Credit* lists several factors that affect exchange rates, whereas *High Price* emphasizes only one, many authors infer that Ricardo was an extreme Bullionist.

Hicks developed the inference as follows: Ricardo claimed that only an increase in the money supply could affect the price of bullion and the foreign exchange. This shows that he used a metallic money model, and that he failed to recognize the role of credit. Thornton, by contrast, understood the workings of a credit system, and in particular he understood that "real causes have monetary effects." For this reason, Thornton recommended that Britain's monetary system be managed by a central bank "whose operations must be determined by judgement, and cannot be reduced to procedure by a mechanical rule." Ricardo reached different conclusions about monetary policy because his model was too simplistic: "Thornton does believe in the necessity of monetary management; on

of the 100-percent marginal reserve requirement (House of Commons, *Report from the Select Committee on Bank Acts, Part II: Appendix and Index*, 1857, App. 12). For an account of the crisis, see Fetter 1965, 208–210.

[36] The extreme Bullionist position uses a strict version of the quantity theory characterized by a constant velocity of circulation, a dichotomy between the real and monetary sectors, and rigid proportionality between the money supply and the price level.

that crucial matter he is on the same side as Keynes – on the opposite side from Ricardo" (Hicks 1967, 165–166).[37]

Fetter sees a continuous line from the monetary model of Ricardo's *High Price* to the 1844 Bank Charter Act. He infers that Ricardo and Thornton differed across the entire gamut of monetary theory and policy because Ricardo attributed the depreciation of sterling in 1811 to an excessive issue of paper money:

> What Ricardo did, in the heat of controversy over the credit policy of the Bank of England, was to strip from existing theory Thornton's refinements on Hume and come up with a simplistic proposition that had a tough cutting edge in the polemics of the day: depreciation of English money on the foreign exchanges was entirely the result of the expansion of the note issues of the Bank of England. This was not the theory of Henry Thornton, it was not the theory of the Bullion Report.... Ricardo was the doctrinal father of the Currency Principle that wished to tie changes in the currency supply to changes in the specie holdings of the Bank of England; whereas Henry Thornton, and the Bullion Report of which he was a coauthor, anticipated much of the Banking Principle in their recognition of the need for discretionary action by the Bank of England (Fetter 1969, 74–75).[38]

Viner associates Ricardo with the standard Bullionist position insofar as he believed that "a circulation exceeding in amount what, under otherwise like conditions, could have been maintained under a metallic standard, was in excess" (Viner 1937, 125–127). With respect to the causes of an unfavorable foreign exchange and the export of bullion, however,

---

[37] Other authors reach similar conclusions. Peake writes: "Properly interpreted, [Ricardo's *High Price of Bullion*] is first and foremost a challenge to the monetary theory and policy of Henry Thornton. Theoretically, Ricardo challenged Thornton by developing a strict quantity-theory, neutral money analysis which resulted in his well-known dichotomization of the economy into goods and money sectors, with no role for money other than to determine the general level of prices.... At the policy level, Ricardo argued that discretionary monetary policy inherently involved overissue and could be corrected only by resumption of specie payments" (Peake 1978, 202–203).

[38] Horsefield connected Ricardo's position in *High Price* to the 1844 Bank Charter Act: "Exponents [of the 1844 Act] held, with Ricardo, the rigid Quantity Theory explanation of the link between the volume of currency, the level of prices, and the level of the foreign exchanges; they ignored, again with Ricardo, the influence of deposits on prices and gold movements, and influences from natural causes (such as bad harvests) on the rate of exchange" (Horsefield 1944, 114–115).

Sayers reached similar conclusions: "Ricardo was the father of the system adopted by the Bank of England after its internal revolution at the beginning of the 'forties and, after Peel's conversion, embodied in the famous Bank Charter Act of 1844.... This emphasis [on long-run forces] prevented him from realizing the potentialities of banking policy...he must share responsibility for the Bank Charter Act of 1844 which gave the English currency system its peculiar form and also retarded the development of central banking" (Sayers 1953, 64–65).

Viner places Ricardo at the extreme end of the Bullionist camp, describing his theory as: "foreign remittances would have no effect on the exchanges whether under convertibility or inconvertibility;" without a fall in the exchange "the demands of England and the rest of the world for each other's products would necessarily so immediately and completely adjust themselves to extraordinary remittances as to result . . . in the maintenance of equilibrium in the balance of payments without the aid of specie movements;" and "if under inconvertibility there appeared a depreciation of sterling exchange, this was evidence of excess issue of currency" (Viner 1937, 139, 142).[39]

Notwithstanding these strong statements by respected economists, not all authors infer that Ricardo was an extreme Bullionist. Bladen is critical of Viner's interpretation, questioning whether Ricardo actually accepted the "so-called Ricardian theory of the mechanism of adjustment" (Bladen 1974, 173). He approves of Ricardo's focus on "the Bank and its duty to regulate the notes issue with a view to counteracting exceptional conditions in foreign trade," as opposed to Thornton's approach, which emphasized the effects of foreign remittances and corn imports and thereby "distracted attention from the real issue, the standard" (174). Sowell observes that the strict quantity theory, the centerpiece of the extreme Bullionist position, cannot be found in Ricardo's works: "The idea that the price level is rigidly linked to the quantity of money by a velocity of circulation which remains constant through all transitional adjustment processes cannot be found in any classical, neoclassical or modern proponent of the quantity theory of money. . . . A fixed velocity of money was a straw man attacked by Keynes. . . . [Moreover] short-run changes in velocity were thought of as more abrupt, and potentially catastrophic in their effects on real variables" (Sowell 1974, 58–60). Abundant evidence suggests that Ricardo viewed short-run monetary disturbances as potentially devastating to the macroeconomy,[40] as well as unsettling to the affairs of firms and individuals.[41]

---

[39] Viner inserts the caveat that Ricardo, in later years, allowed that factors other than an overissue of currency could affect the foreign exchange (Viner 1937, 139–141).

[40] Ricardo acted as though he believed monetary contraction would depress trade (Hicks 1967, 161). It followed that deflation, if necessary, should be gradual to minimize real disturbances (Niehans 1990, 103).

[41] At the microeconomic level, Ricardo appreciated the short-run neutrality of money, including the fact that the full effects of monetary fluctuations manifest with a time lag (Ahiakpor and Carr 1982, 147; Ahiakpor 1985, 19; Niehans 1990, 103). Among the effects he considered were the extent to which discounting activities by the Bank of England tended to redistribute trade capital and income (Ahiakpor 1985, 19). Taxation

Ricardo's recommendations for monetary policy were designed to stabilize the money supply and prices. His ingot plan reduced the monetary contraction associated with resumption by minimizing the amount of gold required by the Bank of England (Laidler 1989, 69). He recommended permanent devaluation[42] rather than a return to the ancient standard if sterling fell more than 5 percent below its par with gold (Viner 1937, 203). He also proposed that the payments of the quarterly dividend on the national debt be effected by warrants in order to minimize the monetary contraction that always occurred in the days preceding the dividend (Viner 1937, 204; Hollander 1997, 658). In a similar vein, the association between Ricardo and the Currency School is not universal, as authors have recognized the case for discretionary policy in *Economical and Secure Currency* (Robbins 1968, 128; Niehans 1987, 420–421). Viner came to a similar conclusion based on Ricardo's *Plan for a National Bank*, "[Ricardo] recommended that the managers of the currency should engage in open-market operations when expansion or contraction of the currency was desirable" (Viner 1937, 206).

A final point in evaluating Ricardo's status as a monetary theorist is his failure to ascribe to the Bank of England the duties of a lender of last resort. (The lender of last resort is the ultimate source of credit for an economy, the financier responsible to sustain a country's banks and commerce when all other sources of credit fail. The function is often performed by a country's central bank.) Thornton's *Paper Credit* refers to the Bank of England as the country's central bank and recommends that the Bank operate as a lender of last resort (Thornton 1802, 126–128). By contrast, in his *Plan for a National Bank*, Ricardo does not mention the concept. Because of this omission some authors infer that he "failed to recognize the vital role of the Bank of England as lender of last resort" (O'Brien 1975, 152). The point is best articulated by Sayers: "It is significant both of Ricardo's general position and of his view of the Bank directors that neither in published work nor in private letters did

---

also entered his analysis insofar as monetary shocks altered relative prices in a world with differential property and excise taxes (Hollander 1979, 480; Ahiakpor and Carr 1982, 147; Ahiakpor 1985, 20; Niehans 1990, 103; Marcuzzo and Rosselli 1994, 1256). Not just taxation, but any fixed component of cash flow – owing, for example, to long-term contracts or fixed income streams – served to redistribute income during monetary fluctuations (Ahiakpor 1985, 20; Niehans 1990, 103; Marcuzzo and Rosselli 1994, 1256). Finally, he knew that a redistribution of income, resulting from any of these causes, altered the pattern of final demand (Hollander 1979, 480; Ahiakpor 1985, 19).

[42] His recommendation of temporary devaluation was incorporated in the Resumption Act (Robbins 1976, 72).

he make any reference whatever to the special responsibility of the Bank as a prop to the market in times of trouble – as, we should say, a lender of last resort" (Sayers 1953, 63).

In actual fact, the Bank was not Britain's lender of last resort. It acted as any commercial concern and protected its capital by withdrawing credit in crises. The Bank's conduct in this regard has been well documented: "The realization of [the Bank's] responsibilities to provide cash in times of emergency was delayed by the action of the government in issuing Exchequer bills to merchants in distress during the crises of 1793 and 1811. The demand for such aid was renewed in 1825, and it was only after Liverpool had very firmly refused that we hear the last of it. The evil consequences were twofold for the Bank was blinded to its natural responsibility, and the public was encouraged to look to the government for aid" (Morgan 1943, 8).[43] The criticisms of Ricardo on this point are thus muted. All that can be said is that Ricardo never attributed to the Bank of England a role it did not perform, a role it expressly rejected, and a function actually carried out by the Exchequer.

Economic Growth

The distribution of income in a growing economy is a second theme in Ricardo's works; it reflects his concern for Britain's working poor. Ricardo's model of economic growth depicts wages as a function of the supply of and demand for labor. ("Capital" was the term he used for the demand for labor.[44]) Institutional factors that discouraged investment – he specifically identified the corn laws and high taxes – tended to reduce wages. So did laws such as the poor laws that subsidized the multiplication of the poorest families. For these reasons, Ricardo saw free trade, low taxes, and prudential decisions about child-bearing as essential to the welfare of the laboring poor.

Wages were also affected by the pattern of final demand – specifically by the shift between wartime and peacetime spending. The Napoleonic Wars were labor intensive, and for twenty years created a ready demand

---

[43] There was a partial repudiation of the Bank's position as lender of last resort in 1795. The Bank again lent tentatively in the panic of 1825–1826 (Hawtrey 1932, 119–122), and only because the government refused to issue Exchequer bills (Fetter 1965, 118–120).

[44] Classical economists made a further distinction between "fixed" and "circulating" capital. The distinction is one of degree, circulating capital being a more immediate source of employment for laborers.

for services.[45] With the peace of 1815, however, wartime spending ceased and 400,000 troops went home, immediately to discover that British consumers wanted not soldiers, but manufactured goods. It followed that monies formerly paid as wages to soldiers were now divided between manufacturing workers and the owners of factories. Ricardo thought that the shift in demand from services to manufactured goods at least temporarily reduced the derived demand for labor.

Even without a change in the pattern of final demand, it was possible that capitalists would substitute machines for labor in response to rising wages. Ricardo developed this insight – termed the "Ricardo effect" – in the chapter "On Machinery" in the third edition of his *Principles of Political Economy*.[46] He rightly perceived the secular substitution of capital for labor. Berg (1980, 21–24) shows that the proportion of fixed capital composed of machinery increased dramatically in the early nineteenth century, particularly in cotton and textiles – the industries to which Ricardo refers in his "On Machinery" chapter (1:390–391). That chapter also notes that technological change can make it profitable to substitute machinery for labor although wages remain constant: "the discovery and use of machinery may be attended with a diminution of gross produce; and whenever that is the case, it will be injurious to the labouring class, as some of their number will be thrown out of employment, and population will become redundant, compared with the funds which are to employ it" (390). Samuelson (1989) presents a rational reconstruction of Ricardo's model to show that viable inventions can reduce gross national output. Hicks likewise elaborates on how technical progress can depress the demand for labor: in response to a labor-saving invention, there will be a first round of investment as capital embodying the invention is brought into production. If the switch to fixed capital is so strong that there is a net decline in circulating capital, the demand for labor will fall. In the longer term, however, use of the invention is likely to raise profits, and higher profits tend to increase the rate of investment, which, it is to be expected, will give rise to an increase in the demand for labor (Hicks 1969, 148–165, 169–171; see also Hollander 1979, 346–355).

---

[45] Ricardo understood that factor intensities vary from one industry to another. His model of economic growth – described later – assumes uniform capital–labor ratios across all sectors. The purpose of the assumption is to make the model tractable; it does not betray a lack of subtlety in his analysis.

[46] The term "Ricardo effect" was coined by Hayek (1942, 127–152). The term has subsequently been applied to a number of concepts (Ferguson 1973, 1–13).

For Ricardo, the poor laws, taxes, and agricultural protection impinged on per capita economic growth. Ricardo was well acquainted with the operation of the poor laws. He collected Parliamentary reports on the welfare system, and his first appointment upon entering the House of Commons was to the Committee on the Poor Laws. His published works describe the incidence of the poor rates[47] and the effects of payments on the habits of the poor (Ricardo, 1:105–109). His opinion, which remained constant, was that aid should be refused to all persons except those who absolutely needed it because "the population can only be repressed by diminishing the encouragement to its excessive increase" (7:125).

Ricardo's statements about public spending were likewise based on his concern with long-term development. He thought that governments wasted resources – except when developing infrastructure – and thereby slowed the rate of economic growth. Moreover, a high level of public expenditure inevitably led to high taxes. After the war, taxes were an immediate problem. The interest charges to fund the postwar debt required taxes that "hung like a mill-stone round the exertion and industry of the country" (5:21, 33). Britain's war debts were supposed to be repaid through the operation of a sinking fund. The scheme failed, however, because the amount of debt redeemed annually bore no relation to the government's fiscal surplus or deficit. The Chancellor of the Exchequer simply decreed that the government would repurchase certain of its securities and then borrowed monies to do so. Ricardo deplored the churning public debts in his article "Funding System" written for the *Encyclopedia Brittanica*, published in 1820. His frustration with Britain's high taxes and with the incompetence of the sinking fund led him to propose the redemption of the national debt by a one-time levy on capital.

Ricardo's plan for the capital levy never matured. He described in broad terms an assessment on capital that would equal the market value of the national debt, but he never defined the term "capital." Possibly he intended an assessment only against real property; his suggestion that "manufacturers and landholders would want large sums for their payments into the Exchequer" implies as much (6:197). If so, the scheme was grossly unfair because it left untouched financial assets, foreign

---

[47] Chapter 18 of Ricardo's *Principles of Political Economy* is titled "Poor Rates." It addresses the incidence of the poor rates as a tax. It does not speak to the fundamental point of whether the poor laws subsidized the rearing of children who were not otherwise supported.

investments, personalty, and the future earnings of artists, professionals, and others with special skills. Ricardo also underestimated the distress of property owners who would be forced to sell farms and factories on short notice. He assumed that the former owners of public stock – whose financial assets had just been purchased by the government – would eagerly buy lands and manufactures dumped on the market, and that the hundreds of thousands of transactions entailed could be executed efficiently (5:34). In the event, the proposal was received with skepticism and did much to undermine his credibility.[48] (The capital levy is not addressed in later chapters.)

The capstone of Ricardo's work was his analysis of the effects of the corn laws on the distribution of income and on economic growth. High prices during the war made it profitable for British farmers to cultivate poorer land (extending the margin of cultivation) and to farm more intensively land already being used (extending the intensive margin of cultivation). With every extension of the margins, the real costs of producing food – that is, the costs in terms of the resources needed to produce a given amount of food – increased because of diminishing returns to labor and capital, the variable inputs. By the end of the war, marginal production costs were two to three times higher in Britain than on the Continent; the rents of intramarginal lands, those properties better situated and more fertile, rose proportionately.

When the war ended and foreign corn was again imported, farms plummeted in value. The landed gentry, who held disproportionate sway in Parliament, fought to protect their prosperity. In the face of widespread and violent opposition, Parliament approved the Corn Bill of 1815, which prohibited the importation of foreign corn except under extreme conditions. Ricardo's *Essay on Profits* (1815), *Principles of Political Economy* (1817), and *Protection to Agriculture* (1822) were born of the foment surrounding the bill. These works developed a model of economic growth that explains how, in an industrial country with a growing population, tariffs on agricultural produce slow the rate of economic growth and, at the same time, redistribute income from the laboring poor to wealthy landowners. [In the interests of full disclosure, the rational reconstruction of Ricardo's model in the pages that follow – sometimes termed the

---

[48] J. L. Mallet writes in his diary for 19 Dec. 1819: "Ricardo's notion of repaying the National Debt by a tax on real property seems at best a wild sort of notion; and it was not very discreet to let it out in an accidental manner in a speech upon the employment of the poor" (Ricardo, 8:147n).

"new view" – is that developed by Hicks and Hollander (1977). It is not the only interpretation of Ricardo's model.]

Ricardo's analysis of the corn trade was revolutionary. It undermined received wisdom – specifically, Smithian analysis – about the effect of the corn laws on the allocation of resources and on the distribution of income. In the chapter "Of Bounties" in the *Wealth of Nations*, Adam Smith concluded that tariffs neither benefited landlords nor harmed laborers and manufactures, save possibly by making British goods less competitive abroad. He also thought that tariffs had no effect on domestic production.

Smith's conclusions derive from the following analysis. He assumed a uniform worldwide price of corn, measured in silver. He further assumed that the silver price of corn regulated all other prices: money wages, rents, the price of raw materials, and the prices of manufactured goods.[49] Money wages depended on the costs of sustaining laborers, so a rise in the price of corn led to a rise in money wages. The price of corn determined the rent of corn-producing land, rent being calculated as the silver price of corn, less wages, less the necessary profits paid for the use of machinery and improvements to the land. The price of corn also established rents for land used in the production of raw materials, for in response to a rise in the price of corn, landlords would shift land from the production of raw materials to the production of corn, and this transfer would continue until such time as the shortage of raw materials had so increased the prices of these materials that returns to both uses of land equalized at a new, higher level. Smith assumed that manufactured goods were priced at average cost, cost being the summation of wages, profits, and the expenses of raw materials. Crucial to his theory, he treated profits as exogenously determined and thus concluded that a rise in the silver price of corn – by raising wages and the prices of raw materials – would likewise raise the prices of manufactured goods (Smith 1776, 545–547). Because a rise in the silver price of corn does not alter relative prices in Smith's model, he saw no way for tariffs on corn imports to change the allocation of resources. Further, his model predicts that rising corn prices do not affect landlords' purchasing power or the real wages of labor. At most, Smith thought that the corn laws would raise the nominal prices of domestically produced

---

[49] Prior to the publication of Ricardo's *Principles*, the Smithian view was widely accepted. In his otherwise able work, *An Essay on the External Corn Trade*, Robert Torrens writes that a rise in the price of corn raises the money price of labor, which, in turn, raises the money price of all commodities, leaving relative prices, real wages, and profits unchanged (Robert Torrens 1815, 81–82).

commodities and thereby "discourage more or less [the exports] of every sort of industry" (Smith 1776, 547).

Ricardo's *Principles of Political Economy* is a critique of Adam Smith's theory of value[50] and of the conclusions Smith drew from his theory in the chapter "Of Bounties" in the *Wealth of Nations*.[51] Chapter 1 of the *Principles* demonstrates the fundamental errors of Smith's model: the assumption that the price of corn regulates rents, wages, and all other prices; and the assumption that profits are exogenously fixed. Ricardo's critique proceeded in stages. He assumed that labor inputs – regardless of the skill of the laborers or the difficulty of the task – could be reduced to a single metric. He deliberately chose not to take into account differences in the durability of fixed capital, and he assumed that capital and labor were used in uniform proportions in all industries,[52] including in the production of gold, which he took as the measure of value. With these simplifications, his model became tractable but without losing its predictive power – he hoped – because variations in the capital-to-labor ratio or differences in the durability of capital had "comparatively slight" effects (Ricardo, 1:35–36, 44–45). He also took as given, and so did Smith, that the long-run competitive price of a commodity is its minimum average cost of production. With these assumptions it follows that commodity prices are proportionate to relative labor inputs. (This is a modified version of the labor theory of value, taking into account the use of capital.)

---

[50] Writing to Mill in Dec. 1816, Ricardo stated: "In reading Adam Smith, again, I find many opinions to question, all I believe founded on his original error respecting value. He is particularly faulty in the chapter on bounties" (7:100). The specific error to which Ricardo referred was that "the price of corn regulates the price of all other things" (7:105).

[51] Ricardo originally intended the *Principles* to be an expanded edition of his *Essay on Profits* (6:249). He later determined that a complete treatise better suited his purpose, and to this end he chose to concentrate on "where my opinions [about the principles of rent, profit, and wages] differ from the great authority of Adam Smith, Malthus, &c." (6:316). Chapters 1–6 of Ricardo's *Principles* are the critique of Smith's theory of value and its implications for the distribution of income and allocation of resources.

[52] Ricardo in other contexts relaxed the assumption of uniform factor proportions; this led to startling discoveries, such as that a rise in wages would lead to a change in relative prices, even a reduction in the prices of commodities produced at high capital–labor ratios. He came also to understand that with differential factor proportions, a change in the pattern of final demand – seen for instance in the transition from wartime to peacetime production – altered the distribution of income. Similar reasoning led him to recognize the secular substitution of capital for labor in response to rising real labor costs (1:395), and to recognize that the shift to capital-intensive modes of production contributed to Britain's rapid industrialization and slowed the rate of growth of the demand for labor.

Ricardo next addressed the effect of rising wages on prices. Smith committed a fallacy of composition in his chapter "Of Bounties." He assumed that rising wages affect the aggregate economy exactly as rising wages affect a single industry;[53] in consequence he believed that higher wage costs could be passed to consumers in the form of higher prices. Ricardo avoided the error by reasoning as follows: in an economy with uniform factor proportions, an across-the-board increase in wages causes profits to fall in all industries.[54] But profits fall uniformly, so no differentials in profit rates emerge that would entice capitalists to shift resources from one use to another.[55] With no change in the allocation of resources, the supplies of all commodities remain constant and relative prices remain unchanged.[56] It follows that a rise in the costs of subsistence does not, via a rise in money wages, lead to higher prices for manufactured goods.[57]

Having rebutted in Chapter 1 the errors of Smith's analysis, Ricardo proceeded in Chapters 2–6 of the *Principles* to illustrate the perverse effects of the corn laws on the trend path of factor returns and on the rate of economic growth. He does so by refining Smith's concept of land scarcity. According to Smith, in undeveloped regions, such as the North American

[53] If wage costs rise in a single industry, profits in that industry fall, and capitalists, alert to profit opportunities elsewhere, shift resources to other uses. As resources leave the industry, production declines and the price of the commodity rises until such time as the wages, profits, and rents earned in that industry equal the wages, profits, and rents available elsewhere.

[54] Ricardo, 1:307ff.

[55] Smith was familiar with the principle of the competitive allocation of resources, whereby the owners of productive factors are alert to the rents, wages, and profits that can be earned in different industries and allocate their resources to the most profitable uses. Smith stated the principle in his chapter "Of the Natural and Market Price of Commodities": "If at any time [the quantities supplied] exceed the effectual demand, some of the component parts of its price must be paid below their natural rate. If it is rent, then the interests of the landlords will immediately prompt them to withdraw a part of their land; and if it is wages or profit, the interest of the labourers in the one case, and of their employers in the other, will prompt them to withdraw a part of their labour or stock from this employment. The quantity brought to market would soon be no more than sufficient to supply the effectual demand" (Smith 1776, 65).

[56] The distinction between general and relative prices was the most difficult element of the corn-profit model for Ricardo. Concerning an early draft of the *Principles*, he wrote to Malthus: "If I could overcome the obstacles in the way of giving a clear insight into the origin and law of relative or exchangeable value I should have gained half the battle" (7:20). In the end, he made the distinction clear by treating gold as the measure of value and by assuming that it was produced with the same capital–labor mix as all other commodities.

[57] Ricardo could have achieved the same result by assuming a given purchasing power of money or a constant price level, but this was beyond his technical ability (Blaug 1980, 421).

colonies, only land the "most fertile and most favourably situated" is cultivated (1776, 106). Capital in these regions yields high profits, encouraging investment and creating a high demand for labor, which leads to high wages. At the next stage of development, "[w]hen the most fertile and best situated lands have been all occupied, less profit can be made by the cultivation of what is inferior both in soil and situation." Even so, Smith envisioned that the pace of investment would outstrip the rate of growth of population, bringing a rise in real wages. "The wages of labour do not sink with the profits of stock" (106–107). The culmination of this process was a stationary state with a constant population and no net investment. "In a country which had acquired that full complement of riches which the nature of its soil and climate, and its situation with respect to other countries, allowed it to acquire . . . both the wages of labour and the profits of stock would probably be very low" (109). Smith's analysis falls short in that he does not explain the transition from a state of rapid investment and rising real wages to a state of zero investment and low wages. Ricardo and Malthus contributed to the theory of economic growth by showing how the transition occurs: as population expands, increasing land scarcity drives up the costs of subsistence; the rising costs of the wage basket erode profits, cutting the rate of capital accumulation below the rate of population growth; stationarity sets in as real wages and profits fall simultaneously to their minima (Hollander 1984).

Ricardo set out his model as follows. Chapters 2 and 3 of the *Principles* treat rent as a differential surplus. Lands of the lowest quality earn no rents because Ricardo assumes that land can only be used for one purpose – raising corn. Farmers bring land under cultivation until marginal yields suffice to pay only wages and a minimum return to capital. Lands of higher quality do earn rents, the measure of rent being the differential between production costs per unit of output on marginal and superior lands.

Chapter 4 elaborates on the inverse wage–profit relation. Ricardo distinguishes between market and natural prices: market prices are actual prices; natural prices equal long-run minimum average costs, where costs include the returns necessary to keep resources employed in a particular industry. The distinction is central to Ricardo's explanation of the competitive allocation of resources. When the market price is higher (or lower) than the natural price, land, labor and capital are compensated more than enough (or not enough) to retain them in a specific use. Industries with high returns attract resources; industries with low returns decline. The resultant change in an industry's output, either by increase or decrease, causes the market price to better approximate the natural price. Smith described the principle of the competitive allocation of resources in his chapter "Of the Natural and Market Price of Commodities." He failed to apply the principle in the chapter "Of Bounties," however.

Chapter 5 of the *Principles* explains the subsistence wage. Market wages depend on the demand for labor relative to its supply. High wages might persist indefinitely; but because high wages stimulate population (a key assumption and perhaps not correct), there is ever a tendency for wages to approach subsistence. Wages remain high only while the rate of growth of the demand for labor equals or exceeds the rate of growth of population.

Chapter 6 "On Profits" summarizes Ricardo's assessment of the corn laws: barriers to corn imports raise the costs of subsistence. Higher costs lead to higher money wages. (For short intervals, real wages might fall so rapidly that money wages decline while necessities become more dear. This circumstance cannot persist, however, and money wages must eventually rise with the costs of subsistence.) High wages erode profits. As profits disappear, capitalists see no incentive to further investment, and the economy stops growing.

Ricardo saw free trade as the only answer to stationarity. Under a regime of free trade, domestic cultivation would not increase as Britain's population grew. Instead, foreign corn would be imported in exchange for British manufactured goods, given that Britain had a comparative advantage in manufacturing.[58] The principle was first enunciated by Robert Torrens in *An Essay on the External Corn Trade*:

> If England should have acquired such a degree of skill in manufactures, that, with any given portion of her capital; she could prepare a quantity of cloth, for which the Polish cultivator would give a greater quantity of corn, than she could, with the same portion of capital, raise from her own soil, then, tracts of her territory, though they should be equal, nay, even though they should be superior, to the lands in Poland, will be neglected; and a part of her supply of corn will be imported from that country (Torrens 1815, 264–265).

In his chapter "On Foreign Trade," Ricardo adapted Torrens' concept[59] to compare the prospects for economic growth under systems of free trade and protection. Given Britain's comparative advantage in the production

---

[58] Comparative advantage consists in having lower opportunity costs than your trading partners in the production of specific commodities.

[59] Ruffin (2002) argues that Ricardo developed the theory of comparative advantage before Torrens and that Torrens' *Essay* of 1815 is incomplete inasmuch as it fails to make explicit the assumption that factors of production are immobile between countries.

of manufactured goods, Ricardo rightly anticipated that under a regime of free trade Britain would export manufactured goods in exchange for agricultural produce. Corn prices would fall to the world price.[60] Assuming constant returns to scale in manufacturing, the costs of obtaining food for a laborer – that is, the costs of the manufactured goods that would be exchanged for the laborer's food – would not rise as Britain's population grew. With a fixed cost of foodstuffs – and assuming a constant psychological level of subsistence – there was no reason for money wages to rise secularly.[61] Profits would not fall as the population expanded and investment could continue without limit.

Ricardo's opposition to the corn laws was not limited to his *Principles of Political Economy* and *Essay on Profits*. In Parliament, he served prominently on the House of Commons Agricultural Committee of 1821, where he coordinated the testimony of witnesses such as Thomas Tooke, who opposed the corn laws. He also aggressively cross-examined witnesses holding a contrary view. When, in 1822, the Agricultural Committee was stacked with protectionists, Ricardo responded to the committee's report by writing *Protection to Agriculture*, a persuasive, empirical work repudiating the committee's opinions. The pamphlet was well received, even among government ministers, and sold four editions. It was also Ricardo's last contribution to the controversy surrounding the corn laws, as the national debate turned elsewhere during his final months in Parliament.

Almost everything in the preceding account of Ricardo's model of economic growth – the "new view" – differs from the interpretation of Ricardo's model put forward by Piero Sraffa, editor of Ricardo's *Works and Correspondence* and author of the Marxian classic, *Production of Commodities by Means of Commodities*. The principal differences are these: in Sraffa's interpretation, there is no scope for demand–supply analysis so that equilibrium prices need not satisfy the equation of supply and demand, there are no economic agents, there is no optimization and no competitive allocation of resources, the wage rate is exogenously

---

[60] More correctly, the relative price between corn and other traded commodities would be the same in England as on the Continent. Ricardo did not elaborate on what the actual terms of trade would be; he lacked the analytical tools to do so. It was another thirty years before John Stuart Mill explained how international terms of trade are determined.

[61] Ricardo understood that the level of psychological subsistence might not be fixed. Money wages would rise permanently if laborers – striving for a higher standard of living – delayed marriage and child-bearing. Money wages would also rise if the rate of growth of the demand for labor increased beyond the rate at which the population was rising. Neither scenario posed a problem. Both were desirable because the condition of laborers would be improved.

determined and the profit rate emerges as a physical ratio independent of relative prices (Hollander 2001, 21–23). In short, there are no traces of neoclassical economics in Sraffa's Ricardo.

Ricardo's model, as interpreted by Sraffa, describes a cycle of continuous reproduction. At the start of the cycle, commodities are advanced, including the means of subsistence for laborers. "Productive" activities transform these commodities into outputs. The relative values of inputs and outputs are determined by the "difficulty of production," where difficulty is measured by the labor embodied in the commodity. A surplus arises from the production process because the labor embodied in the outputs at the end of the cycle exceeds the labor embodied in the commodities advanced at the start. This surplus is the source of profit; thus profits are created by production, not by exchange. The profit rate depends only on technological factors that determine the ratio of the labor embodied in inputs to the labor embodied in outputs.[62]

Between Sraffa and the new view lies a broad, populated field. Authors disagree, for example, about the exact way Ricardo distinguished between general and relative prices. In the model as interpreted by Hollander, all commodities, including the "invariable measure of value," are produced at identical capital–labor ratios. According to Blaug, however, commodities are produced at different capital–labor ratios, the "invariable measure of value" being produced at the "mean of the entire spectrum of capital–labor ratios in the economy" (Blaug 1980, 421). Chapter 1 of the *Principles* supports both interpretations. The distinction is perhaps not crucial; as Blaug points out, the inverse wage–profit relationship obtains under either interpretation. Yet noting the distinction alerts readers to the lack of consensus.

On the issue of wages, Hollander's reconstruction sees real wages moving at levels above subsistence in an advancing economy, rising or falling depending on the relative growth rates of labor and capital, and then declining to subsistence at the terminal stationary state. The *Principles* support Hollander's view but not consistently. "Ricardo's treatment of wages in the *Principles* was eclectic," observes Peach (1993, 115), for he often spoke as if the subsistence wage was the relevant wage. Peach further

---

[62] In Ricardo's *Principles of Political Economy*, the profit rate is determined by the labor embodied in inputs relative to the labor embodied in outputs. In his earlier *Essay on the Influence of a Low Price of Corn on the Profits of Stock*, the profit rate is determined by the corn embodied in inputs relative to the corn embodied in outputs (Sraffa 1951; see also Hollander 1995b).

notes that the prime objective of Ricardo's model – to show that pro-gressively diminishing agricultural returns irreversibly depress profits – is demonstrated more forcefully when the relevant wage is the subsistence wage (Peach 1993, 8, 113–115).[63] On the weight of these two points, Peach concludes that the relevant commodity wage for purposes of interpreting Ricardo's growth model is the subsistence wage.

Concerning the predictive power of Ricardo's model, the new view sees profits and wages falling to their respective minima, but the model does not predict the variables' actual paths. The model also does not permit predictions about the onset of stationarity because it allows for the possibility of improvements in farming that postpone stagnation – perhaps indefinitely. The new view contrasts with traditional interpretations, which see Britain's economy moving inexorably and mechanically to stationarity in the immediate future:

[Ricardo's model is] designed to prove one central proposition: that the exis-tence of the Corn Laws, which hindered the import of corn, caused resort to inferior land at home, involving a fall in the average and marginal products of labour and capital and hence bringing about a stationary state in the not very distant future. Smith had envisaged a stationary state, but it was nothing like imminent and its achievement was not mechanical. Ricardo on the other hand had provided a mechanical model to establish its fairly immediate likelihood (O'Brien 1975, 41).

In the traditional view, Ricardo's model was valuable precisely because of the strong predictions it yielded. He wanted to emphasize the downward trend of profits under the corn laws because this was his central argument against protection (Peach 1993, 8).

A final point of disagreement concerns the inclusion (or absence) of neoclassical elements in Ricardo's model. O'Brien (1975, 37–41) inter-prets Ricardo's model as a sequential account of pricing and distribution characterized by one-way causal relationships. Demand enters the model in a primitive sense; it has zero price elasticity. This contrasts with the new view, which claims that Ricardo used demand–supply analysis with a downward-sloping demand curve, he employed the concept of dimin-ishing marginal productivity, and he used both marginal analysis and a

---

[63] In the new view of Ricardo's model, the commodity wage basket is variable. Whether real wages rise or fall depends on the rate of capital accumulation as compared with the rate of population growth. This interpretation allows for the possibility that the com-modity wage might fall faster than the money price of corn rises. In such an event, the money wage would fall (and profits rise) even as land scarcity becomes more pronounced.

theory of general interdependence in his description of the competitive allocation of resources. The new view is beyond the pale for traditional interpreters: "asserting that 'Ricardo's model involves the use of something akin to the equilibrium conception of marginalist theory in the context of distribution' seems to me going much too far" (O'Brien 1981, 14).

The Law of Markets

The most controversial aspect of Ricardo's work concerns the law of markets, sometimes referred to as "Say's law."[64] The law is not a single proposition, but consists of a number of statements about the relationship between production and purchasing power. At its most basic, the law states that production creates purchasing power. The concept is best illustrated in the context of a barter economy where each participant seeks to exchange his wares for those of others. In this setting, supply creates the ability to demand, and this demand is always effectual because goods trade immediately one for the other.

The analysis thickens with the introduction of money. For in a monetary economy, each trade is a double exchange: a person sells goods for money, then later trades the money for goods and services. Because the value of the initial sale can be stored in the form of money, the seller's ability to demand is not always immediately exercised. It follows that when the people of a country attempt to hoard cash by forestalling purchases, products of all types might be supplied with no one to buy them. Classical economists referred to this situation as a "general glut" – a period of economic stagnation, accompanied by high unemployment, idle farms and factories, and a "glut" of unsold commodities of all types.

The most extreme form of Say's law, termed "Say's identity," denies the possibility of general gluts. It holds that supply always and everywhere creates an effectual demand. Excess supplies of particular commodities are offset by excess demands in other sectors.[65] Even particular gluts are quickly eliminated as the pattern of national output adjusts to the pattern of demand. The identity formulation fails because it cannot explain periods of depression and unemployment; it is also inconsistent with a

---

[64] For a thorough but concise explanation of Say's law, see Skinner (1967) and Baumol (1977).

[65] The mathematical formulation of this idea was presented by Lange (1942) using the identity $\Sigma P_i X_i = 0$, for $(i = 1, \ldots, n)$, where P_i represents the price of good (i), X_i represents the excess demand for good (i), and the summation occurs over all goods in an economy.

monetary economy. The identity only obtains if the demand for money never changes (Lange 1942, 53). For this to hold true, however, money cannot be a store of value. By implication, if money is not a store of value, then each person acquiring cash immediately spends it, driving prices to infinity. Thus, any model incorporating Say's identity reduces to a barter economy in which the failure of effective demand is impossible by definition (Patinkin 1948, 136). Moreover, because Say's identity is inconsistent with finite prices, it is also inconsistent with the quantity theory, which assumes a determinate price level (Patinkin 1951).

A more plausible formulation of the law, termed "Say's equality," holds that supply eventually gives rise to an effectual demand, though it may be necessary for the price level to fall before consumers purchase excess products. Classical economists, with the possible exception of James Mill, accepted the equality version of the law, which allows for general gluts.[66] These economists disagreed, however, about (1) the causes of general gluts, (2) the likelihood of their occurrence, (3) the ability of Britain's economy to correct itself through changes in prices and in the allocation of resources if a general glut ever happened, and (4) whether Britain actually suffered a glut after the Napoleonic Wars.

Robert Malthus was a great believer in general gluts. He thought Britain experienced one that lasted from 1813, at the close of the Napoleonic Wars, until 1821 or 1822. He attributed economic distress to several factors: (1) a fall in aggregate demand occasioned by a drop in the incomes of landlords and farmers, (2) the cessation of wartime spending, (3) a contraction of the money supply, and (4) possibly "oversaving." (In classical economics, the term "oversaving" refers to excessive investment, not to hoarding, that is, the amassing of cash by a refusal to spend.) For Malthus, the process of economic adjustment was too slow to compensate for a want of aggregate demand; with this in view, he recommended that the government impose taxes, spend the proceeds, and thereby bring aggregate demand and supply into balance.

David Ricardo was a skeptic by comparison. He considered a general surfeit of commodities unlikely. In the event a glut occurred, he thought the balance between demand and supply would be quickly restored by a fall in wages and prices. With respect to the causes of postwar economic

---

[66] For classical economists generally, the demand for money is a function of uncertainty (Corry 1962, 43, 44, 98). Money served as a store of value (Ahiakpor 1985, 18) and might be hoarded in times of alarm (Sowell 1974, 62). Smith and Say, notably, made explicit assumptions about hoarding (Skinner 1969, 180–181; Hollander 1979, 68, 80, 84).

distress, Ricardo and Malthus largely agreed. Both recognized the hardship occasioned by volatile corn prices, the cessation of wartime spending, and monetary instability. Ricardo's analysis diverged most from Malthus on the question of oversaving. He understood what Malthus meant by oversaving, but thought it impossible in practice because oversaving required irrational investment. J. B. Say raised the same objections. Much of what has been termed the "general glut debate" reflects the critique by Ricardo and Say of Malthus' oversaving thesis; the critique is central to both Ricardo's (vol. 2) *Notes on Malthus* and Say's (1821) *Letters to Malthus on Political Economy*. As regards Britain's economic state, Ricardo refused to characterize postwar conditions as a general glut. He identified, instead, a series of exogenous shocks that depressed specific industries and at times the whole economy. At no point did he concede there had been a reduction in consumer demand.

Ricardo's views translated into a particular agenda for public policy: he opposed any fiscal stimulus of output and employment. In this regard, he was concerned not merely with short-run demand but also with the long-term effects of government spending on economic growth. He believed that high levels of government spending, financed ultimately by high taxes, impeded the accumulation of capital and slowed the rate of growth of the demand for labor. He considered high taxes an immediate problem, observing in Parliament that more than 10,000 wealthy Britons emigrated to the Continent after the war to avoid taxes, taking their entrepreneurial abilities and capital with them – and this happened at a time when investment was urgently needed. Thus, even though he recognized the theoretical possibility of a short-term stimulus from government spending, he opposed expansionary fiscal policy because current conditions did not warrant it and because of concern about its effects on economic growth.

Related to the efficacy of fiscal policy is the concept of "Ricardian equivalence." This is the proposition that the government's choice to finance public spending by taxes or debt has no effect on consumer behavior. Authors associate Ricardo with this concept because Chapter 17 of his *Principles*, "Taxes on Other Commodities than Raw Produce," states that the value of a lump-sum tax in the current period equals the present value of the future debt payments that must be made if the government raises the same funds by borrowing.[67] The passage does not imply that

---

[67] To my knowledge, James Buchanan (1976) coined the term "Ricardian equivalence." For a detailed description of the concept see Andrew Abel (1987).

Ricardo treated debt and taxes as equivalent from the consumer's perspective. In fact, he believed that consumers, in their immediate spending decisions, do not take into account the future tax burden entailed by public debts. For this reason, and because he was concerned about the slow accumulation of capital, he recommended that the government finance all its expenditures by taxes. It would make consumers less inclined to spend unproductively and more inclined to invest (Ricardo, 1:247).

A final proposition under the rubric of Say's law concerns the adequacy of demand in the long run: in the secular period there will always be effectual demand for a country's output, no matter how vastly it increases. Ricardo stated the proposition in Chapter 21 of his *Principles*, "Effects of Accumulation on Profits," capping his argument that if the corn laws were repealed, Britain's economy could grow without limit. The chapter specifically rejects Adam Smith's prediction that Britain's economy would stagnate because of the "increasing competition of capitals."[68] Smith believed that profits must fall secularly because consumers would never purchase the output of a vast industrial economy at prices that afford capitalists the incentive to further investment: "As capitals increase in any country, the profits which can be made by employing them necessarily diminish.... There arises in consequence a competition between different capitals" (Smith 1776, 384; see also pages 100–113). Smith relied on an error of composition; he assumed that just as investment in a single industry heightens competition and cuts profits, so, too, investment in the aggregate raises competition and erodes profits. His analysis overlooked the fact that investment in the aggregate gives rise to a corresponding increase in purchasing power that is effectual in the secular period.

Ricardo addressed again the long-run sufficiency of demand in his *Notes on Blake*, a critique of William Blake's *Observations on the Effects Produced by the Expenditure of Government During the Restriction of Cash Payments* (1823). Blake adopted Smith's increasing competition of capitals thesis as the centerpiece of his explanation as to why aggregate demand in Britain would always be deficient unless Parliament annually authorized massive debt-financed expenditures.

---

[68] Adam Smith advanced two arguments as to why the economy would eventually reach stationarity. He attempted to show how land scarcity would lead to a point of no net investment (and low profits) and a constant population (earning subsistence wages). Smith also thought that stationarity would occur even without a rise in the cost of subsistence because of the "increasing competition of capitals."

The secondary literature offers widely divergent interpretations of Chapter 21, "Effects of Accumulation." Hollander recognizes that the chapter addresses the long-run sufficiency of aggregate demand, and that it is not concerned with short-run phenomenon (Hollander 1979, 510–513). The emphasis on demand in the secular period is natural because the *Principles* address the effects of agricultural protection on the distribution of income over time, an issue altogether separate from the adequacy of demand in the short run (Sowell 1963, 193, 202). Stigler concludes from the chapter that "Ricardo developed the law of markets along [James] Mill's line," but he recognizes the sophistication of Ricardo's statement: "In this form the law of markets is no longer a truism, it is the proposition that general equilibrium of the economy, with prices equal to costs (including 'profits'), is compatible with any level of real income. It would be more appropriate to call this the Mill–Ricardo Law than Say's Law" (Stigler 1953, 595).

Other authors interpret Chapter 21, especially pages 290–293 (Ricardo, vol. 1), as a simplistic statement of the law of markets; according to Peach (1993, 134): "The 'law of markets' received its formal blessing from Ricardo in the chapter 'Effects of Accumulation on Profits and Interest' in the *Principles*. . . . The steps in his reasoning should be familiar: commodities are supplied only with a view to demanding other commodities [290]; . . . and all money income is spent either by the direct recipients, or by those to whom they lend their unspent money balances, thus implying that aggregate net savings are zero [291]." Blaug takes a similar view, citing page 290 as evidence that "at no time did he permit himself to conceive of a break in the income stream through the influence of hoarding" (Blaug 1958, 78). He also interprets Ricardo's *Notes on Blake* as a statement about the short-run sufficiency of aggregate demand (79).

Opinions in the secondary literature again vary on the question of "oversaving." Malthus believed that rapid investment might lead to an increase in national output for which there was no corresponding increase in aggregate demand. Oversaving in this sense has nothing to do with hoarding or a shift in the demand for money (Hollander 1997, 514–526). Yet modern authors have been thrown by the word "saving." Because Ricardo rejected Malthus' theory, they conclude that he "denied that saving could ever involve a deficiency of demand" (Corry 1958, 41). Interpreted this way, Ricardo's *Notes on Malthus* seem to advance the identity version of the law of markets.

Authors disagree about whether Ricardo's attitude toward fiscal policy comports with the identity or the equality version of the law of markets. Ricardo opposed any fiscal stimulus to output and employment, even during the depression of 1819. He argued that Parliament would merely transfer resources from one employment to another, and that by doing so it would discourage investment and economic growth. Authors who associate Ricardo with the equality formulation of the law observe that his statements about fiscal policy are based on a concern over long-term economic growth. Given the classical distinction between productive and unproductive expenditure, he would have found it "beyond comprehension that someone should recommend wasteful expenditure as a way of generating wealth" (Baumol 1997, 219; Kates 1997, 197). By contrast, authors who associate Ricardo with Say's identity are likely to associate him also with the "Treasury view" of fiscal policy – or the idea that an increase in government spending cannot cause an increase in aggregate economic activity. Referring to a speech by Ricardo during the depression of 1819, Hutchison writes: "Here again is Ricardo urging upon the House of Commons the obvious practical conclusion to be drawn from the Law of Markets, that public works could not possibly help to remedy the depression... the doctrine against public works was, of course, eventually to become by 1929 'the orthodox Treasury dogma steadfastly held'" (Hutchison 1952, 75–76). "No economist who preceded Ricardo and no other economist of the English-speaking world from his time until Keynes so delighted in making sweeping policy recommendations from assumptions of his own choosing" (Fetter 1969, 83). His "assumptions" dictated a policy of "unambiguous... laissez faire" (Peach 1993, 141), a view continuously reinforced by his "pathological feeling that the government did everything badly" (Fetter 1969, 73).

The final and most important basis for associating Ricardo with a particular version of the law of markets concerns his interpretations of the events of the postwar period. Ricardo attributed postwar economic crises to a series of exogenous shocks, the most important one being the transition from wartime to peacetime production. In his view, Britain responded quickly to these shocks; therefore, a prolonged period of unemployment never occurred. A few authors commend the analysis. His was the "first systematic attempt to reconcile the facts of depression and unemployment with Say's Law" (Sowell 1972, 29). The transition from wartime to peacetime production was bound to be difficult, especially for agriculture (Schumpeter 1954, 693). Furthermore, Ricardo rightly observed that the agricultural crises of 1813–1816 and 1820–1822 resulted from abundant harvests and a glut of imported corn (De Marchi 1970, 263). He also correctly attributed a measure of postwar distress to mishandling of the currency by the Bank of England (O'Brien 1981, 29).

Most historians of economics, however, accept a stylized account of the postwar period according to which all branches of trade were stagnant, unsold commodities glutted markets, and laborers suffered chronic unemployment. The crisis is thought to have originated in a collapse of aggregate demand at the end of the war, later aggravated by the ruinous policy of resumption, which necessitated a severe monetary contraction. For these authors, the empirical merit of Ricardo's analysis goes unnoticed. Blaug remarks that Ricardo attributed the several postwar crises to exogenous shocks: "It is not surprising then that the periodic alternation of booms and slumps was not appreciated by economists until the third or fourth decade of the nineteenth century. Earlier it was possible to argue, as Ricardo did, that every crisis arose out of adventitious and nonrecurring circumstances. The depressions of 1811, 1816–17, and 1818–19 could be explained by pointing to obvious exogenous factors such as the Bank Restriction Act, the strains of waging war, the difficulties of postwar conversion, or the influence of the weather in producing poor or abundant harvests. It took some time before old habits were shed" (Blaug 1958, 98). Peach dismisses Ricardo's claim that the adjustment from wartime to peacetime caused economic hardships: "The fact [that funds were being hoarded and not invested in new ventures] seems to have been regarded as almost immaterial" (Peach 1993, 133–134). Concerning the effects of the Resumption Act, Ricardo failed to recognize "the cause of the contemporary troubles, alleging all sorts of explanations other than the obvious one of contraction of the circulation" (Robbins 1976, 72–73). Robbins likewise dismisses the severity of the disruptions caused by the 1815 Corn Bill: "How greatly superior in good sense is [Malthus'] attitude to that of Ricardo, bombinating away in a stratosphere of abstract logic which led him to attribute the post-war depression in part at least to agricultural protection" (Robbins 1967, 260).

The comparison between Ricardo and Malthus is commonly made when attributing to Ricardo an extreme version of the law of markets. Malthus' works show plainly that he rejected Say's identity. He held that Britain was mired in a general glut because of a chronic shortfall in consumer demand, and that the appropriate response was for Parliament to raise taxes to finance public works. Central to Malthus' account was his belief that wages and prices were downwardly rigid so that Britain's economy had no inherent ability to respond to unemployment. Given the stylized account of postwar conditions, Malthus seems an empirically oriented economist who anticipated the revelations that would unfold in the *General Theory*. Consequently, it was the "almost total obliteration of Malthus' line of approach and the complete domination of Ricardo's" that proved such a disaster to the progress of economics (Keynes 1933, 95, 98).[69]

Authors who share Malthus' perspective also take issue with Ricardo's belief that Britain's economy adapted quickly to the shocks it experienced. "Beginning in 1815, [Ricardo] made a series of predictions that prosperity would soon come to England. The prediction was continuously wrong and it was no compliment to his intelligence that after 1820 he blamed the distress on the abundance of harvests" (Stigler 1953, 596). Of the four predictions cited by Stigler, the first was made on 27 June 1815 at a time when tax reports indicate the economy was expanding. The second and third predictions were made on 25 December 1815 and 15 July 1816. There was severe distress at both periods, but it was short-lived. Agricultural districts returned to prosperity by April 1816 after a sudden rise in corn prices; trade and manufacturing centers were again working by the spring of 1817. Ricardo made his final prediction on 7 August 1817 during a period of general prosperity – agricultural prices were high, foreign trade had recovered, and manufactures were approaching full employment. With respect to Stigler's comment that Ricardo blamed "distress after 1820 . . . on the abundance of harvests," it should be noted that there was no general distress after 1820. Britain saw a continuous expansion of its trade and manufacturing from the third quarter of 1820 through mid-1825.

Conclusion

The chapters to follow contribute to the secondary literature by, first of all, giving a detailed account of economic conditions in Britain in the post-war decade.[70] The historical chapters are integral to our assessment of

---

[69] The comment is surprising because in his earlier *Tract on Monetary Reform* (1923) Keynes described how Ricardo spoke in clear tones the voice of instructed reason regarding the issue between deflation and devaluation (Keynes 1971, 124).

[70] The chapters are essential because texts covering the industrial revolution – however defined – as well as statistical works by Gayer et al. (1953) and Dean and Cole (1967) do not offer a month-by-month account of the events relevant to Ricardo's development. Similarly, books and journal articles about specific industries – such as coal, cotton, iron, railways, and wool – the banking system, the poor laws, and agricultural protection are too narrow in scope for our purpose, which requires precise information about every aspect of the economy.

Ricardo as an empirical economist. Authors who associate Ricardo with Say's identity and a primitive version of the quantity theory assume that he failed to recognize that Britain's economy was depressed for the entire postwar decade and that the crisis resulted from a shortfall in consumer demand. In this light, Ricardo's agenda for public policy seems irresponsible because he opposed expansionary fiscal measures, while urging a return to the gold standard. How someone so intimately involved in the finance and politics of London could recommend policies that ignored contemporary reality has been explained by Blaug as the result of "an abstract and deductive" method that kept Ricardo from relying on empirical evidence to test his conclusions: "the divorce between theory and facts was probably never more complete than in the heyday of Ricardian economics" (Blaug 1958, 187). Others assert that Ricardo was so enamored of deductive reasoning that he denied the existence of the postwar depression.[71] His ruinous agenda for public policy, based on a disregard of the practical consequences of those policies, has been termed the "Ricardian vice" – the methodological error of "piling a heavy load of practical conclusions upon a tenuous groundwork" (Schumpeter 1954, 1171).

Chapters 2 and 3 show that there was no chronic depression in the postwar years. Instead, Britain suffered a series of exogenous shocks. An agricultural crisis prevailed from the harvest of 1813 to the spring of 1816, and two depressions befell trade and manufacturing. The first lasted from the fall of 1815 to early 1817; it was occasioned by the collapse of Britain's foreign markets and by the transition from wartime to peacetime production. The second began early in 1819 and continued through the spring of 1820; it resulted from sudden setbacks in foreign trade and, to a lesser extent, from the Bank of England's returning to the gold standard. A subsequent agricultural crisis occurred between 1820 and 1822. Britain's economy recovered quickly from each of these shocks. Wages and prices remained flexible. There was no sustained period of high unemployment. Apart from temporary crises, real wages may have been depressed because of an abundance of labor relative to the demand for it. Several factors contributed to the disproportion between labor and capital: high taxes, the corn laws, the poor laws, and, perhaps, also the trend toward mechanization.

Chapters 2 and 3 draw almost entirely from primary sources. My familiarity with these sources enabled me to recognize references in Ricardo's

---

[71] See Bonar (1885), 212–213; Mitchell (1949), 135; Maital and Haswell (1977), 364; Peach (1995), 6.

works to Parliamentary reports and contemporary periodicals. For example, and as explained in Chapter 4, I found that Ricardo used tax data when estimating the size of the government's pending loans. As an economist he used the same data to measure aggregate economic activity. The Report of the Finance Committee of 1817, Peel's reports as Home Secretary in 1822 (*Hansard* 2s, 7:1014) and 1823 (*Hansard* 2s, 9:925), and certain speeches by Lord Liverpool[72] alerted me to the fact that in the early nineteenth century, tax data were used to approximate changes in national income. Chapter 4 explores the range of Ricardo's sources and shows how, as a financier, his success depended on being well informed about public finance, monetary policy, and foreign and domestic commerce.

Chapter 5 explains how Ricardo applied his model of economic growth to contemporary events. Most important, it shows that Ricardo's account of the postwar period relied on a distinction between temporary and permanent causes of distress. Temporary causes included the transition to peacetime production, reversals in foreign trade, and monetary shocks. The permanent cause of distress was a disproportion between the supply of labor and its demand. In following the secondary literature,[73] I overlooked this distinction; then in *Hansard*, I found an address by Lord Grenville in which he attributed distress to "temporary causes" as well as to those of a "more permanent view." Knowing that Ricardo commended Grenville's speech,[74] I reread his treatment of the 1819–1820 depression. There I found the same parallel analyses of short-run and long-run conditions. The reports of the Poor Law Committees of 1817, 1818, and 1819 confirmed my revised interpretation of Ricardo, for the committees described "permanent" aspects of economic distress in terms identical to those in Ricardo's correspondence and speeches.

Chapter 6 takes up the law of markets. In keeping with the weight of secondary literature, the chapter shows that the macroeconomic analysis in Ricardo's *Principles* and pamphlets suffers because it does not integrate his insight that aggregate demand might, in theory, be deficient and that,

---

[72] Notable are speeches given on 26 May 1820 and 26 Feb. 1822.

[73] Hollander (1979, 518) states that Ricardo switched from one explanation of the postwar depression to another: "By the end of 1819 Ricardo felt obliged to alter his diagnosis. In his speeches of December we find no reference to capital immobility, but rather the emphasis is placed upon an inadequacy of capital supply relative to population.... But by mid-1820 Ricardo had reverted to his original argument that the postwar problem in manufacturing was entirely due to capital misallocation." Winch (1987, 81) similarly does not distinguish between temporary and permanent causes of the postwar distress.

[74] See Ricardo's letter of 10 Jan. 1820, reprinted in Heertje (1991, 523).

in practice, the hoarding of cash sometimes occurs. My position diverges from the literature that supposes that Say's identity colors the whole of his work, including his account of the postwar depression. Ricardo's analysis of contemporary crises was excellent. He was well informed and rightly characterized what he observed – namely, that Britain's economy adapted quickly to a series of exogenous shocks from 1813 to 1822.

With respect to monetary theory and policy, Chapter 7 shows that Ricardo was not an extreme Bullionist. He was well aware of the potential causes of changes in foreign exchange rates and in the price of gold. I further conclude that Ricardo was not a father of the Currency School and of the 1844 Bank Charter Act. It is true that his *Plan for a National Bank* influenced the act. However, the act's crucial element – the repudiation of discretionary monetary policy – finds no support in his monetary pamphlets. Ricardo also recognized the nonneutrality of money and it is for this reason that he endorsed the discretionary management of a convertible currency pegged to gold.

TWO

The Business Cycle of 1815–1818

Britain began the transition from wartime to peacetime production in 1813. Months of fighting remained, but with the Grand Army lying decimated on the Russian steppe, trade resumed a semblance of normalcy. This meant that foreign corn was again imported and with it came lower prices. British farmers felt the change immediately. Malthus held that the fall in corn so eroded the money incomes of landlords and farmers as to depress Britain's economy for nearly a decade. The pages to follow show that his theory is untenable. There was an agricultural crisis, as Malthus understood, but the consequent fall of agricultural expenditures was counteracted by a high demand for exports. Not until foreign markets collapsed in mid-1815 did Britain experience a general depression.

The postwar crisis lasted less than twenty-four months, from the summer of 1815 to the spring of 1817. The upper turning point of a speculative expansion occurred as early as March 1815 (Gayer, Rostow, and Schwartz 1953, 110). Tax reports suggest the date could be later, in July or August. What is certain is that a general depression was underway by the fall of 1815. Members of Parliament and the commercial press attributed the depression to reversals in foreign trade. Their explanation is substantiated by tax reports that show that general economic activity fluctuated in tandem with Britain's trade. The crisis was worsened by a sudden drop in military expenditures of £53.5 million annually, or 18 percent of aggregate demand, and by the demobilization of 400,000 soldiers. Economic recovery began the spring of 1817 when the demand for exports returned to normal. Favorable conditions continued through 1818.

The Bank of England received much abuse for its postwar monetary policy. Though *de facto* a central bank, it behaved like an ordinary commercial enterprise, withdrawing discounts at the depth of the depression in 1816, then expanding credit in the subsequent boom – essentially conducting a procyclical policy. The Bank also mishandled the return to the gold standard. It initiated a partial return to cash payments in 1816, but increased the note circulation so greatly in 1817 (even after the foreign exchange became unfavorable) that it was forced to suspend cash payments in April 1819. Had it not been for the Resumption Act, the Bank might never have returned to gold. In the event, the achievement was delayed until 1821.

An Agricultural Crisis: Fall 1813 to Spring 1816

"But, above all things, wine upon table at dinner," thundered Cobbett in his *Weekly Political Register*, "that is an unnatural and bad state of society in which farmers can even think of doing these things." With little foreign competition and a growing population, British farmers flourished during the war. Two decades of high corn prices permitted a country lifestyle that was profligate by some accounts and comfortable by any measure. High prices also produced a "rage for farming," as Brougham described it, that was attended by unprecedented investments in land and agricultural machinery, causing "a vast portion of land to be thrown into cultivation which had before been untilled," and extending the intensive margin of cultivation (*Edinburgh Review*, June 1816, 259–261). There were 1700 Enclosure Acts in the years 1800 to 1819, as compared with 2200 in all other decades from 1720 to 1829 combined (Porter 1836, 155–156). In terms of acreage, from 1793 to 1801 landholders enclosed 273,891 acres of common pasture and wastes, or 30,432 acres annually on average. By contrast, 793,743 acres were enclosed between 1802 and 1815, or 52,838 acres annually (Barnes 1930, 106).

Each extension of the margin of cultivation widened the disparity between production costs in Britain and those on the Continent. Secretary of the Board of Agriculture Arthur Young testified before the 1814 House of Commons Committee on the Corn Laws[1] that the expense of cultivating 100 acres of arable land had increased from £411 in 1790 to £547 in 1803 and again to £771 in 1813 – a nominal rise of 90 percent.[2]

---

[1] House of Commons 1814, *Minutes of Evidence . . . Select Committee on Petitions Relating to the Corn Laws of This Kingdom*, 80–83, in *Parliamentary Papers* 1813–1814, 3:274–277, MF 15.15.

[2] In real terms, the rise in production costs was less than 90 percent because an inflation of about 40 percent – as measured by the price of gold – occurred from 1790 to 1813. Gold increased from £3 17s. 10 1/2d. to £5 10s. per ounce.

Accordingly, he stated that the remunerative price of wheat could not be less than 87s. per Winchester quarter; 34s. was his estimate for oats.[3] By comparison, Prussians purchased wheat for under 30s. per quarter and sold oats for 10s. (see App. C.3). Even in Hamburg and Rotterdam, the average price of wheat was below 50s. Because of this disparity, the House of Commons Committee on the Corn Laws concluded that "there is scarcely any price in our own market, which, under circumstances of a general abundance in the other parts of Europe, would be sufficiently low to prevent an importation of corn from those foreign parts."[4] Notwithstanding the threat of foreign competition, British farmers remained optimistic as the war ended. The ports were open,[5] yet prices continued to be high.[6] Moreover, the Corn Laws of 1791 and 1804 had demonstrated the landlords' strength in Parliament[7] and there was every reason to be confident that additional measures could be adopted as needed.

The climate of optimism prevailed until the fall of 1813 when the first in a series of agricultural shocks occurred. Wheat prices, long above 100s. per quarter, turned in anticipation of an abundant harvest. As the harvest came in, wheat dropped below 100s.; it fell past 80s. in November. The combined weight of foreign imports and the stock remaining from 1813 kept prices under 80s. through 1814 and below 60s. for most of 1815 (see App. C.1). The immediate effects were severe[8] because a third of the populace was directly employed in agriculture.[9]

---

[3] Evidence of the disparity in production costs between England and the Continent supported the arguments of protectionists who wanted a more restrictive corn law (Mitchison 1959, 62).

[4] House of Commons 1814, *Report of the Select Committee on Petitions Relating to the Corn Laws*, 6, in *Parliamentary Papers* 1813–1814, 3:200, MF 15.15. Similar findings were made by the House of Lords Committee on Grain and the Corn Laws (1814).

[5] The Corn Law of 1804 permitted importation at any domestic price. Wheat was subject to a high tariff (24s. 3d.) at prices below 63s., but above 63s. the tariff became insignificant. Because wheat prices remained high during the war, the 1804 law never came into effect. This fact is discussed at length in Barnes (1930, 89, 121). Hollander (1997, 868–870) provides a valuable summary of the various corn laws.

[6] Four successive harvests failed starting in 1809. The price of wheat reached 155s. per Winchester quarter in Aug. 1812. It did not fall below 100s. until Sept. 1813 (see App. C.1).

[7] Spencer Walpole estimated the voting power of the landed gentry at about 150 (Smart 1910–1917, Vol. 2, 37).

[8] William Spence wrote that the best grain was sold at a loss, even ignoring rent charges (1815, 2). Malthus described the situation as far worse and more extensive than any mercantile distress that ever took place in the country (1815a, 7).

[9] See the census reports for either 1811 or 1821.

After much wrangling,[10] Parliament approved a fiercely protectionist[11] corn law. The bill prohibited foreign imports unless the country was on the verge of famine. It was an infamous piece of legislation.[12] The clamor soon faded, however, when the abundant harvest of 1815 cut wheat prices to 55s. (see App. C.1). The position of farmers grew worse after a late drought forced the sale of large numbers of cattle (Smart 1910–1917, 1:435). Low prices of corn and stock caused a reduction in the demand for agricultural land to such an extent that in some districts marginally productive farms were abandoned *en masse*: "The tenants are throwing up their farms in bodies; selling their little stock, and quitting the country. Large tracts of country are literally laid waste, as if the ravages of pestilence, or famine, or war, had swept every thing away before them; and proprietors, who used to receive thousands a year of rent,[13] have now not nearly so many hundreds, and, in some cases, scarcely any thing at all" (*Edinburgh Review*, June 1816, 257).

Country banks felt the crisis as landlords, farmers, and land speculators defaulted on mortgages.[14] There followed a twenty-four month financial

[10] On 22 Mar. 1813 – before corn prices began to fall – a select committee was appointed to inquire into the corn trade of the United Kingdom. The committee proposed the free export of corn from Great Britain and Ireland, but nothing came of these proposals (Barnes 1930, 117–118). Debate in Parliament on the corn laws resumed on May 5, 1814 under conditions opposite those in 1813. The House of Lords Committee on the Growth, Commerce and Consumption of Grain (1814) reported twice, but made no policy proposals (Barnes 1930, 129–130). The House of Commons Committee on the Corn Laws (1814) endorsed agricultural protection. Its recommendations formed the basis of the 1815 Corn Law, which passed the Commons on 10 Mar. 1815. Third reading in the Lords occurred on 20 Mar. The bill received royal assent on 23 Mar. (Smart 1910–1917, 1:451–453).

[11] The bill of 1815 prohibited the importation of wheat at prices below 80s. per quarter, but allowed duty-free importation once domestic prices exceeded this threshold for three consecutive weeks. By comparison, the Corn Law of 1804 only prohibited imports when the domestic price of wheat exceeded 63s. per quarter. With respect to other types of corn, the law of 1815 permitted the importation of barley at 40s., oats at 26s., and rye, peas, and beans at 53s. The law allowed importations from Quebec and the North American colonies at rates 25 percent below those for foreign corn (Lowe 1822, App., 128–129).

[12] The total number of signatories to Parliamentary petitions against the 1815 Corn Law amounted to 1,817,000, whereas 10,000 petitioners lobbied for the legislation. On 6 Mar. 1815, riots against the bill began in London and continued for several days; some lives were lost. Robinson, the Vice President of the Board of Trade and the man who introduced the nine resolutions on which the 1815 law was based, had his home sacked ("Chronological Arrangement of Remarkable Occurrences for the Year 1815," *Scots Magazine*, Jan. 1816, 19).

[13] By 1816 rents, generally, had fallen by a third to a half (Fussell and Compton 1939, 194).

[14] The country banks had overextended credit for speculative land purchases and agricultural improvements because everyone assumed that land was a safe investment (Buer

debacle:[15] "The importations of foreign corn, subsequent to the opening of the Dutch ports in 1814, by occasioning a great decline of the price of the principal article of agricultural produce, produced an unprecedented degree of distress, first among the farmers and latterly among the country bankers. It is estimated that, in 1815 and 1816, no fewer than 240 private banking companies either became altogether bankrupt, or, at least, stopped payment" (*Edinburgh Review*, July 1821, 477–478).[16] Twenty-five banks failed during the latter half of 1814; that many again collapsed in 1815; and an additional twenty-six became bankrupt over the first half of 1816.[17]

In spite of the severity of the agricultural depression, the crisis was short-lived. Corn began to rise in January 1816, increasing rapidly so that by April, renters were returning to once-abandoned farms (*Annual Register*, 1816, Chronicle 55). By August 1816, wheat sold above 80s. per quarter. After the harvest of 1816 failed, British farmers enjoyed two and a half years of extreme prices. For eight months, wheat even surpassed 100s. per quarter (see App. C.1). The ports were open but foreign supplies never appeared because the Continent was also in famine (Tooke and Newmarch 1838–1857, 2:14–18). In Rotterdam, the average price of wheat for 1817 was 104s. sterling per quarter (see App. C.3).

Aggregate business conditions did not correspond with the fluctuations of agricultural prices. The peak of a long boom in aggregate activity occurred in the summer of 1815 – two years into the agricultural depression and months before its lowest depths. The ensuing cyclical trough of aggregate activity occurred in September 1816 – a time when agriculture was again prospering and wheat prices were above 80s. At the next cyclical peak, September 1818, wheat sold for 80s. In the subsequent trough, September 1819, it sold for 73s. Given the timing of these events, aggregate business conditions seem more aligned with fluctuations in foreign trade than with the state of British agriculture. This is not to suggest that agricultural demand was unimportant, but changes in the consumption

---

1921, 161). Prior to 1814, the banks had been flourishing. In 1813, only eight of the nearly six hundred country banks in England and Wales became bankrupt.

[15] The country-banking crisis began in July 1814 as a consequence of the fall in corn prices. Reversals in foreign trade in the autumn of 1814 created additional troubles, but exports increased again in the spring of 1815, and it was not until the collapse of foreign demand for home goods in 1815 that there were widespread bank failures as a result of speculative investments in foreign trade.

[16] A similar description of the crisis appears in the *Edinburgh Review*, July 1819, 54.

[17] *Report from the Committee of Secrecy on the Bank of England Charter*, App. 101, in *Parliamentary Papers* 1831–1832, 6:599, MF 35.39–45.

of landlords, farmers, and agricultural laborers were frequently offset by variations in the demand for exports.

The Postwar Depression: Fall 1815 to Spring 1817

As the allied powers neared victory, British merchants anticipated a renewed demand for their exports. The manufacture of exportable commodities proceeded with such intensity that wages and commodity prices rose from late 1813 through the spring of 1815. The tremendous demand for goods enabled workmen in some districts "to raise their wages twice in a week" (*Scots Magazine*, Nov. 1813, 854). This state of affairs continued for some time: "Commercial speculation in all branches has been uncommonly active since the battle of Leipsic, and especially since the passage of the Rhine by the allied powers" (*Scots Magazine*, Feb. 1814, 83).

Initially, the speculations seemed justified. The quantities of goods exported in 1814 exceeded those of any previous year.[18] Aggregate exports increased by another 20 percent in 1815 (see App. D.1). In addition, British military demands for manufactured goods remained high till late 1815, as Parliament voted a vigorous campaign, and even after the Hundred Days, large expenditures were required to support the allied occupation. In a Parliamentary address on 20 February 1815, the Chancellor of the Exchequer described conditions as "the most flourishing period which the history of this country presented" (*Hansard* 1s, 29:860). His assessment is confirmed by the continued rise in money wages at a time – 1814 and early 1815 – when the price of subsistence was declining (Tooke and Newmarch 1838–1857, 2:5, 6).

Under normal circumstances, the speculative boom would have been checked by a lack of credit facilities. However, the Bank of England had extended its circulation farther than usual, allowing an increase in both commercial credit and country-bank issues.[19] The Bank did not deliberately increase private credit – its commercial discounts were modest during the final years of the war (see App. A.6) – but as the conflict intensified in violence and expense, fiscal pressures forced the government to demand liberal advances from the Bank, leading to an increase in the

---

[18] The boom in exports is evident in the report on customs and excise revenues reprinted in *Scots Magazine*, Sept. 1815, 657.

[19] Country banknotes were convertible upon demand into Bank of England notes. They could not be issued without limit because they would be returned to the issuing banks if they became depreciated relative to Bank of England paper. The increase of country notes is evident in Parliamentary reports of 1814 and 1815 (see App. B.1 and B.2).

circulation of its paper[20] and abetting the investments in foreign trade that followed (Acworth 1925, 71).

The prosperity of trade and manufacturing began to ebb in the summer or perhaps early fall of 1815 as foreign demand proved less than anticipated.[21] Continental powers emerged from the war "in a state of comparative poverty and distress" (*Edinburgh Review*, Feb. 1816, 136). Moreover, the Continent was not as dependent on British manufactures as before the war because competitive industries had developed during the years of the Continental System (Gayer et al. 1953, 121). Barriers to foreign trade[22] further hampered British exports, as did renewed competition for Mediterranean markets.[23] Competition from Continental merchant marines in the Mediterranean alone forced more than 800 British ships and 10,000 British sailors out of employment (Smart 1910–1917, 1:461, 462). Because of the reversals in foreign trade in 1815, British commodities glutted markets in Europe and the United States, reducing prices "far below the original cost" (*Annual Register*, 1815, Chronicle 176). In a Parliamentary speech of 9 April 1816, Brougham commented on the "rage for exporting goods of every kind" in 1814 and 1815 that caused English goods to be "a dead weight without any sale at all; and either no returns whatever were received or pounds came back for thousands that

---

[20] The Bank's financial assistance to the government increased steadily from 1807 through the end of the war. The circulation of banknotes increased as well, from £17,205,344 in Feb. 1807 to £27,024,049 in Aug. 1815 (House of Commons 1819, *Second Report from the Secret Committee on the Expediency of the Bank Resuming Cash Payments*, App. 3 and 10).

[21] Gayer assigns the peak of the business cycles to Mar. 1815 (Gayer et al. 1953, 110). Tax data, however, show that general economic activity continued to increase through the third quarter of 1815 (see App. E.2). Trade with the Continent was depressed by June 1815 (*New Monthly Magazine*, July 1815, 579), but a strong demand for commodities to export to the United States prevented a further decline in prices (*New Monthly Magazine*, Aug. 1815, 90). Through the end of the summer it seemed like conditions might improve: "the continental markets generally indicate an improvement in the price of most of our export articles of merchandize, both colonial and manufactured, [causing] the prices here to be fully supported" (*New Monthly Magazine*, Sept. 1815, 184).

[22] In 1816, the United States levied duties of 25 percent on commodities that could be amply produced domestically and 20 percent on those that could not (Smart 1910–1977, 1:495).

[23] During the war, the Dey of Algiers had been allied with Britain, providing the British merchant marine a monopoly of the Mediterranean trade because the Barbary pirates preyed upon all but English ships. This privileged position ended when, in a "fit of magnanimity," British forces commanded by Lord Exmouth attacked Algiers, destroyed the pirates, and opened the Mediterranean to trade (Smart, 1:461).

had gone forth . . . [leading to] a prodigious diminution in the demand for manufactures and indirectly, a serious defalcation in the demand for the produce of land" (*Edinburgh Review*, June 1816, 263). Many bankruptcies ensued.[24]

The importance of foreign trade to postwar conditions should not be underestimated. Gayer remarks that "we have here a crisis the basis of which was prior investment in consumption goods for export and re-export" (Gayer et al. 1953, 117). The official value of goods exported – a measure that reflects quantities traded not market prices – declined by 17 percent from 1815 to 1816. The market value of exports declined by £10 million – about 20 percent – over the same period (see App. D.1). The state of foreign trade was thoroughly documented in government reports[25] and in the commercial press.

Even without a collapse in trade, the postwar transition would have been difficult. Upon the peace of 1815, military expenditures "suddenly diminished by about fifty millions[26] a year" (*Edinburgh Review*, June 1816, 262). The reduction in government spending accounted for nearly 18 percent of aggregate demand, as compared with estimates of British national product: £232 million in 1801, £301 million in 1811 and £291 million in 1821 (Dean and Cole 1967, 166). The effects of demobilization were particularly serious: "The reduction of the army and navy at this particular period, and the return of many soldiers and sailors to their friends just when there was a difficulty of finding employment was a considerable aggravation of the distress, rendering the employment of ordinary labourers more difficult, besides throwing these also on the public market of labour" (*Scots Magazine*, July 1817, 493). By comparing the number of soldiers employed by the British military (see Table 2.1) with the male population of Great Britain – which the census of 1821 estimated at six million and of whom two and a half million were below the age of fifteen – it appears that the 413,000 soldiers discharged after the war accounted for more than 10 percent of the male labor force.[27]

---

[24] The number of bankruptcies rose sharply. Commissions of bankruptcy in the years 1814 to 1818 were as follows: 1814, 1612 bankruptcies; 1815, 2284; 1816, 2731; 1817, 1927; and 1818, 1245 (*Journal of the House of Commons* 1822, 77:1305).

[25] A list of these reports, which came to sixty pages in 1816, appears in the Appendix to the *Journal of the House of Commons*.

[26] The reduction in annual government expenditures between 1814 and 1817 was £53.3 million.

[27] The numbers for soldiers, sailors, and marines in service appear in Acworth (1925, 23). Population figures are taken from the census returns for 1811 and 1821: *Abstracts of Population Returns for 1811*, 509; in *Parliamentary Papers* 1812, 11:543; and *Enumeration*

Table 2.1. *Enrollment in*
British Fighting Services

Year	Soldiers, Sailors, Marines in Service
1814	534,351
1815	365,392
1816	178,724
1817	121,168

The reduction of military spending also affected the 100,000 laborers in war-related industries (Lowe 1822, 62). The ironworks, in particular, suffered "extensive ruin" as the annual average price for pig iron at the forge fell from £6 0s. 0d. in 1814 to £3 16s. 0d. by 1816 (Gayer et al. 1953, 128). Even in April 1817, when most manufactures were reviving, Brougham presented a petition signed by almost the whole laboring population of Birmingham – 11,000 signatures had been obtained in forty-eight hours – pleading for relief (*Hansard* 1s, 36:21).[28]

Timing of the Postwar Depression

Treasury accounts indicate that from the quarter ended July 1813 through the quarter ended October 1815, customs, excise, and property tax revenues steadily increased.[29] This reflects the general prosperity that prevailed through the end of the conflict. The subsequent reversals in foreign trade and domestic manufacturing were manifest in falling tax revenues starting the fourth quarter of 1815. The depth of the crisis seems to have occurred in mid-1816.[30] An increase in excise revenues the first quarter of

---

and Parish Registers of Great Britain according to the Census of 1821, 542–543, in *Parliamentary Papers* 1822, 15:582–583.

[28] In March 1817, Brougham cited statistics to demonstrate the situation in Birmingham: "of a population of 84,000, about 27,500 were receiving parish relief. Of the work people, one third were wholly out of employ and the rest were at half work. The poor rates had risen to between £50,000 and £60,000 a year, a sum exceeding what the inhabitants paid in income tax" (Smart, 1:595).

[29] This occurred notwithstanding the fact that £1.1 million in customs duties were repealed over the twenty-four month period (*A Return of the Gross and Net Amount of All Taxes Repealed, Expired or Reduced in Each Year since the Termination of the War*, in *Parliamentary Papers* 1833, 32:637–653, MF 36.239).

[30] Customs returns for the third quarter of 1816 were down by about 30 percent as compared with 1815; excise returns had declined nearly 17 percent. Gayer assigns the depth of the depression to Sept. 1816 (Gayer et al. 1953, 110).

1817[31] signaled an end to general distress. The subsequent economic expansion peaked in either the third or fourth quarter of 1818, depending on whether one attaches more weight to customs or excise figures. General prosperity continued through January 1819 (tax reports are reproduced in App. E.2).

Tax reports permit historians to trace the business cycle. They also indicate how economic fluctuations would have been perceived at the time. For though Britain did not have national income statistics in the modern sense, members of Parliament and financiers in the City used tax reports to estimate changes in aggregate economic activity.[32] The Finance Committee of 1817, for instance, gauged the severity of the depression by comparing tax revenues in 1816 with revenues of the four preceding years:

The nature and extent of the distress which has prevailed throughout those classes of the community which constitute the bulk of the population, were too strongly impressed upon the minds of Your Committee, to admit of the supposition that under such circumstances the Revenue could have been productive in an ordinary degree.... the revenue derived from articles of most general consumption must be injured by the calamity of a deficient harvest [in 1816]; and the distress proceeding from this cause had followed immediately that rapid fall of prices by which the agriculture of the kingdom had been so greatly depressed and had in conjunction with the effect produced upon the commerce and manufacturing industry of the country by the sudden changes which had occurred in the political state of Europe.

Your Committee are enabled to present at one view a statement of the comparative productiveness of each branch of the Revenue in the year 1816 and for the four several years which preceded it. The result of this comparison will shew that the Revenue in the year 1816 was considerably less productive than in the year 1815.... It will further be observed that the receipt of the year 1815 was an extraordinarily large one.... Your Committee [are] fully impressed with the belief

---

[31] From the second quarter of 1816, I consider customs and excise revenues rather than total revenues because with the repeal of the property tax in March 1816, total revenues declined far below wartime levels. The amount of excise duties collected in 1817 was less than in 1816, but this does not indicate that aggregate economic activity was reduced. It instead reflects the fact that £2.9 million in excise taxes were repealed in 1816 (*A Return of the Gross and Net Amount of All Taxes Repealed, Expired or Reduced in Each Year since the Termination of the War*, in *Parliamentary Papers* 1833, 32:637–653, MF 36.239).

[32] There are frequent references in *Hansard* to the "tax abstracts" that appeared quarterly when Parliament was in session. Appendix E.1 lists the dates on which tax reports were presented to Parliament. The House of Commons Finance Committee was another source of information on matters relating to public finance. At each session of Parliament, the committee reported the government's income and expenditures from the previous fiscal year and estimated expenditures and tax revenues for the current and upcoming fiscal years.

that the unfavourable returns of the Revenue in the year 1816 are essentially referable to the general distresses of the Country. (*Report of the Select Committee on Finance* 1817, 121–124, in *Parliamentary Papers* 1817, 4:143–146, MF 18.21)

In estimating revenues for 1817, the Finance Committee was more optimistic because an economic recovery seemed to be underway:

Of the degree in which some melioration may already have taken place, it would be premature to state any distinct opinion. [The Committee] have, however, thought it right to call for such information as could be acquired upon this very important point from some of the persons most conversant, practically, with the Manufacturing and Commercial Industry of the Country; and the opinions of these persons as to the actual commencement or the early prospect of returning activity are upon the whole encouraging. Your Committee feel warranted . . . in expressing as belief that a favourable alteration is already manifesting itself throughout the Country. (*Report of the Select Committee on Finance* 1817, 125, in *Parliamentary Papers* 1817, 4:147, MF 18.21)

The assessments of the Finance Committee concerning the severity of the depression in 1816 and the recovery of 1817 were confirmed by the commercial press. To my knowledge, the first mention of a general depression appeared in the *Scots Magazine* of October 1815 under the heading "The Causes of Our Domestic Embarrassments, and of the Depreciation of Property."[33] The *Edinburgh Review* noted in February 1816 an "unprecedented stagnation in almost every branch of our industry" (Feb. 1816, 136). The *Review* later reported that "at no former period of the history of this country was so great and so general a distress ever known to prevail. . . . During the last twelve or eighteen months the country has been suffering severely in every direction; in its agriculture and its manufactures; its home trade and foreign commerce" (June 1816, 255–256). The article attributed the crisis to unfounded speculations in 1814 and early 1815, but observed that the reversals in foreign trade were unrelated to the agricultural depression, which resulted from "over cultivation, enclosures and improvements" combined with "some of the best harvests that had ever been known" (262). A third article in the *Review* echoed the two preceding but also mentioned that "the labourer now has to struggle against low wages and dear provisions" (Dec. 1816, 374).

---

[33] Editors of the *Scots Magazine* were evidently not concerned about a general depression over the summer of 1815. The *Scots'* Commercial Reports for August and September 1815 covered, respectively, the Newfoundland trade and the first opium sale of the year for the East India Company in Calcutta.

The Distressed State of Laborers

The reference in the *Edinburgh Review* to laborers reflects the unemployment, starvation, and civil unrest prevalent in manufacturing districts.[34]
Violence erupted in May 1816 as rioters protested the rising price of corn
by "the breaking of threshing machines, the destruction of barns and
corn stocks and by malicious fire-raising" (*Scots Magazine*, June 1816,
469). The outburst was understandable because a sudden rise in corn
prices – from 53s. to 100s. per quarter over twelve months – coincided
with high unemployment and declining wages: "In the course of this disastrous period . . . all the evils to which the labourer was formerly exposed
were necessarily aggravated by the scarcity of subsistence" (*Edinburgh
Magazine*, Aug. 1817, 39).

Faced with high prices, a general depression, and structural unemployment, laborers directed their frustration toward the bugbear of machinery. Legally, their only recourse was to petition Parliament for relief, as
in these examples.[35]

In consequence of the extensive introduction of Spring Looms into the department
of the Woollen Manufactory . . . they can no longer provide for themselves and
their families, a great number of them having been thereby thrown out of employ
and are reduced to the humiliating necessity of seeking parochial aid (*Petition
of Cloth Weavers of Somerset, Wilts and Gloucester*, 6 Feb. 1817, *Journal of the
House of Commons* 1817, 72:32).

[Petitioners] heretofore maintained themselves and their families, but in consequence of the extensive introduction of Machinery into that department of the
Woollen Trade, they are no longer able to (*Petition of Inhabitants of Leeds relating
to the Use of Machinery*, 11 Feb. 1817, *Journal of the House of Commons* 1817,
72:49).

A petition of several Clothworkers of the County of Gloucester, complaining of
the use of Machinery in the manufacture of Cloth was presented and read (*Petition
of Clothworkers of Gloucester*, 5 Mar. 1817, *Journal of the House of Commons*
1817, 72:138).

The petitioners hoped that a Parliamentary committee would inquire into
their complaints and perhaps even limit the use of machinery in their

---

[34] The Chronicle of the *Annual Register* (1817) gives a detailed account of the unrest. For a
summary of the government's response, including the suspension of the Habeas Corpus
Act and the renewal of the "Gagging Bill," see Smart, 1:548–550.

[35] General indices to the *Journals of the House of Commons* for 1801–1820 and 1820–1837
provide partial lists of petitions. The greatest number of petitions relating to machinery
appeared in 1817.

trades. Their petitions were heard and sometimes considered,[36] but the political process held little promise. By contrast, the outright destruction of machinery brought certain and visceral rewards.[37] Frequent violence forced Parliament to enact strict penalties against machine breaking.[38]

As the depression continued, laborers turned to radical political solutions. Protests in some districts bordered on open insurrection. The House of Commons appointed the Committee of Secrecy on Papers Presented to the House Sealed Up (1817) and the House of Lords formed the Secret Committee to Consider Several Papers Sealed Up in a Bag (1817) to examine the revolutionary schemes of secret societies, which, it was supposed, intended "a total overthrow of all existing Establishments, and a division of the Landed, and extinction of the Funded property of the Country."[39] Parliament's concerns may have been justified, judging by the machinations uncovered, which included the hoarding of pikes, looting of gunsmiths, and even a cabal to raid the Tower of London and Bank of England.[40] In Manchester the conspirators actually designed "to set fire to the factories in the town [and] it was declared by one of the conspirators, that this atrocity was intended for the purpose of increasing the prevalent distress, in the hope of thereby adding to the numbers of the discontented, by throwing the workmen out of employment."[41] The government met these threats, real and imagined, by suspending the Habeas Corpus Act and by reimposing the Act of 1795 for the prevention of seditious meetings.

---

[36] Here is a partial list of Parliamentary committees that investigated controversies surrounding mechanization: Committee on the Petitions of Calico Printers, 1803–1804; Second Committee . . . Calico Printers, 1806; Committee on Petitions of Cotton Weavers, 1810–1811; Committee on Framework Knitters Petitions, 1812; Committee on Machinery for Manufacturing Flax, 1812–1813; Second Committee . . . Manufacturing Flax, 1817; Second Committee . . . Framework Knitters, 1819.

[37] The Chronology of the *Annual Register* (1816) provides accounts of specific acts of machine breaking.

[38] In the 1816 session, Parliament passed the Bill for More Effectual Punishment of Persons Riotously Destroying or Damaging Buildings, Engines, and Machinery in Collieries and Mines. Similar legislation had been approved earlier: the 1812 Bill for More Exemplary Punishment of Persons Destroying Stocking or Lace Frames or Other Machines and the 1813–1814 Act for Punishment of Persons Destroying Stocking or Lace Frames.

[39] House of Commons, *Report from the Committee of Secrecy*, 19 Feb. 1817, in *Parliamentary Papers* 1817, 4:3, MF 18.20.

[40] House of Commons, *Report from the Committee of Secrecy*, 19 Feb. 1817, in *Parliamentary Papers* 1817, 4:4–5, MF 18.20.

[41] House of Commons, *Second Report from the Committee of Secrecy*, 20 June 1817, in *Parliamentary Papers* 1817, 4:10, MF 18.20.

Economic Recovery and the Prosperity of 1818

The government responded in gentler ways too, approving the Employment of the Poor Bill in May 1817, whereby Exchequer bills were loaned through a board of twenty-one commissioners[42] to fund "the employment of the present unemployed population" (Flinn 1961, 88).[43] Financially the project was a success; when presenting the budget the following year Vansittart noted that "there was a sum of £21,448 arising from the profits resulting from the loan of £1,000,000 of exchequer bills granted last year to promote public works and for the general employment of the poor; which profits the commissioners for managing that loan had already paid into the exchequer; and much more was expected to be returned in the course of the current year" (20 Apr. 1818, *Hansard* 1s, 38:211). As a remedy for economic distress, however, the project was less impressive. Not only were funds not directed to the most affected areas of the north and the midlands, but also by the time the commissioners began to evaluate applications for loans – the first applications were received on 24 June 1817 (Flinn 1961, 89) – aid was superfluous.[44]

Economic recovery began early in 1817. Private relief works in Edinburgh began to close in April for want of applicants, and by mid-July business periodicals pronounced a *bona fide* recovery:

On the 7th April, a meeting was called to take into consideration the propriety of continuing or discontinuing the further employment of labourers.... it was essentially necessary to adopt some mode of terminating this artificial aid during the summer, now that the pressure of the winter was over, and when a renewal of employment, to a certain extent, had taken place ... if circumstances did not authorize our stopping now, it seemed impossible to say we could cease at any later period; for every thing indicated that a return of employment was already commenced ("Report of the Committee for Affording Relief to the Labouring Classes in Edinburgh," *Scots Magazine*, July 1817, 493).

We state again, with much pleasure, that our intelligence from the different Manufacturing districts continues favourable. Trade is reviving slowly;[45] and the best proof of it is that all the workmen are now in employment. Wages have also risen,

---

[42] The board was later known as the Public Works Loan Board. At the outset it had twenty-three commissioners, several of whom were friends of Ricardo: Thornton, Baring, Tierney, and Bosanquet (*Hansard* 1s, 36:574).

[43] Vansittart proposed the measure on 28 Apr. 1817. It was approved in May 1817 (*Hansard* 1s, 36:569,818).

[44] The Employment of the Poor Bill did not receive royal assent until 16 June (Flinn 1961, 82).

[45] The quantities of goods exported changed little in 1817. Orders were higher, however, as reflected in the surge in exports in 1818 (see App. D.1).

though, we doubt, not yet in proportion to the prices of provisions. In Glasgow and some other places, those charitable establishments which had been formed for distributing soups, &c. have been given up as no longer necessary (*Blackwood's Edinburgh Magazine*, July 1817, 444).

The revival of domestic manufacturing continued through 1818:

Lead and Iron Mines, almost abandoned, are resuming their former activity. The value of land is increased, and general confidence seems fast approaching, and settling upon a sure and solid foundation.... The Cotton manufactures of the United States and Continental Europe have sunk before our own, and left us undisputed masters of this lucrative branch of trade. The general exports of this kingdom during last year will be found greatly to exceed in quantity most, if not all, those of every preceding year. Manufactures flourish and increase: work is abundant, and all hands employed. The wages in some branches are in comparison to the still high price of some necessaries of life, as yet but low, though much increased; while in most others these are not only good, but liberal (*Blackwood's Edinburgh Magazine*, Jan. 1818, 464).

The business sections of the *Edinburgh Magazine* contained similar accounts of full employment (Jan. 1818, 92) and the "improvement in the condition of the labouring classes" (Apr. 1818, 391). By the fall of 1818, even the ironworks were operating at capacity, with "foreign orders being so great that they cannot be completed with sufficient celerity" (Sept. 1818, 291). Government statistics confirm the accounts in the commercial press. In 1818, real exports advanced £4.7 million, or 11 percent, as compared with exports in 1817 (see App. D.1); imports increased by £6.1 million or 20 percent.

Monetary Policy of the Bank of England

The Bank of England received much abuse for its postwar policies. An early point of criticism concerned the Bank's failure to respond to the collapse of private credit in the depression of 1816. The criticism was justified because at this critical period, the Bank sharply curtailed discounts. A second controversy surrounded the Bank's decision in 1817 to advance £12 million in notes to the government on the security of Exchequer bills. The advance occurred just as the economy was returning to full employment, and it initiated a further – and unnecessary – round of inflation. Both criticisms are addressed below.

With the decline in agricultural earnings starting in 1813, landlords and farmers failed to repay many loans contracted during the war. A crisis among country banks in rural districts ensued. Distress spread to manufacturing centers when foreign markets collapsed in late 1815. The combined effects of the two shocks produced what McCulloch described as "the prodigious diminution of bank paper.... In that period, above 240 country banks became altogether bankrupt, or at least stopped payment. The Board of Agriculture estimated that in the county of Lincoln alone above three millions of bank paper had been withdrawn from circulation; and the total diminution of the currency during 1814, 1815 and 1816, has never been estimated at less than twenty millions, though it probably amounted to much more" (*Edinburgh Review*, Dec. 1818, 65). McCulloch's account agreed with evidence presented to Parliament by Francis Horner showing that "from the accounts on the table,[46] he was convinced that a greater and more sudden reduction of the circulating medium had never taken place in any country.... The reduction of the currency had originated in the previous fall of the prices of agricultural produce. The fall had produced a destruction of country bank paper, to an extent which would not have been thought possible without more ruin than had actually ensued" (*Morning Chronicle*, 2 May 1816). The Bank of England lent no support to the country banks. Instead, at the height of distress, between January and December 1816, the Bank reduced trade bills and notes under discount from £19.1 million to £6.5 million (Gayer et al. 1953, 132).

The sudden withdrawal of banknotes brought the foreign exchange to par and reduced the market price of gold to £3 18s. 6d. (see App. C.4). Gold might have returned to par, except that the Bank of England committed to purchase bullion above the Mint price. The Bank's decision to purchase gold at a premium caused it to accumulate a hoard of more than £10 million (see App. A.2), a treasure so immense that in November 1816 the directors initiated a resumption of cash payments at the ancient Mint price for all £1 and £2 notes issued before 1812. No demand for specie occurred in response to this offer. The Bank made similar commitments in April 1817 and September 1817[47] and, according to Tooke, the prospects for a complete and permanent resumption of cash payments appeared good: "It is quite clear that the value of paper had been virtually restored,

---

[46] Horner referred to an account of stamps on country banknotes presented to the House of Commons on 1 May 1816. The report covered the period Oct. 1813 to Oct. 1815. By law, banks were required to purchase stamps – which meant paying a per-unit tax – for the promissory notes they issued.

[47] In April, the Bank promised to pay in cash £1 and £2 notes dated prior to 1816. In Sept., the Bank promised to pay in cash all notes of any denomination dated prior to 1817 (Smart, 1:616).

and that the Bank was in 1817 in a position looking only to the amount of its treasure relatively to its circulation, extended as this was, to resume cash payments" (Tooke and Newmarch 1838–1857, 2:50).

Notwithstanding the favorable circumstances, the Bank did not effect a complete resumption of cash payments at par in 1817 and, in fact, failed to accomplish the task until 1821. Opponents of the Bank questioned how there could have been a four-year delay in implementing a policy that was practically in place in 1817. The answer, as outlined in what follows, involves a complicated sequence of disruptions in foreign exchange markets coupled with an ill-timed expansion of the money supply caused by a £12 million advance from the Bank to the government to finance the Exchequer's fictitious sinking fund.

Because of an exodus of capital and vast importations of corn, sterling reversed its course on the foreign exchange in March 1817. By July 1817 it became profitable to export gold (see App. C.4). There followed a rapid depletion of the Bank's hoard (see App. A.3 and A.4) because all notes of the Bank of England dated prior to 1 January 1817 were at that time convertible. Under normal circumstances, the Bank would have contracted its notes to raise the value of sterling on the exchange, but this policy was not followed. Instead, the government forced the Bank to increase its circulation via a £12 million cash advance on Exchequer bills during the summer of 1817. The issues of country banks expanded in turn (see App. B.1). The metallic component of the money supply may also have increased because the Bank issued more than £1 million in gold coin and the Mint issued £4.2 million in new silver coin during 1817 (see App. A.3 and B.4).

The fall of sterling in 1817 occurred partly in response to an exodus of foreign and domestic capital and partly because of the need to make sizeable remittances abroad for the corn and commodity imports of 1817 and 1818. The exodus of capital was caused by investors on the Continent who had purchased millions in British funds during the war, but then withdrew their wealth as peace returned. Table 2.2 shows the magnitude of these transfers of capital. The account pertains to foreign holdings of British government debt; other types of foreign investment are not included.

Loans raised in Britain by Continental powers contributed to the outflow of capital. France negotiated loans to pay the installments of its war indemnity. Russia, Prussia, and Austria borrowed funds for postwar reconstruction, including the recovery of their monetary systems, all of which returned to a metallic standard (Gayer et al. 1953, 162). Table 2.3

Table 2.2. *Foreign Holdings of British Debt*

Report Date	Foreign Ownership of British Funds
29 February 1816	£17,334,458
31 August 1816	17,235,150
1 March 1817	15,892,711
30 August 1817	13,305,397
28 February 1818	12,729,618
31 August 1818	12,486,913

Source: House of Commons, *Second Report from the Secret Committee on . . . Cash Payments* 1819, App. 43, in *Parliamentary Papers* 1819, 3:354, MF 20.29.

breaks down by country and year the amounts of funds raised in London by Continental powers. British citizens invested more than £7 million in these loans. Their willingness to supply foreign governments with capital was partly caused by low interest rates in the home market. Both Thomas Tooke and Nathan Rothschild, in testimony before the 1819 House of Commons Committee on Resumption, cited low returns as one cause for the flight of capital.[48] Alexander Baring made a similar observation before the House of Lords Committee on Resumption: "The difference in the rate of interest in this country and in foreign countries, has undoubtedly occasioned considerable transfers of capital abroad. Nor do I think that it is likely to discontinue, whether new loans are made there or not, as long as the same disproportion continues to exist between the value of capital in this and other countries."[49] In total, no less than £12 million in capital was transferred to the Continent during 1817 and 1818.[50]

In addition to the exodus of capital, extensive imports of corn and other commodities helped turn the foreign exchange. Tooke reported that a "scarcity of corn and of nearly all the leading articles of consumption"

[48] House of Commons, *Minutes of Evidence Taken before the Secret Committee on . . . Cash Payments* 1819; Thomas Tooke's testimony, 125–132; Rothschild's testimony, 157–163; in *Parliamentary Papers* 1819, 3:129–136, 161–167, MF 20.27.

[49] House of Lords, *Minutes of Evidence Taken before the Lords Committees Appointed to Enquire into . . . Cash Payments* 1819, 103, in *Parliamentary Papers* 1819, 3:469, MF 20.30.

[50] The detailed examination of capital flows is warranted not only because capital flight interrupted the return to cash payments but also because the transfers of wealth to the Continent supported the view that Britain's economic woes were partly due to a deficiency of capital. This view had implications for both agricultural and fiscal policies and supported the members of the opposition in Parliament who claimed that the corn laws and high taxes discouraged domestic investment.

Table 2.3. *Loans Raised in Britain by Continental Powers*

	1817	1818
France*	£12,041,364	£15,014,166
Russia	1,106,875	2,966,145
Prussia		2,790,000
Austria[†]		4,100,000
Holland		1,818,181
Private European Loans		16,000,000

*Baring Brothers served as loan contractors for the Austrian loan in 1818 and for the French loans in 1817, 1818, and 1819.
[†]The financial demands by Austria–Hungary and Russia were high because these nations were returning their currencies to silver standards (Hawtrey 1934, 341).
Source: Statement of British and Foreign Loans, Contracted in 1817 and 1818, dated 7 May 1819. *Journal of the House of Lords* 1819, 52:374.

was evident in Britain by early 1817 (Tooke and Newmarch 1838–1857, 2:61). The scarcity stemmed from the poor harvest of 1816 and the drop in foreign trade and domestic production during the depression of 1816. Shortages brought rising prices, accompanied by "the usually exaggerated speculations connected with them, which continued through the greater part of 1818" and resulted in "importations of enormous magnitude" (2:61). The official value of imports rose by £6.1 million, about 20 percent, from 1817 to 1818 (see App. D.1). Imports of principal commodities increased by even greater percentages (see Table 2.4 and App. D.2 and D.3).

In response to the exodus of capital and the imports of 1817, the foreign exchange turned against Britain in July 1817. Exporting gold became profitable and the Bank gradually lost its reserves – about £400,000 per month

Table 2.4. *Imports of Commodities*

Commodity	1817	1818
Barley (qtrs.)	161,811	722,843
Beans (qtrs.)	5,850	120,779
Oats – Foreign (qtrs.)	478,994	989,749
Oats – Irish (qtrs.)	699,281	1,429,535
Wheat – Foreign (qtrs.)	1,030,829	1,586,030
Wheat – Irish (qtrs.)	115,794	228,709
Raw Wool (lbs.)	14,700,000	26,400,000
Raw Cotton (lbs.)	126,000,000	179,000,000

on average from October 1817 through March 1819 (see App. A.3). Normally the Bank would have contracted its notes, but this was not possible because in mid-1817 the Bank, under protest, granted the government a £12 million cash advance.

Why the government required so large an advance is not immediately obvious in that the fiscal demands of 1817 were moderate. The national deficit for the year ended 5 January 1818 was only £1.1 million as compared with total government expenditures of £58.7 million (see App. E.3). The explanation for the government's action centers on the Exchequer's sinking fund. A true sinking fund requires a budget surplus. Britain enjoyed nothing like a budget surplus during the latter years of the war. Yet millions were applied to the official sinking fund to redeem public debt during Vansittart's tenure at the Exchequer. To maintain the appearance of such a fund, the government regularly sold Exchequer bills in the open market, or to the Bank of England, then applied the revenues from these sales to repurchase long-term bonds. The government would later issue new bonds and use the proceeds to purchase Exchequer bills. William Huskisson captured the absurdity of this system in a letter of protest to Lord Liverpool in February 1819:

The mystery of our financial system no longer deceives anyone in the money market; selling Exchequer Bills daily to redeem funded debt daily, then funding those Exchequer Bills once a year, or once in two years, in order to go over the same ground again; whilst the very air of mystery and the anomaly of large annual or biennial loans in times of profound peace, create uneasiness out of the market, and in foreign countries an impression unfavourable to the solidity of our resources.... Whatever surplus of revenue we possess must be our real sinking fund; be its amount great or small (Acworth 1925, 79).

Vansittart's sinking fund wrought havoc in financial markets because the government's annual loans were larger than necessary and because the money supply was liable to increase suddenly in situations such as occurred in 1817 when the government sold £12 million in Exchequer bills to the Bank to finance its purchases of funded debt.

The depression of 1819–1820 would have been less severe had the Bank of England not advanced millions to the government in 1817. A more restrictive monetary policy would have checked the increase of country banknotes and the speculative boom in foreign trade in 1818. The Bank also would have been able to arrest inflation, turn the foreign exchange, and reverse the outflow of gold. However, instead of contracting its notes, the government "in effect paid off some £12 millions (nominal) of Funded Debt by borrowing notes from the Bank of England to the required amount!" (Acworth 1925, 78, 79).[51] Tooke was highly critical of these maneuvers: "if the increase of about £700,000 in Bank Notes in the first half of 1817 was excessive under the circumstances described, what is to be said for the prudence of the further increase which took place, to the extent of nearly two millions on the average of the following six months, when all the circumstances tending to make the former amount excessive were in full operation?" (Tooke 1823, 1:155–156). Because of the depreciation of sterling, the Bank continued to lose bullion until April 1819 (see App. A.3 and A.4) when, at the request of the Resumption Committees, cash payments were ordered stopped:

The state in which the Bank found itself in the Years 1816 and 1817 appears to have induced the Directors, in the latter year, to signify by two successive notices their intention to pay in Cash all Notes of dates antecedent to the 1st of January 1817. The effect of this measure has been to produce a considerable drain of the Treasure previously collected by the Bank . . . the Committee are decidedly of the opinion, that all practicable and advantageous operations for that purpose [Resumption] would be impeded instead of being promoted by a continuance under the present circumstances of the partial payments to which the Bank is at present liable; and they presume most strongly to recommend to the House that such payments should immediately be suspended by legislative authority.[52]

Because it mismanaged the money supply, the Bank found itself no better positioned to resume cash payments in April 1819 than it had been immediately following the war, and far worse positioned than it had been in 1817. From the spring of 1817 to January 1819 the market price of gold rose from £3 18s. 6.d. per ounce to £4 3s., the highest price since November 1815 (see App. C.4). Concurrently, the Bank lost its bullion hoard, which declined from £11.8 million in October 1817 to £3.8 million in April 1819 (see App. A.2). Government ministers attributed the failed attempt at resumption to two causes already mentioned: loans to Continental powers and unusually high imports of corn (Acworth 1925, 80). The opposition blamed the Bank's failure on the £12 million it extended

---

[51] Acworth and Tooke argued that because of the Bank's advances, the money supply was higher than it otherwise would have been, and thus the foreign exchange was more adverse and the pressure on the Bank's gold reserves was greater than necessary. The actual circulation of Bank of England notes increased less than 10 percent in 1817 (Account of the Average Amount of Bank Notes in Circulation in each Quarter of a Year, from 1792 to 1832, *Digest of Evidence on the Bank Charter* 1832, App. 12): £27,138,290 on 31 Mar. 1817; £27,541,200 on 30 June 1817; £29,504,080 on 30 Sept. 1817; £28,915,940 on 31 Dec. 1817.

[52] House of Lords, *First Report by the Lords Committee . . . Cash Payments* 1819, in *Parliamentary Papers* 1819, 3:365, MF 20.29.

to the government in 1817. In doing so, they were keen to emphasize the dangers of having the government and the Bank jointly manage an inconvertible currency (Smart 1910–1917, 1:614–624). They were also keen to emphasize the government's failure to commit to a metallic standard.

By law[53] cash payments were to resume six months after the signature of a definitive peace treaty. Such a treaty was signed on 30 May 1814, and Vansittart accordingly proposed that cash payments resume on 25 March 1815 (June 1814, *Hansard* 1s, 28:628–629). The Chancellor reversed his decision, however, in February 1815[54] on the grounds that "the Restriction Act must be continued at least until the account of our foreign expenditure could be wound up, and until the state of our exchange and of the bullion trade should be further improved" (*Hansard* 1s, 29:697, 711, 790, 1203).[55]

Following Napoleon's escape and the Hundred Days, peace treaties were ratified on 29 November 1815. According to the original Bill 44 Geo. III, cash payments were to resume in May 1816 – and indeed they might have, for the market price of gold was then at £4 per ounce and the foreign exchange had become favorable in June. Despite the opportune circumstances, "It was notorious that the bank had not taken steps for the resumption of cash payments" (3 May 1816, *Hansard* 1s, 34:247). The government consequently extended the Bank restriction until 5 July 1818 so that the Bank would have "sufficient time for all necessary preparations" (*Hansard* 1s, 34:243–244, 404–407).[56]

The deadline for restoring cash payments was postponed again during the session of 1817, this time until 1 October 1818 (*Annual Register* 1817, Chronicle 87). However, when Parliament convened in 1818, Vansittart announced that "the Bank had made ample preparation for resuming its payments in cash . . . [and] he knew of nothing in the internal state of the country or in its political relations with foreign powers which would render it expedient to continue the restriction. . . . [Yet,] there was reason to

---

[53] The original Orders in Council appeared on 26 Feb. 1797 and were confirmed by Bill 37 Geo. III, which was thereafter continued and/or amended nine times. Bill 44 Geo. III. extended resumption till six months after ratification of a definitive treaty of peace. For a list of these various acts, see the *Index to the Journals of the House of Lords, 1780–1819*.

[54] Bill 54 Geo. III, c. 99 renewed the Bank Restriction Act until 5 July 1816 (*Hansard* 1s, 29:1203); it was passed in Mar. 1815.

[55] Horner and Tierney led the opposition to the Bank restriction in the House. When the bill to continue the restriction was finally approved, Horner noted that "from the silence of the governor of the Bank of England . . . he looked to the event of the resumption of cash payments with any thing but hope and satisfaction" (*Hansard* 1s, 29:1203).

[56] Bill 56 Geo III, c. 40 prolonged the Bank restriction. Parliament approved it in May 1816.

believe that pecuniary arrangements of foreign powers[57] were going on of such a nature and extent as might probably make it necessary for parliament to continue the restriction" (29 Jan. 1818, *Hansard* 1s, 37:115).[58]

In January 1819, for the fifth and final time, the government proposed to extend the Bank restriction. It reversed its position days later when there emerged a general consensus in Parliament in favor of convertibility (Smart 1910–1917, 1:674). The government also feared that the Whigs would capitalize on the Bank restriction in the upcoming election. In a letter of 23 January 1819, Huskisson wrote: "L[iverpool] is in one of his grand fidgetts. Yesterday he said if Tierney were to beat us, it would be fatal." Liverpool accordingly changed his position on the question of resumption, to the delight of his opponents: "When the noble earl said that a fixed standard of value was necessary for this great mercantile country he only repeated what [the earl of Lauderdale] and the noble lords around him had been contending for the last 12 years and what the noble earl [Liverpool] had uniformly contradicted. The noble earl's doctrine had always been that Bank paper had never depreciated in value. . . . [Though now] he congratulated himself, the House, and the country upon such a convert to sound principles on a question of such importance."[59]

There can be no doubt that the continuation of the Bank restriction on the grounds of its expedience to the government and the Bank invited support for legislation to restore the gold standard. For it was understood that if convertibility was not restored, nothing would prevent the government from forcing the Bank to extend its circulation again and again, with no foreseeable end to monetary instability and inflation.

Conclusion

Aggregate economic conditions over the business cycle of 1815 to 1818 accord more closely with fluctuation in foreign trade than with changes in the fortunes of British farmers. An agricultural depression began in the

---

[57] This is a reference to the loans raised by foreign powers in Britain (see discussion, p. 139).

[58] On 9 Apr. 1818, the government officially moved to continue the Bank restriction (*Hansard* 1s, 37:1230). In response, Grenfell made an able speech, describing the conditions favorable to resumption in 1816 and early 1817, and attributing the failed attempt at resumption to the increase of banknotes in the autumn of 1817 (*Hansard* 1s, 37:1251–1252).

[59] Statement by the Earl of Lauderdale in the House of Lords on 21 May 1819 (*Hansard* 1s, 40:628–629).

fall of 1813 and continued through the spring of 1816. As it happened, the drop in agricultural income and the consequent reduction in agricultural demand were offset by a high demand for exports so that a state of general depression was forestalled until the fall of 1815. The return of high corn prices in 1816 did not produce a rise in agricultural demand sufficient to bring the economy out of the depression. The aggregate economy did not recover till foreign demand increased in early 1817.

The Bank of England conducted a procyclical monetary policy in the postwar years. It failed to support private credit during the country-banking crisis of July 1814 to July 1816; it even withdrew commercial discounts at the height of distress. Moreover, although the Bank was positioned to resume cash payments at the ancient par in 1816 and actually declared some of its notes convertible, the attempt to restore the gold standard failed because the Bank extended an advance of £12 million to the government just as the foreign exchange became unfavorable. In the following months the Bank lost two thirds of its hoard, leaving it no better prepared to resume cash payments in 1819 than it had been immediately after the war. Because the Bank and the government mishandled the paper pound so badly, intense opposition to the Bank restriction developed in Parliament. The government, fearing that the Whigs might capitalize on the restriction, permitted the Lords and Commons to convene committees to enquire into the possibility of restoring the gold standard. The 1819 Resumption Act, which required the Bank of England to make its notes convertible at the ancient par, was the result of the investigations of these committees.

THREE

The Business Cycle of 1818–1825

This chapter describes the business cycle of 1818 to 1825. The depression phase of the cycle, which lasted from February 1819 to May 1820, was caused by a coincidence of shocks in the principal markets for British exports: the Bank of France caused a financial panic on the Continent by precipitously cutting discounts; war erupted in Spanish South America; and numerous failures occurred among the small banks of the United States. The Resumption Act of 1819 likely aggravated the situation. For although the Bank of England did not reduce the money supply as it returned to gold, it might have extended credit more liberally had the act not been in effect. Some historians speculate that the depression resulted from a failure of demand in the home market. Tax reports show that this did not occur.

The account in this chapter corrects the misconception in the secondary literature that Britain's economy was continually depressed during the decade following the war. The depression of 1819–1820 lasted only seventeen months. It ended in May 1820 when exports returned to normal levels. Britain's economy then expanded for five years, driven by a burgeoning foreign trade. Even at the depth of the crisis in 1819, not all sectors were depressed. Agricultural communities went largely untouched.

Only after the general depression ended did corn prices begin to fall. From mid-1820 through 1822, corn dropped more than 30 percent. The landed interests in Parliament, with a chorus of crude inflationists, attributed the fall to the Resumption Act.[1] They argued that resumption

---

[1] The opponents of resumption were also Ricardo's principal critics: Mathias Attwood, Henry Brougham, William Cobbett, Sir John Sinclair, and Charles Western.

caused a general deflation and that the appropriate remedies were to abandon the gold standard and to adopt a more protectionist corn law. The following pages introduce the factions vying for control of Britain's monetary and agricultural policies. Particular emphasis devolves to the 1821 House of Commons Committee on Agriculture, for within its proceedings the battles over resumption and the corn laws reached a near-fevered pitch.

This chapter also discusses the Poor Law Committees of 1817, 1818, and 1819. The committees are important for two reasons: first, Ricardo based his analysis of the sufferings of the poor on the committees' work, and second, the committees' investigations supported the idea that wages were low because of a low capital-to-labor ratio. This conclusion had further implications for agricultural and fiscal policies, as it was believed that high taxes and agricultural protection discouraged domestic investment.

Onset of the Depression of 1819–1820

Britain began to recover from the immediate postwar depression in early 1817. General prosperity continued through 1818, and even in January 1819 there were only favorable reports in the commercial press.

The accounts from the manufacturing districts are not less flattering.... orders were never known to be greater than at present... and the weavers are in full employment (*Edinburgh Magazine*, Nov. 1818, 483).

The iron works in particular, which two years ago were in so lamentable a state of distress are now so well employed that they cannot execute their orders (*Edinburgh Magazine*, Jan. 1819, 91).

The agricultural interests of this country are recovered from their severe depression.... All our manufactures are in full activity.... The extension of our trade from the additional and increasing arrivals and departures from every port is truly great and cheering (*Blackwood's Edinburgh Magazine*, Jan. 1819, 497).

As further evidence of the general prosperity, the speech of the Lords Commissioners on behalf of the Prince Regent at the opening of Parliament on 21 January 1819 asserted that "the trade, commerce, and manufactures of the country are in a most flourishing condition [and] the favourable change which has so rapidly taken place in the internal circumstances of the United Kingdom affords the strongest proof of the solidity of its resources" (*Bulletins of State Intelligence*, 1819, 15). The statements were confirmed by members of the House in the subsequent debate on the address (*Hansard* 1s, 39:17–65).

Foreign demand might have sustained the boom in exports and the 1819–1820 depression might never have happened, except that in October 1818, "a sudden and great fall of the French funds occurred[2] [so that] combined with the great and sudden fall of the prices of grain on the Continent, extensive failures occurred in Paris, Marseilles and other parts of France as also in Holland and in Hamburg in 1818 before any indication had appeared of discredit or of any material pressure on the money market in this country" (Tooke and Newmarch 1838–1857, 2:94–95). Concurrently, war broke out in Spanish South America, and the United States struggled through a banking crisis. The troubles of foreign markets were noted by contemporary journals[3] and caused concern, but confidence remained in the resilience of the home market.

Actual events proved more harsh. Real exports for 1819 declined by £11.3 million or 25 percent relative to the exports of 1818 (see App. D.1). The collapse of foreign demand, in turn, caused a depression in domestic trade and manufacturing so that "numerous and extensive failures, which began in the latter part of 1818, continued more or less through the earlier part of 1819. Importers, speculators and manufacturers were successively ruined" (Tooke and Newmarch 1838–1857, 2:77). Brittania's prospects faded in the spring fog:

Since our last publication, we are happy to see, that our accounts of the extensive trade and flourishing revenues of our country are borne out by the highest authority.... [However,] a time of commercial pressure and difficulty is marching hard after many, and will soon overtake individuals (*Blackwood's Edinburgh Magazine*, Feb. 1819, 630).

The pressure upon some branches of our trade has been very great, [but] we are mistaken if it lasts long, and are also convinced that the greatest danger is over, as there is every prospect of permanent tranquility among the nations of Europe (*Blackwood's Edinburgh Magazine*, Mar. 1819, 761).

---

[2] The bullion hoard at the Bank of France began to dwindle during the summer of 1818 when a high demand for bullion in Russia, Prussia, and Austria coincided with an overextension of the Bank's circulation (Jenks 1927, 38). To protect its hoard the Bank curtailed discounts, "refusing to discount any paper having more than forty-five days to run, as compared with the normal ninety days" (Hawtrey 1934, 341). This action resulted in a complete collapse of the money market, imperiled the loan of 179 million francs that had just been contracted with Barings, and threatened to prevent France from meeting her indemnity obligations.

[3] *Blackwood's* commercial report for Jan. 1819 (496–498) noted conditions in the United States and South America: "Numerous and extensive failures are daily taking place – confidence is shaken – money is not to be had, and mercantile concerns wear a most unfavourable aspect throughout the Maritime States of America [and] our former great and lucrative trade with Spanish South America remains subjected to the greatest vexations, vicissitudes and uncertainty from the nature of the sanguinary and destructive warfare there carried on."

Concurring with *Blackwood's*, the editors of the *Edinburgh Review* attributed "the principal, as well as the immediate cause of the distress of the manufacturing and commercial classes, to [the] falling off in the Continental demand" (July 1819, 53). The *Review* considered the crisis to have been aggravated by the extensive speculations in exportable commodities in 1818, made possible by an increase in private credit that might have been checked if the currency had been convertible: "We have experienced, in the course of the last eight years, three periods of universal distress, viz. the years 1812, 1816 and 1819; and although many circumstances may have concurred to produce it, there can be no doubt that the general practice of overtrading[4] which was the natural consequence of the paper system, has been the main cause of that glut of goods and also of labour in the market which has occasioned the fall of prices and of wages, which is at the root of our present distress" (Jan. 1820, 57).

The importance of reversals in foreign trade should not be underestimated. *Blackwood's* blamed the crisis on "the situation of foreign nations, and the condition to which these were reduced," principally referring to Continental powers, the regions of Spanish South America, and the United States – markets to where unprecedented levels of British exports had been shipped:

The bubble is burst and brought ruin on thousands and the United States will find they are as yet too young and unsettled a state to carry on their trade and improvements by a banking system or a paper currency . . . The trade to Spanish South America is completely cut up (*Blackwood's*, Sept. 1819, 747).

The accounts from those foreign markets on which our commerce chiefly depends, is gloomy and distressing indeed. By the immense extension of our manufactures we have indeed overstocked almost every market, but this will be found to proceed more from the inability of these nations, owing to recent political events and convulsions, to find the means of trade, than that their wants have been over-supplied (*Blackwood's*, Oct. 1819, 108).

Compounding the crisis, merchants miscalculated the home demand for foreign goods. Vast stocks of imports remained from 1818, causing the prices of imported commodities to fall sharply from January 1819 through December 1820.[5]

---

[4] "Overtrading" referred to the import, export, or production of commodities in excess of the quantity saleable at a profit. In 1819 it was recognized that both imports and exports had been too great.

[5] According to the Gayer et al. (1953) Index of Wholesale Prices of Imported Commodities, imported goods declined in value from Nov. 1818 (index 133) to Feb. 1821 (index 101). For a return of the prices of specific commodities, see the House of Commons, *Report*

Table 3.1. *Imports into Great Britain*

Year	Sugar (cwts.)	Raw Wool (lbs.)	Raw Cotton (lbs.)	Tea (lbs.)	Silk (lbs.)
1816	3,760,548	8,100,000	93,900,000	36,234,380	1,137,922
1817	3,795,550	14,700,000	124,900,000	31,467,073	1,177,693
1818	3,965,947	26,400,000	177,300,000	20,065,728	2,101,618
1819	4,077,009	16,200,000	149,700,000	22,881,957	1,848,000
1820	4,063,541	10,000,000	149,300,000	30,147,994	2,642,000

The losses on cotton–wool imports alone were £3 million. *Blackwood's* estimated total losses "on all exports and imports since last year at fifteen millions" (Feb. 1819, 630; July 1819, 498). The connection between excessive imports and the collapse of prices was widely recognized, for in addition to commercial reports such as *Blackwood's*, there were Parliamentary accounts for every branch of trade.[6] Table 3.1 is based on trade figures in the *Journal of the House of Commons*.[7] Without considering any other commodities, the data for sugar, wool, cotton, and silk explain the movement in the Gayer imported commodity price index, which employs the following weights: sugar (16.6%), cotton (16.3%), wool (11.9%), tea (11.1%), and silk (6.1%). The importations of cotton, wool, and silk increased enormously from 1816 to 1818. Although sugar imports remained stable, the stock on hand at the end of 1819 was still "very considerable," leading to a fall in price of about 15 percent from January 1819 to January 1820 (*Blackwood's*, Jan. 1820, 473). The price of Bengal cotton fell almost 11 percent over the period,[8] and Georgia cotton declined by a fourth, owing to continued importations from the United States and India:

Cotton. There have of late been very considerable arrivals from the United States and more are daily expected (*Blackwood's*, Feb. 1820, 591).

Cotton – The cotton market continues heavy, and the India Company having declared a further quantity for sale on the 17th instant, has added to the general stagnation of the trade (*Edinburgh Magazine*, Mar. 1820, 287).

---

from the Committee of Secrecy on the Bank of England Charter 1832, App. 92 and 93, in *Parliamentary Papers* 1831–1832, 6:581–583, MF 35.45.

[6] The *Journal of the House of Commons* (1819) contains 130 pages of reports on foreign trade.

[7] For data on a wider range of commodities, see App. D.2.

[8] The prices of sugar, cotton, and other commodities are quoted in House of Commons, *Report from the Committee of Secrecy on the Bank of England Charter* 1832, App. 92 and 93, in *Parliamentary Papers* 1831–1832, 6:581–583, MF 35.45.

The increase in importations was not limited to wool, cotton, and silk. According to official values – that is, the government's measure that reflected quantities of goods traded as opposed to the market value of those goods – imports for home consumption increased 57 percent from 1816 to 1817 and by another 30 percent from 1817 to 1818 (Tooke and Newmarch 1838–1857, 2:62).

Trade statistics and anecdotes suggest that the depression of 1819–1820 was largely caused by overtrading. Supporting this conclusion, tax records show that domestic consumption of the principal commodities remained constant. According to a Parliamentary address by Lord Liverpool, "It is material to consider whether the distressed state of the commerce has grown out of any diminution in our internal consumption. . . . there is no ground for believing that any part of the distress which pervades our internal commerce has arisen from a reduction in the use of any of the great articles of consumption" because tax reports indicated practically no diminution in the consumption of tea, coffee, tobacco, malt, or spirits and "It was the same with articles on which there had been no increase of taxation, consumed by all classes such as candles, paper, hides, skins, soap, salt, bricks, etc." (26 May 1820, *Hansard* 2s, 1:568–570).[9] Tax reports and trade statistics bring into question the view that the postwar depression resulted from a chronic shortfall of consumer demand. The evidence suggests, rather, that the 1819–1820 depression corrected excessive investments in foreign trade.

British Agriculture and Manufacturing in 1819

Blackwood's describes the initial months of 1819 as "the most disastrous in the commercial annals of Great Britain" (Feb. 1820, 591). But not all industries languished. The annual average prices for British wheat were 94s. in 1817, 84s. in 1818, and 73s. in 1819.[10] The Corn Law of 1804 deemed 64s. a threshold high enough to ensure profits. Even when wheat declined to 63s. in January 1820 after an "early and abundant harvest," the price of corn in Britain still exceeded prices on the Continent and farmers suffered only relative to their former extravagance (*Blackwood's*, Sept. 1819, 746 and App. C.3).

---

[9] Excise returns show that Liverpool's statements were correct (Marshall 1833, 2:14–15).

[10] Account of the Average Price of All Sorts of Grain in Each Year, *Journal of the House of Commons* 1821, 76:1032.

The prosperity of British agriculture was further attested by the 1832 Committee of Secrecy on the Bank of England Charter, which characterized 1819 as a year of "Great Manufacturing and Commercial [but not Agricultural] Distress."[11] No less an authority than Lord Liverpool held the same opinion: "If Certain manufacturing districts are excepted . . . I have never known the country in general since the conclusion of the war in a more prosperous situation . . . But I must now reverse the picture, and I must say that nothing can be worse or more alarming than the state of those parts of the country which I first excepted."[12]

Manufacturing districts were indeed troubled. As British exports became unsaleable, manufactures curtailed production and employment. The financial press reported "general gloom" and "great stagnation in the manufacturing and commercial world." *Blackwood's* characterized manufacturing wages as "dull and low" (Apr. 1819, 110). Signs of recovery appeared in June (*Blackwood's*, June 1819, 365), but proved deceptive: "In this publication we had hoped to have been able to have given an account of the revival of trade, and more cheerful prospects for the commercial interests of the country. We are disappointed. The stagnation of all kinds of business continues, and is extreme, perhaps unprecedented. Numerous and severe failures cover the face of the manufacturing districts with distress and dismay, while the dreadful depreciation of all manufacturing property has swept away from thousands the labour and the profits of years" (July 1819, 498). Conditions deteriorated further; by September "[manufacturing prices] are so low and the number of hands so great, we fear there is but a faint prospect of workmen speedily obtaining comfortable wages" (*Edinburgh Magazine*, Sept. 1819, 284). The *Edinburgh Review* provided a similar account: "When we examine into the condition of the labouring classes in this country, we immediately perceive that their distress arises from want of employment" (Oct. 1819, 452). High unemployment coincided with a fall in manufacturing wages (*Edinburgh Review*, May 1820, 332–334):

The wages of weavers in Glasgow, which, when highest, had averaged about 25s. or 27s. a week, had been reduced in 1816 to 10s.; and in 1819 to the wretched pittance of 5s. 6d. or 6s.

    [In Coventry] those in employment, such as had frames of their own, and who worked 16 hours a day, were only in the receipt of 10s. a week; the second class,

---

[11] House of Commons, Committee of Secrecy of the Bank of England Charter 1832, *Digest of Evidence on the Bank Charter*, 4.

[12] Letter from Lord Liverpool to Canning, 23 Sept. 1819 (Aspinall 1959, 11:333).

whose frames were furnished by the master manufacturers, earned in all about 5s. 6d.; and the third, or inferior class of workmen, only from 2s. 9d. to 1s. 6d. a week.

The frame-workers of Nottingham . . . after working from 14 to 16 hours a day, only earn from 4s. to 7s. a week.

Commercial reports are important because they show that wages adjusted quickly to changes in the level and pattern of final demand.[13] The dynamic adjustment of wages is not revealed in indices compiled by modern authors[14] because these indices are annual averages based on broadly defined industries with limited allowance for geographic variations in wages.

Radical political figures capitalized on the distress of 1819 to further the cause of Parliamentary reform – or leveling. On 16 August 1819, the day of the Peterloo massacre, Sydney Smith wrote: "If trade does not increase, there will be a war of the rich against the poor" (Smart 1910–1917, 1:690). According to *Blackwood's*, "The alarming situation of all the manufacturing districts has put a complete stop to business. In extensive districts of the country, it is completely suspended, and terror and alarm now occupy the minds of thousands. . . . People at a distance from and unconnected with the manufacturing districts have no idea of the terrible dangers and principles which assail the peaceable part of the community in those places" (Dec. 1819, 351). Fractious political assemblies "proved so attractive to the manufacturing classes, under the irritation produced by low wages and a deficiency of employment, that the spirit rapidly diffused itself through the counties of York, Lancaster, Chester, Nottingham, and Leicester . . . gaining at length the important town of Birmingham" (*Annual Register*, 1819, 104). When Parliament reassembled on 23 November 1819 the Prince Regent cited "seditious practices . . . incompatible with the public tranquillity" as grounds for "such measures as may be requisite for the counteraction and suppression of a system, which, if not effectually checked must bring confusion and ruin on the nation" (*Annual Register*, 1819, 116). The crisis is fully documented in the *Papers Relative to the Internal State of the Country*, reprinted in the *Journal of the House of Commons* 1819–1820, 75:595–612. The *Papers* describe the condition of manufacturing districts, the inflammatory activities of political reformers, and random incidents of defiance. Parliament responded with

[13] Further evidence on wages is contained in Smart 1910–1917, 1:724–725.

[14] See the indices compiled by Kondratieff, Tucker, Bowley, and Wood. The indices are reproduced in Mitchell and Deane (1962, 348–349) and in Gayer et al. (1953, 135, 167, 203).

the so-called Six Acts, "forming a system of force, terror and coercion," according to Earl Grey (*Annual Register*, 1819, 129), and instituting what Tierney decried as "an attack upon the very vital principles of the British constitution" (*Annual Register*, 1819, 130–131).

Orders for British textiles returned to normal levels the summer of 1820.[15] There occurred a corresponding increase in the demand for manufacturing labor. From June on, the commercial press voiced no doubts about the recovery:

Several manufacturing houses could employ many more weavers than they can find at the present prices (*Glasgow Journal*, June 1820).

We are happy to learn from Sheffield that the trade of that place has materially revived and there is every prospect of a further amendment. Many able hands, who have been for the nine or twelve months past supported by parochial support, are now in full work (*Edinburgh Magazine*, Aug. 1820).

You will be sorry to hear the trade and manufactures of these counties (round Manchester) are materially mended and are mending. I would not mention this to you if you were not a good Whig; but I know you will not mention it to anybody (Letter by Sydney Smith, Oct. 1820, quoted in Smart 1910–1913, 1:740).

Total exports for 1820 increased by £5.5 million; imports were also higher (see App. D.1). Britain's foreign trade continued to expand in 1821; the official value of exports increased by £2.5 million. "The improvement which had begun in the course of the preceding year, to show itself in the state of our manufactures, still continued. In Yorkshire and Lancashire, the seats of the woollen and cotton manufactures, the working classes found regular employment, and received a liberal remuneration for their services. Other branches of industry were not equally prosperous. The iron trade[16] was still in a very depressed state; and petitions setting forth the decay of the principal branches of industry in Birmingham were at an early period introduced" (*Annual Register*, 1821, 69). Cotton and wool prices were lower after 1818, but an increase in output sustained profits and employment (Gayer et al. 1953, 154–156).

---

[15] Though in Apr. 1820 *Blackwood's* reported that "the same languor continues to operate upon every other article of commerce," by May its editors noted that "In the manufacturing districts trade in general may be stated as better [and] work is more abundant."

[16] Iron prices declined from 1818 through 1821 (Gayer et al. 1953, 151, 152, 177). However, Mitchell's figures on the output of pig iron show that British production increased from 280,000 tons in 1819 to 390,000 tons in 1821 and to 450,000 tons in 1823 (Mitchell 1988, 280).

Tax reports[17] show an increase in aggregate demand starting the third quarter of 1820. Total customs and excise duties fell in 1819, notwithstanding new excise duties of £3 million. By July 1821, however, customs and excise revenues surpassed the levels at which they had peaked in 1815 (see App. E.2). Revenues remained steady for the next four years in spite of the fact that £12 million in taxes expired or were rescinded from 1821 through 1825.[18] The increase in tax revenues improved the government's fiscal situation, which saw a budget surplus of £1.5 million in 1820, £3.2 million in 1821, £3.4 million in 1822, and £4.3 million in 1823 (see App. E.3).

The Condition of the Poor

The distressed position of laborers in the postwar years was partly caused by temporary conditions such as reversals in trade and manufacturing. The condition of laborers was further compromised by "permanent" causes – meaning, laws and institutions that tended to increase the supply of labor relative to the demand for it. Committees in both Houses[19] concluded that, among these causes, the poor laws encouraged starveling families to have more children than they could support.

Your Committee cannot but fear, from a reference to the increased numbers of the poor, and the increased and increasing amount of the sums raised for their relief that this system is perpetually encouraging and increasing the amount of misery it was designed to alleviate (House of Commons, *Report from the Select Committee on the Poor Laws* 1817, 4).

The committees' views were widely publicized (see App. F). From 1814 to 1818, the *Scots Magazine* featured fourteen articles on the management of the poor. The *Edinburgh Review* published seven articles between 1817 and 1821, interpreting the poor laws and describing their practical aspect. Reviews of the first and second reports by the Society for the Suppression of Begging appeared in the *Scots Magazine* (Jan. 1814, Feb. 1816, Sept. 1816). The *Scots* (Nov. 1816) also delved into the education of the

---

[17] Tax data were published quarterly when Parliament was in session (see App. E.1 for a list of reports).

[18] House of Commons, *A Return of . . . all Taxes Repealed, Expired or Reduced in Each Year since the Termination of the War* 1833, in *Parliamentary Papers* 1833, 32:637–653, MF 36.239.

[19] The House of Commons Committees on the State of Mendicity in the Metropolis in 1815 and 1816, the House of Commons Committees on the Poor Laws in 1817, 1818, and 1819, and the House of Lords Committee on the Poor Laws in 1817.

lower orders, as did the *British Review* (Feb. 1817). Similar writings on mendicity, vagrancy, and the abuse of charities fostered a widespread belief that charitable assistance encouraged vice[20] but did nothing to redeem the existing squalor:

> Every public and proclaimed provision, for the relief of general indigence, is not only utterly incompetent to the attainment of its object, but has the effect of perpetuating and extending the very distress which it proposes to alleviate (*Edinburgh Review*, Mar. 1817, 2).

> [The poor laws] relax the natural excitements to industry and foresight, and thus multiply the instances of wretchedness beyond its power of relieving them (*Edinburgh Review*, Feb. 1818, 262).

England's welfare system originated with the Poor Law of 43 Eliz. I, which levied poor rates on "every inhabitant, parson, vicar and every occupier of land" according to the assessed value of his real property so as to provide "a convenient stock of flax, &c. to set the [able bodied] poor to work; and also competent sums for and towards the relief of the lame, impotent, &c".[21] Relief was administered in several forms. The workhouse system was the most notorious. A typical workhouse was inhabited by orphans, single women with dependent children, the aged, and the infirm – persons who, in exchange for shelter and subsistence provisions, were set to some type of manufacturing work (Boyer 1990, 22–23). Able-bodied laborers were eligible for "outdoor" relief – that is, assistance outside the workhouse. Under the Speenhamland system – also known as "allowances in aid of wages" – unemployed and underemployed laborers were guaranteed a minimum weekly income determined by the price of bread and the size of the laborer's family. In 1824, 41 percent of parishes paid allowances in aid of wages (Boyer 1990, 10–11). Child allowances were paid to laborers who had a minimum of three, four, or five young children. The exact rules varied from one parish to the next. A typical parish might assist a father with four children under the age of twelve, paying a weekly sum of 1.5s. for each child at and beyond the fourth (Boyer 1990, 154). Given that in 1819 manufacturing workers earned 4s. to 10s. per week, having an additional child raised household income by at least 15 percent. Child allowances were most common in the agricultural

---

[20] The House of Commons *Report of the Committee on the State of Mendicity in the Metropolis* 1816 illustrates the popular view with a recitation of the "evils attending mendicity" (3–4).

[21] House of Commons, *Report from the Select Committee on the Poor Laws* 1817, 4, in *Parliamentary Papers* 1817, 4:4, MF 18.28.

counties of the south, being provided by 90 percent of parishes in 1824 (Boyer 1990, 15). Many parishes also provided seasonal assistance under the roundsmen system whereby laborers worked for local farmers at reduced rates. The parish made up the difference between the cost of subsistence and the wage earned by the underemployed laborer.

By the nineteenth century, the poor laws were obsolete. According to the statutory definition of real property – "lands, houses, tithes, coalmines or saleable underwoods" – manufacturers and those with monied capital paid almost no poor rates. Nonresident landlords were likewise exempt, and tenants, though they could be compelled to pay, were often deemed too impoverished. As a result, resident landlords suffered a disproportionate tax burden. Concerning this liability, Brougham observed that "in one parish, every individual, with a single exception, was wholly ruined; this gentleman had to pay the whole poor-rates of the parish, and his income was accordingly entirely absorbed" (*Edinburgh Review*, June 1816, 257). Liberal judicial rulings made the poor rates even more burdensome. The phrase "a convenient stock of flax, &c. to set the poor on work," for instance, was interpreted to require public works on a scale sufficient to employ all the able-bodied poor in a given parish. The Rev. Phillip Hunt testified before the Select Committee on Laborers' Wages in 1824 that poor rates were also used to finance the system of roundsmen, whereby unemployed laborers were sent, in rotation, from farm to farm, "to work for such farmers [but] to have their wages paid, in whole or in part, out of the poor rates."[22] In some districts, the poor rates even subsidized wages paid to manufacturing laborers:[23]

---

[22] *Report from the Select Committee on Labourers' Wages* 1824, 36. Similar observations were made by the Lords Committee on the Poor Laws in 1817: "The effect of the system of roundsmen has been to throw upon the general [poor] rates of parishes . . . a very considerable proportion of the wages of that labour, the charge of which ought to have been defrayed by the individuals for whom it was performed" (House of Lords, *Report of the Lords Committees on the Poor Laws* 1817, 9, in *Parliamentary Papers* 1817, 5:99, MF 19.25).

[23] House of Commons, *Minutes of Evidence Taken before the Committee Appointed to Consider Petition Relating to Ribbon Weavers*, 3–6, in *Parliamentary Papers* 1818, 9:7–10, MF 19.46. It is important that economic historians not ignore the fact that some persons receiving poor relief were employed. For otherwise there is a risk of overestimating the extent of unemployment. Blaug has stated that "in an era when the number of individuals on public relief hovered steadily around one million (about 10 per cent of the population of England and Wales), the existence of a hard core of surplus labour must have been taken for granted" (Blaug 1958, 75). While Blaug has correctly noted the extent of poor relief, it would be a mistake to infer that all those receiving assistance lacked employment. To the contrary, many were partly employed, and others fully employed by masters who

Question: How is it possible that goods can be manufactured at so low a rate ... that you can purchase goods so much cheaper than you can manufacture them?

Answer: The masters that encourage the half-pay system, get their goods made at half-pay; some get them manufactured at full thirty per cent. lower than I do.

Question: Then you conceive the poor's rates pay the difference of wages?

Answer: Yes ... they even have to support, in part, those who work for me. (Testimony of John Robinson, House of Commons, *Minutes of Evidence taken before the Committee Appointed to Consider Petition Relating to Ribbon Weavers* 1818, 36).

Because the poor rates depleted households' disposable incomes, Parliament concluded that the poor laws also reduced the private demand for labor:

The greater part, Your Committee believe, of the sums of money which are now forced into the poor's rate, and undergo a compulsory, and for the most part unprofitable distribution, would probably be restored to their natural channel, giving thereby an increased activity to labour, under the interested but beneficial superintendence of their owners; from which would necessarily result a rise of wages (House of Commons, *Report from the Committee on the Poor Laws* 1819, 9).

Contributions ... would otherwise have been applied more beneficially to the supply of employment. And as the funds which each person can expend in labour are limited, in proportion as the poor rate diminishes those funds, in the same proportion will the wages of labour be reduced, to the immediate and direct prejudice of the labouring classes (House of Commons, *Report from the Select Committee on the Poor Laws* 1817, 4).

The abuses of England's welfare system went unchecked because the Law of 43 Eliz. I provided no guidelines by which to determine the amount of the poor rates or the extent of relief. "All the various details of the system – the mode of making the assessment, the species of property to which it was to be extended – were either left entirely to their [churchwardens] discretion, or no precise rule was prescribed for their conduct; nor was any adequate security provided by the law for the upright administration of the funds which they were empowered to raise" (*Edinburgh Magazine*, Aug. 1817, 34).[24] In some instances churchwardens so liberally provided

managed to shift part of their wage costs to the poor rates. Blaug's articles on the Poor Laws are discussed later.

[24] The ambiguity of the law frequently gave rise to legal challenges to the decisions of the churchwardens so that, in 1815 alone, "the money expended on law-suits amounted to £285,000" (*Edinburgh Magazine*, Aug. 1817, 34).

from the poor rates that persons laboring at low wages were induced to abandon regular employment (House of Commons, *Report from the Committee on the Poor Laws* 1819, 7–8).

The poor law system of England and Wales was contrasted with that in Scotland where, in most regions, contributions to the poor were only compulsory during periods of distress and the demand for aid increased only in districts where regular tax levies for support of the poor existed:

The Committee have thought it right to examine evidence respecting the management of the Poor in Scotland; where, though a power exists by law to impose a compulsory assessment for the relief of the Poor, recourse has seldom been had to it [because] considerable sums are raised by regular collections at the churches, which are applied to the purpose of relieving the Poor at the discretion of the minister and elders (House of Lords, *Report of the Lords Committee on the Poor Laws* 1817, 10).

The Committee of the General Assembly of the Church of Scotland state, "That it is clear to them, that in almost all the country parishes which have hitherto come under their notice, where a regular assessment has been established, the wants of the poor and the extent of the assessment have gradually and progressively increased" (House of Commons, *Report from the Select Committee on the Poor Laws* 1817, 4–5).

The popular press agreed that the Scottish relief system, which was not institutionalized but relied on private donations except during emergencies, produced "the comparative exemption of Scotland from the burdens and the miseries of Pauperism" which occurred under the largesse of the English poor law (*Edinburgh Review*, Mar. 1817, 9).

On the basis of much testimony, poor rate returns, and a comparison between the English and Scottish systems, the Poor Law Committee of 1819 recommended stringent eligibility requirements for relief. However, the committee postponed any reforms until the immediate crisis in trade and manufacturing ended: "It is not at a moment like the present, when from a concurrence of circumstances, the Country is unusually embarrassed by the number of persons without employment, that it should be attempted to bring this better system at once into operation. . . . That the market for labour is in many parts of the kingdom at present much overstocked, does not admit of dispute; nor does Your Committee believe that in other parts the demand is greater than the supply" (House of Commons, *Report from the Committee on the Poor Laws* 1819, 8).[25]

---

[25] The amendments to the Poor Law 59 Geo. III c. 12 that Parliament approved in March 1819 provided for the appointment of salaried public officials to administer the poor rates

The committee apprehended no short-term solution to the disproportion between labor and capital apart from emigration. However, to this end Parliament voted £50,000 to establish settlers on the Cape of Good Hope. Settlements were also proposed for the Australian continent and New South Wales (*Annual Register*, 1819, iv). The committee hoped that the extension of public education would cause a decline in the birth rate, and that this would coincide with investments creating jobs, so that "the demand and supply of labour should be nearly balanced, and the wages of labour become a more adequate remuneration of industry" (House of Commons, *Report from the Committee on the Poor Laws* 1819, 9). The committee's conclusions correspond exactly with Ricardo's position on poor relief.

The secondary literature has examined whether the poor laws relieved or worsened Britain's humanitarian crisis. Several hypotheses have been tested, the most relevant being: did poor relief increase the incidence of marriage? did poor relief raise fertility? did poor relief deter laborers from emigrating from the impoverished agricultural counties of the south to London and the industrial north? and did poor relief depress laborers' wages?

Mark Blaug concluded from a study of county-level data that "simply not much can be said" about the effect of the poor laws on population (Blaug 1963, 173). Poor relief may have exerted a slight effect on population, but if so it acted by lowering the rate of infant mortality, not by raising the birth rate. With respect to wages, he concedes that "on the face of it, it seems that the Speenhamland policy depressed agricultural wages between 1795 and 1824," but he claims that "this should not be submitted as evidence that subsidies depressed wages. On the contrary, the causal relationship seems to run the other way: wages were only subsidized when, for other reasons, they were too low to provide a minimum standard of living" (Blaug 1963, 168–169). Blaug later reiterated his conclusion: "the Old Poor Law was essentially a device for dealing with the problems of structural unemployment and substandard wages in a lagging rural sector of a rapidly growing but still underdeveloped economy" (Blaug 1964, 229).

Arthur Redford examined the persistence of a disparity between rural and urban wages not accounted for by differences in the costs of living.

---

because this task was becoming too great for the unpaid churchwardens and overseers. The act also charged overseers of poor relief to "take into consideration the character and conduct of the person to be relieved, distinguishing . . . between the deserving, and the idle, extravagant, or profligate poor" (Rose 1971, 67–88).

He identified several factors that deterred internal migration: the relatively more generous distribution of poor relief in agricultural parishes, the law of settlement under which poor laborers could be deported to their home parishes, and the difficulty and expense of traveling from the southern counties to the north. Of these factors, poor relief was the most important: "Why should there be a recurrent scarcity of labour in the manufacturing districts, where wages were comparatively high, while in the agricultural counties of the south there was a vast, inert mass of redundant labour subsisting on starvation wages or on the pauper's dole?... The most obvious impediment to the adjustment of the labour supply was considered to be the restrictive effect of the poor laws in binding a man to his parish of settlement" (Redford 1976, 84). The practice of paying wages out of the poor rates was prevalent in Norfolk, Suffolk, Huntingdon, Beford, Buckingham, Surrey, Dorset, Wilts, and Devon – the counties where a surplus of agricultural labor was most evident (Redford 1976, 94).

James Huzel (1980) used data from individual parishes to test whether poor relief affected marriage rates, fertility, and the mobility of labor.[26] He concluded that poor relief had no appreciable effect on fertility or the incidence of marriage. Contrary to the results obtained by Blaug and Redford, Huzel found that poor relief did not deter mobility, nor did it reduce the rate of infant mortality. George Boyer (1990) provide a critique of the studies of Blaug, Redford, and Huzel. Like Huzel, he used parish-level data from the 1831 census; he also used the 1834 *Report on the Poor Laws*. However, Boyer added to his model demographic variables – including population density and the availability of housing – not considered in the earlier studies. Using the refined model, he obtained results remarkably similar to Malthus' conjectures that poor relief increased fertility: "Parishes that began allowances at three children experienced birth rates 25% greater than those of parishes without allowances, other things equal" (Boyer 1990, 163). On the question of mobility, Boyer concluded that poor relief did not significantly affect the migration of laborers from the agricultural counties to London and the north (191).

---

[26] Huzel (1980) obtained data on marriages, births, and infant mortality from the unpublished parish returns for the 1831 census. Information concerning the allowance system came from the *Report from His Majesty's Commissioners for Inquiring into the Administration and Practical Operation of the Poor Laws* 1834. He determined patterns of migration using census data.

Monetary Contraction and the 1819–1820 Depression

Given that the Resumption Act of 1819 coincided with a period of general depression, there were allegations that the return to gold caused the depression. Alderman Heygate "imputed the distresses to the great diminution of the currency, which had been for a long time gradually going on. When nine millions had been withdrawn from the circulation, great mischief and distress must have been the result" (24 Dec. 1819, *Hansard* 1s, 41:1582). Again in May 1820, and as became characteristic of the inflationists, Ellice claimed that monetary deflation had been from 30 to 50 percent (*Hansard* 2s, 1:193). He was supported by Alexander Baring, who called for a bimetallic standard (*Hansard* 2s, 1:196)[27] in order to devalue the currency.[28]

Members of Parliament who supported the act pointed out that monetary deflation could not be traced to resumption. For not until the resolutions on resumption passed the House of Lords without division on May 24, 1819, and Peel's nine resolutions on resumption were accepted by the House of Commons on May 26 was the act assured passage. By comparison, domestic prices declined from February to June and then stabilized.[29] The inflationists answered that the Bank of England anticipated the outcome of the debate on resumption and withdrew its notes months before the act passed: "It had been said that the act of 1819 had not occasioned distress, because the distress had begun before it passed; but, the preparation for carrying it into effect had begun long before the bill had received the sanction of parliament. That bill merely prevented prices from taking a backward course. The evils which the measure had caused in its contemplation and subsequent execution were incalculable" (Sir Francis Burdett, *Hansard* 2s, 7:408–409). Contrary to Burdett's claim,

---

[27] Baring repeated his proposal for bimetallism in February and March 1821 (*Hansard* 2s, 4:535,1327), but seemed to have abandoned the idea later (*Hansard* 2s, 5:132).

[28] Baring proposed allowing the Bank to pay "either in gold or in silver" at the Mint price. Presumably he intended the ancient parity, 1 to $15^{2096/10,000}$, though he may have considered the parity of the new coinage, 1 to $14^{2878/10,000}$ (House of Lords, *Reports Respecting the Bank of England Resuming Cash Payments* 1819, App. C.10). The important point is that the market ratio of gold to silver on 8 May 1820 was 1 to $15^{8/10}$ so that regardless of whether the old or new Mint regulations applied, the market price of silver was lower relative to its Mint price than the market price of gold relative to its Mint price. Thus, a bimetallic standard would have permitted the Bank to devalue the currency by paying its notes in silver, the cheaper of the two metals.

[29] The Gayer et al. (1953) domestic price index is 123.8 for June 1819 and 121.2 for June 1820.

the Bank made no attempt to contract its notes.[30] The Bank's circulation increased from £25,126,704 in February to £25,252,680 in August; indeed, "It was in this very interval, ending in August 1819, in which there is not the vestige of preparation for cash payments, by a contraction of the circulation, that the principal part of the fall of prices, resulting from the large importations had taken place" (Tooke and Newmarch 1838–1857, 2:97). During the fall of 1819, the Bank withdrew some of its notes (see App. A.1). However, it is difficult to determine whether the total circulation declined, because at the same time, the Mint issued £1.2 million in new silver coins and the Bank added £694,380 in gold coins (see App. B.4 and A.4). The combined circulation of Bank of England notes, silver coins, and gold sovereigns declined at most by 3 percent, from £30,824,512 in the fourth quarter of 1818 to £29,949,633 in the fourth quarter of 1819 (see App. B.6).

Modern economists might suggest that rational agents, anticipating the decline in prices upon the return to gold, attempted to increase their cash holdings and, in so doing, initiated the deflation that followed. The suggestion is plausible except for the fact that until May 1819 there was no reason to believe that Parliament would approve the act. Starting in 1814, the government repeatedly promised to restore the gold standard, but nothing came of these promises. When the committees on resumption were appointed in February 1819, it was not a foregone conclusion that Britain would return to gold. Even as late as 5 April 1819 when the committee from the House of Commons tabled its first report, there was no sign that resumption would pass, for the committee recommended only that the Bank suspend the limited cash payments it began in 1816.

Landlords and Inflationists

In the summer of 1820, a period of deflation began in Britain; it lasted two years and amounted to 37 percent.[31] Any informed person

---

[30] There was no need for the Bank to contract its notes in 1819. The act stipulated that cash payments were not to begin until Feb. 1820 and then only at the current gold market price of £4 1s. per ounce. Convertibility at the ancient par was not scheduled to begin until May 1821.

[31] The fall of prices is shown by several indices. The index of wholesale prices of domestic commodities published in Gayer et al. (1953, 469) is the best index because it provides monthly data, based on a wide range of commodities, spanning a long period of time, and weighted according to actual consumption. Also, the Gayer index consistently measures price fluctuations because it is based on a single source, the *Price Current Lists*. Of the other indices, Silberling's (1923) provides quarterly data and is based on 35 commodities,

would have been aware of the deflation. The prices of principal commodities were reported monthly in popular magazines and daily in the major newspapers.[32] Parliament used a wide range of indices (see App. C.7).

Gayer records a domestic price index of 126 for May 1820 as compared to 79 for May 1822. In these calculations, agricultural commodities weighed heavily: wheat (26%), oats (17%), mutton (16%), and beef (8%). Wheat, which had been selling for 74s. per quarter in August 1820, declined to 55s. by December. The slide continued for another two years with wheat falling to 46s. in December 1821 and finally to 38s. in December 1822. Oats experienced a similar fall. Mutton declined by more than 60 percent from January 1819 to July 1822. Beef prices fell 50 percent over the same period.[33] The prices of corn and livestock remained higher in England than on the Continent (see App. C.2 and C.3). Nevertheless, because the margin of cultivation in England was overextended and marginal costs of production were inordinately high, the fall of prices brought upon farmers "ruin of an irretrievable character" (*Annual Register* 1820, 65).

Inflationists attributed the agricultural crisis to the Resumption Act. They fought against the perception that low corn prices resulted from abundant harvests and Irish imports. They took pains to show that monetary contraction had caused a general depression, and that the only solution to the crisis was to devalue the currency.

The fall of prices on some of the principal articles of manufactures and commerce since 1818, may be taken to have been: Iron, from £13 to £9 10s.; copper, from £140 to £98; cotton, from 1s. 7d. to 10d.; sugar, from 90s. to 60s.; hemp, flax, tallow, wines, oil have fallen in similar proportions (Mathias Attwood, 9 Apr. 1821, *Hansard* 2s, 5:105).

The contraction of the circulating medium was the cause of the present distress.... The diminution of the value of produce was not confined to agriculture: a similar diminution was to be found in the value of all other commodities.... Nothing but the repeal of the act of 1819 would give relief to the agriculturalists (Charles Western, 29 Apr. 1822, *Hansard* 2s, 7:199).

---

as opposed to 78 commodities in Gayer. The Schumpeter index (1938) is based on fewer commodities still and uses contract prices paid by institutions. The Rousseau index (1938) presents only annual data and the overall index is an unweighted average of indices developed for agricultural and industrial products.

[32] Appendix C.5 gives prices as reported in *Blackwood's*.

[33] Mutton and beef prices are drawn from House of Commons, *Report from the Committee of Secrecy on the Bank of England Charter* 1832, App. 92.

Attwood and others asserted that monetary deflation caused a fall in prices unmatched by a corresponding decline in tithes and poor rates so that agriculture languished under a tax burden that had increased by some estimates as much as 50 percent.[34]

There is no truth, therefore, in the opinion that any fall in prices peculiar to agricultural produce has taken place. The fall in prices has been universal and not particular. The leases of the tenants, the mortgages of the landowner, [and] taxation pressing heavily on agricultural labour . . . will render the difficulties of the agricultural community more permanent (Mathias Attwood, 12 June 1822, *Hansard* 2s, 7:977).

According to Charles Western, "during the depreciation of money, the rents of estates had doubled, but incumbrances had doubled and taxes had quadrupled. . . . But what was the state of the landlord now? His income was again reduced to one half, and all their fixed payments remained" (*Hansard* 2s, 6:1444). Western also claimed that deflation had caused an unjust redistribution of property insofar as the real value of the national debt had increased to the benefit of stockholders – "monied men" – at the expense of landholders.

Pressure mounted for Parliament to remedy the crisis. In 1820 landholders sought to alter the method of calculating the average price of corn. The change would have made the existing corn law more prohibitive, though without raising the 80s. nominal threshold.[35] In 1821 measures were brought forward to replace the corn law altogether, to repeal the Resumption Act,[36] and even to repudiate the national debt.[37] Attwood explicitly sanctioned devaluation (*Hansard* 2s, 5:124–125). Western urged Parliament to "rip up the law of 1819" (*Hansard* 2s, 6:1444). Brougham adjured the House to repudiate the national debt with what one observer described as "parasitical zeal" (*Annual Register* 1822, 98). And Burdett recommended that all contracts signed prior to the Resumption Act be

---

[34] Baring, in a speech directed at Ricardo, intimated that deflation had been "not less than from 25 to 33 per cent. In some instances he should say that it had risen to a third and even 50 per cent" (*Hansard* 2s, 5:92).

[35] This proposal was made by the 1820 Agricultural Committee. The Committee's report was largely ignored, however, because Parliament was preoccupied with the trial of Queen Caroline.

[36] The Petition of the Merchants of Birmingham, which received wide support, effectively called for a repeal of the Resumption Act (*Hansard* 2s, 4:530).

[37] The proposal was made in a Parliamentary address by Curwen supporting the Petition of the Merchants of Birmingham on 8 Feb. 1821 (*Hansard* 2s, 4:528).

forcibly renegotiated.[38] Fortunately, the schemes to repudiate the national debt and devalue the currency never matured.[39] However, landholders did win a new corn bill in 1822.[40]

The inflationists consistently misrepresented or ignored data on the circulation of gold and silver coins. Their foremost spokesman, Mathias Attwood, estimated that the money supply had fallen by "one-fourth or one-fifth," causing a deflation that "approached nearly to one-half: [though] the hon. member for Portarlington denies that prices will fall except in proportion to the reduction of money" (*Hansard* 2s, 7:981). By comparison, contemporary reports show that the aggregate of specie and Bank of England notes increased from £30 million in the fourth quarter of 1819 to £36 million at the close of 1822 (see App. B.6). Attwood could have checked any number of reports on the coinage. Parliamentary accounts of the silver coin issued by the Mint permitted accurate estimates of the silver circulation (see App. B.5). There were comparable accounts for copper.[41] The value of British gold coin issued by the Bank of England up to April 1819 was reported by the committees on resumption (see App. A.3). The Bank did not indicate how many sovereigns it issued after April 1819, but there were reports in 1818, 1819, 1822, and 1823 on the value of gold coin produced by the Mint.

Members of Parliament who supported resumption and who opposed extending agricultural protection responded to the inflationists with two arguments. First, they pointed out that although agricultural profits had

---

[38] Sir Francis Burdett called for a reduction in taxation, a reduction in the money terms of all contracts – especially mortgages – and a repudiation of the national debt proportionate to the degree of monetary deflation, which he estimated at not less than 20 percent (*Hansard* 2s, 7:956–957).

[39] In the debate on the Bank Cash Payments Bill, Baring moved that "a select committee be appointed to consider the provisions of 59 Geo. III, c. 49, [the Resumption Act] and to report their opinion to the House, whether it would be expedient to make any alteration in the said act" (*Hansard* 2s, 5:92–93). His proposal was negatived 141 to 27. Similarly, his proposal to repudiate the national debt was condemned as "objectionable both in justice and policy" (*Hansard* 2s, 4:539).

[40] The Corn Law of 1822 had no practical significance. By its own terms it only took effect when the domestic price of wheat reached 80s. per quarter. The price of wheat never attained this level and the bill was superseded by another corn law in 1828 (Smart 1910–1917, 2:117).

[41] A Parliamentary report on copper coins created at the Mint appeared on 24 May 1819 (*Journal of the House of Commons* 1819, 74:1123). A report on copper coins forged by a Mr. Bolton – who was given the contract to make them – appeared on 3 June 1819 (*Journal of the House of Commons* 1819, 74:1124).

fallen, foreign trade and manufacturing prospered – the inference being that corn was low because of causes specific to agriculture and not because of a decline in domestic expenditure associated with the Resumption Act. Second, they identified the principal causes of low corn prices: a series of bumper harvests and corn imports from Ireland.

In answer to Brougham's claim that resumption had caused a general depression, Huskisson stated that "the manufacturers, and the working classes generally, were in a state of comparative ease and comfort. . . . He defied any man upon any other principle to account for the known fact, that the produce of the taxes upon consumption was gradually and steadily rising" (29 Apr. 1822, *Hansard* 2s, 7:207). Peel advanced the same argument in response to a petition from the agriculturalists of Wiltshire: "Distress was only partial . . . the [Resumption Act] should be fairly tried, not by its effect upon a particular interest, but by its effect upon the state of the whole interests of the country. He [cited] the state of the manufacturing interest, the state of the poor-rates, the comforts enjoyed by the manufacturing population, and the tranquillity prevailing in the manufacturing districts. . . . He could not admit partial distress to be a fair criterion; and, next, he would not admit even that partial distress to be occasioned by the bill" (3 Apr. 1822, *Hansard* 2s, 6:1455). Peel later described how the continued rise of exports led to an increase in manufacturing production – even at the ironworks – and consequently to full employment at good wages (12 June 1822, *Hansard* 2s, 7:1014–1015). The prosperity alluded to by Huskisson and Peel was undeniable: "The contented state of the working classes in 1821 and 1822, and not to mention the great increase of the revenue in those years, attest the comparative well-being of the bulk of the community in periods of what those who are interested in high prices and high rents are pleased to characterize as agricultural distress" (Tooke and Newmarch 1838–1857, 2:74). The King's speech of 1823 further described the "increasing activity which pervaded the manufacturing districts and the flourishing condition of commerce in most of its principal branches." The working classes were well employed, the poor rates were down, and cotton was booming (*Hansard* 2s, 9:925). Agricultural prices remained low in 1823, but complaints about agricultural distress became less frequent, perhaps because of a corresponding decline in rents (Smart 1910–1917, 2:144). Conditions were even better the following year, which Smart describes as one of "great prosperity everywhere" (183).[42]

---

[42] Because Ricardo died in Sept. 1823, there is no need to give a full account of the events of 1824 and 1825.

The principal cause of the agricultural crisis was an excessive supply of agricultural produce. British ports closed against foreign wheat in February 1819 and against all other grains in August 1819.[43] Landlords expected prices to rise when the ports closed, but this did not happen. Instead, prices remained steady then fell precipitously at the harvest of 1820. Parliament appointed an agricultural committee in 1821 to investigate the fall of corn. The committee concluded that the enormous harvest of 1820, combined with corn shipments from Ireland, occasioned the agricultural crisis. Corn prices declined further in 1821 because of the stocks that remained from 1820,[44] another abundant harvest and yet more imports from Ireland (see App. D.3). Wheat fell to 55s. per quarter by December 1821 and, after a third excellent harvest, to 38s. in October 1822 (App. C.1).

Experts on commodity markets,[45] David Hodgson among them,[46] testified before the 1821 Agricultural Committee about the enormity of the harvest of 1820. By Hodgson's estimate, the harvest exceeded an average crop by five bushels per acre, or 15 percent[47] (House of Commons, *Minutes of Evidence Taken before the Select Committee . . . Depressed State of Agriculture* 1821, 263–264):

Question: Have you any objection to state to the Committee, upon any scale you may have formed, what has been the comparative productiveness of the crops of the last six years?

Answer: None whatever; the crop of 1815, according to the method explained, gave a result of 37 Winchester bushels per acre; 1816 gave 25 1/16; 1817 gave 33 4/10; 1818 gave 32 and 4/16; 1819 27 7/16; 1820 37 1/16.

---

[43] There is one exception to the prohibition on imports. The ports opened to foreign oats from Aug. to Nov. 1820. During that short interval 700,000 quarters of oats were brought from the warehouses to the domestic market (House of Commons, *Report from the Select Committee Appointed to Inquire into . . . the Distressed State of Agriculture* 1822, 5).

[44] Tooke reports that because of the magnitude of the harvest of 1820, "there was as much corn left in the country [in Apr. 1821] as generally in common years there is after the harvest." Wheat from 1820 continued to appear in the market for the next three years (Tooke and Newmarch 1838–1857, 2:82).

[45] Corn factors were individuals or partnerships who speculated in corn. To gauge prices months in advance, teams of statisticians were sent to farms throughout the kingdom to assess the state of the crop, measure the weight of the grain, etc. Corn factors were better informed about affairs in agriculture than anyone else because their livelihood depended on such expertise.

[46] Hodgson was a corn factor at Cropper, Benson, and Company in Liverpool. In a letter to Trower dated 21 Apr. 1821 Ricardo described Hodgson, along with Thomas Tooke, as "our best informed witness" (Ricardo, 8:370).

[47] Hodgson stated before the 1821 Agricultural Committee: "The average acreable produce will be about thirty-two" quarters of wheat (*Minutes of Evidence* 1821, 264).

Hodgson also testified that the extent of cultivation increased[48] in 1819 and 1820 as farmers switched from livestock to grain (House of Commons, *Minutes of Evidence Taken before the Select Committee . . . Depressed State of Agriculture* 1821, 265):

Question: What are your reasons for supposing an extension of growth to have taken place within the two or three last years in the United Kingdom?

Answer: I apply it to the crops of 1819 and 1820; it appears from documents which I will submit to the Committee, that there has been a very great falling off in the slaughter of cattle in the towns of Liverpool, Manchester, Birmingham, Leeds and Sheffield, in the last two years . . . of $15^{1/4}$%.

Parliament subsequently estimated that the crop of 1820 was sixteen million quarters. An average harvest was twelve million quarters; a deficient crop, as seen in 1816, about nine million (Marshall 1833, part 2, 90).

The effects of the harvest of 1820 were compounded by the importation of Irish corn (see Table 3.2).[49] William Huskisson, author of the report of the 1821 Agricultural Committee, stated that if no alteration had been made in the corn trade with Ireland, the pressure of the glut might never have been felt by the English grower (Smart 1910–1917, 2:62). The amount of Irish corn imported in 1820 was first published in a Parliamentary report of March 1821.[50] Data from this report, and others that followed, are reproduced in Table 3.2.

Mathias Attwood denied that "importations from Ireland . . . an abundant harvest [or] the importation of a few millions of foreign grain" caused the agricultural crisis (9 Apr. 1821, *Hansard* 2s, 5:110–111). However, as Thomas Tooke explained before the Agricultural Committee, a fall of prices was inevitable given the combination of an inelastic domestic demand for corn and a vast increase in the supply (*Minutes of Evidence* 1821, 228):

Question: Has your attention been particularly turned toward the effect produced on the price of corn by abundance?

---

[48] Even Thomas Attwood, an inflationist and brother to Mathias Attwood, in his testimony of 10 Apr. before the Agricultural Committee admitted that there had been an increase in tillage after 1816 (*Minutes of Evidence* 1821, 245). Ricardo was pleased by the inconsistencies of Attwood's testimony; he wrote to Trower that Attwood's "claims to infallibility have been sifted by Huskisson and myself" (Ricardo, 8:370).

[49] The data in the table come from App. D.3. The same information, up to Apr. 1821, appears in the *Report from the Select Committee . . . Depressed State of Agriculture* 1821, App. 8 and 19.

[50] Reports were presented to Parliament on 2, 12, and 28 Mar. See the Appendix to the *Journal of the House of Commons* 1821.

Table 3.2. *Imports of Irish Corn*

Year	Imports of Irish Wheat: Grain & Flour (qtrs.)	Imports of Irish Oats: Grain & Flour (qtrs.)
1815	584,156	708,496
1816	426,172	795,585
1817	115,794	699,281
1818	228,709	1,429,535
1819	498,880	948,208
1820	1,073,371	1,040,917
1821	1,664,575	1,379,038
1822	1,598,167	673,755

Answer: I have reason to think…that a deficiency or excess in the [corn] supply, compared with the average consumption, is attended with a still greater difference of price than that of most other articles.

Question: Can you state to the Committee, any facts on which that opinion is grounded?

Answer: I have made the following extracts relative to the prices of wheat and the quantities exported and imported.

Tooke produced evidence showing the correlation between the supply of corn and its price from 1671 through 1817 (*Minutes of Evidence 1821*, 229–232). He found that because of an inelastic demand for corn, "the effect on price is in a ratio very much beyond the excess or defect of quantity" (229). Colquhoun estimated the quarters of grain, including seed, consumed annually in Britain to be 9,170,000 of wheat, 6,335,000 of barley, 16,950,000 of oats, 685,000 of rye, and 1,860,000 of beans and peas (*Edinburgh Review*, Jan. 1820, 175). Irish wheat imported in 1821 and 1822 accounted for 20 percent of home consumption. Irish oats imported in 1820 and 1821 filled 10 percent of Britain's consumption.

The increase in the supply of corn would not have caused such a severe fall in prices if domestic producers had been able to export. However, the margin of cultivation in Britain was overextended to the point that when corn prices were ruinous to British farmers, they still could not compete on the Continent. The disparities in production costs between Britain and the Continent had been documented by the House of Commons Committee on the Corn Laws in 1814. They were shown again by Castlereagh, the Foreign Secretary, who presented to Parliament in March 1820 detailed accounts of corn prices at major European ports.[51]

[51] Castlereagh requisitioned a second report in Apr. 1821 – a fact Ricardo was pleased to report to McCulloch: "Mr. Huskisson tells me that Lord Castlereagh has written to all our consuls and ambassadors abroad for an account of the prices of corn in foreign countries

The evidence Castlereagh obtained from British consuls (see App. C.3) shows that average wheat prices did not exceed 20s. per quarter from 1820 onward in Russia and Prussia, Britain's principal sources for imported wheat. In Holland and Prussia oats traded for as little as 5s. per quarter. Additional evidence was presented to the 1821 Agricultural Committee by Hodgson and Tooke concerning corn prices at Continental ports and the shipping costs to Britain from these ports (*Minutes of Evidence 1821*, 224–227, 270–271, 284–286).

Prices on the Continent were so low that British farmers could not export. As Tooke observed though, the demand for corn in the home market was inelastic, making prices highly volatile.[52] In the event of an abundant harvest, there being no vent for exports, domestic production glutted the market, causing a ruinous fall in prices. On the other hand, in the event of a deficient harvest, as happened during the war and the famine of 1816, prices were likely to exceed 100s.

The Corn Law of 1815 did not stabilize commodity markets. It prohibited imports when the domestic price of wheat was below 80s, but once prices reached this threshold the ports opened and foreign corn could be imported duty-free for three months. The Agricultural Committee of 1821 recognized that, in the event of a deficient harvest, the domestic price of corn would rise and then – as soon as the ports opened – fall precipitously under a deluge of foreign corn.[53] Speculators lodged enormous quantities of foreign corn at British ports (see App. D.4), at which point the corn

for a series of years which will be laid before parliament as soon as it arrives" (21 Apr. 1821; Ricardo, 8:374).

[52] The table below shows the annual range of wheat prices from 1813 to 1822. The data come from two sources: Account of the Weekly Average Prices of Barley, Oats, Rye and Wheat from 4th January 1813, to 24th February 1816, *Parliamentary Papers* 1816, 14:391–393, MF 17.83, and Account Showing ... Average Price of Wheat ... Highest and Lowest in Each of the Years from 1815 to 1826, *Parliamentary Papers* 1826–1827, 16:13, MF 29.128.

Year	Price Range (s. per qtr.)	Year	Price Range (s. per qtr.)
1813	73–129	1819	64–78
1814	62–82	1820	53–73
1815	54–70	1821	46–70
1816	53–103	1822	38–50
1817	74–112		

[53] In his testimony of 6 Apr. 1821 before the Agricultural Committee, Tooke stated that "in the event of a short crop, I should take for granted that prices will rise to the importation price of 80s." (*Minutes of Evidence*, 232).

was not legally imported. Once the ports opened, it could be "imported" simply by transferring it to another warehouse. For example, between 15 August and 16 November 1820, some 727,000 quarters of foreign oats, or 5.8 million bushels, were admitted for home consumption (*Report from the Select Committee . . . Depressed State of Agriculture* 1821, App. 22). The stocks of foreign corn warehoused in Britain remained consistently high because profits to be made in the home market outstripped those on the Continent where prices were lower by one-third to one-half.

Parliament kept detailed accounts of corn prices on the Continent. These accounts show that the prices of wheat, rye, barley, and oats fell almost 70 percent from 1818 through 1824 (see App. C.3). The inflationists were loath to admit that corn had fallen abroad. For if corn declined 70 percent in Rotterdam, Hamburg, and St. Petersburg, it must have fallen because of factors unconnected with resumption. Moreover, it was reasonable to suppose that these same factors – good weather and abundant harvests – were at work in the home market. Speaking to a motion made by Charles Western on the currency, Attwood stated that "the hon. member[54] had asserted that prices on the continent had fallen to as great an extent as in this country; that of course this could only have been occasioned by abundant production; and he had asked whether we should find in France so great an absurdity as a demand for a reduction of taxes on the ground of an abundant harvest and a glut of corn? [However,] the question as to foreign prices, was one on which much misstatement had taken place, and on which it was of importance to have the real facts before them" (10 July 1822, *Hansard* 2s, 7:1613). Even assuming, Attwood continued, that there had been a fall of prices on the Continent, he was certain that it had been caused by the Bank of England's purchases of bullion which "materially deranged the monied system of Europe" (*Hansard* 2s, 7:1614).

In spite of Attwood's objections, there was no doubt that corn prices had fallen abroad. The reports Castlereagh obtained from Britain's consuls indicate that prices of wheat and rye began to decline in 1817, barley and oats in 1818. The reports also show that the fall of corn prices on the Continent was at least as severe as in Britain.[55] Table 3.3 indicates

---

[54] Attwood refers to David Ricardo.

[55] Macleod presents a similar argument: "The low prices of that year [1822] had nothing to do with the act of 1819 [because] the prices of all sorts of agricultural produce were equally depressed all over the continent of Europe. . . . At Vienna wheat which was 114s. in March 1817, fell in September, 1819, to 19s. 6d.; at Munich wheat fell from 151s. in September, 1817, to 24s. 5d. in September, 1820. The same phenomena were observed in Italy" (Macleod 1902–1906, 2:103).

Table 3.3. *Annual Average Wheat Prices*
at Foreign Ports

Port	1817 (s. sterling)	1822 (s. sterling)
Archangel	57.2	14.2
St. Petersburg	56.6	29.9
Konigsberg	57.7	22.8
Hamburg	80.0	27.5
Rotterdam	104.4	35.0

the annual average prices of wheat, converted to British shillings, at foreign ports (see also App. C.3).

Concerning Attwood's claim that monetary operations in Britain "deranged the monied system of Europe," there is again no supporting evidence. Attwood suggested that gold purchases by the Bank of England
in preparation for resumption bid up the world relative price of gold,
which, in turn, caused a monetary contraction on the Continent and the
fall of corn. His argument is not supported by the timing of price fluctuations on the Continent as compared with the international movement
of gold.

The sharpest decline of prices on the Continent occurred between 1817
and 1820 (see App. C.3). For most of this interval, Britain was exporting
gold. (Sterling traded below par from June 1817 until August 1819, making
it profitable to export gold.[56]) The export of gold should have raised
prices on the Continent, not reduced them. Moreover, even after the
foreign exchange became favorable, the Bank did not acquire significant
amounts of bullion until April 1820. Tooke summarized the rebuttal to
the inflationists in the following terms:

It was reserved for the opponents of Peel's bill to discover "that the operations on
English currency must have materially deranged the monied system of Europe."[57]
And these operations on English currency are said to have been "such a reduction,
forcibly made in the amount of money in circulation as was fully adequate to
occasion that fall in prices." But if the influence of such a cause could have the
effects ascribed to it, its operation would, in the cases cited, of the fluctuation
of prices between 1815 and 1820, have been in an exactly opposite direction to
that which is inferred. For it has been seen, that bullion was flowing largely into
this country, coincidentally with the great rise of prices on the Continent in 1816

[56] The Bank of England alone lost £8 million of its hoard (see App. A.2).
[57] Tooke cites Mathias Attwood's Parliamentary speech of 10 July 1822.

and 1817; and that if flowed out of this country in 1818 and 1819, coincidentally with the great and rapid fall of prices on the Continent (Tooke and Newmarch 1838–1857, 2:92–93).

There was also little correlation between gold purchases by the Bank and fluctuations in British domestic prices. In February 1819, the quantity of gold coin and bullion in the Bank amounted to £4,354,000; by September 1819 it was £3,570,000 (see App. A.2). Yet this is the interval when the greatest fall in prices occurred. It should be noted that the Mint coined only £3,574 in sovereigns and half-sovereigns in 1819, a quantity too small to affect the market price of gold (see App. B.4).

Monetary Contraction and the Deflation of 1820–1822

No one except the ardent inflationists claimed that the agricultural crisis was a strictly monetary phenomenon. Even so, contemporary reports suggested that there had been some monetary deflation and, to this extent, the burden of taxes and mortgages on land had increased. The combined circulation of gold, silver, and notes of the Bank of England remained stable. Reports from the Stamp Office, though, indicated that the circulation of notes among country banks was sharply reduced, from £20.5 million in 1818 to £8 million in 1822 (see App. B.1). Parliament later discovered that the country-bank circulation declined by no more than 12 percent. However, this information was not known at the time, so even the strongest proponents of resumption, Ricardo among them, were concerned about the fall in the country-bank circulation.

The circulation of Bank of England notes declined after resumption because people exchanged banknotes for gold and silver.[58] From 1819 to 1823, £16.6 million in coins were issued this way (App. B.6), all of which remained in circulation. Silver coin was not melted or exported owing to a 6-percent seigniorage that made it unprofitable to melt at prices below 5s. 6d. per ounce, which price it reached only briefly in February 1819 (see App. C.4). Gold coins were not melted or exported after May 1819 because the rise of sterling on the foreign exchange made smuggling

---

[58] Private persons could carry gold to the Mint to be coined or they could purchase gold coin at the Bank of England. For an ounce of gold the Mint would produce coin worth £3 17s. 10 1/2 d. and return it to the owner after several weeks. Because of the time lag, it was more convenient to obtain gold at the Bank. In this way, the Bank sold £13,749,898 in gold coin from May 1821 through the end of 1823. During the same period the Mint issued only £10,930 to private persons (see App. A.4).

Table 3.4. *Minimum Circulation of Specie and Bank
of England Notes*

1819 – £29,949,633	1821 – £33,063,069	1823 – £40,556,157
1820 – 30,213,933	1822 – 36,092,157	

unprofitable. Sterling traded well above par by April 1820; therefore, sovereigns were repatriated "directly into circulation, so as not only to displace some of the small notes, but to form an addition to the whole circulation. According to this view, the amount of the circulation in 1820 would not vary materially from what it had been in 1819.... [And] there is no doubt, that in 1821 and still more in 1822, the basis of the currency, as consisting of Bank of England notes and gold coin, exceeded in amount what it had been in 1819" (Tooke and Newmarch, 2:101). Table 3.4 shows the minimum circulation of specie and Bank of England notes in the years 1819 through 1823. The actual circulation was higher because of the repatriation of British gold coins smuggled out of the country before July 1819.

Once gold began to be imported, the Bank's hoard increased rapidly.[59] An indication of the amount of treasure accumulating at the Bank came in March 1821 when it petitioned the government for the power to redeem its notes in British gold coin two years ahead of schedule.[60] (Up to this point banknotes were convertible only into gold bars weighing 60 oz.) The government agreed, bringing forward the Cash Payments Bill. The request aroused suspicion that the Bank had amassed an enormous hoard, but nothing could be verified because the actual values of the Bank's hoard were not reported until 1832.[61]

The rise of sterling and the influx of gold were, in themselves, favorable circumstances. However, there was concern in Parliament that the strength of the pound reflected too restrictive a monetary policy by the Bank of England. The Bank never altered its policies in response to resumption; it continued to discount commercial notes at 5 percent. When the market rate of profit fell below 5 percent, as seems to have

---

[59] Between Mar. 1820 and May 1821 the Bank's gold reserve increased from £4,964,000 to £13,329,000 (see App. A.2).

[60] The Resumption Act forbade the Bank to redeem its notes in coin before 1 May 1823. However, once the Bank accumulated a sufficient hoard there was no reason for it not to redeem its notes with sovereigns. The Bank Cash Payments Bill permitted the Bank to do so starting 1 May 1821.

[61] See the House of Commons, *Report from the Committee of Secrecy on the Bank of England Charter* 1832, App. No. 5, in *Parliamentary Papers* 1831–1832, 6.

happened in 1819, the demand for discounts nearly ceased. By 1820, the Bank's commercial discounts were one-fifth what they had been in 1810 (see App. A.6). Taken in isolation, the change was benign. But because it coincided with the reports from the Stamp Office indicating that the country circulation was sharply reduced, the change occasioned some disquiet.

The government at first urged the Bank to reduce its discount rate; the Bank refused. In the alternative, the government proposed[62] to increase the money supply by borrowing £4 million from the Bank on an advance of Exchequer bills, and then loaning the £4 million to finance agricultural investments (Smart 1907–1917, 2:66). Liverpool justified the measure, stating:

It was allowed on all hands that if it should turn out that the circulating medium was inadequate to the wants of the country, it would be better to increase it through the medium of discounts than by a further issue of Exchequer Bills. . . . It does appear very extraordinary to His Majesty's Government . . . that at this moment when the market rate of interest is not more than 4 per cent., the Bank refuse to discount at a lower rate than 5. . . . An immense quantity of treasure must have been flowing into the coffers of the Bank of England. The quantity of gold thus locked up by the Bank and their refusal to discount at less than 5 per cent. must certainly be very injurious to them, and if to them, to the public at large, more specifically to that distressed part of the public, the agricultural interest. Finding it impossible, however, to induce the Bank to lower the rate of interest on their discounts, conformably with the expectations held out in 1819, His Majesty's Government resolved on borrowing £4 millions on Exchequer Bills from the Bank with a view to applying that sum in some manner to the relief of the country (26 Feb. 1822, *Hansard* 2s, 6:715).[63]

The government intended "to get these 4 millions into general circulation" with the hope that this would "extend and quicken the general circulation" (*Hansard*, 433). The proposal was attacked by members of the House on the grounds that it would be "*pro tanto* a repeal of the bill of the right hon. gentleman opposite (Mr. Peel)" and that it would lead to another round of inflation, accompanied by a fall in the foreign exchange and a loss of the Bank's gold reserve (*Hansard*, 489). The matter was resolved on 21 June 1822 when the Bank reduced its discount rate to 4 percent. The

---

[62] Debate on the matter began 29 Apr. 1822. Smart devotes an entire section to this and other attempts to undermine the Resumption Act (Smart 1910–1917, 2:77–78, 92–100).

[63] For a discussion of surrounding events see Acworth 1925, 105–106.

government, in response, abandoned its efforts to "extend and quicken the circulation."

Conclusion

Crises in the United States, Spanish South America, and Continental Europe caused a reduction in the demand for British exports that triggered a general depression, starting in February 1819. The suffering of manufacturing districts was acute but short-lived. When foreign demand returned to normal in mid-1820, manufacturing districts began to amend. Inflationists attributed the depression to a contraction of the money supply caused by the Resumption Act. However, the crises in trade and manufacturing began before Parliament considered the act. And at no time did the Bank of England change its lending policies in response to resumption.

When the prices of agricultural commodities collapsed in 1820, inflationists again claimed that the country was in the throes of a general depression caused by monetary deflation. They proposed to devalue the currency and increase barriers to foreign trade. Members of Parliament who supported free trade and the gold standard pointed out that there was no general depression – trade and manufacturing were by this time prospering – and that agricultural prices had fallen from obvious causes: the abundant harvests of 1820, 1821, and 1822 and corn imports from Ireland. Moreover, the money supply was not reduced. The Bank of England withdrew several million of its notes, but these had been replaced entirely by gold and silver coins. The only grounds for admitting some degree of monetary deflation were reports from the Stamp Office indicating a reduction in the country-bank circulation. It was discovered a decade later that the country circulation declined by at most 12 percent between 1818 and 1823. Likewise, documents in the archive of the Bank of England reveal that £14 million in sovereigns and half-sovereigns were issued by the Bank from 1821 through 1823, more than compensating for the withdrawal of the Bank's notes. Still more sovereigns were repatriated, and these, combined with silver issuing from the Mint, extended the money supply steadily from 1819 onward.

If the Bank can be faulted for the manner in which it implemented the Resumption Act it is only in the fact that it could have cut interest rates sooner. Lower interest rates would have spurred economic growth, and probably would have relieved some of the pressure on agriculture. But, given the limits of central banking in the early nineteenth century and the fact that the Bank of England was a private institution, "that would have involved a conception of Bank policy and a subtlety of action which the Old Lady of Threadneedle Street had not yet attained even a hundred years later, under not dissimilar circumstances. Neither the tools nor the attitude necessary for a successful compensatory banking policy existed" (Rostow 1942, 19).

FOUR

Ricardo as an Empirical Economist

Ricardo was brilliant in the City, first as a stock jobber (1793–1818) and later as a loan contractor (1806–1819).[1] He was also a long-time associate of prominent Whigs, who arranged for his election to Parliament in 1819. As a trader and financier he acquired a thorough knowledge of public finance, foreign and domestic commerce, and the determinants of the money supply. In Parliament he developed further expertise as a member of Commons committees studying agriculture and the poor laws. The depth of Ricardo's knowledge is shown by the highly empirical character of his published works, starting with his letters to the *Morning Chronicle* and concluding with his posthumously published *Plan for a National Bank*. The only one of his works that does not have a distinct empirical element is the *Principles of Political Economy*. This chapter describes Ricardo's insight into the economic and political milieu of Georgian England.

The Business of Loan Contracting

In 1806, Ricardo joined a select group of financiers in the City of London whose *raison d'etre* was to underwrite the allied campaign against France. Contractors submitted bids at auctions held annually, or at most at intervals of two years, at Downing Street under the supervision of the Chancellor of the Exchequer. The syndicate that tendered the highest bid earned the right to purchase the government's entire bond offering. Prospective

---

[1] An overview of Ricardo's business transactions appears in Sraffa's article "Ricardo in Business" (Ricardo, 10:67–91).

financiers prepared their bids by looking to current and future market conditions. Future conditions mattered because installments on loans were paid over a period of months during which time bond prices were likely to fluctuate to the loss or gain of the syndicate.[2] Given these risks, Ricardo necessarily kept informed about factors affecting both the demand for and supply of loanable funds.

The demand for funds in London was occasioned primarily by loans for the British government. Foreign powers also negotiated loans in the City. Occasional sales of previously issued government debt were a smaller, but still important, element in the demand for funds. Sraffa records that it was common practice for loan contractors to depress bond prices prior to auctions by "selling out the stock which they owned and also in making sales of stock of which they were not possessed. The sales would depress the price against the day of the contract, so as to make the new stock obtainable as cheaply as possible" (Ricardo, 10:77–78). Records in the Bank of England indicate that the Bank, at the government's behest, also manipulated bond prices. In June 1804, for instance, William Pitt asked the Bank to purchase Exchequer bills so as to "reduce the discount within moderate limits"; the Bank agreed.[3] The Bank also resolved the next year to purchase Exchequer bills "whenever they may judge such bills press upon the market."[4]

Ricardo understood the effects of the government's financial decisions on the market. He described in the *Principles* the consequences of both extensive borrowing in wartime and rapid debt reduction in peacetime: "In time of war, the stock market is so loaded by the continual loans of Government, that the price of stock has not time to settle at its fair level, before a new operation of funding takes place, or it is affected by anticipation of political events. In time of peace, on the contrary, the operation of the sinking fund . . . elevates the price of stock and consequently depresses the rate of interest on these securities below the general market rate" (1:298). The statement refers to a sinking fund resulting from a government budget surplus – meaning, "an excess of revenue above

---

[2] Ricardo's success on the loan of 1815 attests to this fact. The loan, which was the last one of the war and the largest at £36 million, was arranged just days before Waterloo. Upon news of the battle reaching London, the Omnium rose from a 2.5-percent premium to a 13-percent premium. Ricardo, as a contractor for the loan, had all his money invested in stock at this point, earning a profit the *Sunday Times* estimated at "upwards of a million sterling" (Ricardo, 10:84).

[3] Bank of England, *Minutes of the Court of Directors*, 21 June 1804, G4/30.

[4] Bank of England, *Minutes of the Court of Directors*, 24 Oct. 1805, G4/31.

expenditure" (4:193–194). In practice, Britain's sinking fund was an accounting fiction.[5] But it was expensive, and Ricardo observed in his *Funding System* (1819) that because Government loans were unnecessarily large, "the contractor must make a large purchase and he must wait before he can make his sale of ten millions to the commissioners. He is induced then to sell much more largely before the contract which cannot fail to affect the market price" (4:173).[6] Because of the effects of government borrowing on interest rates, Ricardo was forced to monitor closely the government's financial needs and the size of the Exchequer's intended sinking fund.

The government's loan of 1819 illustrates how responsive interest rates were to changes in the demand for funds. The auction for this loan occurred on 9 June 1819, at which time the Resumption Act had already passed first reading in both Houses. Being concerned about its ability to resume cash payments according to the schedule contained in the act, the Bank of England made clear its intent to refuse its customary advances to loan contractors after the auction. In consequence, and fearing that contractors would be unable to pay monthly installments of the intended £24 million loan, the government reduced the loan to £12 million. The decision caused an immediate rise in the price of stock, which did not escape Ricardo's attention since he bid at the auction: "In lieu of a loan of twenty-four millions from the contractor, there was one only of twelve millions; and as soon as this arrangement was known, previous to the contract, the stocks rose 4 or 5 per cent., and influenced the terms of the loan in that degree" (4:173).

Bond prices also depended on the supply of loanable funds, which, Ricardo understood, was affected by political events, conditions in foreign and domestic commerce, and fluctuations in the money supply. He attributed the financial panic of 1797 to "political alarm" (3:365),[7] and

---

[5] During the Liverpool Administration (1812–1827) disbursements from the sinking fund were set arbitrarily. The fund bore no relation to the government's budget surplus or deficit. The Chancellor of the Exchequer simply decreed that the government would redeem bonds to a certain value and then borrowed monies to do so.

[6] In Parliament, Ricardo noted that as a loan contractor, it was in his interests to see the fund maintained as it ensured high premiums to the contractors. Consulting the "advantage of the country," however, he opposed its continuation (Ricardo, 5:4–6).

[7] Malthus similarly acknowledged the influence of war on markets. One day after Waterloo he cautioned Ricardo that "Should the allies be successful at the commencement of the campaign, Omnium will certainly rise very considerably, but on the other hand if Bonaparte should begin prosperously, I think there might be a panic which would occasion a rapid fall." His concern was great enough that Malthus sold his £5000 share of the Omnium before news of the battle reached London, after which time the Omnium rose to a 13 per cent. premium (Ricardo, 6:231–233).

likewise noted "the great effect" that a pending conflict between Russia and Turkey in 1821 "would have on the price of the public securities" (9:39). As an illustration of the influence of domestic commerce on financial markets, he credited low interest rates in 1817 to the relocation of capital from wartime to peacetime production: "May not the derangement which the different employments of capital have experienced from the termination of the war have thrown an unusual quantity in the market to seek new occupations. Although there is no amount of capital which may not be employed in a country there is probably an interval while it is seeking its ultimate destination, during which it particularly operates on the rate of interest. May we not be experiencing such an interval now when so different a direction is given to capital from the change from war to peace?"[8] The vigor of Britain's foreign trade similarly affected the market: "In our case the market rate of interest has been lowered by causes which may be considered permanent . . . and also by causes which may be considered temporary such as the derangement of foreign commerce; that as the last of these causes shall cease to operate by things getting into their natural order the rate of interest will have a tendency to rise" (Heertje 1991, 522).

Ricardo further understood how changes in the monetary base disturbed private credit and thereby, at least temporarily, altered interest rates. Critics sometimes confuse his comments about the long-term effects of a change in the money supply on the rate of interest – he said there were no effects – with the immediate results of that change. But Ricardo carefully distinguished between the short and the long run:

I do not dispute, that if the Bank were to bring a large additional sum of notes into the market and offer them on loan, but that they would for a time affect the rate of interest. . . . It is only during the interval of the issues of the Bank and their effect on prices that we should be sensible of an abundance of money; interest would, during that interval, be under its natural level; but as soon as the additional sum of notes or of money became absorbed in the general circulation, the rate of interest would be as high, and new loans would be demanded with as much eagerness as before . . . To suppose that any increased issues of the Bank can have the effect of permanently lowering the rate of interest and satisfying the demands of all borrowers so that there will be none to apply for new loans . . . is to attribute a power to the circulating medium which it can never possess (Ricardo, 3:91–92).

He referred again to the effects of monetary expansion in Chapter 21 of the *Principles*: "If by the discovery of a new mine, by the abuses of banking, or by any other cause, the quantity of money be greatly increased,

---

[8] Letter from Ricardo to Grenfell, 27 Aug. 1817 (Heertje 1991, 521).

its ultimate effect is to raise the prices of commodities in proportion to the increased quantity of money; but there is probably always an interval, during which some effect is produced on the rate of interest" (1:198). The reference to "abuses of banking" suggests that Ricardo treated the notes of country banks as part of the money supply. He never described the causal relation between the activities of country banks and interest rates, but in the financial crisis of 1815, he recognized how the precarious situation of country banks affected the demand for notes of the Bank of England: "there has been a considerable rise in the value of money which I think has been effected by the many failures of country banks, which has increased the use of Bank of England notes in the country both as a circulating medium and as a deposit against the alarm which always attends extensive failures in the country" (6:343).

The importance of monetary fluctuations to Ricardo as a loan contractor cannot be overestimated. Interest rates could not be permanently altered by changes in the monetary stock (1:298; 3:88, 92, 150; 5:130, 445). But the bond auction occurred on a particular day and its outcome depended on the rate of interest prevailing that day so that short-term factors – including fluctuations in the money supply – were critical to his estimate of an appropriate bid: "It is the market price on the day of bidding for the loan which governs the terms on which the loan is negotiated. It is looked to both by the minister who sells and the contractor who purchases" (4:173). The importance of market conditions is further evident in that on the day of the auction, contractors were known to send runners to and from the City to report current stock prices to them at Downing Street even while the auction was proceeding (10:76).

Contemporary Sources of Information

Ricardo had ready access to information on current and expected demands for loanable funds. Loans to foreign powers and large stock sales in the City were reported twice weekly in *The Course of Exchange*, a newsletter to which he subscribed. The British government's demand for funds could be estimated by comparing its tax revenues and projected expenditures. Each quarter the Treasury reported the revenues generated by customs, excise taxes, the property tax, and other taxes. (App. E.1 lists taxation reports presented to the House of Commons from 1815 to 1823.) That Ricardo was acquainted with these reports is clear from his correspondence and Parliamentary speeches (5:315; 6:304; 9:158). Exact expenditure figures were published with a lag of one fiscal year, but accurate estimates of future government spending were available from any of several sources: the reports of finance committees, Parliamentary votes on expenditures,[9] or the annual budget report by the Chancellor of the Exchequer.[10] Once Ricardo estimated the government's demand for funds – and given his sense of the market's readiness to supply funds – he could predict changes in interest rates. He intimated as much in a letter of August 1814 to Malthus: "The fall in the Omnium is to be attributed to our continued expenses and the expectation of another loan before the payments on the present are completed" (6:119).[11]

The short-term supply of funds depended on changes in the monetary base composed of specie and Bank of England notes. The circulation of banknotes could be monitored easily. The Bank reported the number of its notes outstanding at least twice annually. In years with extended Parliamentary sessions, such as 1819, as many as six updates appeared.[12] (App. A.1 lists the reports presented to Parliament on the monthly circulation of banknotes.) Parliament published less frequent but still adequate reports on the silver coinage (see App. B.5). Neither Parliament nor the Bank released any information about the circulation of gold coin.

The Mint regularly reported the value of the gold coins it had manufactured (see App. B.5). The Mint coined almost exclusively for the Bank of England,[13] so it was known how many sovereigns and half-sovereigns the

---

[9] The Government submitted spending proposals for the upcoming fiscal year to Parliament, which then voted whether to accept the estimates, thereby approving funding. These estimates were public information, being listed in the Appendix to the *Journal of the House of Commons*. The *Journal* for most Parliamentary sessions contains about 200 pages of expenditure estimates.

[10] The target level of the sinking fund was another factor to consider in estimating the size of pending government loans. During Vansittart's (1812–1822) tenure at the Exchequer the intended level of fictitious sinking fund was announced in his annual budget address.

[11] The commercial report for Mar. 1815 in the *New Monthly Magazine* (p. 187) suggests this was a common means of estimating future interest rates: "The expectation of a considerable loan being required for the service of the present year, will tend to prevent much if any further rise in the funds till the contract for the loan is completed. The following comparative statement of the receipts of revenue for the years 1813 and 1814, places the resources of the country in a very gratifying and satisfactory point of view, taken from official documents as laid before Parliament."

[12] App. A.1 lists the monthly circulation of Bank of England notes and indicates the dates on which reports appeared.

[13] As to this fact, see "An Account of All Sovereigns and Half Sovereigns Coined at the Mint for Persons Other than the Bank of England," *Parliamentary Papers* 1830, 17:371, MF 32.131. Anyone was permitted to take bullion to the Mint to have it melted into sovereigns, but the production of coins took several weeks. The Bank, by contrast, was always ready to buy gold – at £3 18s. 6d. per ounce before resumption; at £3 17s. 6d. after

Bank received. The Bank, however, gave no indication as to how many sovereigns it issued to the public or how many were added to its hoard. Under pressure from Parliament in 1797, 1810, and 1819, the Bank published an index showing fluctuations in its bullion reserve. Ricardo was familiar with the index.[14] Yet neither he, nor anyone outside the Bank, knew that the standard interpretation of the index overestimated the value of the hoard (Klein 1997, 78–79). The index was only deciphered after the discovery of a document in the Bank's archive showing levels of the bullion hoard on specific days matched with the corresponding index numbers (Klein 1997). A note at the bottom of the document reads: "This Scale was given to the Deputy Governor, who did not deliver it to either of the Committees [meaning the House of Commons and House of Lords Committees investigating Resumption in 1819]."[15]

At the Bank Court on 21 March 1822, the governor of the Bank reported changes in the total amount of banknotes and sovereigns in circulation from March 1820 to March 1822 (Ricardo, 4:232n). The governor did not distinguish between notes and coin, but given that the Bank's note circulation was known, Ricardo calculated by subtraction that the Bank issued sovereigns worth £7.5 million between May 1821 and March 1822. A report from the Mint indicated that it coined £14 million in gold between April 1819 and February 1822 (*Journal of the House of Commons* 1822, 77:1148). Because £7.5 million were distributed to the public, Ricardo guessed that the remaining £6.5 million were added to the Bank's hoard.

The whole amount of circulation both in London and the country does not probably much exceed 32 millions, of which there are nearly 16 millions of Bank of England notes of 5 pounds and above, 7,500,000 of sovereigns, and nine millions of country Bank notes. If this be true there has been little or no falling off in the amount of Bank of England notes and coin together since 1819. By a return laid before the H of Commons more than 19 millions of sovereigns have been coined since 1817. During the period that the Bank so foolishly issued coin, when it was advantageous to export it, they got rid of 5 millions of sovereigns, so that if these were all exported more than 14 millions of sovereigns must now be in the country (9 June 1822, Ricardo, 9:201–202).

---

the act took effect. Because of the convenience of trading with the Bank, gold merchants preferred it over the Mint.

[14] Ricardo used the index of 1810 in *Secure Currency* (1816) to estimate the Bank's profitability (4:99–101). He cited the index of 1797 in *Plan for a National Bank* (1823) to show that the Bank's discounts to merchants comprised a small fraction of commercial lending in London (4:279). He described the index as "the ingenious calculator" (4:415–418).

[15] Bank of England, *Memorials, Contracts, Accounts for Parliament*, C66/1, 24–25.

Ricardo's estimates were remarkably precise. The actual value of sovereigns issued between May 1821 and March 1822 was £9.1 million. The total value of the Bank's hoard – of which sovereigns constituted a part – amounted to £11 million (see App. A.2 and A.3).

By 1821, two categories of gold coins circulated: coins newly issued from the Bank of England and coins of an earlier vintage that had been exported during the depreciation of sterling and then repatriated when sterling surpassed its intrinsic par on the foreign exchange. The fact that gold coins were imported or exported en masse in response to slight variations in exchange rates made it difficult to calculate changes in the monetary base. The government kept an account of gold shipped to and from the country lawfully. However, smuggling was the practice of the day, leaving no record. To develop a sense of the international traffic in gold, Ricardo conferred with several friends who were bullion merchants.

Mr. Goldsmid[16] informs me that at the period of the improvement in the exchange about Christmas last there were no importations, as far as he knows, of gold from France. A small quantity was imported from Lisbon. I have consulted Wetenhall's list and the following [table enclosed] appear to be the variations in the exchange and the price of gold about Christmas last (Ricardo to Malthus, 29 Aug. 1812, 6:85).

At one point he seems also to have attempted to interview smugglers:

I have been making enquiries concerning a bullion merchant. I find that the trade is mostly carried on by a class of people not particularly scrupulous in their modes of getting money, and I am told that they would not be very communicative, particularly on the subject of their exports. There are however some well informed merchants who know a great deal of the trade without themselves being actively engaged in it, to whom I hope I shall be able to introduce you . . . Mr. Mushet will dine with us on Sunday (Ricardo to Malthus, 22 Mar. 1813, 6:90).

Goldsmid was an important source for Ricardo. He shared nonpublic information about international gold shipments, and being a bullion broker for the Bank of England, he may also have indicated to Ricardo the scale of the Bank's transactions in gold. The "Mr. Mushet" mentioned in the second letter is Robert Mushet, Master of the Mint. He was a friend of Ricardo's and a founding member of the Political Economy Club. It is uncertain what strictures, if any, governed the release of proprietary information by the administrators of the Mint, but Mushet included a

---

[16] Isaac Lyon Goldsmid and Aaron Asher Goldsmid were partners in the house of Mocatta and Goldsmid, bullion brokers for the Bank of England (Ricardo, 6:85n).

wealth of data in his pamphlets and he may have shared with Ricardo additional facts about the gold trade. Without private sources of information, the extent of the international traffic in bullion could only be estimated using random accounts from mints on the Continent, as for example, when Alexander Baring reported to the House of Commons Committee on Resumption that "in France it appears by the report of the minister of finance that there has been carried to the Mint of France in the sixteen months preceding the 31st December last, gold to the amount of 125 millions of francs (being equal to about 5 millions sterling) . . . . Of that gold, upwards of three-fourths was in coin from this country; and this operation has continued during the present year, though the amount of the importations of this year has not been reported."[17]

Ricardo's knowledge of the money supply is significant for his analysis of postwar events. For, among other things, he would have known that the Bank failed to support private credit during the depression of 1816. This is confirmed by the fact that he did not dispute Sir John Sinclair's assertion in *The Means of Arresting the Progress of the National Calamity* (1817) that Britain's economic crisis was due to a contraction of the money supply.[18] Ricardo also knew that the circulation of Bank of England notes remained stable during the first half of 1819, when the depression of 1819–1820 began and when most of the deflation associated with that crisis occurred. He stated as much before Parliament on 9 June 1820, saying: "The reduction of bank-notes within the last year did not exceed £2,000,000; that reduction of £2,000,000 was all that was necessary to bring about that state of the currency which all had united with the finance committee in desiring to see obtained" (5:61). Finally, he knew that the monetary contraction – if any – occasioned by the Resumption Act could not have caused deflation to the extent alleged by Attwood, Western, and their allies. At the time the Bank resumed cash payments, it appeared from James Wetenhall's biweekly publication, *The Course of the Exchange*,[19] that gold was trading 5 percent higher relative to silver

---

[17] Baring's evidence appears in the second report of the House of Commons Committee on Resumption, which Peel presented to the House on 6 May 1819 (*Hansard* 1s, 40:155).

[18] In a letter to Sinclair of 4 May 1817, Ricardo stated: "Thank you for your pamphlet, which I have read with attention. I agree with you that a part of our distress has been occasioned by the reduction of the circulation" (7:151).

[19] Ricardo subscribed to the *Course of the Exchange*. So did everyone else. Government reports on gold and silver prices and the foreign exchange always cited Wetenhall as the definitive source.

than when the Resumption Act passed. Ricardo attributed the rise in gold to unnecessarily large purchases of bullion by the Bank of England[20] – something he had hoped his ingot plan would preclude. Because of the disparity between gold and silver, he conceded to the inflationists that resumption had caused deflation of 10 percent: 5 percent to bring the paper pound to par and an additional 5 percent owing to a rise in gold (19 Mar. 1821, 5:95; 7 May 1822, 5:165).

Ricardo ceded further ground to the inflationists in 1822 in light of reports from the Stamp Office that indicated a reduction in the circulation of country-bank notes: "there has been little or no falling off in the amount of Bank of England notes and coin together since 1819, but Country Bank notes have diminished to the amount of £7.5 millions ... it is a great reduction" (9 June 1822, 9:201). According to the stamp estimates, the country-bank circulation declined by 60 percent between 1818 and 1822, from £20.5 million to £8 million (see App. B.2). If the stamp report was accurate, the money supply was significantly reduced and the claims of the inflationists became increasingly plausible. It was shown years later that stamp reports were not accurate, but as Ricardo could not have known this, his recontre against the inflationists lost its hard cutting edge.

In the early nineteenth century there were six hundred country banks in England and Wales. Another eighty country banks operated in Scotland along with the three Scottish chartered banks. The banks answered to no central body and no attempt was made to gather data from individual banks about the volume of their issues. What little information existed on the country circulation came from the Stamp Office, which recorded the number of stamps purchased by the banks for their promissory notes.[21] The Stamp Office could not measure the actual circulation of country notes because it was not known how many of these notes had been destroyed or how many were held by the banks as reserves. Instead it

---

[20] Ricardo stated before Parliament: "If the Bank contemplated paying in gold coin in 1823, as they were now by law required, they must purchase a quantity of gold for that purpose; and to this cause was to be attributed the present disproportion between the price of gold and silver" (2 Feb. 1821, 5:70).

[21] Stamps were a per-unit tax levied mostly on items made of paper: newspapers, banknotes, bills of exchange, medical licences, etc. The Stamp Office, at irregular intervals, provided data on the amount of money that had been paid in stamp taxes on country-bank notes; a higher tax was paid on notes of greater value. Stamp reports usually distinguished among notes of different denominational categories: less than £1 1s., from £1 1s. to £2 2s., from £2 2s. to £5 5s., and, by increasing increments, up to £100. (Stamps were also paid on cards, dice, and race horses.)

Table 4.1. *Index of Country Bank Issues*

1818 – 100	1822 – 88.34
1819 – 98.29	1823 – 88.10
1820 – 94.16	1824 – 95.41
1821 – 93.05	1825 – 102.28

relied on arbitrary assumptions about the correlation between the number of stamps sold and the circulation of country notes. Mr. Sedgwick, Chairman of the Stamp Board, summarized these assumptions in his testimony before the House of Lords Committee on Resumption in 1819:[22] "It is supposed that a Country Banker may usually have about One Tenth of the whole Amount of his Notes in his Coffers as a Reserve, and Nine Tenths in Circulation. The Notes of a Country Banker are supposed to last, on the average Three Years[23] . . . the Reserves of the Current Year will, of course, be thrown into Circulation in the next Year."

In 1832, the Committee of Secrecy on the Bank of England Charter obtained accurate data on the country circulation. Henry Burgess, secretary of the Country Bankers' Committee, presented to the Committee of Secrecy accounts from one hundred twenty-two country banks,[24] which showed that the circulation of country notes remained stable from 1818 through 1825 (see App. B.1).[25] Table 4.1 reports Burgess' data as index numbers (1818 = 100). The discrepancies between the stamp reports compiled by Sedgwick and the actual returns presented by Burgess resulted from the unrealistic nature of the assumptions of the Stamp Office, particularly the assumption that notes lasted on average only three years. Concerning this assumption, Burgess stated that it was not unusual for

---

[22] House of Lords, *Reports Respecting the Bank of England Resuming Cash Payments* 1819, App. F.7, in *Parliamentary Papers* 1819, 3:774, MF 20.34.

[23] It was known that £1 and £2 notes tended to be so worn by the end of three years that they were no longer negotiable (House of Lords, *Reports . . . Cash Payments* 1819, App. F.6, in *Parliamentary Papers* 1819, 3:773, MF 20.34).

[24] Unlike reports from the Stamp Office, Burgess' data accurately reflected fluctuations in the circulation of country-bank notes (House of Commons, *Minutes of Evidence Taken before the Committee on the Bank of England Charter* 1832, 413): "*Question:* Should you think that the account of these 122 Banks gives a fair view of the operations of the whole body of the Country Bankers of England and Wales? *Answer:* Perfectly fair. *Question:* And you think the general result drawn from this scale would correspond with the result of all the Bankers of England and Wales, if you had returns from them? *Answer:* I think it would with great accuracy."

[25] Macleod cites Burgess' figures as evidence that price fluctuations after 1819 were not due to changes in the volume of country-bank notes (Macleod 1902–1906, 2:105).

bankers to continue reissuing notes for four, five, or six years and that because of the great number of notes stamped in 1818, country bankers "did not consequently get any large amount of new stamps for some years subsequent to the passing of the Act of 1819" (House of Commons, *Minutes of Evidence Taken before the Committee on the Bank of England Charter* 1832, 444–445). Burgess' testimony is supported by the fact that from 1819 through 1822 the country-banking system did not experience the sort of crisis that would have caused a reduction of 60 percent in its circulation. The number of bank failures in 1819 was not unusual. From 1820 through 1824 country banks enjoyed even greater stability.[26]

Bankruptcies among country banks were reported by periodicals to which Ricardo subscribed.[27] Based on these reports he could have gauged the severity of the country-banking crisis in 1814–1816. He might also have been aware of the relative stability that prevailed in the country system thereafter. However, Ricardo's writings make no reference to bankruptcy reports, and it is not known whether he used them. (The data contained in these reports are summarized in App. B.3, which lists the number of bankruptcies among country banks that occurred monthly from 1812 through 1830.) Anecdotal evidence on the country banks appeared in several issues of the *Edinburgh Review*. Its contributors described the collapse of the country-banking system in 1814–1816 and provided estimates of the extent of monetary contraction; Ricardo subscribed to the *Review*.

Much as with the country circulation, the state of commercial credit – composed of bills of exchange and nonbank promissory notes – could not be measured precisely. Reports from the Stamp Office on "Bills of Exchange" and "Promissory Notes Not Re-Issuable" were published in 1819, 1821, and 1823 (see App. B.7), but they only indicated the number of bills or notes that had been stamped. The reports said nothing about the proportion actually circulating. Table 4.2 summarizes accounts from the Stamp Office.

Neither Ricardo nor anyone else could have measured a sudden credit contraction such as would occur during a financial panic when large numbers of bills would have been temporarily withdrawn. It is not known whether Ricardo read the reports from the Stamp Office pertaining to

---

[26] Thirteen country banks failed in 1819; these failures occurred evenly throughout the year, indicating no period of extreme pressure. Four banks failed in 1820; ten in 1821 (see App. B.3).

[27] *Blackwood's*, *Edinburgh Magazine*, *Morning Chronicle*, and *Times* all listed bankruptcies.

Table 4.2. *Stamp Office Accounts*

Year	Amount of Stamps Issued on Bills of Exchange
1818	£ 589,331
1819	575,782
1820	544,978
1821	527,877
1822	519,203
1823	535,847
1824	556,919
1825	597,080

private credit. In his testimony before the House of Commons Committee on Resumption in 1819, he correctly stated that commercial credit had been reduced in 1816, but this reflected only on his general impression of what had occurred, because no Stamp Office report on the state of commercial credit in 1816 had been issued up to that time (Ricardo, 5:419).

Ricardo's Interest in Public Policy

Ricardo's interest in public policy began long before he entered Parliament. From his August 1809 article on bullion in the *Morning Chronicle* to his posthumous *Plan for a National Bank*, his writings, with the exception of the *Principles*, centered on current political controversies. Accordingly, he came to study matters not directly related to loan contracting, such as the operation of the poor laws, the effects of the corn laws on economic growth and the distribution of resources, the treatment of Catholics, public education, and child labor. This section describes the information relevant to public policy that was available in the commercial press and in government reports.

Newspapers and magazines were important sources for Ricardo. During a tour on the Continent he instructed Mill and Bentham to save papers for him, saying afterward: "I was very much obliged to you and to Mr. Bentham for the loan of the month's newspapers – I have read them with very great interest and will return them when we meet in London" (7 Aug. 1817, 7:170). Of these papers, both the *Times* and the *Morning Chronicle*[28] reported on agriculture, the foreign exchange, and the prices

---

[28] The Sraffa index contains twenty-four references to the *Times* and thirty-four references to the *Morning Chronicle*.

of funds. Political events, and particularly the activities of Parliament, were also regular features in the *Times*.

With respect to monthly magazines, *Blackwood's Edinburgh Magazine* and the *Edinburgh Magazine* (originally the *Scots Magazine*) contained data on prices and financial markets along with detailed reports on agriculture, manufacturing, and foreign trade. His correspondence indicates that he received *Blackwood's* at Gatcomb during 1818 and perhaps during 1817 (7:219, 326, 332, 362). McCulloch mentions *Blackwood's* in their correspondence of 1819 and 1822[29] (8:25; 9:205–206). Correspondence also reveals that Ricardo was reading the *Edinburgh Magazine* in 1818 (7:315, 362).

Of the policy-oriented periodicals to which Ricardo subscribed, the most important was the *Edinburgh Review*. There are one hundred twenty-five references to the *Review* in his *Works*. The editors of the *Review* gave significant attention to current political debates, especially to the controversies surrounding resumption, corn tariffs and the poor laws (see App. F).[30] Ricardo also subscribed to the *Quarterly Review*,[31] a journal that Fetter describes as "only less important than . . . the *Edinburgh [Review]* in tracing the development of English economic controversy" (Fetter 1958, 47).[32] Most economic articles in the *Quarterly Review* pertained to monetary policy[33] and the poor laws. It also featured discussions of Britain's general economic state in 1815, 1820, and 1823 (see App. F).

Ricardo's use of these periodicals has great relevance to his knowledge of postwar events. The *Edinburgh Review* and the *Scots Magazine* described the extent and causes of the first agricultural depression. The magazines also documented the timing and severity of the general depression of 1815–1817. Ricardo's first reference to the general depression, in a letter of 25 December 1815, repeats the arguments of an essay titled "British Finances" in the October 1815 edition of the *Edinburgh Review* (6:344–345). Concerning the economic recovery of 1817 and the

---

[29] *Blackwood's* editor had a personal dislike for McCulloch and attacked him in several articles.

[30] The *Review* was founded by Sydney Smith, Francis Jeffrey, and Francis Horner as an instrument of political suasion and "from the first issue it appeared in the blue and buff colors of the Whig party" (Fetter 1953, 233).

[31] There are fourteen references to the *Quarterly Review* in Ricardo's *Works*; he subscribed from 1816 through 1822.

[32] The *Quarterly Review* was a Tory journal founded to counteract the influence of the *Edinburgh Review* (Fetter 1958, 47).

[33] Ricardo would have noted the articles on monetary policy because his pamphlets were, in several instances, being reviewed.

prosperity of 1818, the commercial sections of *Blackwood's* and the *Edinburgh Magazine* provided comprehensive coverage. They also chronicled the depression of 1819, and the subsequent expansion from 1820 through 1824.

The reports of Parliamentary committees proved another valuable source for Ricardo. Although there is no definitive list of the reports he owned, his correspondence suggests that he kept informed about a wide range of subjects:

I applied the morning after I saw you to the proper officer in the Vote Office of the House of Commons, to get you a set of Parliamentary papers, but I am sorry to say without success ... To console you under your disappointment I can assure you that it will give me great pleasure to lend you, whenever you may want them, any of my papers or reports. The report of last year respecting the employment of children in Manufactures should have been sent to you in town the other day ... This year there have been very few reports, – the only one of importance is a very thick one containing the laws in reference to Roman catholics[34] in the different Protestant countries of Europe. If you would like to have this, as well as the one before named, I will send them to you (Ricardo to Trower, 30 Mar. 1817, 7:146).

I thank you for your offer to lend me some of the Reports; and I am disposed to trouble you so far as to beg the use of the Police Report,[35] that on education,[36] and on the employment of Children in Manufactures[37] (Trower to Ricardo, 28 Apr. 1817, 7:150).

I have read the report of the Committee of the House of Commons on the Poor Laws[38] with much satisfaction – I am glad to see sound principles promulgated from that quarter, though I should have been still more pleased if they had insisted more strongly on an efficient remedy ... All the principal Reviews write well on this subject. In the last number of the British [Review] there is a very good review of the Commons' report (Ricardo to Trower, 10 Dec. 1817, 7:219).

The poor law report referred to by Ricardo was the report of the Commons Committee of 1817. This report was preceded by two reports on the *State of Mendicity in the Metropolis* in 1815 and 1816 and was followed by two further Commons committee reports on the poor laws in 1818 and

---

[34] *Report from the Select Committee on Laws Respecting Roman Catholic Subjects* 1816, in *Parliamentary Papers* 1816, 7:1–544, MF 17.33.

[35] *Report from the Committee on the State of the Police of the Metropolis* 1816, in *Parliamentary Papers* 1816, 5:1–388, MF 17.23.

[36] *Report from the Select Committee on the Education of the Lower Orders in the Metropolis* 1816, in *Parliamentary Papers* 1816, 4:1–324, MF 17.17.

[37] *Report from the Select Committee on the State of Children Employed in the Manufactories of the United Kingdom* 1816, in *Parliamentary Papers* 1816, 3:235–522, MF 17.12.

[38] *Report from the Select Committee on the Poor Laws* 1817, in *Parliamentary Papers* 1817, 6:1–170, MF 18.28.

1819. Apart from the fact that Ricardo owned Poor Law Committee reports, we can infer his interest in England's welfare system because his first appointment upon entering Parliament was to the Poor Law Committee of 1819.

Ricardo must have been informed about the history of the poor laws and their legal interpretation. He would have known that resident landlords paid a disproportionate amount of the poor rates and even subsidized the wages of manufacturing laborers. From the Poor Law Report of 1817 he would have learned that in the districts in England and Wales where compulsory provisions for the poor were most generous, the number of persons receiving relief was greatest. This was in marked contrast to Scotland, where poor relief came from voluntary contributions except in times of crisis and where no increase in the number of persons seeking poor relief had occurred.[39] These facts became important in his analysis of the depression of 1819–1820, for he concluded that the extreme hardships of the poor were, in part, caused by an undue increase in the supply of labor resulting from too liberal provisions from the poor rates.

The corn laws were another, and more contentious, topic of Parliamentary inquiry. Ricardo read[40] the Parliamentary reports on the corn laws that appeared during the agricultural crisis of 1813–1816: the first and second *Reports Respecting Grain and the Corn Laws* from the House of Lords[41] and the House of Commons *Report from the Select Committee on Petitions Relating to the Corn Laws*.[42] The Commons report focused on the "extension and improvement of the agriculture of the United Kingdom"; agricultural production costs; a remunerating price for domestic growers; and the competitive threat of Continental producers. The Lords reports explored the same subjects in less depth.

Both reports established factual points critical to Ricardo's interpretation of the 1813–1816 agricultural crisis: that vast tracts of formerly

---

[39] The conclusions of the poor law committees were reinforced by articles in magazines such as the *Edinburgh Review, Quarterly Review*, and *Scots Magazine*, which described the English poor laws and their many shortcomings, especially as contrasted with the successful poor relief system in Scotland (see App. F).

[40] To Malthus in Aug. 1814, Ricardo asked: "Have you read the report of the Lords Committee on the corn question? It discloses some important facts, but how ignorant the persons giving evidence appear to be of the subject as a matter of science" (6:130). Because he read the *Minutes of Evidence*, which includes the testimony of more that two dozen witnesses, we can assume that he was acquainted with the contents of the actual report, which is only a few pages.

[41] 25 July 1814, *Parliamentary Papers* 1814–1815, 5:1035–1335, MF 16.24.

[42] 26 July 1814, *Parliamentary Papers* 1813–1814, 3:195–342, MF 15.15.

waste land had been brought under cultivation during the war and that, at the same time, additional capital had been applied to land already being farmed. Many witnesses before the committees commented on extensions of both the extensive and intensive margins of cultivation: "within the last twenty years a very rapid and extensive progress has been made in the Agriculture of the United Kingdom . . . great additional capitals have been skilfully and successfully applied, not only to the improved management of lands already in tillage, but also to the converting of large tracts of inferior pasture into productive arable land, and the reclaiming and inclosing of fens, commons and wastes, which have been brought into a state of regular cultivation" (House of Commons, *Report from the Select Committee on Petitions Relating to the Corn Laws* 1814, 3). Another observation of the Lords and Commons committees was that improvements had occurred in techniques of husbandry and that these improvements had made possible the production of higher yields. The final point made by the committees was that British agriculture could not compete with foreign producers.

The committees of 1814 attributed the vast importations of corn to the fact that foreign producers had lower production costs, on average, than British farmers. The Commons committee established that "80s. per quarter is the lowest price which would afford to the British grower an adequate remuneration. The Evidence [supporting this finding] is inserted at length in the *Minutes*; and the names [of witnesses] will be found to include many of the most eminent surveyors and land agents from different parts of Great Britain, as well as some persons who have been long and very extensively engaged in the Corn Trade, and several occupiers of land distinguished for their practical knowledge" (House of Commons, *Report. . . on the Corn Laws* 1814, 4–5). Witnesses also testified that corn on the Continent could be produced with so little expense that "there is scarcely any price in our own market, which, under circumstances of a general abundance in the other parts of Europe, would be sufficiently low to prevent an importation of corn from those foreign ports at which a considerable supply is annually accumulated for exportation only" (House of Commons, *Report . . . on the Corn Laws* 1814, 6). Given the contents of these reports, Ricardo could not have been ignorant of the state of agriculture at the close of the war, nor would he have been uninformed about the causes of the 1813–1816 agricultural crisis. His *Essay on Profits* (1815) reiterates the committee's arguments, including that "improvements in agriculture, or in the implements of husbandry lower the exchangeable value of corn" (6:19), and again, that "great improvements have been made in agriculture, and that much capital has been expended on the land, it is not attempted to deny; but, with all those improvements, we have not overcome the natural impediments resulting from our increasing wealth and prosperity, which obliges us to cultivate at a disadvantage our poor lands, if the importation of corn is restricted or prohibited" (6:32).

Ricardo's analysis of the agricultural crisis was not a matter of abstract theorizing, but reflected an appreciation of current conditions.[43] Perhaps most telling is his dispute with Malthus about whether low corn prices caused a general depression.[44] Malthus alleged that the postwar reduction in the expenditures of landlords and farmers so reduced aggregate demand as to cause a depression lasting almost a decade. Ricardo responded to Malthus with a clever argument. He used tax reports to approximate recent changes in economic activity then inferred from the available reports that the fall in corn had not caused a general depression: "It is dangerous to listen to reports respecting briskness or slackness of trade. It is I believe certain that the revenue has been uncommonly productive the last quarter which is no indication of diminished trade. . . . You appear to me to attribute effects much too great to the fall of raw produce which has lately taken place" (17 Oct. 1815, 6:304). The excerpt alludes to the Treasury report on quarterly government tax receipts that appeared on 11 July 1815 (*Journal of the House of Commons* 1814–1815, 70:726). Ricardo rightly cited the report because it shows that both customs and excise revenues increased from the third quarter of 1813, the quarter when agricultural prices began to decline, through the second quarter of 1815, the most recent quarter for which returns were available. Without

---

[43] Ricardo also kept informed about agricultural issues because his friends were foremost among the pamphleteers, writing both for and against agricultural protection. Ricardo read Lauderdale's *Letter on the Corn Laws* (1814), though he disagreed with Lauderdale's analysis of the effects of protection (6:169, 189). He read at least four works by Torrens on money and the corn laws: *Essay on Money and Paper Currency* (1812); *Essay on the External Corn Trade* (1815); *Letter to the Rt. Hon. Earl of Liverpool on the State of Agriculture of the United Kingdom* (1816); and *Letters to the Earl of Lauderdale* (1816). He repeatedly referred to these works in his correspondence with Trower (17 Apr. 1815, 6:212; 23 Feb. 1816, 7:24; 24 Apr. 1816, 7:28). Ricardo also expressed approval for Edward West's *Essay on the Application of Capital to Land* (1814) which addressed agricultural protection (9 Mar. 1815, 6:179; 18 Sept. 1818, 7:298). As for Malthus' pamphlets on the corn laws, they are too important to relegate to a footnote and are taken up in Chapter 5.

[44] On 16 Oct. 1815, Malthus wrote to Ricardo: "Is it possible for above half the national income to fall very greatly in price, without affecting the demand and the other half. I confess I feel no doubt that the main cause of the present slackness of trade is the diminished incomes of the landlords and farmers" (Ricardo, 6:303).

a change in tax rates – and there had been no change[45]– an increase in customs and excise revenues could not have occurred unless preceded by an increase in economic activity. Given the coincidence of low corn prices and a robust general economy from the harvest of 1813 through the second quarter of 1815, he concluded that Malthus' interpretation of events was flawed.

Ricardo used tax data to gauge aggregate conditions throughout his career. Treasury reports were particularly useful to rebut the inflationists' argument that resumption caused a general depression. The rise of customs and excise revenues, starting the third quarter of 1820, showed that aggregate conditions were prosperous. Ricardo referred McCulloch to the tax abstract that appeared on 6 February 1822, stating: "The country – on the whole – is in a flourishing condition, our wealth is daily increasing. Every thing indicates that our manufactures are in a progressive state of improvement, and from the produce of the revenue I should conclude that their prosperity more than makes up for the losses and adversity of the agricultural class" (9:158). He deployed similar arguments to demonstrate to Charles Western and Mathias Attwood that resumption did not cause the collapse of corn prices:

Could the agricultural interest be ruined by an alteration in the value of money, without its affecting, in the same manner, the manufacturing and commercial interests of the country? If corn fell 30 per cent from an alteration in the value of money, must not all other commodities fall in something like the same proportion? But had they so fallen? Was the manufacturing interest so distressed? Quite the contrary. Every thing was flourishing, but agriculture. The legacy duty, the probate duty, the ad valorem duty on stamps, were all on the increase;[46] and certainly, if a raised value of money had lessened the value of property, less might be expected to be paid generally upon transfers of property. The state of the revenue was to him (Mr. Ricardo) a satisfactory proof, if every other were wanting, of the erroneous conclusions of the hon. Gentleman (Parliamentary debate, 11 June 1823, Ricardo, 5:315).

The fact that Ricardo gauged changes in aggregate economic activity according to tax reports is no small matter because, as has already been shown in Chapters 2 and 3, the consecutive periods of depression and expansion of the postwar decade are mirrored in the fluctuations of customs and excise returns.

[45] House of Commons, *A Return of . . . all Taxes Repealed, Expired or Reduced in Each Year since the Termination of the War* 1833; in *Parliamentary Papers* 1833, 32:637–653, MF 36.239.

[46] It is not clear which of two reports Ricardo used since tax abstracts appeared on 10 Feb. 1823 and again on 10 Apr. 1823. The abstracts contained the same information, except that the April report included the most recent quarterly update.

Ricardo in Parliament

In the autumn of 1815, Pascoe Grenfell, a prominent Whig and member of Parliament,[47] enlisted Ricardo's support in the campaign to end the Bank restriction. He suggested a pamphlet on the subject and to this end provided Ricardo with a wealth of information, including historical documents on the Bank of England, reports detailing financial arrangements between the Bank and the government, current reports of banknotes in circulation, reports on the Bank's expenses and revenues, a detailed list of the sources of excess profits for the Bank,[48] and information concerning dividend payments by the directors (Ricardo, 6:242, 257–259, 276–277, 281–284). Ricardo incorporated all these materials into *Secure Currency* (1816). The pamphlet begins with a detailed history of Bank operations; it proceeds to discuss policy recommendations and concludes by criticizing the Bank's excessive profits. The appendices to *Secure Currency* provide estimates of the Bank's financial statements for 1797–1815 and data on the Bank's revenues and its note circulation.

Opponents of the Bank recognized political promise in Ricardo, and from 1816 he became increasingly involved in the Whigs' strategy[49] to restore a metallic standard and to limit the perquisites enjoyed by the Bank. Ricardo was not new to Whig circles. Henry Thornton and Francis Horner had been his friends at least from the time of the Bullion Committee (Ricardo, 6:xxxv). Richard Sharp[50] and John Whishaw[51] shared with Ricardo mutual friends in Malthus and Thomas Smith; they also

---

[47] Grenfell has been described as "a vigilant observer of the actions of the Bank of England, and a great authority on finance. On the latter subject he made many speeches... and it was chiefly through his efforts that the periodical publication of the accounts of the bank was commenced" (*Dictionary of National Biography* 1949–1950, 8:553).

[48] Grenfell emphasized two sources of excess profits: the fact that the Bank did not purchase stamps on their notes as country banks did (25 Aug. 1815, 6:260 and 8 Sept. 1815, 6:266), and the fact that the Bank received a management fee for administering the public debt (20 Sept. 1815, 6:275).

[49] There was coherent development and enforcement of party policy by the early nineteenth century, since "the features of party management had long been in existence" (Aspinall 1926, 389).

[50] Richard Sharp was a Whig member of Parliament, described as being "very active in the background." He served for a time on the finance committee and was also on Horner's bullion committee. At his home Sharp "gathered around him the chief persons of the day and he knew their characters so well that he could hit them off in a moment." He resigned from the constituency of Portarlington to permit Ricardo to enter the House (DNB, 17:1351–1352).

[51] Sraffa notes that John Whishaw was a prominent member in Whig society and that he had been a contemporary of Malthus at Cambridge (Ricardo, 6:66n).

attended the King of Clubs,[52] which Ricardo occasionally visited. Pascoe Grenfell was a friend and political ally from 1815 till Ricardo's death. In the years before his fame, he was acquainted, to a lesser extent, with Henry Brougham,[53] George Tierney,[54] and Lord King.[55]

These acquaintances developed into working relationships as Ricardo gained prominence among the Whigs – a rise evident by early 1818. Lord Grenville's[56] opinion of the *Principles* was "favourable beyond my expectations," according to Ricardo (10 Dec. 1817, 7:220). Grenville's reaction led to their first meeting (probably in March 1818) whereafter Ricardo became an unofficial counselor to him on economic matters (22 Mar. 1818, 6:259; 13 Feb. 1819, 8:19n). Ricardo's ascent continued when on 13 March 1818, Lords Essex and Holland supported his election to Brooks's, the premier Whig club in London (8:28n). By mid-1818 Brougham, Warburton,[57] and Parnell[58] were negotiating with Lord

---

[52] The King of Clubs was comprised mostly of Whig politicians. Malthus became a member in 1812; Ricardo in 1817 (6:87n).

[53] Henry Peter Brougham, Baron Brougham, and Vaux (1778–1868), Lord Chancellor. Brougham joined the *Edinburgh Review* in 1802. He entered Parliament in 1810 and by 1815 was "the most prominent member of the opposition in the commons." Brougham defended Queen Caroline before the Lords in 1820. He was elevated to the peerage and became Chancellor in 1830; as Chancellor he worked diligently, though "he gave some offence by boasting publicly and repeatedly of achievements that he had not performed and that were indeed beyond mortal power" (DNB, 2:1356–1366).

[54] George Tierney (1761–1830) entered Parliament in 1789. He opposed Pitt's financial schemes in a manner Wilberforce described as "truly Jacobinical" and the conflict culminated in a pistol duel between them in 1798. After Lord Grenville's administration, Tierney became more prominent among the Whigs. "His undaunted tenacity, his knowledge of business, his readiness in debate, his clearness of expression gave him great claims to the leadership of his party in the House of Commons . . . in 1817 he became the acknowledged leader of the opposition" (DNB, 19:865–867).

[55] Peter King, seventh Lord King, Baron of Ockham (1776–1833), was active in the House of Lords in opposing the suspension of cash payments and the corn laws. He wrote several pamphlets on the currency, Roman Catholics, and the corn laws (DNB, 11:147–148).

[56] William Grenville, Baron Grenville (1759–1834), entered the House of Commons in 1782; the House of Lords in 1790. He formed the Ministry of All the Talents in 1806, which ended in 1807 because the King objected to Grenville's liberal treatment of Catholics. Grenfell opposed the suppression of Catholics, slavery, and the corn laws (DNB, 8:576–581).

[57] Henry Warburton (1784–1858) was a timber merchant early in life, entered Parliament in 1826, and was a founding member of the Political Economy Club (DNB, 20:753–754).

[58] Henry Parnell, first Baron Congleton (1776–1842) entered Parliament in 1802 and for a time represented the borough of Portarlington. He served on the Bullion Committee and was chairman of the 1813 Committee on the Corn Trade of the United Kingdom. As a colleague of Ricardo's, Parnell supported resumption and the retrenchment of public expenditure (DNB, 15:342–345).

Portarlington (Parnell's brother) on the price for Ricardo's seat in Parliament. At the same time, his correspondence reveals an active role in the Whig campaign to restore a metallic standard:

Mr. Vansittart had a ridiculous project I hear of creating a new circulating medium and legal tender . . . I am told that he has now abandoned it, and indeed it is difficult to believe that he ever entertained so ridiculous a project, tho' my authority for the fact is no less than that of Mr. Tierney (22 Mar. 1818, 6:260).

Tomorrow evening there is to be a long debate in the House of Lords on the Bank Restriction Bill, on which occasion Lord Grenville means to speak. Lord King mentioned to me his idea of proposing that the Bank should be forbid making any dividend on their stock while the price of gold was above the mint price . . . Sir James Mackintosh has been reading Bentham and was just beginning to give me his opinion of the book when we were interrupted (25 May 1818, 6:262–263).

From what you [Richard Sharp] say, I fear that you have some reason to think, that the Bank will not place themselves in a situation to resume cash payments next year. What possible excuse can now be offered, either by the Bank, or by ministers, for not fulfilling the engagement which they have so solemnly contracted? (27 Aug. 1818, 7:291–292).

The inquiry into the state of our currency, and exchanges, is proceeding in both houses very satisfactorily. I have had many conversations with several of the Committees of both Houses – with Lord Grenville, Marquis of Lansdowne, Lord King, Mr. Huskisson, Mr. F. Lewis, Mr. Grenfell and others. All have a very perfect knowledge of the subject (28 Feb. 1819, 8:19).

The reference of 27 August 1818 to the "engagement" of the ministers indicates Ricardo's knowledge of the fact that the government and the Bank had on several occasions pledged to resume cash payments, but just as frequently had reneged on the promise. This fact is crucial to any critique of Ricardo's support for the 1819 Resumption Act.

Ricardo took his seat in Parliament on 26 February 1819. As a member of the House he gained further access to information on national affairs because he could submit motions to Parliament that specific economic reports be prepared and because he participated directly in the proceedings of Parliamentary committees. His first appointment was to the 1819 Committee on the Poor Laws. Inquiries concerning the poor laws historically focused on two issues: the disproportionate tax burden imposed by poor rates on landed interests[59] and the fact that poor relief perpetuated misery in the lower classes by taxing industry and subsidizing procreation. The

---

[59] Chapter 18 of Ricardo's *Principles*, titled "Poor Rates," addresses the tax burden associated with the poor laws (1: 257–262).

committee recognized both problems and suggested sweeping reductions in poor relief, though with the caveat that changes to the laws not occur in 1819 because of the current distress. According to the committee's report, the current distress of the laboring class reflected a low demand for labor at a time when the labor force was expanding. They attributed rapid population growth (along with "sloth" and "vice") to the operation of the poor laws and remarked that the poor rates caused a reduction in households' disposable incomes, which, in turn, led to a drop in the demand for labor.[60] The committee envisaged no short-term solution to the disproportion between labor and capital apart from emigration; long-term solutions were looked for in the education of the lower orders and in an increase of the national capital stock. These facts are relevant because Ricardo's analysis of the sufferings of laborers and the solutions he proposed to their plight are similar to the analysis and proposals put forward by the committee.

Ricardo also served on the agricultural committees of 1821 and 1822. His work on the committees formed the most significant aspect of his Parliamentary career because the conflicts surrounding resumption and agricultural protection centerd on the committees' investigations. Ricardo figured so prominently in the attending debates that when Lord Londonderry (Castlereagh) presented the report of the 1822 Agricultural Committee to Parliament he remarked how his objections to a new corn bill had been "fortified considerably by the discussions which have since taken place on the subject, and more especially by the sanction and confirmation which the opinion I expressed has received in the able work[61] which has recently been published by the hon. member for Portarlington (Mr. Ricardo), whom it is impossible for the House on such questions to have higher authority" (*Hansard* 2s, 7:152). In a subsequent debate on the report, Attwood referred to the "hon. member for Portarlington – and if he referred so repeatedly to the opinion of that hon. gentleman, it was because he was the only individual of equal authority who had given any consistent exposition at all of the causes of agricultural distress . . . although he (Mr. Attwood) did not agree with him, in scarcely any one of the opinions he entertained" (*Hansard* 2s, 7:379).[62]

The report of the 1821 Agricultural Committee demonstrated that unprecedented Irish corn imports and the bumper harvest of 1820 were

---

[60] House of Commons, *Report from the Committee on the Poor Laws* 1819, 7, 9.

[61] Ricardo's pamphlet *On Protection to Agriculture* (1822).

[62] These comments "naturally brought forward the hon. member for Portarlington, as the gladiator, on the other side of the question," noted Londonderry (*Hansard* 2s, 7:396).

significant causes of low corn prices. The report thus refuted the inflationists who argued that monetary contraction had caused a general depression with a corresponding fall in prices. The report also explained how the 1815 Corn Law destabilized agricultural markets: the law prohibited imports when the domestic price of wheat was below 80s. per quarter but allowed unlimited, duty-free importation once the price of wheat exceeded 80s. Ricardo concurred with the findings of the committee of 1821.

He attributed "the temptation to import into this country" to the discrepancy between corn prices in Britain and on the Continent (*Protection to Agriculture* 1822, 6:242). Corn could be imported quickly because it was kept in warehouses at British ports. The upshot was that once wheat surpassed 80s., the market was liable to be "overwhelmed with foreign corn" (8:350). Given the inelastic domestic demand for corn,[63] sudden importations of as much as 15 percent of annual consumption had a ruinous effect on domestic farmers. Ricardo's concerns were well known; Lord Londonderry stated that "No member of that committee [1821 Agricultural Committee] went further in allowing the extent of that danger [sudden corn imports] than the hon. member for Portarlington" (Ricardo, 5:157n).

Ricardo further understood that in the event of an abundant harvest, Britain's own production would glut the home market, there being no vent for the surplus. Marginal production costs were so high that even when prices were ruinous, British farmers could not compete on the Continent (Parliamentary speech, 8 Feb. 1821, 5:74). The extent to which corn prices were lower on the Continent was well known, being described first before Lords and Commons Committees on the Corn Laws in 1814, and later before the Commons Committee on Agriculture in 1821. To emphasize the point, Ricardo requested accounts of foreign corn prices. The first account was laid before Parliament on 9 March 1820; an updated version was ordered by Castlereagh in April 1821 (8:374).

The importation of Irish corn was another factor explored by the 1821 Agricultural Committee. After hearing testimony about Irish imports, Ricardo described Irish farmers as "the most formidable" of all rivals, surpassing the farmers of Poland, Russia, and America (21 Apr. 1821, 8:369).

[63] Ricardo was especially pleased with Tooke's testimony before the committee because Tooke argued that the domestic demand for corn was inelastic: "Mr. Tooke who is a good political economist gave us some valuable information of the effect of abundance on price.... This is in fact the present cause of the great depression in the price of corn. A little effect may be ascribed to the currency; but abundance is the great operating cause" (Ricardo to Trower, 21 Apr. 1821, 8:370–371).

He even included in Appendix B of *Protection to Agriculture* (1822) a table showing the shipments to the port of London of Irish wheat, barley, oats, beans, and peas, and the average prices of these commodities from 1817 through the first quarter of 1822 (4:270).

The final contribution of the 1821 Agricultural Committee was that it documented a general decline in corn prices both on the Continent and in England from 1818 through 1821. The fact proved important because, given the timing of international gold flows compared to the timing of fluctuations in corn prices on the Continent, it became evident that the decline in foreign corn could not have been caused by a monetary contraction in Britain – which is what the inflationists were then claiming.

Because of his ongoing polemic against the inflationists, Ricardo was eager to show that corn prices could be low in consequence of an abundant supply. To this end he brought to the 1821 Agricultural Committee witnesses and data that would substantiate the arguments he had advanced in the House. According to Tooke, "I was summoned to give evidence before that Committee at the instance of Mr. David Ricardo, who was a member of it. The purpose of my evidence was to state reasons for believing that the Low Price of Corn, and the consequent distress of the agricultural interests, were sufficiently accounted for by the Abundance of the supply" (Tooke and Newmarch 1838–1857, 2:66–67). Ricardo also called Edward Solly before the committee. At the conclusion of Solly's testimony, he wrote a favorable account to McCulloch: "Mr. Solly, the other merchant I called, gave some valuable information respecting the price of corn in Poland, and in the Prussian Ports, and also regarding the expenses of conveying corn from the interior, to the Ports of Embarkation, and from those Ports to London" (25 Apr. 1821, 8:374).

Ricardo also served on the Agricultural Committee of 1822. That committee, however, produced no new evidence and its main purpose was simply to recommend revisions to the existing corn law. The only new data in the committee's report were updates on the quantity of corn warehoused at British ports.[64]

One other committee on which Ricardo served deserves mention: the 1822 Committee on Public Accounts. The committee had been appointed to develop accounting procedures for the government so that reports on public income and expenditure, the national debt, and foreign trade

---

[64] Despite the want of Parliamentary reports in 1822, information on the state of agriculture was still publicly available. Both *Blackwood's* and the *Edinburgh Magazine* provided thorough reports on agriculture and the corn market.

would be understandable and consistent from year to year. The problems in the national accounts were identified by the committee as follows: "The principal and most prominent defect in the present form of the Accounts is that they neither do nor can exhibit any Balance between the Income and Expenditure of the year . . . this defect is also attended with the further inconvenience that it allows the possibility of the existence of errors which [cannot] be detected."[65] Public accounts were a valuable source of information to Ricardo because they included data on public (taxation) income, public expenditures, funded and unfunded debts, and trade and navigation.[66] Ricardo was familiar with the public accounts even before his appointment to the committee in 1822. On three occasions in 1820 and 1821, he asked the government for more comprehensible accounts (5:67, 100, 116). And in 1822, he complained that "it was impossible that the Members of the House could come to any knowledge of the real state of the country" on the basis of the existing reports (5:139). His opinions were widely respected and it was acknowledged that the measures Parliament adopted to correct errors in the accounts were suggested by Ricardo: "Mr. Lushington, in the course of his reply, said that the balance-sheet format was adopted at the suggestion of an hon. member (Mr. Ricardo), and was deemed to be the most compendious way of stating the accounts" (Ricardo, 5:145).

Ricardo also kept informed about committees on which he did not serve. Of these, the most important were the House of Commons committees on finance, for they used tax reports to approximate changes in aggregate economic activity. Ricardo was familiar with the reports of these committees[67] and adopted the same measure of economic activity. Similarly, he gave attention to the committees on foreign trade, appointed in 1820, 1821, 1822, and 1823 to investigate topics that ranged from conditions in specific branches of trade to the operation and maintenance of port facilities. Ricardo had hoped to advance the cause of free trade as

---

[65] House of Commons, *Report from the Select Committee on the Public Accounts of the United Kingdom* 1822, 1–2.

[66] See the appendix to the *Report from the Select Committee on the Public Accounts of the United Kingdom* 1822.

[67] He refers to the fourth report from the 1817 Select Committee on Finance (4:304n) and the first report from the 1819 Select Committee on Finance (4:193; 5:65). The report of 1817 was important because it measured the severity of the depression of 1815–1817; it also showed that the depression began in late 1815 and was ending by early 1817. The report of 1819 was important because it established conclusively the prosperous state of the country in 1818.

a member of the trade committees and was frustrated when the House failed to appoint him (Ricardo to McCulloch, 13 June 1820, 8:196–197). And finally, the 1819 Committee on Frame Work Knitters, appointed in response to a long campaign by laborers against the introduction of machinery, could not have escaped Ricardo's notice. During the years Ricardo studied political economy, many Parliamentary committees were convened in response to petitions against machines or in response to the destruction of machinery in disturbed manufactures. Ricardo was fully aware of the public controversy surrounding machinery and addressed the issue at least four times in Parliament (5:30–31, 68, 93, 302–303).

Conclusion

Ricardo was well informed about economic and political events in Britain. As a bond trader and financier he was knowledgeable about monetary fluctuations, national finances, and, to a lesser extent, foreign trade and domestic commerce. He thus came to the field of political economy with an established empirical background. His interest in public policy complemented the understanding he developed in the City. Serving in Parliament capped his development as an economist because he was forced to defend his policies, and did so on the basis of tax abstracts, reports on the coinage, accounts of the Bank of England's circulation, and Parliamentary studies of the poor laws and domestic agriculture.

FIVE

Ricardo's Analysis of Postwar Events

Ricardo distinguished between temporary and permanent causes of the economic distress of the postwar years. Short-term crises he attributed to exogenous shocks. He believed that Britain adapted quickly to these shocks, that wages and prices were flexible, and that capitalists were alert to shift resources to profitable industries. The immediate postwar distress occurred because of the transition from wartime to peacetime production. The transition was complicated by failures among the country banks and by reversals in foreign trade. The depression of 1819–1820 was primarily caused by a collapse of Britain's foreign markets. And contrary to Malthus' assertions, there was no lack of consumer demand. Regarding the agricultural crisis of 1820–1822, Ricardo marshaled evidence to show that prices in the home market were below marginal production costs owing to a glut of corn from Ireland and a series of bumper harvests. His purpose was to discredit inflationist writers who blamed the fall of corn on the new gold standard. Ricardo disapproved of the manner in which the Bank of England implemented the Resumption Act, but too much depended on the certainty of gold and there was no going back. Also, he knew that the combined circulation of banknotes and coin remained stable as the Bank returned to gold, so the inflationists must have erred in claiming that prices had fallen 50 percent generally.

Ricardo attributed the "permanent" aspect of Britain's trouble to an abundant supply of labor relative to the demand for it. Comments on a speech by Lord Grenville illustrate the parallel streams of his analysis:

I hope your Lordship will not think I take too great a liberty, in expressing my satisfaction at finding that my opinions on the causes of the present distresses, concur with those which your Lordship has so ably stated in the pamphlet before me.[1] The distress which proceeds from the misapplication of capital, and the miscalculation of demand by our manufacturers may, it is to be hoped, be slowly removed, but that which arises from the disproportion between capital and population will necessarily be of a more permanent description (Ricardo to Grenville, 10 Jan. 1820, quoted in Heertje 1991, 523–524).

Implicit in Ricardo's letter is the idea that capital investment creates jobs. He recognized the theoretical possibility that capital might displace labor; but as a practical matter he associated a high stock of physical capital with a high demand for labor.

The distinction in Ricardo's work between temporary and permanent causes of postwar crises is significant. Yet it has been overlooked by commentators who attribute to him a lack of consistency.[2] This chapter shows there is no lack of consistency; instead he offered parallel analyses of short-term shocks and institutional problems.

Permanent Aspect of Britain's Economic Trouble

Ricardo identified three institutional factors tending to either retard the accumulation of capital or encourage an excessive increase in population. High taxes and the corn laws discouraged domestic investment, whereas the poor laws subsidized the expansion of the labor supply and thereby depressed wages:

He conceived that the distress was chiefly to be ascribed to the inadequacy of the capital of the nation to carry on the operations of trade, manufacture, and commerce. But why was the capital more inadequate now than formerly? If the profits on capital were higher, and labour more productive in other countries,

---

[1] Grenville stated before Parliament that the "temporary causes of depression" were a reduction in exports, owing to "distresses of foreign nations," combined with "hazardous and groundless speculations" in trade (30 Nov. 1819, *Hansard* 1s, 41:452–453). His speech later appeared as the pamphlet about which Ricardo commented. Upon receiving Ricardo's letter, he responded: "I am unaffectedly gratified by knowing that the general view which I take of the causes of the present distress is sanctioned by your high authority" (11 Jan. 1820, Ricardo, 8:150).

[2] Hollander makes such an inference: "By the end of 1819 Ricardo felt obliged to alter his diagnosis [of the depression]. In his speeches of December we find no reference to capital immobility, but rather the emphasis is placed upon an inadequacy of capital supply relative to population which is explained in terms of low profitability due in turn to agricultural protection... But by mid-1820 Ricardo had reverted to his original argument that the postwar problem in manufacturing was entirely due to capital misallocation" (Hollander 1979, 518). Winch similarly fails to differentiate between "temporary" and "permanent" causes of the depression (Winch 1987, 81).

it could not be doubted that capital would be transferred to those countries: no proposition in Euclid was clearer than this. Now, he thought they had greatly aggravated this evil by bad legislation, and he had formerly mentioned instances. He had referred to the corn laws as one example; and however unpopular the doctrine might be with some gentlemen, he would state his opinion freely, that he believed the corn laws to have materially increased the evil. These laws had tended to raise the price of sustenance, and that had raised the price of labour, which of course diminished the profit on capital (Parliamentary address, Dec. 1819, Ricardo, 5:38).

Notwithstanding his concern, Ricardo did not believe – as some of his contemporaries did – that Britain was on the verge of secular stagnation.[3] Writing to Trower in 1816, he stated, "we are happily yet in the progressive state, and may look forward with confidence to a long course of prosperity" (7:16–17). Again in 1821, in response to McCulloch's concern[4] that the country had reached the end of its resources, he replied: "I am by no means ready to admit that we may not have a more limited measure of prosperity notwithstanding the continued operation of our corn laws and the continued existence of our debt" (23 Mar. 1821, 8:358).

Corn tariffs discouraged the expansion of the national capital stock, including the wages fund, by raising the real costs of the wage basket and its costs in terms of money. High money wages eroded profits and discouraged investment.[5] In terms of Ricardo's growth model, the causal sequence whereby agricultural protection discourages capital accumulation is as follows: the corn laws prohibit the import of foreign produce, leading to an increase in the demand for domestic corn. Farmers respond by increasing output at both the extensive and intensive margins of cultivation. With each extension, production costs increase because marginal lands are less fertile and because there are diminishing returns to variable

---

[3] See Hollander 1979, 600–605.

[4] In Dec. 1819, McCulloch wrote to Ricardo: "Though very far from being an alarmist I think it must be admitted by all that the situation of the country is now critical in the extreme – With ignorant and despotic ministers, a million of paupers, a taxation three times as oppressive as in any other country in the world, and corn laws forcing the cultivation of the poorest soils and proportionably reducing the rate of profit, it is quite impossible to suppose that this country can bear up under the difficulties with which she is surrounded without a total change of system – It is worse than ridiculous to talk of the present distresses being temporary – They will at least continue as long as the causes by which they are produced" (Ricardo, 8:139).

[5] Hollander recognizes this aspect of Ricardo's argument, observing: "The Corn Laws rendered the profit rate in Britain, and accordingly the rate of capital accumulation, lower at any and every point of time than would otherwise be the case in an open economy" (Hollander 1979, 600). Similar analysis appears in Tucker 1960, 168–171, 178.

inputs (5:49, 167). The corn laws consequently generate an increase in the real costs of a given wage basket (5:50). Manufactured goods, in general, have the same money prices under free trade or protection, so industrial capitalists receive the same gross revenues under either system. Under protection, however, money wages are higher, so capitalists earn lower profits. Ricardo believed this would lead to lower investment than under a regime of free trade:[6] "Corn laws made the price of that necessary of life, grain, higher than in neighbouring countries, and thus interfered with the article which was considered the chief regulator of wages. Where grain was dear, wages must be high, and the effect of high wages was necessarily to make the profits on capital low" (16 Dec. 1819, 5:33). By contrast, his model suggests that profits would not fall secularly under free trade because there would effectively be no land constraint and consequently no increase in marginal production costs as a result of economic growth:

I contend for free trade in corn on the ground that while trade is free, and corn cheap, profits will not fall however great be the accumulation of capital. If you confine yourself to the resources of your own soil, I say, rent will in time absorb the greatest part of that produce which remains after paying wages, and consequently profits will be low. Not only individual profits but the aggregate amount of profits will be diminished, notwithstanding an increase of capital (Ricardo to Trower, 8:208).

There would always be a limit to our greatness while we were growing our own supply of food: but we should always be increasing in wealth and power whilst we obtained part of it from foreign countries and devoted our own manufactures to the payment of it (Parliamentary address, 1822, 5:180).

Domestic lands are limited, but with free trade the extensive and intensive margins only extend until (marginal) domestic costs equal those on the Continent. Thereafter domestic resources are allocated to other sectors – particularly manufacturing – and manufactured goods are exchanged for corn imports.

Related to Ricardo's concern that the corn laws impeded capital accumulation was his understanding that a secular increase in real labor costs could lead capitalists to switch to capital-intensive modes of production or to even transfer resources from labor-intensive to capital-intensive industries.[7] He first mentioned the possibility of an induced change to capital-intensive production in the 1817 edition of the *Principles* (1:61, 349).

---

[6] The same argument appears elsewhere in his *Works*: 1817, 1:122; 1819, 5:32, 38; and 1822, 4:237.

[7] Ricardo's case for the secular substitution of fixed capital for labor has been appreciated by many authors (see Ferguson 1973, 93; Berg 1980, 60; Hollander 1997, 195–196).

He subsequently elaborated on the concept in the machinery chapter added to the 1821 edition: "The consequence of a rise of food will be a rise of wages, and every rise of wages will have a tendency to determine the saved capital in a greater proportion than before to the employment of machinery.... In America where the food of man is easily provided, there is not nearly such great temptation to employ machinery as in England, where food is high and costs much labour for its production . . . with every augmentation of capital, a greater proportion of it is employed on machinery. The demand for labour will continue to increase with an increase of capital, but not in proportion to its increase" (1:395). Ricardo believed that the secular substitution of capital for labor in response to rising real labor costs contributed to Britain's rapid industrialization, and that it slowed the rate of increase in the demand for labor. His statements are astute. Though historians generally assume that the proportion of domestic fixed capital composed of machinery remained stable during the early nineteenth century, records show that the proportion increased from 5 percent in 1750 to 17 percent in 1850 (Berg 1980, 21). Beginning in the 1780s and continuing through about 1840, the introduction of machinery was particularly rapid in cotton and textile industries (Berg 1980, 23–24); these were the industries Ricardo singled out in the *Principles* (1:390–391).

Ricardo believed that a postwar change in the pattern of final demand also contributed to the disproportion between labor and circulating capital. Because different economic sectors operate at different factor intensities, he understood that a change in the pattern of final demand might alter the derived demands for factor inputs and could be detrimental to the employment and/or wages of laborers. He considered this an actual problem after the war as the pattern of final demand switched from labor-intensive services – namely, the military – to capital-intensive luxury goods.[8] The effects of a change in the pattern of final demand were first described in his *Notes on Malthus* (1820): "A society does one or the other in proportion to the demand for either the objects of men's work; or for objects which are almost exclusively produced by machinery ... to the capitalist it can be of no importance whether his capital consists of fixed or of circulating capital, but it is of the greatest importance to those who

---

[8] There is little dispute about the existence of passages in Ricardo's writings that suggest the possible conflict between fixed capital and labor. What is argued in the literature is whether Ricardo's observations on machinery were relevant to his interpretation of the postwar depression (Berg 1980, 70–73, 76). That Ricardo understood that the postwar change in the pattern of final demand potentially could have affected the demand for labor has been noted by Hollander (1995, 196–197; 1979, 519–520).

live by the wages of labour" (2:235–236). There is a subsequent reference
in the third edition of his *Principles* (1821):

In the same manner, a country engaged in war, and which is under the necessity of
maintaining large fleets and armies, employs a great many more men than will be
employed when the war terminates [because] at the termination of the war, when
part of my revenue reverts to me, and is employed as before in the purchase of
wine, furniture or other luxuries, the population which it before supported, and
which the war called into existence, will become redundant and by its effect on
the rest of the population and its competition with it for employment, will sink
the value of wages and very materially deteriorate the condition of the labouring
classes (1:392–394).

Given that the extent of the postwar demobilization was common knowledge and that Ricardo allowed that wartime expenditures were directed
toward labor-intensive services, it is reasonable to infer that he recognized
how the postwar change in the pattern of final demand had affected the
demand for labor. He did not mention whether the sudden reduction in
labor demand might have contributed to short-run excess labor supply,
but this does not negate our inference. For by the time Ricardo was writing in 1820 and 1821, the postwar change in the pattern of demand would
have been manifested in a lower demand for labor, and thus lower wages,
than otherwise.

Early in 1821 – perhaps between 25 January and 12 March (Hollander
1979, 366) – Ricardo recognized that a sudden change in technology could,
in principle, lead to an absolute reduction in the demand for labor, not
merely a reduction in the rate of growth of this demand.[9] A statement of
his new position appeared in the 1821 edition of the *Principles*: "The discovery and use of machinery may be attended with a diminution of gross
produce; and whenever that is the case, it will be injurious to the labouring class, as some of their number will be thrown out of employment and
population will become redundant, compared with the funds which are to
employ it" (1:390). There have been questions in the secondary literature
concerning whether current economic events affected Ricardo's position
on machinery and whether he intended to explain postwar unemployment
or underemployment in terms of sudden technical innovation.

Hollander attributes the change to a purely theoretical discussion
between Malthus and Ricardo on the effects of machinery (Hollander

---

[9] Both Hollander and Berg discuss Ricardo's case for the substitution of machinery for
labor in response to sudden technical progress (Hollander 1987, 103; Berg 1980, 65–66).

1979, 367).[10] This seems to be correct, based on the literary context of Ricardo's discussion of machinery and the historical context in which he was writing. At the close of the *Principles* chapter "On Machinery," Ricardo says that his description of labor-displacing technical change is merely speculative: "To elucidate the principle, I have been supposing, that improved machinery is suddenly discovered, and extensively used; but the truth is, that these discoveries are gradual, and rather operate in determining the employment of the capital which is saved and accumulated, than in diverting capital from its actual employment" (1:395). Moreover, an extensive study of contemporary labor disturbances reveals no event in 1820 or 1821 that would have caused Ricardo to conclude that laborers were being displaced suddenly by machines. The "Battle of Bonnymuir" occurred in April 1820 and there was a violent colliers' strike in Shropshire in January 1821. But riots and machine-breaking had been commonplace since the 1790s and, by comparison, the disturbances of 1820–1821 were mild.

Another aspect of Ricardo's argument concerning the disproportion between capital and labor relates to the high taxes required to finance Britain's war debt. This taxation impeded the accumulation of both fixed and circulating capital:[11] "All taxation had a tendency to injure the labouring classes, because it either diminished the fund employed in the maintenance of labour, or checked its accumulation" (18 June 1819, 5:27). In practice, he did not believe that there had been an absolute reduction in the national capital stock; rather, he thought its accumulation had been slowed (10 Mar. 1821, 5:95). Moreover, capitalists were emigrating to escape the high taxes, thus draining the country of entrepreneurial ability:

The national debt . . . occasioned many persons to emigrate to other countries, in order to avoid the burthen of taxation which it entailed, and hung like a mill-stone round the exertion and industry of the country (9 June 1819, 5:21).

Another cause of the existing disposition to send capital out of the country was to be found in the national debt . . . it became a matter of calculation whether it was worth a capitalist's while to continue in a country where he not only obtained

---

[10] With respect to the influence of John Barton and his *Observations on the Circumstances which Influence the Condition of the Labouring Classes of Society* (1817), Hollander allows that Barton may have sown the seeds of Ricardo's change concerning machinery, but he minimizes Barton's role on the grounds that *Observations* does not refer to a conversion of circulating into fixed capital that would reduce gross produce – the concept central to Ricardo's revised position (Hollander 1979, 357).

[11] Many statements to this effect appear in Ricardo's *Works* (7 Aug. 1817, 7:171; 16 Dec. 1819, 5:33; 24 Dec. 1819, 5:38; 28 Jan. 1820, 8:153n; 29 Mar. 1820, 8:168–169; 1820, 2:452).

small profits, but where he was subjected to a great additional burthen. Every pecuniary motive impelled him rather to quit than to remain (16 Dec. 1819, 5:33).

Ricardo's statements have historical merit. During the three years ended in 1819, more than ten thousand English people emigrated to Paris, drawing millions in capital in tow.[12] The flight of persons and capital occurred, in part, to escape taxation. The problem grew worse when Parliament passed a tax increase of £3 million in 1819, an amount exceeding the combined total of all other tax increases in the decade following the war. To Ricardo it seemed that the corn laws and high taxes invited the loss of investment.

He was also concerned that the population was increasing too rapidly to maintain adequate wages. Although Ricardo had long believed that the poor laws encouraged population growth (27 Jan. 1817, 7:125), he began to emphasize the problem after serving on the 1819 Poor Law Committee:

The distress of the poor is considered as synonymous with diminished resources. Suppose a nation to increase its capital annually at the rate of 2% but that at the same time its population increases at the rate of 2 1/2% is it not clear that there will be annually new demands on its charitable funds? Its annual net revenue . . . would increase but would be accompanied with a diminution of happiness, if not positive misery to the great mass of the people (Ricardo to McCulloch, 29 Mar. 1820, 8:170–171).

I am particularly pleased with your observations[13] on the state of the poor – it cannot be too often stated to them that the most effectual remedy for the inadequacy of their wages is in their own hands (Ricardo to Malthus, 4 May 1820, 8:183–184).

Ricardo's view is plausible given the evidence presented to the Poor Law Committees of 1817, 1818, and 1819. Particularly relevant is the fact that Scotland, which had minimal public relief, was almost exempt from the sufferings of the poor experienced in England and Wales.

The permanent aspects of Britain's crises admitted no easy solutions. There was little scope for reducing government expenditures and thus little scope for cutting taxes. From 1813 to 1823 the annual cost of civil government remained at £10 million, a minuscule 3 percent of national income. Military expenditures had been reduced as far as practicable, from £74 million annually at the end of the war to £15 million thereafter.

---

[12] House of Commons, *Second Report from the Secret Committee on Cash Payments* 1819, App. 43; and "Statement of British and Foreign Loans, contracted in 1817 and 1818," *Journal of the House of Lords* 1819, 52:374.

[13] The reference is to a passage from Malthus' *Principles* (1820) (Ricardo, 2:262).

Interest charges on the national debt – at £30 million a year – formed the largest component of the government's budget. Little could be done to reduce these charges; by 1819 the national debt was £845 million as compared to an annual budget surplus of £1–2 million.[14] Because of the government's need to fund so large a national debt, Ricardo recognized that taxes were not likely to be reduced. However, he thought the tax burden could be minimized by assigning taxes in a way that did not distort the competitive allocation of resources: "We cannot now help living under a system of heavy taxation, but to make our industry as productive to us as possible, we should offer no temptations to capitalists, to employ their funds and their skill in any other way than they would have employed them, if we had had the good fortune to be untaxed, and had been permitted to give the greatest development to our talents and industry" (*Protection to Agriculture* 1822, 4:244).

The poor laws also presented a problem. A sudden change in the system would have consigned marginal families to starvation; without change, however, the poor laws subsidized irresponsible decisions about childbearing. Ricardo settled on a trade-off: continue to support families in the greatest need, but gradually withdraw support.

The ill effects of the poor laws then I suppose to be admitted and their abolition to be desirable the question then is how is it to be effected? Can it be by any other means than by gradually limiting their application, by encouraging the poor man to depend on his own exertions only? Is not this to be done by refusing all relief in the first instance to any but those whose necessities absolutely require it – to administer it to them in the most sparing manner, and lastly to abolish the poor laws altogether? (Ricardo to Trower, 27 Jan. 1817, 7:124–125).

Furthermore, he thought there should be an immediate end to subsidized wages. Under the roundsmen system, agricultural laborers were partly paid from the poor rates. Manufacturing wages were also subsidized. Ricardo believed that farmers and manufacturers reduced the wages they paid to their employees by amounts equal to the subsidies they received from the poor rates. For this reason he endorsed the Poor Relief Bill that would have prohibited the system of roundsmen: "that bill proposed to have the labourer paid in just wages by his employer, instead of having him transferred to the poor-rates" (5:113–114). He expected that once subsidies were removed, the competition among employers for current laborers would be sufficient to raise the rate of wages at least to

[14] See App. E.3 and E.4 for data on public finance.

the subsistence level (Ricardo to Trower, 27 Jan. 1817, 7:124). This rise would occur independently of the effect of the poor laws on population growth.

The corn laws posed a final problem. Because of his concern about the effects of agricultural protection on economic growth and on the allocation of resources, Ricardo urged that the corn laws be abolished. However, many persons were employed in agriculture, and much investment had been made in agricultural land and capital in reliance on the continuation of the protectionist system. To avoid unnecessary hardships to farmers and agricultural laborers, Ricardo proposed that the corn laws be gradually abolished.

It might, however, be desirable, that the farmers, during their current leases, should be protected against the losses which they would undoubtedly suffer from the new value of money, which would result from a cheap price of corn, under their existing money engagements with their landlords.... Although the nation would sacrifice much more than the farmers would save even by a temporary high price of corn, it might be just to lay restrictive duties on importation for three or four years, and to declare that, after that period, the trade in corn should be free, and that imported corn should be subject to no other duty than such as we might find it expedient to impose on corn of our own growth (*Essay on Profits* 1815, 4:33).

At the termination of the war, the obstacles to importation are removed, and a competition destructive to the home-grower commences, from which he is unable to withdraw, without the sacrifice of a great part of his capital. The best policy of the State would be, to lay a tax, decreasing in amount from time to time, on the importation of foreign corn, for a limited number of years, in order to afford to the home-grower an opportunity to withdraw his capital gradually from the land (*Principles* 1817, 1:266–267).

Even with the gradual elimination of the laws there would be a loss of agricultural capital. This Ricardo considered an unfortunate but necessary consequence of the transition:

That some capital would be lost cannot be disputed, but is the possession or preservation of capital the end, or the means? The means, undoubtedly. What we want is an abundance of commodities, and if it could be proved that by the sacrifice of a part of our capital we should augment the annual produce of those objects which contribute to our enjoyment and happiness, we ought to . . . repine at the loss of a part of our capital (4:248–249).

As for agricultural laborers, Ricardo assumed those displaced by the switch to free trade would be absorbed in Britain's manufacturing sector. In fact, he was eager for the transfer of resources from agriculture to sectors with greater demand: "[Malthus] does not sufficiently allow for the effects of a better distribution of the national capital on the situation of the lower classes. It would be beneficial to them, because the same capital would employ more hands; besides, that the greater profits would lead to further accumulation; and thus would a stimulus be given to population by really high wages, which could not fail for a long time to ameliorate the condition for the labouring classes" (4:35). According to this view, industrial-based growth under a system of free trade would raise the demand for labor more than growth under Britain's current system.

Malthus held the opposite opinion. He doubted whether Britain's manufacturing base could absorb the workers displaced from agriculture.

The farmers, in some districts, have entirely lost the little capital they possessed; and, unable to continue in their farms, have deserted them, and left their labourers without the means of employment. . . . In Ireland, it is quite certain, that there are no mercantile capitals ready to take up those persons who are thus thrown out of work, and even in Great Britain, the transfer will be slow and difficult. Our commerce and manufactures, therefore, must increase very considerably before they can restore the demand for labour already lost (Malthus 1815a, 163).

He further believed that the drop in the incomes and expenditures of landlords that would occur because of the transition to free trade would lead to a reduction in aggregate demand.

But if we look at the probable effects of returning peace to Europe, it is impossible to suppose that, even with a considerable diminution in the price of labour, we should not lose some markets on the continent, for those manufactures in which we have no peculiar advantage; while we have every reason to believe that in others, where our colonies, our navigation, our long credits, our coals, and our mines come in question, as well as our skill and capital, we shall retain our trade in spite of high wages. Under these circumstances, it seems peculiarly advisable to maintain unimpaired, if possible, the home market, and not to lose the demand occasioned by so much of the rents of land, and of the profits and capital of farmers, as must necessarily be destroyed by the check to our home produce (1815a, 166).

Malthus reversed his position on agricultural protection once he recognized the relative importance of manufacturing (Hollander 1992).[15] The change is evident in his 1824 article in the *Quarterly Review* titled "Political Economy."By 1824 he concluded that because of the extent of Britain's foreign trade, domestic manufactures could absorb the

---

[15] For a critique of Hollander's discovery, see J. M. Pullen (1995).

workers who would be displaced from agriculture by the abolition of the corn laws.

In the period which has elapsed since the return to peace, the difficulty of finding employment, particularly on the land, has been too notorious to require proof; and if, owing to the extraordinary stimulus given to the population by the previous demand for it, it still continues to increase with rapidity, yet there is reason to think that the present demand would not nearly have kept pace with the rate of increase, and that great distress would have been the consequence, if the happy opening of new and large channels of foreign commerce, combined with the improved views of our government in commercial legislation, had not prepared the way for a renewed demand for labour (Malthus 1824, 287).

Moreover, because of the increasing scale of trade and manufactures, it was important to protect and expand Britain's access to foreign markets. The corn laws threatened the growth of Britain's exports because they undermined the global free trade movement.

At a period when our ministers are most laudably setting an example of a more liberal system of commercial policy, it would be greatly desirable that foreign nations should not have so marked an exception as our present corn-laws to cast in our teeth. A duty on importation not too high, and a bounty nearly such as was recommended by Mr. Ricardo, would probably be best suited to our present situation, and best secure steady prices. A duty on foreign corn would resemble the duties laid by other countries on our manufactures as objects of taxation, and would not in the same manner impeach the principles of free trade (Malthus 1826, 436n).

Malthus approved of Ricardo's proposal for "substantially free trade in corn" (Ricardo, 4:266)."Substantially free trade" involved the elimination of protective tariffs, but the retention of countervailing duties on foreign corn to compensate for the distorting effects on the competitive allocation of resources of taxes peculiar to British farmers:

It must not be supposed, however, that . . . the importation of corn should be at all times allowed without the payment of any duty whatever. . . . whenever any peculiar tax falls on the produce of any one commodity, from the effects of which all other producers are exempted, a countervailing duty to that amount, but no more, should on every just principle be imposed on the importation of such commodity; and further, that a drawback should be allowed, to the same amount also on the exportation of the like commodity (Ricardo, *Protection to Agriculture* 1822, 4:243).

Tithes were an obvious tax paid by British farmers from which foreign producers were exempt. If tithes cost 10s. per quarter, for example, then there should have been a correcting tariff of 10s. per quarter on foreign produce. Similarly, if British farmers chose to export, they should have been paid a drawback – a refund of the monies paid in tithes.

When Malthus recognized that industrial growth was a viable option, he also changed his view on the importance of the consumption of landlords in maintaining a sufficient level of aggregate demand. According to his initial interpretation of the postwar depression, the fall of the incomes of landlords and farmers upon the harvest of 1813 led to such a reduction in aggregate demand that the economy was forced into a depression for the better part of the next decade. Later, however, he saw exports as the crucial element of aggregate demand:

Without [Britain's manufacturing exports] she would be less powerful, and I should certainly add less wealthy, though she might still be as strong in defensive war. It is owing to the abundance of her exports, derived from her skill machinery and capital, that money rents and the money prices of corn and labour are high.... would it not be an impoverishing and very disadvantageous exchange to substitute for the rich capitalists and comfortable and independent traders living upon the profits of stock, a body of dependents upon the landlords? (Malthus to Chalmers, Mar. 1832, quoted in Hollander 1992, 655).

Ricardo all along endorsed industrial-based growth. Malthus converted to Ricardo's position when he recognized that British trade and manufacturing were expanding, while the role of agriculture diminished.

Malthus' Analysis of Postwar Conditions

Historians who associate Ricardo with an extreme version of the law of markets based on his analysis of postwar conditions often give Malthus high praise for his assessment of the same. Malthus treated the years 1815 to 1823 as a single protracted crisis.[16] His analysis is a narrative of cascading economic ruin as losses in one industry – starting with agriculture – trigger losses and unemployment in all others. He believed that the collapse of corn prices, occasioned by the harvest of 1813 and corn imports, caused "a severe shock to the cultivation of the country and a great loss of agricultural capital" (Malthus 1815a, 139–141). Money wages soon declined, but the fall was not sufficient to eliminate unemployment,

---

[16] Link has noted Malthus' confusion on the timing of the postwar depressions: "Malthus dated the postwar slump from 1813 or 1815, and again there seems to have been little recognition that there were shorter fluctuations. Judging by his review of Tooke, Malthus treated the whole period from the end of the war to 1822 or 1823 as a unit, marked by contraction and then by stagnation" (Link 1959, 63).

forcing "a great number of agricultural labourers out of employment,"
notwithstanding "a fall in the price of labour as has already taken place"
(155).[17] There were not enough jobs in trade and manufacturing to absorb the displaced agricultural workers. And Malthus did not believe that
workers could regain full employment without years of additional investments in manufacturing: "In Ireland [and Britain] there are no mercantile
capitals ready to take up those persons who are thus thrown out of work
and . . . the transfer process will be slow and difficult. Our commerce and
manufactures, therefore, must increase very considerably before they can
restore the demand for labour already lost; and a moderate increase beyond this will scarcely make up for the disadvantage of a low money price
of wages" (156).

The reduction of the expenditures of landlords and farmers caused, in
Malthus' narrative, a net drop in the demand for manufactured produce:
"Already in all the country towns, this diminution of demand has been felt
in a very great degree; and the surrounding farmers, who chiefly support
them, are quite unable to make their accustomed purchases" (Malthus
1815a, 161). He implicitly assumed that consumers – who benefitted from
an increase in purchasing power made available to them by the decline
of agricultural prices – failed to increase their expenditures. This led to
"an actual diminution of home demand" (161), which, in turn, prompted
merchants to export excessively. Once foreign markets were inundated
with British goods, the prices of these goods also collapsed, bringing
ruin to merchants and manufactures. His position is summarized in the
Principles:

[The stagnation of effectual demand] commenced certainly with the extraordinary fall in the value of the raw produce of the land, to the amount, it has been
supposed of nearly one third. When this fall had diminished the capitals of the
farmers, and still more the revenues both of landlords and farmers, and of all those
who were otherwise connected with the land, their power of purchasing manufacturers and foreign products was of necessity greatly diminished. The failure
of home demand filled the warehouses of the manufacturers with unsold goods,
which urged them to export more largely at all risks. But this excessive exportation glutted all the foreign markets, and prevented the merchants from receiving
adequate returns . . . from the diminution of the home revenues, aggravated by
a sudden and extraordinary contraction of the currency, even the comparatively
scanty returns obtained from abroad found a very insufficient domestic demand,

---

[17] In a letter to Ricardo of 16 July 1821, he stated: "We know from repeated experience
that the money price of labour never falls till many workmen have been for some time
out of work" (Ricardo, 9:20).

and the profits and consequent expenditure of merchants and manufacturers were proportionably lowered (Malthus 1820, 493–494).

The cessation of wartime government expenditures was, for Malthus, an additional cause of economic distress. He believed that aggregate demand had fallen because private spending did not compensate for the loss of wartime expenditures:

The returned taxes, and the excess of individual gains above expenditure, which were so largely used as revenue during the war, are now in part, and probably in no inconsiderable part, saved. . . . [This] contributes to explain the cause of the diminished demand for commodities, compared with their supply since the war. If some of the principal governments concerned spent the taxes which they raised in a manner to create a greater and more certain demand for labour and commodities, particularly the former, than the present owners of them, and if this difference of expenditure be of a nature to last some time, we cannot be surprised at the duration of the effects arising from the transition from war to peace (Malthus 1820, 499–500).

He also believed that the wartime campaign was labor intensive, that peacetime spending was less so, and that the change in the pattern of final demand tended to reduce the derived demand for labor: "The powerful stimulus which had been given to population during the war continued to pour in fresh supplies of labour, and, aided by the disbanded soldiers and sailors and the failure of demand arising from the losses of the farmers and merchants, reduced generally the wages of labour, and left the country with a generally diminished capital and revenue" (494).[18]

Ricardo denied the central premise of Malthus' analysis: that a decline in the incomes of landlords and farmers in 1813 caused a reduction in aggregate demand, leading to a general depression. He considered Malthus' theory untenable because national economic activity – as measured by tax data – expanded through the summer of 1815.

Malthus first mentioned to Ricardo his concerns about the effects of low agricultural prices on general economic activity in a letter of April 1815: "If the value of the whole raw produce falls compared with manufactured and foreign produce, does not such a fall necessarily involve a diminution of demand for manufactured and foreign produce?" (Ricardo, 1952, 6:208). His conviction as to the effect of declining agricultural prices on aggregate demand was reinforced two months later in a meeting with Lord King: "I saw Lord King last night. He speaks of having heard of very

---

[18] Notwithstanding this observation, Malthus believed that the supply of capital was still excessive relative to the demand for it (Hollander 1997, 596).

general distress among farmers and shopkeepers all over the country. I confess I feel more and more convinced of the unavoidable evils attending a general fall of prices and of the unobserved advantages attending the high prices of corn and labour. [Lord King] said that the view which I took of the effect of such prices on foreign commerce appeared to him to be quite new" (Malthus to Ricardo, 19 June 1815, Ricardo, 6:231). In response Ricardo stated that "the farmers and shopkeepers may suffer very general distress from a sudden and general fall of prices, but I hold that this would be no criterion by which to judge of the general or permanent prosperity of a country" (27 June 1815, 6:234). By the fall of 1815, Malthus was convinced of the existence of a general economic crisis and of his appreciation of its causes: "Is it possible for above half the national income to fall very greatly in price, without affecting the demand and the other half. I confess I feel no doubt that the main cause of the present slackness of trade is the diminished incomes of the landlords and Farmers" (16 Oct. 1815, 6:303). Ricardo answered the next day: "It is dangerous to listen to reports respecting briskness or slackness of trade. It is I believe certain that the revenue has been uncommonly productive the last quarter which is no indication of diminished trade. As you allow that the loss of the sellers is the gain of the buyers, you appear to me to attribute effects much too great to the fall of raw produce which has lately taken place" (17 Oct. 1815, 6:304).

On its face, Ricardo's answer suggests the naive overconfidence in abstract theory of which he has been accused,[19] but his statement was far from naive. For in saying that "the revenue has been uncommonly productive the last quarter" he referred Malthus to the Treasury report of 11 July 1815 (*Journal of the House of Commons* 1814–15, 70:726). That report shows an increase in customs and excise revenues from the third quarter of 1813, when agricultural prices began to decline, through the second quarter of 1815 – the most recent quarter for which returns were available (see App. E.2).[20] Ricardo did not deny the current agricultural crisis,[21] but he understood that without a change in tax rates – and there

---

[19] Hollander critically interpreted the quote, saying: "Ricardo went so far in his reply as to deny the putative facts of excess aggregate supply" (Hollander 1997, 146).

[20] Gayer assigns the cyclical peak of the cycle to Mar. 1815. Tax returns, however, indicate that economic activity increased through the third quarter of 1815 (Gayer 1953, 110).

[21] Ricardo was informed about agricultural conditions. His *Essay on Profits* (1815) cites foreign imports as a cause of low corn prices and warns of future agricultural crises if the corn warehoused in British ports were suddenly admitted for home consumption (4:26, 29, 35). His concern was well founded. Almost one million quarters of foreign corn were imported in 1813 and 1814. This corn, combined with the unprecedented harvest of 1813, glutted the market for the next two years. Corn prices necessarily collapsed given that

had been no change[22] – the increase in customs and excise returns revealed by the Treasury could not have happened unless Britain's economy was growing. The coincidence of low corn prices and a robust general economy from the harvest of 1813 through the second quarter of 1815 showed that Malthus' theory of postwar distress was inadequate.

Ricardo's Analysis of Postwar Conditions

Posing an alternative to Malthus' analysis, Ricardo attributed the depression of 1815–1817 to the change from wartime to peacetime production: "In every change from peace to war and from war to peace there must be great changes in the distribution of capital and much individual distress" (25 Dec. 1815, 6:345). His explanation was reasonable given the magnitude of the transition.[23] He was optimistic that the adjustment process could be completed rapidly. And in this he proved correct. For Britain's economy recovered from the postwar depression by the summer of 1817, within twenty-four months of Waterloo.

The transition from wartime to peacetime production was formidable. Government spending decreased by £53.3 million from 1814 to 1817 – 18 percent of aggregate demand. The decline in war expenditures entailed the demobilization of 430,000 soldiers and the elimination of 100,000 jobs in wartime industries. The soldiers and factory workers suddenly released from employment accounted for at least 15 percent of the male labor force. The upheaval in British agriculture was perhaps of an even greater magnitude. The abundant harvests of 1813 and 1815, added to the corn imports of 1814, caused wheat to fall from a high of 127s. per quarter in February 1813 to 54s. per quarter by February 1816; other produce fell similarly. It was impossible for British farmers to relieve the glut by selling to the Continent because during the war the margin of cultivation had been extended and consequently production costs had increased beyond the point at which they could compete abroad. The fall in corn

demand was inelastic: "The money value of the whole [agricultural] produce would be less than when the quantity was less, and they would have the same money rent to pay. This was the peculiar evil under which the farmers suffered at the termination of the war, when the ports were opened" (*Notes on Malthus*, Ricardo, 2:110).

[22] House of Commons, *A Return of...all Taxes Repealed, Expired, Reduced...since the Termination of the War; and also of all Taxes Imposed* 1833; reprinted in *Parliamentary Papers* 1833, 32:637–653, MF 36.239.

[23] Rostow describes the postwar adjustments at length, concluding that the situation was "economically probably the most wretched, difficult, and dangerous in modern English history" (Rostow 1942, 19).

prices resulted in many bankruptcies and widespread unemployment in agricultural districts. This was no small matter as one-third of the British populace was employed in farming.

The transition to peacetime activity took longer than Ricardo expected, yet he remained certain of its eventual success: "It appears to me that a sufficient time has elapsed to make that new distribution of employments which our altered circumstances have made necessary. The duration of the intervals between marked changes are often much longer than is generally supposed. It proceeds from the opposition which is naturally given to such change . . . the duration of the resistance depends on the degree of information, or the strength of the prejudices of those who offer it, and therefore cannot be the subject of any thing like accurate calculation" (8 Sept. 1816, 7:67). The chapter "On Sudden Changes in the Channels of Trade" in the *Principles* (1817) provides a thorough statement of his analysis, which, in short, is that fixed capital cannot be transferred easily between industries and might be rendered useless by a change in the pattern of final demand, and that laborers will be unemployed as capitalists "are removing their capitals and the labour which they can command from one employment to another" (Ricardo, 1:263).

The commencement of war after a long peace, or of peace after a long war, generally produces considerable distress in trade. It changes in a great degree the nature of the employments to which the respective capitals of countries were before devoted; and during the interval while they are settling in the situations which new circumstances have made the most beneficial, much fixed capital is unemployed, perhaps wholly lost, and labourers are without full employment. The duration of this distress will be longer or shorter according to the strength of that disinclination, which most men feel to abandon that employment of their capital to which they have long been accustomed. It is often protracted too by the restrictions and prohibitions to which the absurd jealousies which prevail between the different States of the commercial commonwealth give rise.

When, however, such distress immediately accompanies a change from war to peace, our knowledge of the existence of such a cause will make it reasonable to believe that the funds for the maintenance of labour have rather been diverted from their usual channel, than materially impaired, and that after temporary suffering, the nation will again advance in prosperity (1:265).

Ricardo thought British industry was particularly liable to this type of distress because of its high capital intensity.

In rich and powerful countries, where large capitals are invested in machinery, more distress will be experienced from a revulsion in trade, than in poorer countries where there is proportionally a much smaller amount of fixed and a much larger amount of circulating capital. . . . It is not so difficult to withdraw a circulating as a fixed capital, from any employment in which it may be engaged. It is often impossible to divert the machinery which may have been erected for one manufacture to the purposes of another (1:266).

His mention of a "revulsion in trade" is not merely hypothetical. There were three aspects to the postwar structural change: the transfer of resources out of wartime industries, the movement of labor and capital out of agriculture, and the adjustment of exports to better approximate foreign demand.

In our case the market rate of interest has been lowered by causes which may be considered permanent such as the accumulation of capital and people and also by causes which may be considered temporary, such as the derangement of foreign commerce; that as the last of these causes shall cease to operate by things getting into their natural order the rate of interest will have a tendency to rise (Ricardo to Grenfell, 27 Aug. 1817, reprinted in Heertje 1991, 521).

At no point did Ricardo attribute distress to a lack of aggregate demand. He was adamant that there were profitable industries and that the solution to Britain's crisis lay in moving resources to where they were required. The low rate of interest following the war was no sign that profits were not available. Instead, interest rates were low because of the difficulty of identifying profitable investments.

May not the derangement which the different employments of capital have experienced from the termination of the war have thrown an unusual quantity in the market to seek new occupations. Although there is no amount of capital which may not be employed in a country, there is probably an interval while it is seeking its ultimate destination, during which it particularly operates on the rate of interest. May we not be experiencing such an interval now, when so different a direction is given to capital from the change from war to peace (Ricardo to Grenfell, 27 Aug. 1817, reprinted in Heertje 1991, 521).

There are considerable intervals during which a low rate of interest is compatible with a high rate of profit, and this generally occurs when capital is moving from the employments of war to those of peace (Ricardo to Malthus, 21 Oct. 1817, 7:199).

Ricardo's comments have some historical basis. In late 1817, interest rates were lower than at any former time in the century.[24] And more important, there were prosperous industries. From April 1816 through 1819, corn prices were high enough to attract substantial amounts of

---

[24] Interest rates were high in 1816 because of the failure of twenty-six country banks from January through July. But when the country-banking crisis ended and calm returned to financial markets, interest rates fell sharply. The long-term yield on British Government Consols (three percent) declined to 3.56 percent in mid-1817. Short-term yields on commercial bills dropped to 4 percent (Homer and Sylla 1991, Tables 19 and 23).

capital. Evidence before the Agricultural Committee of 1821 indicated that tillage increased by up to 15 percent. Similarly, by late 1817 the demand for British exports had revived and manufactures were approaching full employment. Ricardo hailed the return of prosperity in letters to Malthus: "We shall now I hope for some years sail before the wind. You and I have always agreed in our opinions of the power and wealth of the country, – we were not in a state of despair at the discouraging circumstances with which we were lately surrounded. We looked forward to the revival which has taken place" (10 Oct. 1817, 7:192; see also 7:185–186).

The recovery of agriculture and manufacturing validated Ricardo's prediction that Britain would accomplish the postwar transition without a prolonged depression.[25] Unfortunately, the prosperity for which he looked did not endure. A coincidence of shocks to Britain's principal markets annihilated the demand for British exports during the trading months of 1819. In the depression that followed all aspects of Britain's trade and manufacturing suffered. Ricardo described the crisis in detail to his friend Thomas Smith:

You will find the politicians of this country in a very gloomy mood. Commerce is languishing – merchants and manufactures are failing – overtrading has become general and all our markets are glutted with goods. Cotton and many other articles are lower in price here than they can be grown for in the countries where they are produced. Pauperism is increasing and employment cannot be found for the industrious. To crown the whole we are labouring under great financial difficulties, our revenue being insufficient[26] to meet our expenditure (27 Apr. 1819, reprinted in Heertje and Weatherall 1978, 570).

The remark about excessive imports – "cotton[27] and many other articles" – reflects an understanding that there had been miscalculations in foreign trade. The allusion to "markets glutted with goods" likely refers to foreign markets.

---

[25] In Chapter 1, see the discussion of Stigler's criticism. Stigler said: "Beginning in 1815, he [Ricardo] made a series of predictions that prosperity would soon come to England. The prediction was continuously wrong and it was no compliment to his intelligence that after 1820 he blamed the distress on the abundance of harvests" (Stigler 1953, 596).

[26] Though Ricardo does not cite sources, his mention of the "revenue being insufficient" indicates a familiarity with Treasury reports. When writing to Smith, he could have seen two quarterly tax reports for 1819, dated 4 Feb. and 6 Apr. The Feb. report showed an increase in total tax revenues over the previous quarter, though customs returns were down; the Apr. report showed a decline in customs, excise, and total tax revenues. (App. E.2 records the data from both reports.)

[27] Cotton and wool were commodities associated with heavy losses by trading houses – losses estimated at not less than £3 million (*Blackwood's*, Feb. 1819, 630).

From 1819 onward, Ricardo's references to "misallocated capital" did not refer to the transfer of capital from wartime to peacetime industries – which is how these passages are sometimes interpreted.[28] Instead, he used the concept to explain why Britain's merchants and manufactures incurred losses in 1819 and 1820: exports and imports far exceeded demands. He also applied the concept to explain why the price of corn fell after the harvest of 1820: the margin of cultivation was overextended, corn was in surfeit, and prices could not rise till resources were withdrawn from farming.

Malthus criticized Ricardo's explanations of the depression of 1819 and of the subsequent agricultural crisis on two grounds. Like modern authors, he understood Ricardo to mean that Britain's economy was still adjusting from wartime to peacetime production. Malthus rejected this notion because he did not believe the postwar transition could have taken more than four years. Also, Malthus was convinced that the depression stemmed from a chronic shortfall in consumer demand.

The present state of things indeed in England America Holland and Hamburgh still more than in France does appear in the most marked manner to contradict both [Say's] and your theory. The fall in the interest of money and the difficulty of finding employment for capital are universally acknowledged and this fact, none of your friends have ever accounted for in any tolerably satisfactory manner; but what confidence can be placed in a theory, as the foundation of future measures which is absolutely inconsistent with the past and the present state of things (Malthus to Ricardo, 25 Sept. 1820, 8:260).

The difficulty of finding employment for Capital in the countries you mention proceeds from the prejudices and obstinacy with which men persevere in their old employments, – they expect daily a change for the better, and therefore continue to produce commodities for which there is no adequate demand. With abundance of capital and a low price of labour there cannot fail to be some employments which would yield good profits . . . Men err in their productions, there is no deficiency of demand . . . we are guilty of some such folly now, and I can scarcely account for the length of time[29] that this delusion continues (Ricardo to Malthus, 9 Oct. 1820, 8:277).

---

[28] Ricardo's explanation of the hardships attending the transition from wartime to peacetime production has been viewed favorably by modern authors, at least in his account of the years 1815 to 1817. But, by not realizing that there were two distinct business cycles in the postwar decade and by neglecting the miscalculations in foreign trade in 1819 and in corn production for 1820–1822, critics have mistakenly assumed that he analyzed events from 1819 onward in terms of the postwar adjustment of capital (Blaug 1958, 77; Link 1959, 63; Tucker 1960, 125–126; Hollander 1979, 518).

[29] I am not certain what Ricardo knew about the conditions in America, Holland, Hamburg, and France. But, in Britain, the crisis in manufacturing and foreign trade that began in Feb. 1819 was nearing an end by the summer of 1820. It is possible that Ricardo was

The Rev. Benjamin Grey described a conversation during which Ricardo and Malthus expressed their differences at length: "Mr. Ricardo and Mr. Malthus came and entertained us for two hours and upwards with an argument in defence of their respective theories of Political Economy. Mr. Malthus contending that the present distress arose from unemployed capital and Ricardo from misemployed capital which would soon assume its proper channels" (note by Sraffa in Ricardo, 8:334n). Ricardo doubted whether conditions from 1819 to 1822 exhibited a lack of demand for he did not perceive the "symptoms" of a general glut.

Mr. Malthus . . . contends that there may be at one and the same time a glut of all commodities, and that it may arise from a want of demand for all – he indeed argues that this is the specific evil under which we are at present suffering (Ricardo to Trower, 26 Sept. 1820, 8:257).

As I have already said I do not see how stagnation of trade can arise from such a cause . . . Such and such evils may exist, but the question is, do they exist now? I think not, none of the symptoms indicate that they do (Ricardo to Malthus, 21 July 1821, 9:26–27).

Modern authors who accept the stylized history of postwar events echo Malthus' view. For according to that history, Britain's economy was depressed from 1815 through 1822 or 1823 and Ricardo's position has no empirical basis.[30] Hollander describes Ricardo's explanation of events in terms of misallocated capital as "incompatible with the evidence, particularly with the pervasiveness of the depression and the absence of those potentially profitable industries presumed to exist in that account" (Hollander 1997, 608). He repeats passages from Malthus' *Principles* that question Ricardo:

Where is there any considerable trade that is confessedly understocked, and where high profits have been long pleading in vain for additional capital? The war has now been at an end above four years; and though the removal of capital generally occasions some partial loss, yet it is seldom long in taking place . . .

I cannot bring myself to believe that this transfer can require so much time as has now elapsed since the war; and again ask, where are the understocked employments, which, according to this theory, ought to be numerous and fully capable of absorbing all the redundant capital (Malthus 1820, 334–334, 498–499).

---

referring to conditions in domestic agriculture, for corn prices fell sharply after the harvest of 1820.

[30] Many authors admit the validity of Ricardo's misallocated capital explanation in the years 1815 to 1817, but they question what they perceive as his continued use of the argument in 1820, five years after the war ended (Blaug 1958, 77; Link 1959, 63; Tucker 1960, 125–126; Hollander 1979, 518).

Peach alludes to Malthus' letter of 25 September 1820 (quoted earlier) and to Ricardo's response as proof that Ricardo "believed passionately in the practical relevance of his doctrine [the law of markets] to such an extent that he blamed reality for not conforming to the 'model', not vice versa" (Peach 1993, 139–140).

Notwithstanding this critique, Ricardo did not err in his assessment. Tax reports show no decline in the home consumption of basic commodities, not even during 1819. The mistakes in foreign trade were well documented. And perhaps most important, Britain's economy recovered quickly from the depression – just as Ricardo anticipated:

It was not very long ago since they were all in a state of the greatest alarm on account of the distressed manufacturers. It was conceived that our manufacturers were declining and the most gloomy apprehensions were indulged on their behalf. But he took the liberty of intimating his opinion, that those distresses were not permanent; and happily, his predictions had been fulfilled (Ricardo in Parliament, 18 Feb. 1822, 5:133).

Wages and prices were highly flexible. Capitalists were able to shift resources from depressed industries to those that were expanding. For these reasons trade and manufacturing began to improve in 1820 and were prospering by 1821: "In looking at the general state of the country, it was satisfactory to find that, amid the gloom and distress in which the agricultural interests were involved, its foreign commerce was in a flourishing condition" (12 Feb. 1823, 5:247). On all points, Ricardo's description of postwar conditions closely matched actual events.

The empirical aspect of Ricardo's position has been obscured, in part, by his remarks in other contexts. Glaring among these are his statements before the House of Commons Committee on Resumption on 4 March 1819. Responding to sharp questions, he professed ignorance of current events and minimized the potential harm of returning to gold in the midst of a depression:

Question: Are you aware that there is at present a considerable stagnation in trade, and that there has been a great reduction of prices in consequence?

Answer: I have heard so; but I am not engaged in trade, and it does not come much within my own knowledge.

Question: Might not the reduction of prices to the amount of 5% consequent on a reduction of the issues of the Bank be particularly embarrassing if it took place at a period when there appears to have been so great a reduction of prices in consequence of other causes – namely, the excess of speculation and the stagnation resulting from that?

Answer: An alteration in the value of 5% does not appear to me very formidable; but of this matter I do not profess to know much; I have had little practical knowledge upon these subjects (Ricardo, 5:384–385).

Given that Ricardo was informed about the nature and severity of the depression and that he recognized the nonneutrality of money and wanted to minimize the difficulty of returning to gold, his remarks are curious. I will venture two explanations for his testimony.

First, Ricardo may have confined his testimony to subjects of personal expertise. His knowledge of the crisis was necessarily limited in March 1819 because he could have known about reversals in foreign trade for at most four weeks. Moreover, as a conscientious witness, he might have deferred to experts in particular branches of trade, of whom several were called before the committee. Five witnesses before the Lords committee were directly involved in foreign trade: Haldimand, who specialized in trade with Italy and France; Ward, a Mediterranean merchant; Richard Page, who traded with France, Holland, and Flanders; Thomas Tooke, a Russia merchant; and Matthew Fletcher, another Mediterranean merchant.[31] Haldimand, Ward, and Tooke were called before the Commons committee as well, along with three merchants who did not appear before the Lords: John Irving, a general merchant; John Gladstone, who specialized in the East and West Indies trade; and Hieronimus Burmester, a Spanish and Portugal merchant.[32] Ricardo and Nathan Rothschild were the only other witnesses before the committee who were not associated with the Bank of England, the Bank of Ireland, the Mint, or country banks.

A second – and more speculative – explanation for Ricardo's testimony is that he mischaracterized the extent of the current crisis and the risks of deflation so as not to lend credibility to the opponents of resumption. Among these, Alexander Baring was the foremost; Vansittart[33] described his testimony to the committees as "the most important of any" (quoted by Sraffa in Ricardo, 5:352). Baring was not an obvious candidate to

---

[31] Their testimony, which is extensive and detailed, can be found in the *Journal of the House of Lords* 1819, 52:352–476.

[32] Their testimony appears in the House of Commons, *Minutes of Evidence Taken before the Secret Committee on the Expediency of the Bank resuming Cash Payments* 1819, 94–103, 104–113, 153–156.

[33] Vansittart was loath to consider resumption in 1819, and so approved of Baring's opposition to the act. Ministers wanted to prolong the Bank restriction, but they were forced to convene the resumption committees to preempt the Whigs gaining a political advantage after Tierney – leader of the opposition in the Commons – threatened to move for a committee of inquiry on the matter (Hilton 1977, 40).

spearhead the opposition to gold, but his motive becomes clear given the Baring brothers' role in financing the French war indemnity.[34]

In 1816, France proved unable to pay the installments of its war indemnity and was forced to arrange financing for the remainder of the debt. The British government unofficially, and Wellington overtly,[35] urged that Barings contract the necessary loans. This was done and Barings negotiated a series of loans at or exceeding 100 million francs. The final loan, arranged in October 1818, was to be paid during the initial months of 1819 (Jenks 1927, 35–39). The scheme began to unravel, however, only days after the final loan was contracted, when the Bank of France curtailed credit to protect what remained of its bullion hoard. The resulting financial crisis threatened to undermine the credit of the French government, bankrupt Barings, and postpone indefinitely the final installment of the indemnity. To avert such a catastrophe, the French extended the time for Barings to pay the loan to eighteen months, and the allies agreed to more generous terms for the indemnity in accord with the declining price of stock (Jenks 1927, 39–40). However, Barings still faced the task of selling the loan, so when Alexander returned from Paris in February 1819 he was unnerved by the possibility that resumption might actually occur. Mallet discussed the matter with him and noted in his diary: "Narrower means of credits, a closer system of discounts, a return to a sound currency in this great commercial country could not fail affecting all Europe for a time; and it is for a time and for that very time that Baring wants facilities of every kind."[36] Baring testified to the Resumption Committees that cash payments ought to be delayed four or five years (Hilton 1977, 43). To this end he emphasized the hazards of appreciating the currency – then about 4 percent below par – while deflecting attention[37] from the fact that Baring Brothers had profited by more than a million sterling from the French loans and wanted to sell the final installment as dearly as possible (Jenks 1927, 36).

[34] Article 4 of the Definitive Treaty of Peace stipulated that France was to pay the allied powers in installments an indemnity of 700 million francs (*Annual Register*, 1815, 412).

[35] Wellington's interest was due to the fact that proceeds from the indemnity funded the army of occupation in France under his command.

[36] J. L. Mallet's diary entry of 2 Mar. 1819, cited by Sraffa in Ricardo, 5:352n.

[37] Opening his testimony to the Lords Committee on Resumption, Baring described himself as a "merchant in general business." He omitted any reference to his involvement in Baring Brothers or to the fact that he had just returned from France, having negotiated a loan on behalf of the French government for 179 million francs. Baring's testimonies of Mar. 3, 4, 9, and 10 are recorded in the *Journal of the House of Lords* 1818–1819, 52:389–409.

Ricardo was aware of all this.[38] It is possible that he might have minimized the hazards of resumption so as not to reinforce Baring's testimony. Also, Baring was a competitor. Mallet provides this account of a meeting at Ricardo's home in London: "Everyone is full of Mr. Baring's evidence before the Lord's Committee. Admirable as to principles, but letting out all sorts of difficulties as to the practicability of resuming Cash payments; and hinting that it cannot be done in less than four or five years. Everyone agrees that it is knocking the thing on the head; and that such an extension of time is tantamount to doing nothing."[39] Whether Ricardo feigned ignorance before the Commons committee so as not to lend credibility to the opponents resumption cannot be determined from his extant works. What is certain is that he understood the threat Baring posed to stabilizing the money supply.

The Role of Money in Postwar Crises

During the nineteenth century, Britain's money supply consisted of coins, produced by the Mint, and the notes of private banks. The banks, including the Bank of England, served the interests of their shareholders. The circulation was thus liable to fall during crises when the banks withdrew credit. The depression of 1815–1817 was no exception.

The cessation of wartime expenditures combined with losses in foreign trade sent Britain's economy into a depression late in 1815. Malthus and Ricardo were soon aware that the money supply had fallen. Malthus thought the contraction originated with the Bank of England; he wrote to Ricardo asking: "Pray has there been any account lately of the number of Bank of England notes in circulation? It has been said I understand that they have been much diminished lately, which is one great cause of the fall of prices. Is this so?" (Ricardo, 6:303). Ricardo answered that it was not: "The last return of Bank notes in circulation was I think larger than any that preceded it. I have not the paper in London but I think the circulation of Bank notes then [May 1815] amounted to 28,000,000 or more" (17 Oct. 1815, 6:304). The "last return on Bank Notes" is the

---

[38] Ricardo made significant investments in the French Rentes over the summer of 1817. He sold two-thirds of his holdings in Aug. 1818. The withdrawal of credit by the Bank of France in Oct. 1818 caused Rentes to trade at a deep discount, at which point Ricardo reinvested in them (Ricardo, 10:99–101).

[39] Mallet's diary entry of 6 Mar. 1819 is mentioned by Sraffa in Ricardo, 8:18n.

30 May report from the Bank of England (see App. A.1). The account shows no appreciable change.

Though the Bank of England kept its circulation steady, Ricardo saw that failures among the country banks were "a cause of much mischief all over the Kingdom" (10 Sept. 1815, 6:268), which "occasioned much ruin and distress" (*Secure Currency* 1816, 6:73).[40] Bank failures sparked panic in rural districts, leading to further reductions in the country-bank note circulation and, in some instances, to desperate attempts to hoard Bank of England notes.

I have very little doubt but that there has been a considerable rise in the value of money which I think has been effected by the many failures of country Banks, which has increased the use of Bank of England notes in the country, both as a circulating medium, and as a deposit against the alarm which always attends extensive failures in the country (Ricardo to Trower, 25 Dec. 1815, 6:343).

In some of the accounts of the amounts of bank notes in circulation at certain periods which I have seen, the one and two pound notes vary, very remarkably, relatively to the notes of a higher value, which may be occasioned (not that I know that it is) by the increased or diminished credit of the country banks. It appears, in 1815, that the amount of notes above five pounds was about thirteen millions, while those under five pounds were above nine millions ... the same sort of inequality appears to affect the notes of the amount of ten and twenty pounds which may be supposed to be that description of notes which, as well as those of five pounds and under, are used chiefly in the country circulation, upon occasions of the discredit of the country banks (Ricardo before the House of Commons Committee on Resumption, 1819, 5:389–390).

Ricardo agreed with Sinclair, an inflationist writer, that "a part of our distress has been occasioned by the reduction of the circulation" (4 May 1817, 7:151). Testifying before the House of Lords Committee on Resumption, he again noted that a reduction in private credit in 1816 contributed to a deflation "much more considerable" than 4 percent and that a deflation so severe must cause "some little inconvenience" (5:416, 419).

Money played a lesser role in the depression of 1819–1820. The circulation of the Bank of England remained stable through 1818 and the spring

---

[40] Country-bank failures occurred from June 1814 through June 1816. Banks in agricultural districts were affected first. Banks in manufacturing towns began to fail after the demand for exports collapsed. Notwithstanding the "ruin and distress" caused by Bank failures, Ricardo believed, based on tax abstracts, that aggregate economic activity continued to expand through mid-1815. (This remark in *Economical and Secure Currency* would have been written in Aug. or Sept. of 1815 in the midst of the banking crisis.)

of 1819. Its circulation decreased 20 percent during the fall of 1819 as private persons traded banknotes for silver coin. Yet the combined circulation of banknotes and coin declined only from £30.8 million at the end of 1818 to £29.9 million at the close of 1819 (see App. B.6). Ricardo knew the money supply was stable,[41] so in Parliament he described the monetary contraction associated with resumption as "totally inadequate" to have produced the current depression in trade and manufacturing (24 Dec. 1819, 5:37).

Ricardo's thoughts about resumption – or more correctly, the Bank's implementation of the act – began to change in 1820. He saw the market price of gold drop below its Mint price and noticed also a rise of sterling on the foreign exchange (9 June 1820, 5:61). He expected the Bank to maintain a circulation sufficient to prevent any fall in the price of gold or rise in the foreign exchange.[42] The Bank was instead passive and allowed the value of paper to rise. It followed that when Alexander Baring presented the petition of the merchants of London and called for a bimetallic standard that would have devalued the currency, Ricardo's response was limited. He could not deny the occurrence of monetary deflation, but merely asserted that the extent of deflation did not warrant abandoning the gold standard. Shortly after the debate, he mentioned to Sinclair that "the public has suffered much pressure from the limitation of circulation, but Parliament is not responsible for more than about 5 or 6 per cent. of that pressure" (11 May 1820, 8:186).

Ricardo's misgivings about how the Bank was implementing resumption were confirmed the spring of 1821 when it became evident that the Bank had accumulated millions in gold. The Bank was secretive about its bullion hoard, but Ricardo noticed a growing disproportion between the market price of gold and the market price of silver, which he attributed to purchases of gold by the Bank:

If the Bank contemplated paying in gold coin in 1823, as they were now by law required, they must purchase a quantity of gold for that purpose; and to this cause

---

[41] Ricardo bid for the government loan of 9 June 1819 and so carefully studied reports from the Bank concerning its circulation. Seven reports appeared in 1819 on these dates: 1 Feb., 3 Mar., 28 Apr., 24 May, 6 July, 3 Dec., and 23 Dec. We know Ricardo looked at the reports because in a Parliamentary speech of 9 June 1820, he expressly stated that "the reduction of bank-notes within the last year did not exceed £2 millions" (5:61).

[42] Ricardo stated many times in later years that this was his expectation in 1819 (1821, 5:516–519; 1822, 9:140–141; 1822, 5:200–201; 1822, 4:225).

was to be attributed the present disproportion between the price of gold and silver (2 Feb. 1821, 5:71).

What was it that at that moment produced the variation between the metals, to the higher price of gold? Was it not the operations of the Bank? That corporation were so timid . . . had taken alarm and had made great and unnecessary purchases of gold (8 Feb. 1821, 5:75–76).

Evidence confirming his suspicions appeared on 19 March 1821 when the government, at the request of the Bank, proposed the Bank Cash Payments Bill to allow the Bank to pay its notes in specie instead of ingots. The professed purpose of the bill was twofold, according to Vansittart, (1) to prevent the forgery of small banknotes by gradually substituting coin for these notes and (2) to reverse the "drain which was made by the Bank on other countries for the precious metals . . . because that drain rendered the circulation of other countries more restricted" (19 Mar. 1821, *Hansard* 2s, 4:1315–16). The forgery argument was obviously a ruse, for as Ricardo pointed out, "such a plan would be wholly ineffectual . . . whether the issues consisted altogether of Bank-notes, or half in Bank-notes and half in sovereigns, the danger of forgery would be the same" (19 Mar. 1821, *Hansard* 2s, 4:1331).[43] But to the bill in general he raised few objections. The issuance of coin was at variance with the ingot plan – designed to minimize the Bank's purchases of bullion – but the damage had been done. The Bank's unnecessary purchases had already raised the relative price of gold. Dispensing the hoard as specie posed no additional threat:

The Bank had strong prejudices against the [ingot] plan and immediately commenced purchasing bullion and coining money, and were absolutely forced to come to the legislature for permission, last year, to pay in specie, as they had accumulated a large quantity of coin. After they had been foolish enough to do so, it became a matter of indifference whether parliament agreed to their request or refused it – indeed it was more desirable to comply with it – the evil had already been done by the purchase and accumulation of gold, and no further mischief could arise from the substitution of the coins (in circulation) for the paper which they were desirous of withdrawing (3 Jan. 1822, 9:141).

Learning of the Bank's accumulation of gold,[44] Ricardo revised his estimate of the extent of monetary deflation – which had earlier been 5 or

---

[43] The number of forgeries had been high since 1812; there was nothing unusual about the practice in 1820 (see App. A.7). It is thus odd that not until 1821 did the Bank discover the need to issue coin as a means to prevent forgery.

[44] From the same information, Ricardo was also able to approximate the increase in the Bank's hoard. Given a 5 percent decline in the paper price of gold (from £4 2s. to £3 17s. 10.5d.) and a 10 percent rise in the foreign exchange, he estimated the increase of

6 percent (11 May 1820, 8:186) – arriving at a figure of 10 percent. His calculation assumed a constant relative price of silver, so that changes in the nominal price of silver, which he determined by looking at the foreign exchange with France, would reflect the appreciation of sterling: "The surest test [of deflation] was the rate of the foreign exchanges; and if his hon. friend looked at what a pound sterling was worth in 1816 in the silver coin of France and what it was now worth, he would find it difficult to make out a variation of more than 10 per cent" (18 Mar. 1821, 5:95). He knew that the world relative price of silver might have changed because of the current war in South America, which "impeded the regular supply of the precious metals to Europe," but there was no way to determine if this had occurred (12 June 1822, 5:205).[45] In any event, the extent of deflation was at least double what he had anticipated in 1819, prompting this note to Malthus: "I very much regret that in the great change we have made from an unregulated currency to one regulated by a fixed standard we had not more able men to manage it than the present Bank directors. If their object had been to make the revulsion as oppressive as possible, they could not have pursued measures more calculated to make it so than those which they have actually pursued" (9 July 1821, 9:15). Ricardo was apprehensive about the Bank's return to gold. Given the nonneutrality of money and what appeared to be a severe reduction in the circulation, he blamed the Bank for a measure of economic distress.[46]

It was undeniable that the manner in which the Bank had gone on purchasing gold to provide for a metallic currency had materially affected the public interests . . . His hon. friend had said, that whilst the Bank was obliged to pay its notes in gold, the public had no interest in interfering with the Bank respecting the amount of the paper circulation, for if it were too low, the deficiency would be supplied by the importation of gold . . . In this opinion he did not entirely concur, because there might be an interval during which the country might sustain great inconvenience from an undue reduction of the Bank circulation . . . before it [gold]

the world relative price of gold at 5 percent. Assuming then that the world demand for gold was unit elastic, and assuming that the international gold stock amounted to £400 million, Ricardo figured that the Bank of England had amassed a hoard of £15 to £20 million (12 June 1822, 5:209–210). The accuracy of this estimate reflects favorably on his empiricism, for the Bank purchased gold worth £16 million between mid-1819 and June 1822 as compared with his estimate of £15 to £20 million.

[45] According to figures compiled by British consuls, bullion exports from Mexico in 1820 and 1821 were higher than usual. Similarly, the production and export of bullion from South America did not seem to have diminished (Marshall 1833, 2:173).

[46] His view is repeated in comments of Dec. 1821 (5:519) and Jan. 1822 (9:140) and in *Protection to Agriculture* (1822, 4:225).

was coined the currency would be at a very low level, the prices of commodities would fall and great distress would be suffered. Something of this kind had in fact happened. The Bank entirely mismanaged their concerns in the way in which they had prepared for the resumption of cash payments; nothing was more productive of mischief than their large purchases of gold (5:199–200).

Too restricted a circulation hampered economic activity in 1820. Whether he considered tight monetary policy a problem in 1821 or 1822 is less clear. At the very least, he thought monetary contraction had aggravated the agricultural crisis by causing corn prices to fall an additional 10 percent (2 Mar. 1821, 8:350; 19 Mar. 1821, 5:95; 11 Dec. 1821, 9:122–123; 25 Jan. 1822, 9:152; 7 May 1822, 5:165).

Ten percent is a formidable deflation. Ricardo allowed for so severe a monetary contraction because reports from the Stamp Office indicated that the country circulation had fallen by half:

The country circulation is I believe very much reduced, and I trust it is issued by bankers of character and property. I have not much fear of their being shaken by a return to specie payments (5 Mar. 1822, 9:176).

The whole amount of circulation, at the present moment, both in London and the country, does not probably much exceed 32 millions, of which there are nearly 16 millions of Bank of England notes of 5 pounds and above, 7,500,000 of sovereigns, and nine millions of country Bank notes. If this be true there has been little or no falling off in the amount of Bank of England notes and coin together since 1819, but country Bank notes have diminished to the amount of 7,500,000£ ... How badly has this business been managed! (9 June 1822, 9:201–202).

The Stamp Office estimated that the country circulation declined from £15.7 million in 1819 to £8.4 million in 1822 (see App. B.1). It was not until the investigation of the Committee of Secrecy on the Bank of England Charter in 1832 that Parliament obtained data from the banks themselves. Henry Burgess, representing the banks, reported that after Parliament passed the Resumption Act the country circulation declined at most 12 percent – far less than originally believed.

Possessed of accurate information about the country circulation, Ricardo could have opposed the inflationists more effectively. As it was, when Baring called for devaluation of the currency by the adoption of a bimetallic standard (*Hansard* 2s, 4:523–529, 1317–1328), or when Baring and Attwood together urged that the Resumption Act be overturned (*Hansard* 2s, 5:91–130), Ricardo was obliged to refer to alternative explanations for the fall of prices and, by a circuitous course of reasoning, he argued that monetary contraction had not caused more than 10 percent deflation. His alternative explanations focused on the increased supply of agricultural produce beginning in 1820.

Nonmonetary Causes of Low Corn Prices

British corn prices were extremely volatile in the years 1813 through 1823, ranging from a high of 128s. per quarter to a low of 38s.[47] Attending this volatility, two periods of ruinously low prices occurred from fall 1813 to spring 1816 and from fall 1820 through 1822. The second period is relevant to resumption.

When prices collapsed in 1820, Ricardo blamed the decrease on a glut of domestic corn. However, he was at a loss to explain how farmers so grossly miscalculated the demand for their output (9 Oct. 1820, 8:277; Dec. 1820, 8:334n). He did not learn about the extent of the harvest of 1820 or the quantities of Irish corn being imported until the hearings of the 1821 Agricultural Committee. The committee documented to Ricardo's satisfaction, and often at his instance, that "abundant harvests...the vast importations from Ireland...[and] the late improvements[48] in agriculture" combined with extensions of the margins of cultivation[49] caused the glut of corn (19 Mar. 1821, 5:94; 1822, 4:259). He repeatedly mentioned these causes in private correspondence, Parliamentary debates, and in *Protection to Agriculture* (4:259–261; 5:108, 125, 151; 8:369; 9:157).

Unlike the inflationists, who argued that higher tariffs or repeal of the Resumption Act would end the agricultural crisis, Ricardo thought that the 1815 Corn Law ensured both agricultural depressions and unstable prices.[50] Under the corn laws, the margin of cultivation had been extended – and real production costs increased – to the point that British

---

[47] "An Account Showing the Respective Weeks in which the Average Price of Wheat Was Highest and Lowest," *Parliamentary Papers* 1826–1827, 16:13, MF 29.128.

[48] Technical progress in the methods of cultivation did not contribute to the agricultural depression, because these changes led to reductions in production costs. Technical improvements did, however, lead eventually to lower corn prices.

[49] The margin of cultivation increased during the war, contracted in the 1813–1816 agricultural depression, then increased again in response to a prolonged period of high corn prices. Wheat prices surpassed 70s. in May 1816 and remained high, selling for 73s. per quarter even in Sept. 1820.

[50] In *Protection to Agriculture* (1822), "the weight of emphasis was placed by Ricardo upon the excessive grain-price fluctuations engendered by the protective system...[And] In the Commons a very great deal of attention was paid by Ricardo to the question of corn price instability due to protection" (Hollander 1979, 553, 601, 647).

farmers could never profitably export to the Continent: "It was certainly desirable that those engaged in the production of corn should have a vent when an excess of supply existed. When two or three good harvests followed in succession, we might, if prices were at all on a level with those on the continent, export it after a fall of three or four shillings a quarter; but at present there must be a destructive fall before it could be sent abroad" (8 Feb. 1821, 5:74). If the harvest was abundant, farmers were ruined because their produce was dumped wholly on the home market, and domestic demand was inelastic. If the harvest failed, prices were exorbitant, but even then, prosperity was short-lived. The ports closed to foreign corn at prices below 80s. per quarter of wheat. When prices exceeded 80s. the ports opened to unlimited, duty-free importation, that often caused the home market to be "overwhelmed with foreign corn" (2 Mar. 1821, 8:350).

To reduce the volatility of prices, Ricardo called for the repeal of the corn laws. He argued that domestic output was too high and that if British agriculture was to become profitable, large tracts of marginal land would have to be withdrawn from cultivation: "He agreed with an observation of a Noble Person [Lord Liverpool] in another place, that part of the distress was owing to too much corn being produced, and agriculture must lessen its produce so as to suit the demand . . . It had been said that importation would throw the whole of the lands out of cultivation. But this was assuming that the remunerating price was for every grower the same; whereas, corn was raised in some lands at 40s. and in others at not less than 70s." (7 Mar. 1821, 5:84–85). "Open the ports, admit foreign grain," he said in May 1820, "and you drive this land [poor or unprofitable soils] out of cultivation; a less remunerating price would then do for the more productive lands" (5:49). He restated his position in *Protection to Agriculture* (1822), attributing low corn prices to "unusually abundant . . . harvests of 1819 and 1820," in addition to "importations from Ireland [that] were unusually great" (4:260). He also observed that "if the [corn] price obtained be less than remunerative, profits will be depressed, or will entirely disappear . . . [and] capital will be withdrawn from the land and the supply will gradually conform to the demand" (4:219). Ricardo understood the risks of eliminating the corn laws, including the risk that landlords and farmers – who had invested millions in farming – would be ruined. For this reason he recommended a gradual dismantling of the protective system (13 Oct. 1819, 8:103; 6 May 1820, 5:44).

Concerning the effects of the 1820–1822 agricultural depression on aggregate economic activity, Ricardo recognized that the fall in corn prices had not caused a general depression.[51] Writing to James Mill, he observed that "if the labouring class, in Agriculture, and Manufactures, are doing well, we must console ourselves for the misfortunes of landlords and tenants – they form but a small proportion of the whole population, and it is no small comfort to reflect that the losses they sustain are more than made up by the prosperity of other capitalists" (9 July 1821, 9:13). Similar statements appear in his correspondence of 1822 and 1823 (9:158, 315). Ricardo also published his views in *Protection to Agriculture*, especially Section 5, which is a direct attack on the inflationists. He began by showing that the fall in corn prices was greater than anything that could have been caused by the Bank of England. He then turned to the profitable state of merchants and manufacturers: "How have they contrived to exempt themselves from this desolating storm? The answer is plain, there is no truth in the allegation. Agriculture has been depressed by causes of which the currency forms only a little part. The peculiar hardships which the landed interest are suffering . . . will continue only while the supply of produce exceeds the demand" (4:230). His arguments had much force. Tax abstracts and commercial reports attested that the 1819–1820 general depression had ended by the third quarter of 1820 (see App. E.2).[52] By comparison, the decline in corn prices and the attending agricultural depression did not begin until October 1820.

Conclusion

Ricardo's analysis of conditions from 1815 through 1823 reflect his detailed knowledge of the shocks that actually occurred. He rebutted Malthus' claim that the agricultural depression of 1813 to 1816 caused a decline in aggregate economic activity; tax abstracts proved that Britain's economy expanded for almost two years after corn prices collapsed. His analysis of the problems associated with the adjustment from wartime to peacetime patterns of final demand is exemplary. Ricardo's remarks

---

[51] He consistently adhered to this view. In the 1820 edition of the *Principles*, for instance, Malthus described a hypothetical situation where, in response to a fall in the price of raw produce, "many labourers will be thrown out of work [and] wages, after a period of great distress, will generally be lower in proportion." Ricardo responded: "If the supply be increased without any diminution of the supply of other things, it cannot diminish the power of the country generally to employ labour, but on the contrary must increase it" (2:229–230).

[52] The amount of money collected from customs and excise taxes increased little after 1820, but this is because tax rates were reduced by one-third from 1821 to 1825.

about "misallocated capital" after 1817 never refer to the transition from wartime to peacetime production – contrary to the interpretation of secondary critics and Malthus. Rather, he believed that merchants miscalculated the demand for both imports and exports in 1819, and that the margin of cultivation in agriculture had been overextended. Throughout his analysis of postwar conditions, Ricardo allowed for the nonneutrality of money. He recognized how the management of the inconvertible pound amplified both depressions and inflationary periods. This fact was central to his support for the Resumption Act. He anticipated that the Bank would return to gold with little difficulty. In this he was disappointed, for the Bank kept interest rates unnecessarily high. Ricardo allowed that a monetary contraction after 1819 caused a drop in prices of perhaps 10 percent. His calculations were based on the best available information about the operations of country banks and the circulation of banknotes and coin. Ricardo's analysis of postwar conditions – being a well-informed account of events that actually occurred – does not lend credence to the idea that he accepted Say's identity.

SIX

The Law of Markets

In the secondary literature, the central question surrounding Ricardo's application of the law of markets is whether he used the identity or the equality version of the law. To reiterate, the difference in the two versions is this: Say's identity is the description of a barter economy where the production of commodities always and everywhere creates an effectual demand. There may be excess supplies of particular commodities, but if so, there are offsetting excess demands in other sectors, so that a universal glut never occurs. Say's equality, in contrast, allows for a temporary glut of all commodities. Aggregate demand may not be sufficient to purchase the economy's output at the current price level, in which case there will be an interval while prices are falling before consumers purchase the surplus. Markets eventually clear, but much distress can be experienced in the interim.

Ricardo applied the law of markets in several contexts – but not consistently. His analysis of postwar conditions used the equality version of the law. He recognized unemployment; he gave valid reasons for its occurrence; and he explained the adjustments necessary to return Britain to prosperity. With respect to the short-term effects of fiscal policy, his model is less sophisticated. "Model" might overstate the level of Ricardo's critique for he assumed full employment with no underlying analysis. He could have reasoned, along lines consistent with Say's equality, that the price mechanism, free of public interference, can eliminate unemployment. Resources may be temporarily idle, but if wages and prices adjust quickly enough, expansionary fiscal measures are unnecessary. This analysis is not present. Instead, Ricardo assumed away the underlying problem and then concluded that no remedy was required. The sufficiency of aggregate demand in the secular period is another theme in Ricardo's works. The issue comes to the fore in Chapter 21 of his *Principles*, "Effects of Accumulation," where he rebuts Adam Smith's argument that England would eventually reach stationarity – a state of zero economic growth – because of the "increasing competition of capitals." Ricardo maintained that there could be no lack of aggregate demand in the long run. Similar reasoning appears in his *Notes* and unfinished review of William Blake's *Observations on the Effects Produced by the Expenditure of Government* (1823). The final context in which Ricardo addressed the law of markets was his critique of oversaving. For Malthus, oversaving referred to the theoretical possibility that the national investment program might proceed too rapidly, leading to the production of commodities for which there was no demand at current prices. Ricardo rejected the idea on two grounds: he did not believe people invested irrationally and he thought Malthus' speculations bore no connection to current conditions.

Expansionary Fiscal Policy

The central theme in Ricardo's statements about fiscal policy is that governments waste resources, except when developing infrastructure, and thereby impede the accumulation of capital and slow the rate of growth of the demand for labor. This theme has generated little controversy in the literature, for it relates to long-run economic growth and has no implications for the short-term effects of expansionary fiscal measures. There is nothing discrepant between a model that allows for unemployment – and perhaps recognizes the need for fiscal stimulus – and a model in which public extravagance over the long term impedes the accumulation of capital. What remains contested is whether Ricardo's statements about the short-term effects of fiscal policy – statements usually associated with the "Treasury view"[1] – imply that he adhered to Say's identity.

When Ricardo considered public spending he was not concerned primarily with the immediate effects of this expenditure on the level

---

[1] The "Treasury view" is the proposition that an increase in government spending will not cause an increase in aggregate economic activity. For the proposition to obtain, an economy must have one or both of these characteristics: (1) every increase of government spending is offset by a corresponding decrease in consumption and private investment so that expansionary fiscal measures cause no increase in aggregate demand and/or (2) the economy's resources are fully employed so that an increase in government spending changes the pattern of final demand but has no effect on aggregate output and instead causes inflation.

of aggregate output, but rather with the question of whether high government spending, financed ultimately by high taxes, was likely to impede or encourage the accumulation of capital.[2] It was his conviction that "by the profuse expenditure of Government, and of individuals, and by loans . . . the country is impoverished; every measure, therefore, which is calculated to promote public and private economy, will relieve the public distress" (Ricardo, 1:246).[3] As Baumol and Kates have observed, Ricardo's argument centered on the classical distinction between productive and unproductive expenditure, productive expenditure (investment) being the engine of economic growth (Baumol 1997, 219; Kates 1997, 197). He opposed public extravagance on the grounds that a deficient national capital, relative to a growing labor supply, was one of the "permanent" causes of the postwar distress. Not only did government expenditure impede the accumulation of capital by taking resources "from the productive industry of the country" and diverting them to "the support of unproductive labourers" (1:244), but also the consequent high taxes encouraged capitalists to emigrate, thereby withdrawing their entrepreneurial abilities and their capital.[4] The reduction of capital, in turn, "diminished the demand for labour [and was] injurious to the working classes" (8:168–169). Ricardo did not oppose taxation and public spending in all instances. He was ready to endorse the development of infrastructure: "Taxes for the benefit of trade itself such as for Docks, canals, Roads, etc . . . are on a different footing from all other taxes and produce very different effects, they may and generally do promote production instead of discouraging it" (28 Jan. 1820, 8:155). Apart from infrastructure projects, he considered public spending uniformly wasteful.

Ricardo was particularly hostile to debt-financed expenditures, for he believed that households treat public bonds as part of net wealth,

---

[2] Churchman concludes that "were Ricardo to have conceded the short-run inapplicability of the Law of Markets, this might be interpreted as opening the floodgates of theoretical support for public extravagance" (Churchman 1999, 654). Her arguments reinforce an earlier interpretation by Tucker (1960, 177).

[3] Ricardo expressed a similar view to McCulloch in 1818 after his article on Ricardo's *Principles* appeared in the *Edinburgh Review*: "I am as great a friend to economy in Governments as you can wish me to be; every guinea that is spent unnecessarily I think is a public wrong, and I should therefore be sorry to give the slightest encouragement to waste and extravagance" (7:286).

[4] "[In] a country which has accumulated a large debt . . . it becomes in the interest of every contributor to withdraw his shoulder from the burthen, and to shift this payment from himself to another; and the temptation to remove himself and his capital to another country, where he will be exempted from such burthens, becomes at last irresistible" (Ricardo, 1:247–248).

ignoring the future tax liability entailed by public deficits. (In modern parlance, he rejected the idea of "Ricardian equivalence.") Public finance affects private spending. Households are more inclined to consume unproductively – and less inclined to invest productively – if the government finances its operations through debts rather than taxes.

> It must not be inferred that I consider the system of borrowing as the best calculated to defray the extraordinary expenses of the State. It is a system which tends to make us less thrifty – to blind us to our real situation. . . . By the system of loans, [the taxpayer] is called upon to pay only the interest of this £100, or £5 per annum, and considers that he does enough by saving this £5 from his expenditure, and then deludes himself with the belief, that he is as rich as before (Ricardo, 3:247).

On the other hand, if the government financed expenditures through taxes, households would attempt to save to the amount of the tax. Ricardo assumed that a household's consumption is inversely proportionate to its tax burden, that for every increase of taxes by £100 there is an offsetting reduction in private consumption of £100. This seemed correct based on his quasiempirical observation that households are loath to reduce their net wealth.[5]

> The desire which every man has to keep his station in life, and to maintain his wealth at the height which it has once attained, occasions most taxes, whether laid on capital or on income, to be paid from income [consequently] If he had been required to pay 100 l. as a tax on income, on wine, on horses, or on servants, he would probably have diminished, or rather not increased his expenditure by that sum (*Principles* 1817, 1:153).

> If an individual were called upon to pay 1000 l. to the income-tax, he would probably endeavour to save the whole of it from his income; he would do no more if, in lieu of this war-tax, a loan had been raised, for the interest of which he would have been called upon to pay only 50 l. income-tax. The war-taxes, then, are more economical; for when they are paid, an effort is made to save to the amount of the whole expenditure of the war, leaving the national capital undiminished (*Funding System* 1819, 4:187).

It is doubtful, as an empirical matter, whether taxes cause a pound-for-pound drop in private consumption. Ricardo's statements about tax-financed expenditures indicate, in modern terminology, that he assumed a marginal propensity to consume from disposable income of one. More likely the marginal propensity to consume out of disposable income is less than one so that an increase of taxes by £100 causes households to reduce consumption by less than £100. But given Ricardo's assumption,

---

[5] This assumption by Ricardo has been noted in the literature (Roberts 1942, 258; Sowell 1974, 67).

tax-financed government expenditures cannot raise the level of national output. Public spending changes the pattern of aggregate demand but there is no change in the level of aggregate expenditure.

Ricardo addressed the short-term effects of specific public expenditure programs in two instances. The first involved Parliament's loan of Exchequer bills to support private credit during the financial panic of 1793. The second involved a loan of Exchequer bills to the manufacturing districts of Scotland during the depression of 1819. The second instance is more familiar to readers.

The depression of 1819 caused severe hardships in the southwestern Scottish counties of Ayr, Renfrew, and Lanark. The reason for the trouble was that in Glasgow, the chief city of the region, 60 percent of the families were employed in trade and manufacturing (Marshall, 1833, 1:13). These were the industries most affected by the fall in the demand for exports. There were no poor rates upon which to support the unemployed, and private contributions were soon exhausted (16 Dec. 1819, *Hansard* 1s, 41:1217). Citizens from Renfrew and Glasgow appealed to Parliament for aid.

Ricardo opposed any relief for Scotland. He cautioned the House against "employing capital in the formation of roads and canals" because "the capital thus employed must be withdrawn from some other quarter" (16 Dec. 1819, 5:32). Based on this text, Hutchison concludes, "Here again is Ricardo urging upon the House of Commons the obvious practical conclusion to be drawn from the Law of Markets, that public works could not possibly help to remedy depression ... the doctrine against public works was, of course, eventually to become by 1929 'the orthodox Treasury dogma steadfastly held' " (Hutchison 1952, 75–76). Hollander also concedes that Ricardo adhered to a full employment model (Hollander 1979, 515).

The question before Parliament was whether to adopt a measure, such as the 1817 Employment of the Poor Bill, by which Exchequer bills would be loaned to municipalities in Scotland as a means to finance public works (16 Dec. 1819, *Hansard* 1s, 41:1225). The municipalities were expected to resell the bills, or use them as collateral to obtain loans, to fund "plans of artificial labour, such as the making of roads, &c" that would create jobs (*Hansard* 1s, 41:1217). Those in Parliament who opposed the plan were concerned that public assistance might interfere with unemployed laborers finding new jobs in the private sector – their being "dispersed and engaged in other Pursuits," as Prime Minister Liverpool observed (Hilton 1977, 83). Liverpool's sentiments were typical. There was a widespread bias against public works on the ground that "they merely diverted resources from a more profitable private sector" (Hilton 1977, 83–84). Ricardo shared this view. He commented that a loan of Exchequer bills to Lanark, Renfrew, or Glasgow to finance public works would "withdraw [capital] from some other quarter."

Ricardo's statements are based on a model of full employment. This fact is remarkable given that he was informed about the current depression and the existence of widespread unemployment. It is possible, as Hutchison stated, that Ricardo recommended public policies based on Say's identity without considering whether the model was consistent with current conditions. An alternative explanation is that Ricardo assumed that laborers displaced from manufacturing would efficiently relocate to other sectors and that public works would only impede the adjustment process. I cannot say that the alternative reading is correct, for there is no textual evidence as to Ricardo's underlying thoughts. He describes a situation of full employment – and nothing more.

In the event, orders for Scottish goods increased soon after the Parliamentary debate in question. By June of 1820 manufactures in the vicinity of Glasgow were returning to regular employment:

It is particularly gratifying to be able to state that the trade of this town continues in progressive improvement. Commercial men are gradually extending their business and are daily getting fairer prospects. Weavers for every kind of fine plain work are in considerable request. The wages of weaving are a little higher (*Edinburgh Magazine*, June 1820, 579; reprinted from the *Glasgow Paper*).

We again notice an improvement in the demand for British manufactures. The advices from Germany continue to announce large sales at the different fairs . . . the simultaneous orders from the West Indies, the United States and the Continent of Europe must have greatly lightened the home market (*Edinburgh Magazine*, June 1820, 579; reprinted from the *Glasgow Chronicle*).

Several manufacturing houses could employ many more weavers than they can find at the present prices (*Edinburgh Magazine*, June 1820, 579; reprinted from the *Glasgow Journal*).

Taking into account the lag of several months between the debate of 16 December 1819 and the point at which Renfrew and Lanark counties and the city of Glasgow launched their relief works, and taking into account the fact that Scottish manufacturers returned to normal production by mid-1820, the succor brought by Parliament to the unemployed of Glasgow and its surrounding counties cannot have been great.

In circumstances similar to those of 1819, the government granted loans of Exchequer bills in 1793 to recover Britain's commerce from financial panic. Bills were loaned to private firms in financial straits. The firms sold the bills – or used them as collateral to obtain loans – and with the proceeds paid employees, bought supplies, and made other expenditures. Ricardo knew that during the panic of 1793 banknotes were hoarded. He also knew that by the government's loan of Exchequer bills, and by their subsequent sale or use as collateral, banknotes that had been hoarded returned to circulation: "If the public [purchased Exchequer bills], then was a portion of the circulating medium of the country which had been withdrawn from circulation [i.e., hoarded] again brought forth by the credit of government being pledged for the parties requiring relief" (*Notes on Bentham* 1810, 3:349). The purchasing power represented by banknotes was withdrawn from aggregate demand when the notes were hoarded; that element of demand was again made effectual when households relinquished their hoards in exchange for Exchequer bills. Ricardo did not explicitly make the link between hoarding and aggregate demand, but it is consistent with his analysis. Moreover, his assessment of the Treasury's policy in 1793 allows for the possibility that by the sale of Exchequer bills the purchasing power latent in private hoards could have been transferred to public coffers, enabling the government to spend and thereby raising the level of aggregate demand.

The secondary literature cites two further examples of Ricardo's opposition to expansionary fiscal measures: his letters to Malthus written in January 1817 that describe the effect of private relief works on the employment of the poor and his testimony before the House of Lords Committee on Resumption when he urged Parliament to not restrict the money supply so greatly as to cause a trade surplus. Excerpts from the letters to Malthus read as follows:

I want to hear your opinion of the measure lately adopted for the relief of the poor. I am not one of those who think that the raising of funds for the purpose of employing the poor is a very efficacious mode of relief, as it diverts those funds from other employments which would be equally if not more productive to the community (3 Jan. 1817, 7:116).

[The present relief works take capital] out of the hands of those who know best how to employ it, to encourage industry of a different kind and under the superintendence of those who know nothing of the wants and demands of mankind and blindly produce cloth or stockings of which we have already too much, or improve roads which nobody wishes to travel (24 Jan. 1817, 7:121).

Hutchison assumes the letters pertain to public works programs and from this concludes "how unhistorical it would be to defend Ricardo on the ground that he was concerned simply with the abstract implications of a pure hypothetical model. He applies the model unmodified to current political issues . . . commenting, at the beginning of 1817, on current policies of relief works" (Hutchison 1953, 89). Hollander likewise infers that "Ricardo drew some clear policy deductions from the basic [full employment] assumption. Thus, in correspondence, the 'Treasury view' is stated in the following terms"; Hollander then cites the two letters (1979, 515).

The letters refer to private charitable ventures, not to public works. The century's first public relief program was submitted to Parliament in April 1817 with the Employment of the Poor Bill; Ricardo's extant writings do not refer to this bill. Ricardo expected that private contributions for the poor diverted expenditures from one channel to another, without increasing the demand for labor. Because he believed that hoarding only occurred during financial crises, the alternative to charity was not hoarding but investing or consuming. Thus private relief works altered the pattern but not the level of aggregate demand. His statements require the assumption of uniform factor proportions, not Say's identity.

As to the second example, Ricardo's testimony before the House of Lords Committee on Resumption set out his concern that the Bank of England would restrict the money supply too severely as it returned to gold. The larger the hoard the Bank chose to acquire, the more it would be necessary for the Bank to curb its circulation. To minimize the Bank's hoard, Ricardo proposed that banknotes be convertible into gold ingots rather than into sovereigns. He surmised that people would be less inclined to withdraw the 60 oz. ingots.

One member of the House of Lords committee took exception to Ricardo's ingot plan. The member wanted the Bank to accumulate a hoard of £18 million; this required an addition of £15 million to the Bank's current £3 million. The member reasoned that £15 million in gold could only be brought to England if the country ran a trade surplus (Ricardo, 5:433).

Question: Suppose we were to resume Cash Payments under a Plan which required that the Bank should provide themselves with only Three Millions of Treasure, would not there be a Demand for 15 Millions less of the Produce and Manufactures of this Country, than would be created by imposing on the Bank the Necessity of providing 18 millions?

Answer: Yes, there would; but as we should export these Commodities without procuring a Return of any other which would contribute to our Advantage, the Gold would not be a very desirable Importation.

The exchange between Ricardo and the member is sometimes cited as evidence of Ricardo's Treasury view of fiscal policy.[6]

Question: Supposing we were to adopt a Plan which should annihilate the demand for 15 millions of our Manufactures, do you suppose that that Portion of Wealth would at all exist, in so far is it is composed of Manufacturing Labour?

Answer: I think it would . . .

Question: Do you mean to say that an extra Demand for the commodities of the Country would not produce any Increase in its Manufactures?

Answer: I should very much doubt whether it would . . .

Question: Will not a great Diminution of the Demand for Commodities prevent his obtaining those Advantages from his Capital, which a great Increase of the Demand for them would secure?

Answer: It may, as far as regards the particular Commodity; but if there is less Production of one Commodity, the Production of another would in a Degree be encouraged (5:434–438).

The testimony does not relate to fiscal policy. Ricardo simply argued that curtailing the money supply enough to cause a trade surplus of £15 million would not be beneficial. It would cause distress and unemployment – and that is what he hoped the ingot plan would preclude.

Aggregate Demand in the Secular Period

One proposition under the rubric of the law of markets is that in the secular period there can be no shortage of aggregate demand, no matter how vastly a country's output increases. In the *Wealth of Nations*, Adam Smith expressed the view that the greater the opulence of a country – as measured by its national capital – the lower the returns to that capital. He reasoned that consumption demand does not keep pace in the long run with the increase in output occasioned by investment. Secular stagnation is thus inevitable because consumption falls short of the level that would purchase the output of a fully developed economy at prices that afford capitalists the incentive to further investment.

The increase of stock, which raises wages, tends to lower profit. When the stocks of many rich merchants are turned into the same trade, their mutual competition naturally tends to lower its profit; and when there is a like increase of stock in

---

[6] Hutchison faults Ricardo for his analysis: "we have Ricardo giving us the Classical Law of Markets in action. It is quite impossible that he is simply concerned with an abstract 'model' or 'first approximation' in which he is excusably omitting to state explicitly all his simplifying assumptions. He is discussing economic policy with practical men in the depressed times of 1819" (Hutchison 1952, 74).

all the different trades carried on in the same society, the same competition must produce the same effect in them all (Smith 1776, 100).

The province of Holland, on the other hand, in proportion to the extent of its territory and the number of its people, is a richer country than England. The government there borrows at two per cent., and private people of good credit at three. . . . the diminution of profits is the natural effect of its prosperity, or of a greater stock being employed in it than before (105).

Smith observed that the greater the investment in a single industry the more competitive that industry becomes; with increasing competition, prices fall, and the profit rate in that industry diminishes. He reasoned that the same holds true in the aggregate, and that additions to the national capital stock inevitably erode profits.

As a practical matter, Smith believed that only China had reached the point of secular stagnation. China reached stationarity sooner than England, and at a lower standard of living than would occur in England, owing to the inferior character of that country's laws and institutions. The specific faults Smith identified were that China "neglects or despises foreign commerce" and "the poor or the owners of small capitals enjoy scarce [security], but are liable, under the pretence of justice, to be pillaged and plundered at any time by the inferior mandarines" (109).

Ricardo challenged Smith's statements about the inevitability of secular stagnation. The error of Smith's analysis lay in assuming that a result observed at the microeconomic level necessarily obtains in the aggregate. Ricardo pointed out that investment in the aggregate need not depress prices because every addition to national output creates an increased ability to demand and in the long run this demand will be effectual.

M. Say has most satisfactorily shewn that there is no amount of capital which may not be employed in a country, because demand is only limited by production (1:290).

Too much of a particular commodity may be produced of which there may be such a glut in the market, as not to repay the capital expended on it; but this cannot be the case with respect to all commodities (1:292).

Profits do not fall secularly unless there occurs a rise in the cost of subsistence. High levels of investment can reduce profits temporarily if the new capitals raise the demand for labor: "There is only one case, and that will be temporary, in which the accumulation of capital with a low price of food may be attended with a fall of profits; and that is, when the funds for the maintenance of labour increase much more rapidly than

population – wages will then be high, and profits low" (1:292). But a high
demand for labor is no threat to profits in the long term.

Other instances where Ricardo addressed the secular sufficiency of aggregate demand are his *Notes* and unfinished review of William Blake's
*Observations on the Effects Produced by the Expenditure of Government
During the Restriction of Cash Payments* (1823). The central premise
of Blake's *Observations* is that neither the increase in prices from 1797
through 1815 nor the postwar crises in trade, manufacturing, and agriculture were monetary phenomena. He attributed wartime inflation solely
to the high level of the government's wartime expenditures and accorded
no role to the monetary policy of the Bank of England. Similarly, Blake
believed that when military expenditures were reduced at the end of the
war, there was not sufficient demand in the private sector to consume national output and that, as a result, Britain's economy fell into a permanent
depression:

We have seen landed proprietors without rents; farmers and manufacturers without a market; the monied capitalist ready to lend, and the merchant not wanting
to borrow; a redundant capital, yet a redundant population; and the industrious
poor compelled to apply, like mendicants, at the parish workhouse.... We have
witnessed a depression of the exchanges. We have had the market price of gold
exceeding the Mint price.... And all this accompanied by a general rise of price
in most of the articles of consumable produce....

I have, however, perfectly convinced my own mind that all the results above
specified may have arisen from causes not necessarily connected with an alteration
in the value of currency; and, moreover, that such other causes are not hypothetical
merely, but have been in actual operation....

I have very little doubt that the whole of these appearances may be traced,
and will be found to have originated in the enormous expenditure occasioned by
the late war (Blake 1823, 1–5).

Blake argued that demand is inevitably deficient because consumers are
too strongly inclined to invest. As capital accumulates, commodities are
produced for which there is no demand.

It appears to me that the error lies in supposing, first, that the whole capital of
the country is fully occupied; and secondly, that there is immediate employment
for successive accumulations of capital as it accrues from saving. I believe there
are at all times some portions of capital... lying wholly dormant in the form of
goods for which there is not sufficient demand. I believe, too, that when capital
accumulates rapidly from savings, it is not always practicable to find new modes
of employing it. Now if these dormant portions and savings could be transferred
into the hands of government in exchange for its annuities, they would become
sources of new demand (Blake 1823, 54–55; reprinted in Ricardo, 4:340).

Blake relied on the concept of the "increasing competition of capitals," which he expressly borrowed from Smith's *Wealth of Nations* (Blake 1823, 57). Hoarding is not part of Blake's model. Instead, he envisioned the ever-increasing production of consumer goods for which there would be no demand. The output of consumer goods rises because households invest in capital goods, but there is no demand for these goods because households are investing rather than consuming. To achieve an equilibrium between the quantities of goods produced and the demand for them – and therefore in order to raise the rate of profits – Blake proposed that the government borrow from capitalists and then consume unproductively. In other words, the government diverts resources from private investment to public consumption.

The purchase of an annuity is a complete proof that the owner of the capital has not the means of employing it advantageously. The loan contractors thus become the channel through which all the accumulations of capital that are feebly employed, or that are without employment, find their way into the hands of government; whence they immediately pass into a state of complete activity amongst the producers who furnish the warlike stores, or such other commodities as the subordinate agents of government require . . . The tendency [of government expenditure] would be to relieve all capitalists from excess of stock; to create a demand for their goods, whilst it diminished the competition of new capitalists, and thus increased both prices and profits (Blake 1823, 62–63).

Ricardo disagreed with the theory behind Blake's argument. He rejected the increasing competition of capitals thesis, for he knew that increased production gave rise to an increased ability to demand commodities. And he thought this demand would be effectual: "It is not necessary that in such a country as England new tastes and new wants should be generated – the old tastes are sufficient for the purpose. Tastes and wants exist already in a sufficient degree, give but the means of satisfying them and demand follows" (Ricardo, 4:344). Saving is also a source of effectual demand because it "becomes a fund for future production" – that is, savings are invested (4:343). In response to Blake's claim that people might become sated with corn and cloth and that the surplus production of these would be thrown away, Ricardo pointed out the distinction between a specific industry and the aggregate economy. There may be "a glut of 2 or 10 commodities" but "there cannot be a glut of all" (4:344).

Ricardo also identified the many factual errors in the *Observations*. First of all, Blake argued that wartime inflation and the fall of the pound on the foreign exchange were not caused by excess paper money but by "internal" and "foreign" expenditures by the British government. His theory ignored the fact that the circulation of the Bank of England increased from £9.8 million in 1797 to £27 million in 1815; it also took no account of the corresponding increase in the circulation of the country banks (Marshall 1833, 179–180). Ricardo knew Blake's account was inaccurate. He had shown years earlier in the *High Price of Bullion* (1810) how the increase in the Bank circulation corresponded directly with the fall in the foreign exchange rate and the rise in the price of gold (3:76–78, 121).

The second half of Blake's *Observations* contends that the reduction of military expenditures at the end of the war caused the "distress that has prevailed since its termination" (Blake 1823, 120). His account is a plausible explanation of the twenty-four months following Waterloo. Ricardo also allowed that capital and labor were not fully employed after the war because of the cessation of war-related expenditures. However, Blake extended his analysis to 1822, ignoring every significant event in the intervening period. He provided no account of the agricultural prosperity that began in mid-1816 and continued into 1819. He did not address the boom in foreign trade and manufacturing from mid-1817 through 1818, or observe that foreign demand collapsed in 1819. He also ignored the return of prosperity in foreign trade and manufacturing in mid-1820. Finally, Blake ridiculed the idea that the abundant harvests of 1820 and 1821 contributed to the second agricultural depression:

The universality of this distress is not to be accounted for on any other supposition [than a general diminution of demand], and can hardly be attributed to abundant harvests for so many years together, in all the different quarters of the globe. More especially as there does not appear to be any conclusive evidence of such abundance, except what is inferred from the lowness of price. Moreover, the lost prices are not confined to corn alone. It is well known that manufactures are less in quantity, and less in price also.... To what then can we attribute this universal effect, but to the general diminution of demand?... To those who imagine consumption not to be a necessary ingredient of demand, and that in order to make a market for commodities, it is only necessary to produce more, these phenomena offer problems not very easy of solution; nor is the difficulty less for those who conceive the previously existing capital to have been diminished by being converted into revenue. Accordingly, every drowning theorist has caught at the various straws that crossed him (Blake 1823, 93–94).

In a subsequent note, Blake criticized Ricardo for asserting that the price of corn was low owing to "a cycle of abundant harvests since the termination of the War" (Ricardo, 4:352).

Modern authors have overlooked the factual mistakes in Blake's *Observations*. Blaug assumes the work contains a theoretically sophisticated analysis of deficient aggregate demand and an empirically based explanation of the postwar crisis:

> The blind spots in Ricardo's thinking are strikingly illustrated by his critical comments on a pamphlet by William Blake which appeared in 1823. Blake was one of a number of writers in the deflationary phase of the bullionist controversy who argued that government spending during the war period had actually stimulated production and augmented capital; the conversion of idle funds into public expenditures by means of taxing "unproductive consumption," while it operated to increase prices, accelerated the rate of economic growth. Hence the postwar deflation was simply the result of the sudden decline in public spending.... Ricardo failed utterly to meet Blake's point that full employment of capital was simply being posited as an assumption (Blaug 1958, 78–79).

Corry describes Ricardo's *Notes on Blake* and the unfinished review as showing "that government spending could not be regarded as an addition to demand. Basically this involves the assumption of full employment, as the following quotation illustrates" (Corry 1962, 165):

> But can Mr Blake's proposition, that with the same capital by means of increased exertion and industry, the increased quantity of commodities, required by Government can be produced without occasioning any diminished supply of commodities in any other quarter? If industry be encouraged in one department it is discouraged in another. . . . If more warlike stores be produced more capital must be employed in that line whether the same labourers do more work or new labourers are employed (Ricardo, 4:356).

The passage assumes full employment, as Corry observes. But whether this is incorrect depends on the argument to which Ricardo was responding. If Blake refers to a potential lack of aggregate demand in the short run, then the assumption of full employment is in error. But if Blake refers to the sufficiency of demand in the secular period, the assumption of full employment is correct. Similarly, if Blake is taken to describe conditions in 1823, it was right to recognize that farmers and manufacturing laborers were fully employed.

Malthusian Oversaving

A preceding chapter described the debate between Ricardo and Malthus over the causes and duration of postwar crises. Malthus explained 'the' postwar depression in terms of deficient aggregate demand.[7] However,

---

[7] Malthus' explanation of 'the' postwar depression remained unchanged in later years except on two points: first, he no longer mentioned the country-banking crisis of 1814–1816;

both in his *Principles* (1820) and in correspondence with Ricardo after 1819, he also discussed the possibility that oversaving could result in falling commodity prices, low profits, and a reduction in the demand for labor. By "oversaving" Malthus referred to too rapid an investment program, not to hoarding. He thought that rapid investment could lead to an increase in production without a corresponding increase in aggregate demand. The upshot would be a fall in commodity prices and the idling of labor and capital:[8]

The consumption and demand occasioned by the persons employed in productive labour can never alone furnish a motive to the accumulation and employment of capital; and with regard to the capitalists themselves, together with the landlords and other rich persons, they have, by the supposition, agreed to be parsimonious, and by depriving themselves of their usual conveniences and luxuries to save from their revenue and add to their capital. Under these circumstances, I would ask, how it is possible to suppose that the increased quantity of commodities, obtained by the increased number of productive labourers would find purchasers (Malthus 1820, 352–353).

According to Malthus, capitalists invest by shifting labor from the production of consumption goods to the production of capital goods – or what was referred to as the "maintenance of productive labour" (352). The nominal purchasing power of the laborers does not change because they have only been reassigned tasks, "as far as the labourers are concerned, there would be no diminution of consumption or demand" (352). But the investment program expands the national capital stock, bringing with it a corresponding increase in production. Assuming that capitalists do not increase their consumption, but continue the investment program, aggregate demand will be insufficient to purchase the greater quantity of goods at current prices (352–353). Unsaleable commodities will, as a result, fall in price, eroding profits and causing unemployment:

In the case supposed there would evidently be an unusual quantity of commodities of all kinds in the market, owing to the unproductive labourers of the country having been converted, by the accumulation of capital, into productive labourers;

and second, he believed that some monetary deflation associated with resumption had occurred as the Bank directors "managed the matter of the currency so ill." Even so, Malthus retained his original position that "there is a further effect of the same kind both here and in America occasioned by the diminution of demand and relative excess of supply, and that more is attributed both to the paper and the Bank directors than belongs to them" (Malthus to Ricardo, 16 July 1821, 9:22).

[8] Hollander devotes an entire chapter to Malthus' views on sustainable growth (Hollander 1997, 514–526).

while the number of labourers altogether being the same, and the power and will to purchase for consumption among landlords and capitalists being by supposition diminished, commodities would necessarily fall in value, compared with labour, so as to lower profits almost to nothing, and to check for a time further production. But this is precisely what is meant by the term glut, which, in this case, is evidently general not partial (354).

Ricardo had been acquainted with Malthus' ideas about capital accumulation since their debate in 1814 concerning "the proportion of production to consumption" and whether effectual demand was likely to change in the same proportion and at the same time as aggregate production (Ricardo, 4:108, 111).[9] He recognized, though, that these discussions were purely theoretical and that Malthus was not explaining actual events in terms of a model that involved excessive investment. His view began to change, however, in early 1820. Writing to McCulloch after Malthus had "passed 2 or 3 hours with me last week," Ricardo complained: "Mr. Malthus continues stoutly to deny that demand[10] is only limited by production – he thinks that capital might be very mischievously augmented in a country... he maintained the opinions which he has long held, and which I cannot but think very far from being the correct ones" (28 Feb. 1820, 8:159–160). Within weeks of this meeting, in April 1820, he read Malthus' *Principles* and concluded – particularly because of arguments in the chapter "On the Immediate Causes of the Progress of Wealth" – that Malthus attributed the current economic distress to oversaving:

The most objectionable chapter in Mr. Malthus' book is that perhaps on the bad effects from too great accumulation of capital and the consequent want of demand for the goods produced. This doctrine naturally leads to the conclusion which Mr. Malthus draws from it. I could not have believed it possible, if I had not read it, that so enlightened a man as Mr. Malthus should recommend taxation as a remedy to our present distresses (Ricardo to McCulloch, 2 May 1820, 8:181).

I differ as much as I ever have done with you in your chapter on the effects of the accumulation of capital... Admitting that you are correct on this [page torn] inference you draw is the correct one... If individuals would not do their duty in

---

[9] Ricardo and Malthus discussed the topic of oversaving again in 1816 and 1817 (7:70, 122).

[10] Ricardo's observation that "demand is only limited by production" does not imply that he thought demand would always be at this limit. The statement means nothing more than that real aggregate demand cannot exceed the real aggregate supply. His intent is illustrated by an early letter to Mill: "You observe that the demand for corn is unlimited. It is clear that you attach a different meaning to the word demand to what I do. I should not call the mere desire of possessing a thing a demand for it, such desires are undoubtedly unlimited, but by demand I should understand a desire to possess with the power of purchasing. If so, demand is limited." (26 Sept. 1811, 6:56).

this respect, Government might be justified in raising taxes for the mere purpose of expenditure (Ricardo to Malthus, 4 May 1820, 8:185).

Ricardo's view of Malthus' position was reinforced by a second reading of the *Principles*, which he described in letters to both McCulloch and Trower: "Mr. Malthus speaks of an indisposition to consume being very common – I say it never exists any where, not even in South America to which he has so triumphantly alluded" (2 Aug. 1820, 8:216), and again, "You will not . . . adopt the great and fundamental error of Mr. Malthus, who contends that there may be at one and the same time a glut of all commodities, and that it may arise from a want of demand for all – he indeed argues that this is the specific evil under which we are at present suffering" (26 Sept. 1820, 8:257). Malthus did little to correct this misunderstanding, for in two letters of July 1821, he seemed to imply that oversaving was a factor in the depression:

We see in almost every part of the world vast powers of production which are not put into action, and I explain this phenomenon by saying that from the want of a proper distribution of the actual produce adequate motives are not furnished to continued production . . . I dont at all wish to deny that some persons or others are entitled to consume all that is produced; but the grand question is whether it is distributed in such a manner between the different parties concerned as to occasion the most effective demand for future produce: and I distinctly maintain that an attempt to accumulate very rapidly which necessarily implies a considerable diminution of unproductive consumption, by greatly impairing the usual motives to production must prematurely check the progress of wealth. This surely is the great practical question, and not whether we ought to call the sort of stagnation which would be thus occasioned a glut (7 July 1821, 9:10–11).

I think we may now be said to agree that a certain amount of unproductive expenditure on the part of those who have the means of setting industry in motion is necessary in order that they may be awarded a proper share of the produce; but you think that in the case of this country the evils we complain of do not in any degree arise from a partial approach to the kind of stagnation above described. On the propriety of applying our principles respecting profits to the case of this country I will not now enter into a discussion, but will only say that the symptoms appear to me exactly to resemble those which would arise from the sudden conversion of unproductive labour into productive, and the diminution of unproductive consumption (16 July 1821, 9:21).

Ricardo mistakenly concluded that Malthus analyzed events from 1820 onward in terms of his theory of sustainable growth, in the sense that capital had accumulated too rapidly, resulting in a glut of output with no corresponding increase in aggregate demand: "I should not make a protest against an increase of consumption, as a remedy to the stagnation of trade, if I thought, as you do, that we were now suffering from too great savings. As I have already said I do not see how stagnation of trade can arise from such a cause.... Such and such evils may exist, but the question is, do they exist now? I think not, none of the symptoms indicate that they do" (21 July 1821, 9:26–27). There are two aspects to Ricardo's response to Malthus. The first concerns whether, in principle, oversaving can occur. The second is his evaluation of whether oversaving was an immediate problem.

In principle, Ricardo considered Malthusian oversaving unrealistic because excessive investment, should it ever occur, would raise wages, transfer purchasing power from capitalists to laborers, and reduce profits, thereby eliminating the motive for further accumulation:

> If capital increased too rapidly for the population, instead of commanding seven eighths of the produce, they might command ninety nine hundredths, and thus there would be no motive for further accumulation. If every man were disposed to accumulate every portion of his revenue but what was necessary to his urgent wants such a state of things would be produced... But the condition of the labourer would then be most happy, for what can be more prosperous than the condition of him who has a commodity to sell for which there is almost unlimited demand while the supply is limited and increases at a comparatively slow rate (*Notes on Malthus* 1820, 2:302–303).

Say raised the same objection to Malthusian oversaving. His views are best articulated in the second of his *Letters to Thomas Robert Malthus on Political Economy* (1821). He cited, as did Ricardo, the third section of Chapter 7 of Malthus' *Principles of Political Economy*, titled "Of Accumulation." Say expressly distinguished between hoarding and saving, where by "saving" he meant investment: "a produce saved is a value withdrawn from an unproductive consumption to add it to the capital, that is, to that value which we consume, or cause to be consumed reproductively" (Say 1821, 36). The essence of his objection is that irrational investment does not occur: "Where the capitals become too abundant, the interest which the capitalists derive from them becomes too low to balance the privations they impose upon themselves by their savings. Safe employment for capital will be difficult to be found; capitals are employed abroad. The common course of nature puts a stop to many accumulations" (Say 1821, 37).

As for the contemporary situation, Ricardo did not consider inadequate consumption a problem, nor did he think there had been excessive investment: "There could be no adequate motive to push production to this length, and therefore it would never go so far ... you often appear to me to contend not only that production can go on so far without an adequate motive, but that it actually has done so lately, and that we are now suffering the consequences of it in stagnation of trade, in a want of employment for our labourers &c. &c., and the remedy you propose is an increase of consumption" (Ricardo to Malthus, 9 July 1821, 9:16). His answer to what he understood to be Malthus' explanation of the current situation was reasonable. He could not accept that oversaving contributed to the depression of 1819–1820 or to the subsequent agricultural crisis. He understood the causes of these events: the collapse of foreign demand in 1819 and a glut of corn in 1820. Moreover, he knew that tens of millions in capital had been withdrawn to the Continent in the decade following the war in consequence of the low profits, high taxes and high wage costs in Britain. And he attributed the sufferings of the working class, in part, to the resultant deficiency of capital relative to the domestic labor supply. That excessive investment was a problem under these conditions seemed absurd.

Ricardo's critique of Malthusian oversaving has been interpreted as evidence that he accepted an extreme version of the law of markets. Based on two passages from Ricardo's *Notes on Malthus*, Corry concludes that he "denied that saving could ever involve a deficiency of demand" (Corry 1958, 41).

By accumulation of capital is meant an increase of consumption by productive labourers instead of by unproductive labourers. Consumption is as certain in one case as in the other, the difference is only in the quantity of productions returned (Ricardo, 2:326–327).

Mr. Malthus never appears to remember that to save is to spend, as surely, as what he exclusively calls spending (2:449).

Both quotes refer to Chapter 7 of Malthus' *Principles*, "On the Progress of Wealth." In that chapter, Malthus advanced his theory that oversaving could produce a general glut of commodities. That Malthus used the term "saving" for investment is clear from the heading of Section 3 of Chapter 7 – "Of Accumulation, or the Saving from Revenue to add to Capital, considered as a Stimulus to the increase of Wealth."

Malthus' oversaving thesis assumes a chronic lack of consumption – owing to consumers being sated – and a pattern of irrational investment. Both assumptions seemed empirically flawed to Ricardo. As a financier, he knew that capitalists did not invest irrationally. And as for consumption in Britain, the evidence from tax abstracts and reports in the commercial press suggested that British consumers had healthy appetites:

It is material to consider whether the distressed state of our internal commerce has grown out of any diminution in our internal consumption.... I trust, that I shall satisfy the House, that there is no ground for believing that any part of the distress which pervades our internal commerce, has arisen from a reduction in the use of any of the great articles of consumption.... Comparing the actual consumption of the last year with the average consumption of the three years immediately preceding [based on tax reports];[11] the result of that comparison is, that, during the last year there has not only been no diminution, but, on the contrary, some increase in the home consumption (Parliamentary address, Lord Liverpool, 26 May 1820, *Hansard* 1s, 1:568–570).

Because the available data showed stable and increasing domestic consumption, even during depressed economic periods, Ricardo's argument that underconsumption was not occurring, had an empirical basis. However, allowing Malthus' assumptions about irrational investment and the inadequacy of consumer wants, Ricardo did not dispute his case for expansionary fiscal policy.[12]

Admitting that you are correct on this [tear] inference you draw is the correct one, and [tear] wise to encourage unproductive consumption. If individuals would not do their duty in this respect, Government might be justified in raising taxes for the mere purpose of expenditure (Ricardo to Malthus, 4 May 1820, 8:185).

If his views on this question be correct – if commodities can be so multiplied that there is no disposition to purchase and consume them, then undoubtedly the cure which he hesitatingly recommends is a very proper one. If the people entitled to consume will not consume the commodities produced, themselves, nor cause them to be consumed by others, with a view to reproduction: if, of the two things necessary to demand, the will and the power to purchase, the will be wanting, and consequently a general stagnation of trade has ensued, we cannot do better than follow the advice of Mr. Malthus, and oblige the Government to

---

[11] Liverpool cited excise returns for "candles, paper, hides, skins, soap, salt, bricks, &c." The fact that the amount of excise duties collected for each of these items increased from 1817 to 1820 is confirmed by detailed statements of excise returns (Marshall 1833, 2:14). Excise taxes received on the twenty-seven items listed in the *Digest of All the Accounts* increased from 1817 to 1820 on every commodity except wine and sweets, and this was because the duties on sweets and wines were reduced in 1818. For a list of tax changes see "A return of the Gross and Net Amount of all Taxes Repealed, Expired, Reduced, or Imposed in each Year since the Termination of the War" in *Parliamentary Papers* 1833, 32:637–653.

[12] Ricardo made a similar remark to Trower upon reading an article in the *Times* endorsing public expenditure: "A writer in the Times of this morning appears to have adopted some of Malthus' principles and the conclusions he draws from them are so wild and extravagant that if we had no other reason for suspecting their fallacy, these would afford them. This writer recommends that we should raise loans now instead of the taxes with which we are burthened and for this sagacious reason, because it will promote expenditure and take off the superfluity of our productions" (2 Mar. 1821, 8:349).

supply the deficiency of the people. We ought in that case to petition the King to dismiss his present economical ministers, and to replace them by others, who would more effectually promote the best interests of the country by promoting public extravagance and expenditure (*Notes on Malthus*, 2:307).

To reiterate, the question at issue in the *Notes on Malthus* was not whether consumers might hoard cash, but whether investment could potentially be excessive. Hoarding was not part of Malthus' analysis in Chapter 7 of the *Principles*. And, at any rate, Ricardo recognized that hoarding actually occurred.[13] He observed that Bank of England notes were hoarded in rural districts as a "deposit against alarm" during the country-banking crisis of 1814–1816. He also recognized hoarding "by timid people" in the early years of the war: "the fact of guineas having been hoarded in 1797 is well established" (3:172, 322; 6:343). Similarly, Ricardo understood that capitalists might hold high cash balances while searching for profitable investment opportunities. He believed that this had, in fact, happened in the years 1815–1817 as capital was "thrown in the market to seek new occupations,"[14] leaving fixed capital temporarily idle and "labourers without full employment" (1:265).

Conclusion

Ricardo did not consistently apply the law of markets. His analysis of postwar conditions relied on Say's equality, while his opposition to expansionary fiscal measures implied Say's identity. In the face of postwar crises, his statements about fiscal policy assumed full employment. He may have believed that the country would adapt quickly to unemployment so that his assumption was approximately correct. Or perhaps he was concerned that the prodigality of government, justified as a short-term expedient, would in the long-term divert Britain's resources from private investment to unproductive public consumption. The textual evidence is not conclusive, for his underlying analysis is fragmented and incomplete.

[13] It was common knowledge that hoarding occurred: "There is scarcely an individual of a class above that which is limited to the means of bare subsistence, who had not a hoard, greater or less, of guineas that were put by as a provision against the various contingencies which were considered as endangering the value of paper, either in degree, as by depreciation, or totally, as by foreign invasion or domestic convulsion," and again, there was a "very extensive practice of hoarding . . . among the inhabitants of those states of the Continent which were either the seat of war or which had issued paper to excess" (Tooke and Newmarch 1838, 2:132–133, 138).

[14] Ricardo to Grenfell, Aug. 1817, Heertje 1991, 521.

Among the fragments lie insights that would justify expansionary fiscal measures. Ricardo acknowledged hoarding. He knew that laborers were often without full employment. He was also adamant that debt-financed government spending increased aggregate consumption. Admitting these factual points, it follows that in the event of a depression caused by a lack of private consumption, the government could sell Exchequer bills – diverting purchasing power from private hoards to public coffers – and then spend the proceeds. The government's actions would raise the level of consumption and the demand for labor. This possibility eluded Ricardo, for the requisite fragments never filtered into his macroeconomic model.

Ricardo's comments on Malthusian oversaving and his critique of the "increasing competition of capitals" thesis found in Adam Smith's *Wealth of Nations* and William Blake's *Observations* do not require an extreme version of the law of markets. He rejected Malthus' notion of oversaving because he did not believe that irrational investment on a grand scale ever occurred. He also knew that Britain's economic troubles in the postwar period could not be traced to too rapid an accumulation of capital. It was just the opposite problem – too little capital relative to the supply of labor – that concerned him. With regard to Smith and Blake, Ricardo understood that in the secular period demand was only limited by production. Smith incorrectly assumed that a result observed in a single industry – where high levels of investment create competition that lowers prices – would obtain in the macroeconomy. Smith failed to appreciate that investment, in the aggregate, gives rise to both an increase in output and an increase in purchasing power. In the long-term, this purchasing power is always a source of effectual demand.

SEVEN

Monetary Policy

Monetary policy affects more than one macroeconomic variable. The money supply influences the domestic price level, foreign exchange rates, real and nominal interest rates, national output, employment in the short term, and the pattern of international trade. The monetary authority cannot simultaneously move all variables to ideal levels. Thus there arises a thorny question: which variable should be accorded priority? Ricardo held that stable prices were the primary objective of monetary policy. This explains his support for the Resumption Act of 1819 – the act that tied sterling to gold and thereby fixed, as far as possible, the purchasing power of the pound. With the gold standard secure – and with it, prices stabilized – Ricardo endorsed the discretionary control of the money supply to compensate for erratic actions by country banks and for variations in the demand for liquidity. The best monetary arrangement was a paper currency, convertible into gold or silver, the management of which was entrusted to the Bank of England or to the commissioners of a national bank. In this respect he differed from the later Currency School, which recommended that the fluctuations of the paper pound mimic those of a fully metallic circulation.

The extent to which Ricardo countenanced discretionary policy has been obscured by passages in the *High Price of Bullion* (1810) where he recommended a restrictive monetary response to supply shocks. In *High Price*, he posited a failure of the harvest that necessitated vast importations of corn and that caused – under the gold standard – a trade deficit funded by an external drain of bullion. Given those conditions, *High Price* advocated a restrictive monetary policy. Ricardo's rationale was that the central bank could not simultaneously defend the gold standard and sustain the prevailing level of credit, and that it was better to suffer the short-term effects of tight credit than to endure the long-term instability of a currency without a standard.

Ricardo's preference for stable prices above all other monetary objectives does not imply that he was blind to the effects of money on output and employment. His ingot plan, his allowance for devaluation if the currency was highly depreciated, and his criticism of the Bank's return to gold all demonstrate that he recognized the nonneutrality of money. The same is true of his proposal to use warrants in paying the dividend on the national debt and of his comments on the Irish banking crisis in 1820.

The concept of lender of last resort does not appear in Ricardo's *Plan for a National Bank*. The omission is curious because he was familiar with Henry Thornton's account of the role in *Paper Credit*. My comments are purely speculative, but I submit that Ricardo omitted any reference to the role of the central bank as lender of last resort because this function was performed by the Exchequer. The Bank was a private, profit-seeking business. In severe financial crises, such as occurred in 1793, 1811, and 1825, the Bank behaved as any other commercial institution and reduced its exposure to risk by withdrawing credit. The duty to sustain credit was thus abandoned to the Exchequer.

The Resumption of Cash Payments

Ricardo carefully considered every aspect of the return to cash payments. He weighed the important matters, including the choice of the standard, the possibility of devaluation, and the timing and means by which cash payments were to be restored, and after much consideration developed a plan by which the Bank of England would gradually return to a gold standard at the ancient par.

The basic question of monetary policy in the postwar period was whether Britain should return to a metallic standard or continue with an inconvertible paper currency. Concerning the ultimate resolution of this issue, Tooke reported that "to the principle of the eventual restoration of the value of paper to gold at £3 17s. 10.5d., there was a pretty general assent" (Tooke and Newmarch 1838–1870, 2:107). The consensus in favor of a standard formed because the Bank of England conducted a procyclical monetary policy, expanding its notes during periods of prosperity, then withdrawing credit during crises. Three episodes highlighted the fact that the inconvertible pound was unstable.

First, the annual average amount of commercial paper under discount at the Bank of England increased from £12,950,100 in 1808 to £15,475,700 in 1809 to £20,070,600 in 1810.[1] The first two years saw a speculative boom in trade with South America – the Spanish and Portuguese having just opened these markets to Britain. Many in Parliament and the City thought the Bank encouraged speculation; Sir Francis Baring said it discounted commercial paper to "clerks not worth £100" (Duffy 1982, 73). Critics associated the Bank's commercial discounts with a rise in the money supply and the onset of another round of wartime inflation. In retrospect, the increase in the money supply probably resulted from the loans[2] and open market purchases with which the Bank financed the war effort. This fact did not come to light till later, however, leaving the impression that the Bank had been irresponsible in its discounts.[3]

The Bank's postwar performance was less exemplary. Chapter 2 described the country-banking crisis and the reversals in foreign trade that plagued Britain's economy in 1815 and 1816. At the depth of the depression, when the country banks and merchants were in greatest need, the Bank sharply reduced commercial discounts. On 1 January 1816, the combined discounts to merchants, manufacturers, and traders amounted to £16,652,923. By 1 January 1817 this figure had fallen to £7,604,345.[4] Such a severe contraction of credit did much to aggravate the crisis; it also incited opposition to the Bank in Parliament and in the City.

The third incident concerned the Bank's advance of £12 million in Exchequer bills to the government at a time – the summer of 1817 – when the economy was nearing full employment. The Bank's directors were opposed to the loan, fearing that it would lead to further inflation. But under pressure from the government they granted the advance. Referring to this event years later, Ricardo noted "how little [the Bank directors]

---

[1] House of Commons, *Report from the Committee of Secrecy on the Bank of England Charter* 1832, App. 59.

[2] The Bank loaned money directly to the government. It also advanced monies to the syndicate that won the contract for the government's loan for a given year. In 1808–1810, Barings and Goldsmid raised £37 million in loans for Great Britain contracted by competitive bidding (note by Sraffa in Ricardo, 10:80–81).

[3] The rise in the average value of commercial paper under discount in 1810 does not signal a flaw in the Bank's policies. The Bank granted credit to merchants for sixty-day periods. If the average value of paper under discount was £20 million, the total value of loans for the year was closer to £120 million. Under these circumstances, slight delays by merchants in repaying the Bank could sharply increase the average value of notes under discount. When the trade with South America foundered, such delays occurred. The *Minutes* of the Bank's Court of Directors for 1810 are filled with pleas from merchants asking for extensions of time to repay.

[4] Bank of England, *Committee on Discounts: Analyses*, C36/20.

have been able to withstand the cajolings of ministers; and how frequently they have been induced to increase their advances on Exchequer bills and Treasury bills, at the very moment they were themselves declaring that it would be attended with the greatest risk to the stability of their establishment and to the public interest" (*Plan for a National Bank*, 4:282). The effects of the Bank's decision in 1817 were amplified the following year when applications for commercial discounts increased and "the Committee in Waiting made no attempt to restrict credit" (Duffy 1982, 80). As a result of the Bank's extensions of credit in 1817 and 1818, the speculative boom of 1818 was prolonged needlessly. The Bank's policies abetted another round of inflation and, given that the foreign exchange turned unfavorably in July 1817, depleted the Bank's hoard. It is, perhaps, with these events in view that Ricardo observed in the *Principles*: "Experience shews that neither a State nor a Bank ever have had the unrestricted power of issuing paper money, without abusing that power: in all States, therefore, the issue of paper money ought to be under some check and control" (Ricardo, 1:356).

The complete statement of Ricardo's opposition to an inconvertible currency – what he termed "a currency without a specific standard" (4:59) – appears in Section 2 of *Secure Currency* (1816). He identified two principal faults. First, Ricardo thought it impossible to regulate the value of an inconvertible currency because "no one has yet been able to offer any test by which we could ascertain the uniformity in the value of a money so constituted" (4:59). He understood that, in theory, a price index could be used to approximate changes in the value of the currency – "judging of its value by its relation, not to one, but to the mass of commodities" (4:59). But practical obstacles made price indices unsuitable: "To determine the value of a currency by the test proposed, it would be necessary to compare it successively with the thousands of commodities which are circulating in the community, allowing to each all the effects which may have been produced upon its value by the above causes. To do this is evidently impossible" (4:60).[5]

Ricardo's second objection to inconvertible paper was that "such a currency ... would be exposed to all the fluctuations to which the ignorance or the interests of the issuers might subject it" (4:59). His support for

---

[5] The idea of a price index was common by 1816. Sir George Shuckburgh Evelyn published an index in 1798 that was used by John Wheatley in 1803 in *Remarks on the Currency and Commerce* and again in 1807 when he proposed indexing contracts (Hollander 1979, 416n). Notwithstanding these facts, Hollander notes that price indices were generally viewed as impractical.

the gold standard centered on this concern. Speaking before the House of Commons Committee on Resumption, he acknowledged that some monetary deflation might follow the return to gold, but the tradeoff seemed favorable when compared to the risks of perpetuating the current system:

I acknowledge there will be some little difficulty in it [Resumption], but a difficulty which does not appear to me very formidable, and one for which we would be more than compensated by the possession of a currency regulated by a known and fixed standard (4 Mar. 1819, 5:396).

I think a very serious inconvenience results from the state of uncertainty: one of the evils attending a paper currency not convertible, is, that it encourages overtrading, and leads us into some of those difficulties into which we should not be plunged, if our paper were corrected by the issues of metals (4 Mar. 1819, 5:397).

Having determined that it was necessary to return to a metallic standard, the next step was to choose a metal. Ricardo desired the least variable standard possible. His concern is evident in that, during the years 1815 to 1819, his choice of a standard changed at least twice in response to new information about the current or expected volatility of the prices of metals. In the *High Price of Bullion* (1810), Ricardo acknowledged that there was no perfect standard of value: "Strictly speaking, there can be no permanent measure of value. A measure of value should itself be invariable; but this is not the case with either gold or silver" (3:65). But in choosing between gold and silver, he suggested a gold standard (3:124). His views changed four years later. The initial version of *Secure Currency* advocated a paper circulation convertible in gold bullion. Upon reading a draft, Malthus opposed the plan on two counts: first, gold prices were more volatile than silver prices, and second, a country having a paper circulation, but minimal reserves, might be forced to stop cash payments during periods of crisis:

What has happened clearly proves that there may be a great demand for the precious metals in times of war and convulsion on account of their superior convenience; and such a demand operating upon a country possessing a small quantity of them must occasion either a great rise of price or an extraordinary and most inconvenient diminution of currency (Malthus to Ricardo, 1 Oct. 1815, 6:289).

If you recollect, we found upon calculation that the value of gold in this country at some periods during the Peninsular war was ten and fifteen per cent higher than at Amsterdam and Hamburgh . . . I am not sure whether I should not myself propose silver instead [of] gold as a standard, to prevent the run upon the bank which might be occasioned by an alteration in the relative value of the two precious metals (Malthus to Ricardo, 15 Oct. 1815, 6:298).

Ricardo accepted Malthus' observation about the volatility of gold and made the appropriate change to Section 3 of *Secure Currency*, adopting a silver rather than a gold standard: "I considered gold and silver as less variable commodities than they really are, and the effect of war on the prices of these metals were certainly very much underrated.[6] ... The fall in the price of bullion on the peace in 1814, and its rise again on the renewal of the war on Bonapartes entry into Paris are remarkable facts, and should never be neglected in any future discussion on this subject" (25 Dec. 1815, 6:344). The "facts" referred to were that "on the Peace of 1814 the price of gold had fallen from 108/- per ounce (1 March) to 90/- (28 June); on the return of Napoleon in 1815 it rose from 89/- (28 February) to 107/- (4 April)" (note by Sraffa in Ricardo, 6:344n).

The second instance in which Ricardo changed his preference occurred after he learned of the increasing application of machinery to silver mining: "it is confidently expected that the introduction of the most perfect machinery known into the silver mines may very considerably lower the value of that metal. If so it is unfit for a standard. The same objections cannot be made to gold" (3 Jan. 1819, 8:3). He repeated this view in testimony before the House of Commons Committee on Resumption:

Question: Can a standard of currency, more invariable in its value than the value of a certain quantity of gold, be established by any system yet discovered?
Answer: By none that I have ever even imagined.
Question: If one metal is preferable as affording a less variable measure, which metal would you recommend?
Answer: I have understood that machinery is particularly applicable to the silver mines, and may therefore very much conduce to an increased quantity of that metal and an alteration of its value, whilst the same cause is not likely to operate upon the value of gold, I have come to the conclusion, that gold is the better metal by which to regulate the value of our currency (5:388, 391).

And again before the Lords Committee on Resumption:

I had at one Time thought Silver would be less variable in Value; but having heard that Machinery is particularly applicable to the working of Silver Mines, and cannot be applied to increase the Quantity of Gold, I now think that Gold is the more invariable metal (5:427).

[6] Section 2 of *Secure Currency* explains why Ricardo came to prefer silver: "In favour of gold, it may be said, that its greater value under a smaller bulk eminently qualified it for the standard in an opulent country; but this very quality subjects it to greater variations of value during periods of war, or extensive commercial discredit, when it is often collected and hoarded, and may be urged as an argument against its use" (4:63).

The fact Ricardo rejected silver as a standard also explains his opposition to bimetallism. After the Resumption Act passed, it would have been politically impossible to return to an inconvertible pound. Devaluation, on the other hand, and particularly devaluation resulting from the adoption of a bimetallic standard, was a distinct possibility.[7] Ricardo understood the threat of devaluation; this is evident in his answers to Alexander Baring's frequent calls for a bimetallic standard: "Were that option [bimetallism] given to the Bank, the person who applied at present for sixty ounces of gold bullion would be told by the Bank that they would not pay him in gold, but in silver, which in its relative value to gold was lower" (8 Feb. 1821, 5:74–78).[8]

Once Ricardo decided on a gold standard, the next question was whether to return to bullion payments at the ancient Mint price or to devalue the currency to the current market price. Given the conditions of 1819, Ricardo proposed that Britain not devalue the pound. His judgment was based on the perceived tradeoff between the hardships of monetary deflation and the injustice to public creditors of permanent devaluation.[9] In instances of a severely depreciated currency, Ricardo allowed that the tradeoff would favor devaluation over restoring the standard.

I never should advise a government to restore a currency, which was depreciated 30 pct., to par; I should recommend . . . that the currency should be fixed at the depreciated value by lowering the standard and that no further deviations should take place. It was without any legislation that the currency from 1813 to 1819 became of an increased value and within 5 pct. of the value of gold, – it was in this state of things, and not with a currency depreciated 30 pct., that I advised a recurrence to the old standard (18 Sept. 1821, 9:73).

If, instead of being at 4l. 1s. bullion had been much higher, he should not have proposed a recurrence to the Mint standard. What he was anxious about, was not to restore the old, but to establish a fixed standard (8 Feb. 1821, 5:73).

However, the currency was not seriously devalued in 1819; gold was selling 3 percent above its Mint price when the Resumption Committees

---

[7] The market prices of gold and silver declined to their Mint values immediately after the Resumption Act received royal assent. In Feb. 1820 silver began falling again, and continued to decline till it was selling at 4 percent below its Mint price. Had Britain switched from gold to a bimetallic standard after Feb. 1820, silver would have become the *de facto* standard and the currency would have been devalued about 4 percent.

[8] Ricardo made similar comments the spring of 1821 (19 Mar. 1821, 5:96; 9 Apr. 1821, 5:106).

[9] On this matter, see Hollander 1979, 424–425, 489, 494–499.

reported. Under current conditions, the tradeoff favored returning to the ancient par.[10]

The time had then arrived (in 1819) for fixing a standard, and the only consideration was as to the selection of the particular standard which ought to be adopted.
They had two courses of proceeding open to them on that occasion; one was either
to regulate the standard by the price of gold at the moment, or to recur to the
ancient standard of the country . . . when the currency was within 5 per cent of
its par value, the only consideration was, whether they should fix the standard at
4l. 2s., the then price of gold, or recur at once to the old standard. Under all the
circumstances, he thought they had made the best selection in recurring to the old
standard (Parliamentary address, 1822, 5:208).

Devaluation seemed fraught with danger because it involved the "sacrifice
of a great principle in establishing a new standard" and "it would be
unjust to all creditors, and proportionally advantageous to debtors" (5:43;
8:186). Also, devaluing the currency would set a precedent for future
devaluations by governments in financial straits: "What security has the
public creditor that the interest on the public debt, which is now paid in
a medium depreciated fifteen per cent., may not hereafter be paid in one
degraded fifty per cent.? The injury to private creditors is not less serious.
A debt contracted in 1797 may now be paid with eighty-five per cent. of
its amount, and who shall say that the depreciation will go no further?"
(3:96).

Devaluation was not warranted because sterling traded only 5 percent
below par when the Resumption Committees convened, it was 4 percent
below par a month later, and 3 percent by the time the committees reported to Parliament (5:11, 385, 416). When the act received royal assent
the requisite amount of deflation was nil. The foreign exchange became
favorable in July 1819; gold reached its Mint price a month later. The
propitious nature of these events caused Ricardo to anticipate almost no
economic suffering before the final return to cash payments:

Gold is I believe at £3 18. pr. oz, – silver at Mint price, and the exchanges nearly
at par. The best friends to the measures lately adopted could not have anticipated
less pressure than what has been hitherto experienced, and I think it but reasonable to hope that the permanent price of bullion will settle at the present rate,
without adding much to the slight difficulties which we have already suffered. Our
opponents, whose prophecies are all proved to be unfounded, now say that we
have had great good luck (8 July 1819, 8:44–45).

[10] This has been recognized in the secondary literature (Sayers 1953, 59; Robbins 1976, 72;
Hollander 1979, 425,488).

Ricardo considered the monetary deflation associated with resumption insignificant when compared with the 20 percent deflation that occurred in the crisis of 1815–1816. He made this point before the House of Commons Committee on Resumption:

> Question: Paper having been, in the Middle of 1815, at upwards of 20 per Cent. Discount, and we having it in Evidence, that Gold at the latter End of 1816 would have been at the Mint Price, had it not been sustained by the Bank at the Price of £3 18s. 6d.; do you not think that the Pressure which the Country sustained at that Period must be much greater than what it will now sustain from Paper resuming its Value upon a Par with Gold, it being now at a Discount of only 4 per Cent; and can you state any Proportion which the Difficulties on one Period are likely to bear in relation to the Difficulties of the other?
>
> Answer: I think the Pressure sustained at that Period was much greater than would be experienced now by a Reduction of 4 per Cent. in the Amount of the Currency (24 Mar. 1819, 5:419).

And again before the Lords Committee on Resumption:

> Question: Do you recollect whether within these last Eight Years we have not frequently seen the Circulating Medium of the Country undergo much more formidable Changes with respect to Value than 4 per cent., within a shorter Period than Six Months, judging of the Value of the Circulating Medium by the Price of Gold?
>
> Answer: In my opinion it has undergone much greater Variations than 4 per Cent.; and in the soundest State of our Currency, it would be liable to such Variations (26 Mar. 1819, 5:441).

Ricardo's one reservation about the resumption legislation was that there was no safeguard to prevent the directors of the Bank of England from curtailing the circulation too severely. He proposed[11] such a safeguard in the form of a provision that would have required the Bank to purchase gold at £3 17s. 6d. But this provision was not included in the act:

> He was only sorry that the Bank was not to be obliged by the resolutions to buy all the bullion offered to them at 3l.17s.6d. lest through excessive caution they might starve the circulation. The Mint, it was true, was to remain open to the public, who might coin the bullion which they obtained from the Bank. Mr. Mushett . . . had stated, that with a capital of 300,000l. the Mint could supply the public with 12,000,000l. a year. Yet a year was a long time to wait for twelve millions, and it might easily happen, that in the interim between the reduction of the Bank issues and the supply afforded from the Mint, the country might seriously feel the deficiency. It was on that account that he wished a resolution inserted to compel

---

[11] Ricardo first stated this proposal in 1811 (6:70–71). He repeated it in *Secure Currency* and in testimony before the House of Lords Committee on Resumption (4:66; 5:454).

the Bank to give its notes for bullion (at 3l. 17s. 6d.) on demand (Parliamentary address, 24 May 1819, 5:13).

Notwithstanding his awareness that the Bank could overreact to resumption, he was confident that this would not occur, for it was in the Bank's interests to maintain an adequate circulation: "If the Bank was desirous to follow their own interest, it was a clear and obvious one: if they were to effect a great reduction in their paper, which he should lament, the consequence would be such a rise in paper and such a fall in gold that individuals would carry their gold to the Mint and endeavour to fill up the circulation with it. As to the alarm felt by his hon. friend it was quite groundless, for there could be no fear but that the Bank would keep up a sufficient quantity of notes, as their own advantage depend upon the issue" (9 June 1820, 5:62). His expectations were subsequently disappointed, but as Ricardo pointed out, there was no way he could have anticipated that the Bank would keep its discount rate above the market rate of profit:

Mr. Ricardo cannot fairly be held responsible for the narrow view, and obstinate prejudices of the Bank of England. He could not contemplate that the Bank would so narrow the circulation of paper as to occasion such a rise in its comparative value to gold and the currencies of other countries as to make the influx of gold into this country unexampled in amount. He could not foresee that they would immediately provide themselves with so large a quantity of gold coin.... He supposed that the reverting from a currency regulated by no standard, to one regulated by a fixed one, the greatest care would be taken to make the transition as little burthensome as possible, but the fact is that if the object had been to make the alteration from the one system to the other as distressing to the country as possible no measures could have been taken by the Bank of England so well calculated to produce that effect as those which they actually adopted (5:518–519; similar comments appear elsewhere 9:140–141; 5:312).

The Resumption Act did not require the Bank to pay its notes in gold until 1820, and even then, payment was to be made at a devalued rate of £4 2s. The Bank was not required to sell bullion at the ancient par until 1821, giving it almost two years to effect the requisite monetary deflation.[12] Having observed that "Peel's bill absolutely prohibited the Bank from paying in specie till 1823," Ricardo concluded that "all the friends of that bill had a right to expect that the Bank would make no preparation for specie payments till 1822" (9:141).

---

[12] The Bank returned to the ancient par according to this schedule (Smart 1910–1917, 1:679): 1 Feb. 1820, at £4 1s. per oz.; 1 Oct. 1820, £3 19s. 6d.; and 1 May 1821, £3 17s. 10 1/2d.

His expectation that resumption would entail no serious deflation was strengthened by the inclusion of his ingot plan in the act. The plan prohibited the Bank from paying its notes in coin; the Bank was instead obliged to pay notes of large denominations in gold ingots. The inconvenience of receiving ingots, Ricardo assumed, would reduce the demands upon the Bank's hoard – thus permitting the Bank to maintain a smaller hoard: "I think there would be no provision of gold necessary beyond that which the bank must now have, however small it may be" (4 Mar. 1819, 5:383). Given this safeguard, Ricardo expected that the Bank would not accumulate gold: "There was nothing in the plan which could cause a rise in the value of gold, for no additional quantity of gold would have been required" (4:224). The ingot plan proved a success – no one wanted the ingots, the Bank sold only thirteen as novelties – but it accumulated a large hoard anyway.

The timing of Ricardo's support for resumption has received much scrutiny in the literature, for Parliament approved the act during a period of general depression. Modern authors question whether returning to gold – and incurring the deflation this entailed – was an ideal policy when faced with unemployment and idle manufactures. The rationale for Ricardo's position was that Britain had to restore the gold standard to curb the instability caused by the Bank's postwar monetary policy. Moreover, there was no choice between passing resumption in 1819 or passing the act at a more convenient time. If Parliament did not approve the act in 1819, nothing would prevent further rounds of inflation. And if inflation occurred, the government was likely to oppose any move to restore the standard. (The government blocked all attempts at resumption in the years 1814 to 1818 on the grounds that the market price of gold was too high and the value of sterling on the foreign exchange was too low.) Moreover, the Resumption Act did not require the Bank to restore the gold standard immediately; it gave the Bank two years to raise the value of its paper. Not until May 1821 was the Bank obliged to redeem its notes in gold ingots at the ancient par. By this point, the depression in trade and manufacturing had ended.

The government began promising in 1814 to end the Bank restriction. Five times the promise was made and deadlines were set and five times the promise was forgotten and deadlines were extended. Even so, because of the depression immediately after the war, commodity prices and the price of gold had fallen enough that the Bank was positioned to resume cash payments by the summer of 1816. Ricardo brought this propitious state of affairs to Malthus' attention: "There can not be a better opportunity than the present for the Bank to recommence payments in specie. Silver is actually under the Mint price. The change is surprising and has been brought about in a very unexpected manner" (24 Apr. 1816, 7:29). Malthus agreed: "I really think that if we don't pay in Specie now, we shall never do it. In the present temper of the Country with regard to Currency, I should not wonder, if a fresh separation between gold and paper should take place, and the ministers should encourage it, as a preparation for an alteration in the coinage" (28 Apr. 1816, 7:30). Malthus' fears were justified; five days later the government won third reading of a bill (56 Geo. III, c. 40) that extended the Bank restriction to July 1818.

The bill initially seemed irrelevant. The Bank ignored it and on its own initiative began paying some notes in gold. Eventually it declared all notes dated prior to 1 January 1817 convertible. At this point, however, just as the return to gold seemed assured, the government exacted from the Bank an advance of £12 million. The resulting increase in the money supply – combined with other factors – sparked a further round of inflation, turned the foreign exchange, and started a run against the Bank's hoard. The Bank's operations were so disrupted that it took another four years for it to be in the same position, relative to restoring cash payments, it had enjoyed in 1816.

Given this background, it is not surprising that Ricardo supported resumption in 1819. Had the act not been approved, nothing would have prevented further episodes of monetary inflation such as occurred in 1810, 1814, and 1818. Government ministers had demonstrated their willingness to demand advances from the Bank rather than make difficult fiscal decisions, even when such advances created inflationary pressure. This fact was repeatedly noted by proponents of the act:

When he heard, from a certain class of persons who had petitioned their lordships, those resolutions objected to as tending to a forced and precipitate reduction of the circulating medium, he could not help considering their objections as proceeding from a wish to prolong, to the utmost, the duration of the restriction; for, if the country was ever to return to payments in specie, he would defy any man to devise a plan more easy, more moderate, or less tending to produce distress than that contained in the resolutions before the House [Ricardo's ingot plan]....

[Formerly] they had only fixed a period at which the Bank should resume payments, without taking measures to compel it to make preparations for doing so ... The Bank had never made the proper preparations at the proper time; they had never so reduced their issues as to bring down gold to the Mint price. They would have followed the same course; they would have again come to Parliament with a special case, and again obtained a farther time, as they had before (Lord King in the House of Lords, 21 May 1819, *Hansard* 1s, 40:640–641).

Restoring a metallic standard was the central achievement of the Resumption Act. A subordinate issue was whether convertibility should begin at the current market price of gold or at the ancient par. Because of his sensitivity to the short-run effects of monetary contraction, Ricardo stated before the House of Lords Committee on Resumption that cash payments should start at the current market price and gradually move to the ancient par:

Question: Do you think, on the whole, that any Inconvenience would arise from prolonging that Period [of returning to Cash Payments at the Mint Price] beyond the Period of 12 Months from July next...

Answer: I think the Advantages to be derived from a Prolongation of the Period would preponderate, provided the Public had complete Security, by obliging the Bank to sell Gold at the present Market Price, against a further Excess of Paper Circulation.

Question: Do you think the Balance of the Advantage of prolongation would extend to a Period of Two Years from July next?

Answer: I think Two Years an ample Time; I should say a less Period; but it may be prudent to consult the Fears of even the most timid (Ricardo, 5:450–451).

His arguments were repeated before the House of Commons Committee on Resumption:

Question: Could you assign any period of time, at the expiration of which this [ingot] plan, in your opinion, could be safely resorted to?

Answer: I think it ought to be immediately resorted to, either at the price of 3l. 17s. 10 1/2 d. or at some other price; because I consider that our currency is in a very unsatisfactory state ... whatever regulation might be resolved on, with respect to the time of paying in the standard of the country, I should certainly recommend the adoption of this plan at some other price in the interval.

Question: That is, the bank should be under an obligation of paying their notes on demand in gold, at the present market price of gold for instance, and of making a gradual reduction in the price of gold which they should issue, until the market price of gold corresponded with the Mint price?

Answer: Precisely so (5:381).

The idea of a gradual return to the ancient standard was not new to Ricardo. He first made the proposal in the *High Price of Bullion* (1810, 3:94). He reiterated the idea to Tierney in 1811 and even allowed four years to attain the ancient value (6:69). Perhaps his clearest statement appears in a letter to Spencer Perceval, who at the time was Prime Minister and Chancellor of the Exchequer: "Let the Bank be obliged to sell gold bullion, for their own notes ... at the rate of £4 15s. per ounce for standard bullion.... An enactment to this effect would secure the public against any depreciation of the currency beyond that to which it has already reached.

The Bank would be at full liberty at their leisure, and after the most mature consideration, to adopt such other means as might be necessary, when no danger should appear even to the most timid, gradually to reduce the amount of their paper" (1811, 6:43–44). The advantage of Ricardo's proposal was that it protected the country against further inflation, but without the distress of too rapid a contraction of the money supply.

Discretionary Monetary Policy

Ricardo's case for discretionary monetary policy appears in *Secure Currency* (1816) and in *Plan for a National Bank* (1824).[13] By "discretion" I refer to a central bank's role in stabilizing prices and in correcting financial crises. The bank acts by altering its discount rate or by trading bullion and government bonds. (If the central bank lowers its discount rate, merchants demand more loans. The money supply rises to the extent the bank grants these loans. The money supply also rises if the bank buys bullion and government bonds.) Discretion in this sense does not require a full-fledged countercyclical policy.

National Bank describes how monetary policy might be conducted by the commissioners of a hypothetical national bank.[14] *Secure Currency* is concerned with the monetary policy of the Bank of England.[15]

---

[13] Many authors recognize the argument for discretion in *Secure Currency* (Viner 1937, 206; Niehans 1987, 420–421; Robbins 1968, 128). Arnon, an outlier in this regard, claims that Ricardo did not understand the need for discretion until 1823 (Arnon 1987, 268; 1989, 12; 1991, 177; 1999, 89–90).

[14] Ricardo's proposals for commissioners who would administer the money supply did not originate in *National Bank*. He developed the idea by 1815: "I am convinced, if the principles of currency were rightly understood, that Commissioners might be appointed independent of all ministerial control who should be the sole issuers of paper money . . . These Commissioners should also have the management of the public debt, and should act as Bankers to all the different public departments. They might invest the 11 millions which is the average of public deposits in Exchequer Bills, a part of which might be sold whenever occasion required" (Ricardo to Malthus, 10 Sept. 1815, 6:268). He afterward stated the proposal in all three editions of the *Principles* (1:362).

[15] The introduction to *Secure Currency* expressly limits the pamphlet's scope to the operations of the Bank: "The following important questions concerning the Bank of England [that] will, next session, come under the discussion of Parliament: 1st. Whether the Bank shall be obliged to pay their notes in specie at the demand of the holders? 2dly. Whether any alteration shall be made in the terms agreed upon in 1808, between Government and the Bank, for the management of the national debt? And, 3dly, what compensation the public shall receive for the large amount of public deposits from which the Bank derive profit?" (Ricardo, 4:51) The subject of the country banks does not appear until the close of Section 4, at which point Ricardo proposes they be subject to a minimum reserve requirement.

Ricardo wrote *Secure Currency* because of concerns about how the Bank, in tandem with the government, managed the inconvertible pound. He concluded that neither body could be trusted with the responsibility: "In all countries, I should think, there exists a repugnance to entrust to Government the power of issuing paper money, and when we consider that perhaps in no instance they have not abused such a power, it is not wonderful that such fears are prevalent" (24 Dec. 1814, 6:165–166). He restated this view in all three editions of the *Principles* (1:362) and in *National Bank* (4:282). Provided banknotes were convertible, however, *Secure Currency* makes a clear case for discretion:

Amongst the advantages of a paper over a metallic circulation, may be reckoned, as not the least, the facility with which it may be altered in quantity, as the wants of commerce and temporary circumstances may require (4:55).

Whenever merchants, then, have a want of confidence in each other, which disinclines them to deal on credit, or to accept in payment each other's checks, notes or bills; more money, whether it be paper or metallic money, is in demand; and the advantage of a paper circulation, when established on correct principles, is, that this additional quantity can be presently supplied without occasioning any variation in the value of the whole currency . . . whereas, with a system of metallic currency, this additional quantity cannot be so readily supplied, and when it is finally supplied, the whole of the currency, as well as bullion, has acquired an increased value (4:58).

Ricardo's earliest writings demonstrate his understanding that the demand for money varies: "the demand for circulating medium is subject to continual fluctuations, proceeding from an increase or decrease in the amount of capital and commerce; from a great or less facility which at one period may be afforded to payments by a varying degree of confidence and credit" (*Reply to Bosanquet* 1811, 3:247). He refers particularly to the years 1797 and 1798 when "the addition of two millions in Bank notes served only to supply the vacuum which the hoarding of money had occasioned; so that there was no real increase to the circulation of those years" (*Reply to Bosanquet* 1811, 3:249). His *Notes on Bentham* also mention "the fact of guineas having been hoarded in 1797" (3:322). *Secure Currency* advocates the discretionary management of a convertible currency in order to counteract the effects of variations in the demand for money: "[Ricardo] argues the merits of a paper circulation . . . because it can meet upward fluctuations in the demand for liquidity without delay and without involving eventual changes in the value of money" (Robbins 1968, 128).

National Bank describes the means by which a central bank responds to fluctuations in the demand for money. The first situation involves a decrease in the demand for money whereby banknotes become "redundant":

> If the circulation of London should be redundant, it will show itself by the increased price of bullion and the fall in the foreign exchanges, precisely as a redundancy is now shown; and the remedy is also the same as that now in operation; viz. a reduction of circulation which is brought about by a reduction of the paper circulation. That reduction may take place two ways; either by the sale of Exchequer bills in the market, and the cancelling of the paper money which is obtained for them – or by giving gold in exchange for the paper, cancelling the paper as before, and exporting the gold (Ricardo, 4:296–297).

A rise in the market price of gold above the Mint price signals when the currency is "redundant." The bank's policy at this point – whether active or passive – makes little difference. The money supply will contract, no matter what the bank does, because the holders of banknotes find it profitable to exchange notes for gold at the bank. A fall of sterling on the foreign exchange also indicates that the circulation is redundant. But here the bank's policy does matter. For by raising the domestic rate of interest, the bank might be able to attract capital from abroad. The influx of capital would raise the value of sterling on the foreign exchange, possibly enough to stop an external drain of bullion. (Ricardo did not understand how manipulating interest rates could counteract an external drain; the insight was developed decades later.)

Should there be an increase in the demand for money, Ricardo understood that the bank's policy makes a great difference. The bank is passive if it neither lowers its discount rate nor engages in open-market operations.[16] The bank exercises discretion by changing the discount rate and by purchasing Exchequer bills and gold – in other words, it takes deliberate measures to increase the number of banknotes in circulation:

> If, on the contrary, the circulation of London were too low, there would be two ways of increasing it – by the purchase of Government securities in the market, and the creation of new paper money for the purpose; or by the importation, and purchase, by the Commissioner, of gold bullion; for the purchase of which new paper money would be created (4:297).

---

[16] The Bank engaged in "open-market operations" when it purchased Exchequer bills in the City.

Concerning the Bank of England and its policies in 1822, Ricardo stated that: "He was very glad to hear that the Bank had at length begun to discount at 4 per cent.; and he thought they should have done so long before. Had they persisted in demanding 5 per cent, they would have been without a single note to cash ... [because of] the market price of the loan of money being lower [than 5%]" (Parliamentary speech, 5:222–223).

By means of discretionary intervention, the Bank of England could maintain commercial credit while preventing deflation and a rise in the relative value of gold. A passive policy did nothing to sustain credit. Worse yet, if the Bank was passive – and especially if its discount rate was above the market rate of profit – the volume of its commercial discounts would fall. This would lead to further reductions in the circulation, and deflation, and it would depress the market rate of profits. In the course of deflation, the market price of gold would fall along with other commodities until it became profitable for merchants to bring gold to the Bank. (The Bank purchased gold at the Mint price.) The greater the accumulation of gold in the Bank, the more the price of gold would increase relative to other commodities – that is, the monetary standard would rise in value – preventing deflation from taking a backward course.

Monetary fluctuations affect output and employment. This was an additional reason to be concerned whether the Bank exercised discretion or remained passive. If there was an increase in the demand for banknotes – as might occur in a financial crisis – and if the Bank of England remained passive, Ricardo recognized that "the prices of commodities would fall, and great distress would be suffered" (5:199–200).

Practical Applications of Ricardo's Monetary Theory

In at least four instances, Ricardo proposed that the central monetary authority – the Bank of England or the Bank of Ireland – adjust the money supply to counteract economic shocks. He understood that either open-market operations or changes in the discount rate would have the desired effect. He first averred to discretionary policy in a letter describing the means by which the Bank could resume cash payments. He recommended that the Bank's circulation not be restricted within arbitrary nominal limits as this might interfere with its ability to exercise discretionary control over the money supply:

Depreciation cannot be effectually checked by any other means than by depriving the Bank of the power which they at present possess of adding indefinitely to the amount of their notes. This might be done in a direct manner, by limiting the amount beyond which their paper should not be issued; but it has been plausibly urged against such a measure that occasions may arise in which *sound policy may require a temporary augmentation of Bank paper, and to deprive the Bank of the power of increasing their notes at such periods might be the cause of considerable distress and difficulty to the mercantile classes* . . . if a greater circulation were required from the operation either of increased commerce, or of embarrassed credit, the bank might augment their issues without producing any effect whatever on the price of bullion, and consequently without exposing the Bank to any inconvenience, or depriving the merchants of that increased accommodation, which might be essential to their operations (Ricardo to Tierney, 11 Dec. 1811, 6:67; emphasis added).

Thus as early as 1811, Ricardo recognized the possibility of managing the money supply. Hollander has questioned whether much emphasis should be given to this letter, for Ricardo himself acknowledged that "this argument does not appear . . . to have as much weight as those who advance it imagine" (Ricardo, 6:67; Hollander 1979, 491). But even ignoring the letter to Tierney, Ricardo's later writings indicate the practical importance he attached to managing the currency.

His warrants scheme for the payment of the quarterly dividend on the national debt is significant in this regard.[17] A severe shortage of funds, with a corresponding spike in interest rates, occurred four times a year as the government amassed cash to pay the quarterly dividend on the national debt. Ricardo's solution to these quarterly crises appears at several points in his correspondence;[18] it receives its fullest statement in *Economical and Secure Currency*: "The national debt has become so large, and the interest which is paid quarterly upon it is so great a sum, that the mere collecting the money from the receivers general of the taxes, and the consequent reduction of the quantity in circulation, just previously to its being paid to the public creditor, in January, April, July, and October, occasions for a week or more the most distressing want of circulating medium" (4:74). The Bank of England intervened to some extent during these quarterly crises by "discounting bills probably very freely" which "considerably lessened the inconvenience to the mercantile part of the community" (4:74). Ricardo approved of the Bank's action (1:299; 6:312), but deemed it

---

[17] Hollander has similarly recognized the warrants scheme: "Ricardo paid much attention to the problems created by the seasonal absorption and release of funds by the Treasury, and made detailed proposals to assuage that 'great mass of mercantile inconvenience' created thereby" (Hollander 1979, 492n).

[18] Malthus (6:299), Grenfell (6:305), and Trower (7:22) all praised the proposal in letters to Ricardo.

inadequate because, notwithstanding its discounts, there were significant swings in interest rates before and after the dividend payment:

> Nevertheless, it is well known to those who are acquainted with the money market that the distress for money is extreme at the periods I have mentioned. Exchequer bills which usually sell at a premium of five shillings per £100 are at such times at so great a discount that by the purchase of them then, and the resale when the dividends are paid, a profit may often be made equal to the rate of 15 to 20 percent interest for money.... This great distress for money is frequently, after the dividends are paid, followed by as great a plenty so that little use can for some time be made of it.... The very great perfection to which our system of economizing the use of money has arrived by the various operations of banking, rather aggravates the peculiar evil of which I am speaking; because, when the quantity of circulation is reduced, in consequence of the improvements which have been adopted in the means of effecting our payments, the abstraction of a million or two from that reduced circulation becomes much more serious in its effects, being so much larger a proportion of the whole circulation (4:74–75).

Ricardo proposed that the Bank provide dividend warrants, payable to the bearer, but also receivable in payment of taxes (4:75–76). He believed most warrants would not be presented to the Bank, but would be applied in payment of taxes, which would obviate the need for collecting and dispersing millions in taxes and dividend payments.

The third application of Ricardo's monetary policy appears in his statements on the Irish banking crisis of 1820. The hazards of banking in Ireland came to the attention of Parliament in 1821 after eleven of fourteen banks in the south of that country stopped payment. The Bank of Ireland refused to expand its circulation to compensate for the monetary contraction that occurred as private banks failed. Because of the Bank's inaction, according to Ricardo, "persons had been under the necessity of incurring the expense of conveying gold coin to Ireland, to remedy an evil arising out of the deficiency of circulation from the failures in the south. If the Bank of Ireland had filled the void so occasioned, as it was their duty to have done, the evil would have been avoided" (2 Feb. 1821, 5:70).

In response to the Irish banking crisis, Parliament approved a sum of £500,000 to be lent through commissioners at 5 percent interest to businesses that could provide adequate collateral. At the same time, the Bank of Ireland reversed its former restrictive policy and began freely discounting commercial notes. As a result of the Bank's action, the shortage of funds in Ireland was much reduced so that Irish businesses applied for only £100,000 of the £500,000 voted by Parliament (5:98).

Upon learning of the Bank's decisive action, Ricardo retracted his former criticism:

[The Bank of Ireland] did seem to him to have acted with a degree of energy, which, if it had been the case of this country, they would have found the Bank of England not ready to have adopted. What was the case of the Bank of Ireland? The stoppage of a number of private banks in the country rendered it absolutely necessary that a very great increase in the circulation, of some sort or another, should be provided. Either the diminution of the circulating medium must be supplied by coin, or a powerful effort must be made by the Bank of Ireland to make up the deficiency by an issue of notes. The Bank of Ireland did make that great effort to the amount, he believed, of 50 per cent; and, from what he had himself heard from the Governor of the Bank of Ireland, that issue would have been increased still farther if those securities had been offered on which the Bank of Ireland usually made their advances (5:99).

Because Ricardo approved of the Bank's increase of its circulation by as much as 50 percent in a time of crisis, it is again evident that he did not want a paper circulation tied directly to gold, but that he allowed some scope for discretionary monetary policy.

There is a final situation showing Ricardo's thoughts on discretion. Ricardo criticized the Bank of England for its passive monetary policy from 1820 onward. He would have preferred for the Bank to have lowered its discount rate. This would have prevented the rise of sterling on the foreign exchange above par; it would have prevented the importation of gold and the accumulation of a vast hoard at the Bank; and it would have kept the value of gold stable relative to other commodities (4:232; 5:312). As Parliament considered the act in early 1819, Ricardo's one reservation about the legislation was that it included no check against an excessive contraction of banknotes. The Bank fixed its discount rate on commercial paper at 5 percent. Ricardo feared that if the market rate of profit declined below 5 percent, the currency might become too restricted: "as the Bank directors were governed by certain traditional limits, or something like limits, in discounting to individual merchants, they might have difficulty in keeping up the requisite amount of currency . . . if they had no other means of supplying the requisite amount of circulation but by discounting bills, he feared the public might suffer from a scarcity of currency" (5:12). If the Bank did "starve the circulation," gold would be brought to the Mint and coined, restoring the money supply to its proper level, but "in the interim between the reduction of the Bank issues and the supply afforded from the Mint, the country might seriously feel the deficiency" (5:13).

This is exactly what happened. The Bank kept its discount rate at 5 percent – a level above the market rate of interest. Its commercial discounts dropped sharply. The total circulation, including coins, remained constant (see App. B.6), but because the economy was expanding rapidly, prices – and notably the price of gold – declined. Many persons brought gold to the Bank – so much gold that between May 1821 and December 1823 the Bank was able to issue £13 million in sovereigns, while retaining a hoard of £14 million.[19] Ricardo criticized the Bank for not maintaining the money supply at a level sufficient to prevent a fall in prices and for acquiring so much bullion as to bid up its world relative price (8 Mar. 1822, 5:143–144).

The directors of the Bank defended themselves on the grounds that the combined circulation of banknotes and sovereigns increased after the Resumption Act passed (see, for instance, the statements of the Governor at the Bank Court, 21 Mar. 1822, in Ricardo, 4:232n). The directors' second defense of their administration of the resumption process was that the Bank had made no attempt to acquire bullion. The Bank had been entirely passive, it only purchased gold brought to the bullion office. Ricardo knew that the Bank had been passive insofar as it made no attempt either to purchase bullion or to contract its issues. He read the pamphlet by Samuel Turner – a director of the Bank – that described the Bank's policy (20 May 1822, 9:197). He even cited the pamphlet in a Parliamentary debate:

Mr. Turner, who had been in the direction for two years, decidedly said, that as to the operations of the Bank, Mr. Peel's bill remained a dead letter. It had neither accelerated nor retarded payments in specie.... Taking into consideration the rule by which the bank directors generally admitted they regulated their issues, namely, the application for discounts, and coupling with that the low rate of the interest of money, the circulation would have been the same, and consequently the distress of agriculture as great, even if that bill had never passed (26 Feb. 1823, 5:254–255).

But what Ricardo understood – and what Viner has pointed out – is that the Bank's supposed passivity was irrelevant, for by keeping its discount rate above the market rate of profit, the Bank effectively adopted a restrictive monetary policy (Viner 1937, 181). When the Bank finally reduced its discount rate in June 1822 from 5 to 4 percent, Ricardo was "very glad to hear that the Bank had at length begun to discount at 4 per cent.; and he thought they should have done so long before. Had they persisted in

---

[19] Ricardo did not object to the Bank issuing coin. The harm was done when the Bank purchased enough bullion to raise the world relative price of gold.

demanding 5 per cent; they would have been without a single note to cash . . . [because of] the market price of the loan of money being lower [than 5 percent]" (5:222–223).

Monetary Response to Aggregate Supply Shocks

The extent to which Ricardo endorsed discretionary monetary policy has been obscured by the appendix to the *High Price of Bullion* (1811) where he recommends that the central bank curb the money supply in response to an aggregate supply shock. The discussion seems inconsistent with statements in *Secure Currency* (1816) that allow for discretion. Viner and Jacob Hollander attribute differences in the pamphlets to a maturing of Ricardo's ideas (Viner 1937, 139–140, 203–206; Hollander 1911b, 431–432). But perhaps the policies outlined in *High Price* can be reconciled with those in *Secure Currency*. For *High Price* addresses an aggregate supply shock, whereas *Secure Currency* is concerned with a monetary contraction, or a withdrawal of private credit, leading to a reduction in aggregate demand. Because the primary objective in both pamphlets is price stability,[20] the credit shocks described in *Secure Currency* call for monetary expansion, whereas the failed harvest considered in the appendix to *High Price* requires monetary contraction to maintain the convertibility of banknotes and the par of the exchange. Ricardo understood that monetary contraction could cause "considerable distress and difficulty to the mercantile classes" and that the Bank could act to prevent such distress (11 Dec. 1811, 6:67). However, this was of secondary importance; restoring the gold standard to protect price stability was the primary concern.

Ricardo's proposal in *High Price* to increase (decrease) the money supply in response to an expansion (reduction) in aggregate supply has merit given the limited ability of the directors of the Bank to conduct discretionary monetary policy in the modern, countercyclical sense – in fact, given their penchant to run the Bank like an ordinary commercial concern and to conduct a procyclical policy. The choice confronting Ricardo

---

[20] His support for this view is stated at length in *Secure Currency* (1816, 4:54–55): "All writers on the subject of money have agreed that uniformity in the value of the circulating medium is an object greatly to be desired . . . It was the comparative steadiness in the value of the precious metals, for periods of some duration, which probably was the cause of the preference given to them in all countries, as a standard by which to measure the value of other things. A currency may be considered as perfect, of which the standard is invariable, which always conforms to that standard, and in the use of which the utmost economy is practiced."

was not whether the monetary authority should adhere blindly to the gold standard, as opposed to mitigating the output effects of the failed harvest, but whether it should retain the semblance of monetary stability afforded by gold or abandon that standard, leaving the Bank – in tandem with the government – to manage the inconvertible pound.

High Price considers how the Bank of England should respond if a deficient harvest leads to vast importations of corn and a fall of sterling on the foreign exchange: "England, in consequence of a bad harvest, would come under the case mentioned at page [53] of this work, of a country having been deprived of a part of its commodities, and therefore requiring a diminished amount of circulating medium. The currency which was before equal to the payments would now become superabundant . . . the exportation of this sum, therefore, would restore the value of her currency to the value of the currencies of other countries. Thus it appears to be satisfactorily proved that a bad harvest operates on the exchange in no other way than by causing the currency which was before at its just level to become redundant" (3:106–107).[21]

In the event of a failed harvest, the Bank of England faced three options: contract the money supply to maintain convertibility and hold the foreign exchange at par; lend freely but maintain convertibility by having a bullion reserve sufficient to fund a prolonged external drain; or suspend convertibility and provide sufficient credit to counteract, at least partly, the output effects of the shock. The merit of the first option – that endorsed by *High Price* – is that it safeguards convertibility and therefore a degree of price stability. The shortcomings of the policy are that it aggravates the output effects of the initial shock, it impinges on the central bank's ability to protect domestic credit, and in extreme cases it can actually worsen the external drain of bullion. As Thornton observed, a severe reduction of credit in response to an external drain could "exceedingly distress trade and discourage manufactures as to impair . . . those sources of our returning wealth to which we must chiefly trust for the restoration of our balance of trade, and for bringing back the tide of gold in to Great Britain" (Thornton 1802, 151–153). For this reason, Thornton recommended that the Bank hold enough bullion to fund an external drain for up to two years – in the event of consecutive failed harvests – so that

---

[21] In Ricardian nomenclature "redundant" signifies a circulation of inconvertible paper exceeding a level that could persist if notes were convertible or if coin also circulated. Similarly, "depreciation" does not mean that money has had "an actual fall of value," but only that there exists "a comparative difference between the value of money, and the standard by which by law it is regulated" (1:149).

the loss of gold would not force the Bank to withdraw credit. In other words, Thornton preferred the second option (152–153).[22] His case for supporting domestic credit is not altogether convincing, however, for he did not expect the Bank of England, as a profit-seeking establishment, to maintain a hoard of the magnitude (£19 million) needed to sustain a two-year external drain (162–164). In a review of *Paper Credit*, Francis Horner also offered no response to a severe external drain. He concluded that "under such a combination of inauspicious circumstances, the usual means of prudence and the rules of ordinary policy might be expected to fail, and necessity would be left to justify those desperate measures which it might suggest" (Horner 1802, 194). As to the third option, suspending convertibility, Ricardo was loath to follow this route. Once released from the gold standard, the Bank had resisted the return to convertibility and had instead mishandled the paper pound in such a way as to actually amplify Britain's economic cycle.

In addition to these three options, a fourth was devised later: the central bank could lend freely at a high rate of interest to stop an external drain without eliminating domestic credit. Under this option, the availability of credit preempts the onset of a financial panic, but the high rate of interest attracts capital from abroad so as to turn the foreign exchange. Ricardo never thought of this option. The proposal did not appear until 1856 in the first edition of MacLeod's *Theory and Practice of Banking* (2:385–393).[23] Also, the fourth option may not have been feasible during Ricardo's lifetime given the usury laws and the primitive state of international capital markets. The usury laws, until 1833, prevented the Bank of England from loaning money – except to the government – at a rate of interest exceeding 5 percent (Ryan 1924, 19–20). Moreover, according

---

[22] Thornton distinguished between an external drain resulting from a high domestic price level and that resulting from temporary circumstances such as a failed harvest. In the first instance, he recommended a gradual monetary contraction; in the second, he allowed that the central Bank might have to permit an unfavorable exchange for some time if necessary to protect domestic credit (Laidler 1987, 634).

[23] Some years later, Macleod made this statement about the policy: "In the first edition of this Work published in 1856, we shewed that there is a Third cause of a drain of bullion, and an adverse exchange, which, however it might be known among commercial men, had never yet, that we have seen, found its way into any commercial book whatever, and most certainly had never been brought forward prominently before the public in Currency discussions. . . . We therefore shewed that the only true method of striking at this demand for gold [an external drain] is by raising the Rate of Discount. . . . This is now the acknowledged principle upon which the Bank of England is managed; and after our work was published, in 1856, the Usury Laws in France were modified in order to enable the Bank of France to adopt it, and, in fact, it is now universally adopted by every Bank in the world" (Macleod 1902, 2:344–347).

to Macleod, communication and travel early in the century were "slow, expensive, and uncertain" so that reversing an unfavorable exchange by raising the domestic short-term rate of interest was impractical "because the cost and delay of the transport of gold would far exceed any profit to be made in the difference of the Rates of Discount." By contrast, at the mid-century "railroads and steamers" reduced the time and expense of transporting bullion, so that "a difference of 2 per cent. between the rates of discount in London and Paris will now draw bullion from one place to the other" (Macleod 1902, 2:347).

Eagly and Smith found a statistically significant association between short-term interest rates in London and Amsterdam, and concluded that even early in the nineteenth century, a rise in the rate of interest of one market would attract funds from the other (Eagly and Smith 1976, 210). Their results, however, are suspect, for they obtained statistically significant results only by dividing the data into subperiods, and of these subperiods, half show interest rates in London and Amsterdam moving in tandem, the other half show interest rates moving in opposite directions. Larry Neal (1987) also studied the integration of financial markets. He compared share prices for the Bank of England, the East India Company, and the South Sea Company – joint stock companies whose shares traded in both London and Amsterdam. Neal found that stock prices in the two cities tended to move together and concluded that the London and Amsterdam markets were highly integrated. The conclusion may be a *non sequitur* because the fact that the prices of a company's stock fluctuate similarly in different markets does not imply that large amounts of capital can be transferred between the markets. Rather, the changes in stock prices might indicate that shareholders in both markets responded rationally to information about corporate earnings.

The Lender of Last Resort

Doubts about Ricardo's ability as a monetary theorist have arisen because of the absence of any reference in his *Plan for a National Bank* to the role of the central bank as lender of last resort. The omission contrasts with *Paper Credit*, wherein Henry Thornton devotes two chapters to the idea that the Bank of England ought to be the ultimate source of credit. Ricardo's oversight is curious because he was aware of the importance of the lender of last resort and even described in his *Notes on the Bullion Report* (1810) how the Exchequer fulfilled the role:

In this crisis, Parliament applied a remedy, very similar, in its effect, to an enlargement of the advances and issues of the Bank; a loan of Exchequer Bills was authorized to be made to as many mercantile persons, giving good security, as should apply for them; and the confidence which this measure diffused, as well as the increased means which it afforded of obtaining Bank Notes through the sale of the Exchequer Bills, speedily relieved the distress both of London and of the country (from the *Bullion Report*; reprinted in Ricardo, 3:349).

The Bank could have pursued an equivalent strategy and thereby obviated the need for the Exchequer to intervene:

If the Bank had been more liberal in their discounts at that period, they would have produced the same effect on general credit as was afterwards done by the issues of Exchequer bills. It would appear that the bank would buy the exchequer bills but would not discount the merchants bills, – or rather they would not advance money to the merchants without the guarantee of parliament. If the bank bought the bills it was then by an increase of circulating medium that public credit was ultimately relieved. If the public and not the bank purchased the bills then was a portion of the circulating medium of the country which had been withdrawn from circulation again brought forth by the credit of government being pledged for the parties requiring relief (*Notes on the Bullion Report*, 3:349).

It was a want of currency which aggravated the evil arising from want of confidence [in 1793]. The issue of commercial Exchequer bills induced the Bank to advance money on them, which they would not have done on other securities (3:399).

The Bank could sustain credit without the intervention of the Exchequer. This was evident, for when the Exchequer did extend loans, "it was by the [consequent] increase of the circulating medium that public credit was relieved."

I submit that Ricardo never attributed to the central bank the role of lender of last resort because the Bank of England did not perform this function. Hayek describes in the introduction to Thornton's *Paper Credit* (1802) how during the eighteenth century "the Bank of England became the Bankers' Bank, the *dernier resort* as Sir Francis Baring described it in 1797, where in an emergency everybody expected to obtain ready money" (Thornton 1802, 38). His account is not altogether correct. It is true that the Bank intervened in minor crises of the eighteenth century, most notably after the collapse of the Ayr Bank in 1772,[24] but the Bank did not regard itself as lender of last resort. Certainly Sir Francis in his *Observations on the Establishment of the Bank of England* (1797) does not make this claim. For though he describes how the Bank of England was, in principle, lender of last resort, Baring makes it clear that in the crisis of 1793, "the Directors caught the panic; their nerves could not

[24] For an explanation of the events leading to the crisis, see Macleod (1902, 2:208–216). Hamilton discusses the intervention by the Bank of England (1956, 8:405–417).

support the daily and constant demand for guineas; and for the purpose of checking that demand, they curtailed their discounts to a point never before experienced, and which placed every part of the commerce of the country in a considerable degree of danger" (Baring 1797, 21–22, 47). The Exchequer was thus forced to extend credit through loans of Exchequer bills. Again, in 1811 and 1825, the Bank refused to grant credit.[25]

The directors of the Bank were not opposed to extending credit; they simply were not willing to extend the Bank's credit. In 1793, for instance, Sir Philip Francis asked the Chancellor of the Exchequer "for what reason the directors of the Bank of England had not been invited to undertake the management and distribution of the relief proposed to be given to the commerce and credit of individuals" (*Parliamentary History* 1793, 30:759–760). Pitt failed to offer a convincing response, leading Fox to suggest that the Bank was unwilling to risk its capital: "It was not quite satisfactory to see that government were obliged to take up what the Bank of England would not touch. . . . He could not help again observing that the bank must have some strong reasons for refusing to discount in the usual way. . . . Who could be more interested in the general credit of the commerce of the country than the Bank of England?" (*Parliamentary History* 1793, 30:762–763). Fox was correct: the Bank was interested in credit and commerce. And its directors did everything in their power – apart from extending loans – to mitigate the shortage of funds. Of the "eminent persons in the city of London" who proposed the issue of Exchequer bills by the government, four served at different times as Governor of the Bank, one other was a director.[26] Moreover, of the twenty commissioners who administered the loans of Exchequer bills on behalf of the government, six had been or were to become Governor of the Bank.[27] In total, eight

---

[25] Speaking of the Bank's policy, Thornton noted: "If there has been any fault in the conduct of the Bank of England, that fault, as I conceive, has rather been, as has just been stated, on the side of too much restricting its notes in the late seasons of alarm, than on that of too much enlarging them" (Thornton 1802, 127).

[26] The names of the men are Samuel Bosanquet, governor 1789–1791 and director 1771–1806; Samuel Thornton, governor 1799–1801, director 1780–1836; Benjamin Winthrop, governor 1802–1804, director 1782–1809; Jeremiah Harman, governor 1814–1816, director 1794–1827; and Thomas Boddington, director 1782–1809. These officials were identified by comparing a list in *Parliamentary History* 1793, 30:753 with Roberts and Kynaston 1995, App. 2.

[27] The names of the men are Edward Darrell, governor 1787–1789 and director 1767–1804; Thomas Raikes, governor 1797–1799, director 1776–1810; John Whitmore, governor 1808–1810, director 1786–1823; William Manning, governor 1812–1814, director from 1790–1831. In addition, Samuel Bosanquet and Jeremiah Harman served as commissioners, bringing the total number of Bank of England governors to six. These officials were

former or future governors of the Bank actively campaigned to see the Exchequer extend credit in its capacity as the lender of last resort.

A similar situation occurred in 1811 when the Select Committee on the State of Commercial Credit recommended a loan of Exchequer bills based on the precedent of 1793: "There appeared a general concurrence of opinion . . . as to the expediency of affording parliamentary relief in the manner in which it was afforded by the issue of exchequer bills in the year 1793" (*Cobbett's Parliamentary Debates* 1812, 19:257). The Bank of England was well positioned to provide assistance but effectively refused, offering credit only on onerous terms. (The conditions are described in Bank of England, *Committee on Discounts: Minutes*, C35/1, 70–71). Huskisson remarked on the Bank's apparent neglect of duty, but apart from him, no one in Parliament – and notably no economist[28] – suggested the Bank should undertake the responsibility of lender of last resort (*Cobbett's*, 19:328–350). Even Henry Thornton supported the Select Committee, though he urged that "the manufacturers should be the persons chiefly benefitted by the proposed measure" (*Cobbett's*, 19:420).

It was against this institutional background and twenty years after *Paper Credit* that Ricardo devised his *Plan for a National Bank*. His omission of any reference to the possible role of the central bank as lender of last resort seems more reasonable in light of the Bank of England's entrenched opposition to the duty.

Conclusion

The chapter reveals Ricardo to be a practical, competent economist. But with a view strictly to the substance of his work, we find it less obvious as to why he became ensconced in the pantheon of monetary economists. His recommendations for monetary policy were orthodox, apart from the ingot plan. The same can be said of the analytic content of his pamphlets – except for his explanation of the mechanism of international debt adjustment. The modest scope of Ricardo's pamphlets contrasts with the sophistication of Thornton's *Paper Credit*.

Thornton provided a more detailed account of monetary instruments. He explained – while Ricardo did not – how the velocities of circulation vary from one instrument to another. Thornton's ideas about monetary

identified by comparing a list in *Parliamentary History* 1793, 30:753, 766 with Roberts and Kynaston 1995, App. 2.

[28] "Economists" as listed in Fetter 1980, App. 3.

policy are also more subtle, that difference being best illustrated by their respective answers to an external drain of bullion. Ricardo countenanced only one response: the Bank of England should curb the money supply to stem an outflow of bullion. He subordinated any concerns about the effects of monetary contraction on domestic credit, output, and employment to the surpassing end of convertibility (and stable prices). In the context of an external drain caused by domestic inflation, Thornton agreed: the only response was a reduction of the circulation. Short-term shocks, such as wartime subsidies to Britain's allies or the importation of corn upon a failure of the domestic harvest, might also lead to the export of bullion. And in such a case, Thornton expressed concern about the consequences of monetary contraction. It was possible that by curbing the money supply, the Bank would so depress domestic commerce as to worsen the balance of trade.[29] Thus, in assessing the monetary response to supply shocks Thornton explored further options: the Bank might amass a hoard sufficient to fund an external drain for up to two years,[30] or the Bank might even suspend convertibility (Laidler 1987, 4:634). Thornton's discussion of the lender of last resort – a subject touched remotely by Ricardo's pamphlets – is also vastly superior.

The irony to which this observation leads is that, as between the two economists, Ricardo's works had the greater rhetorical force and a more lasting influence. Thornton passed from the collective memory of the discipline – till recovered by Hayek – but Ricardo, even in death, was not diminished.

Ricardo made but few additions to the analysis of his predecessors. . . . But the comprehensiveness and the force and skill of his exposition and the assurance and rigor of his reasoning made him at once the leading expositor of the bullionist position. It was largely through Ricardo's writings, moreover, that the bullionist doctrines exercised their influence on the subsequent century of monetary controversy (Viner 1937, 122).

The emblem of his triumph was the split occasioned by the 1844 Bank Charter Act of the Bank of England into Issue and Banking Departments,

---

[29] If the Bank reduced its circulation in these circumstances it might "exceedingly distress trade and discourage manufactures as to impair, in the manner already specified, those sources of our returning wealth to which we must chiefly trust for the restoration of our balance of trade. . . . It is also necessary to notice in this place, that the favorable effect which a limitation of bank paper produces on the exchange is certainly not instantaneous, and may, probably, only be experienced after some considerable interval of time" (Thornton 1802, 152).

[30] "It may be the true policy and duty of the bank to permit, for a time . . . the continuance of that unfavourable exchange, which causes gold to leave the country, and to be drawn out of its own coffers" for up to two years (Thornton 1802, 152–153).

a change based on Ricardo's observation in *National Bank* that issuing banknotes and extending credit are distinct and separable functions.[31] Equally significant, if less obvious, was his role in securing Britain's commitment to the gold standard. By its expositive force and wide circulation, *High Price* helped build a consensus at the time of the Bullion Committee that returning to gold was imperative. Again in 1819 – when the investigation of the Resumption Committees had stalled and serious consideration fell to Alexander Baring's proposal to postpone resumption – it was Ricardo's testimony that created the momentum needed for Peel to bring forward his resolutions. Over the next four years, Ricardo's support for resumption, as against the inflationists and bimetallists, helped preserve the act inviolate. The weight of his reputation remains yet discernible in Peel's negotiation of the 1844 Bank Charter Act. That act sealed Ricardo's significance, for there were no further substantive changes to Britain's monetary system till the Great War (Fetter 1965, 198).

---

[31] Horsefield (1944) explains how Ricardo's proposal was revisited by Torrens in his *Letter to Lord Melbourne* (1837), whereupon it immediately entered the debate that led to the Bank Charter Act.

EIGHT

Conclusion

The preceding chapters show how the Ricardian formulation of macro-economics developed in response to events of the early nineteenth century. Chapters 2 and 3 provide the historical context. Chapter 4 completes the foundation by showing that Ricardo was well informed about Britain's economic and political situation. That he used this knowledge as a basis for his analysis of contemporary events is established in Chapter 5; the chapter also refutes the view that his treatment of postwar crises was a rationalization of the quantity theory of money and the strict law of markets in the face of overwhelmingly contradictory evidence. Chapter 6 shows that in other contexts, Ricardo did not consistently apply the law of markets. Particularly unsatisfactory is his stance toward expansionary fiscal policy, where his analysis consists of nothing more than the assertion that the economy is at full employment, leaving no scope for government intervention. Chapter 7 considers the merits of Ricardo's monetary policy, including his insistence on the gold standard as a means to curb the instability of the paper pound. This chapter offers final thoughts about Ricardo's empiricism, the predictive power of his model of economic growth, and the practicality of his monetary pamphlets.

Ricardo as an Empirical Economist

Ricardo is often contrasted unfavorably with Adam Smith as an empirical economist. Smith is considered the more practical thinker, Ricardo the abstract theorist: "Smith had continuous resort to factual materials while Ricardo's 1815 *Essay* and 1817 *Principles* contain no facts at all" (O'Brien 1982, 7); and again, "If Smith's work had an important empirical dimension, Classical economics in its Ricardian formulation was staunchly theoretical... Complementing this confidence in theory was a relative unconcern amongst leading Classicals with the particular facts of economic life. Classical economics provides a high point (or low point?) of a naive overconfidence in theorising and a cool indifference for the results of empirical inquiry" (Coleman 1996, 207–208).

Analysis of Ricardo's treatment of the postwar transition does not sustain this criticism. Adam Smith summarized the transition process after the Seven Years War in the following terms (1776, 499–500):

> By reduction of the army and navy at the end of the late war, more than a hundred thousand soldiers and seamen, a number equal to what is employed in the greatest manufactures, were all at once thrown out of their ordinary employment; but though they no doubt suffered some inconvenience, they were not thereby deprived of all employment and subsistence. The greater part of the seamen, it is probable, gradually betook themselves to the merchant-service as they could find occasion, and in the meantime both they and the soldiers were absorbed in the great mass of the people.... Not only no great convulsion but no sensible disorder arose from so great a change in the situation of more than a hundred thousand men.... The number of vagrants was scarce any-where sensibly increased by it, even the wages of labour were not reduced by it in any occupation, so far as I have been able to learn, except in that of seamen in the merchant service.

His analysis is correct, for though there was a brief financial crisis the summer of 1763, conditions generally were prosperous (Anderson 1801, 4:8). The Seven Years War probably stimulated British industry (Trebilcock 1969, 477). And this stimulus[1] was not lost in the war's aftermath because foreign demand continued to be robust – particularly for iron, steel, and manufactures (Mitchell 1988, 449, 469). The year 1763 brought London its general ruck of "fury, tumult and virulent libels." But the rabble were not so much disturbed by a commercial depression as by Parliament's passing the "cyder excise" (*Annual Register* 1763, History 34–40), or, in the case

---

[1] The magnitude of the transition after the Seven Years War was, in relative terms, about half as great as after the Napoleonic War: In 1764 Britain's national income was approximately £130 million (Dean and Cole 1967, 156). Annual war expenditures were £18.6 million, or 14 percent of national output (*London Magazine*, Mar. 1763, 142). In 1814, Britain's national income was about £300 million (Dean and Cole 1967, 156). And the government that year spent a combined £70 million (23% of national output) on the military and on subsidies to allied powers (Marshall 1833, Vol. 1, Statement 3). In terms of the numbers of people involved, 410,000 troops were demobilized over a period of three years after the Napoleonic Wars, whereas, according to Smith, 100,000 men were suddenly demobilized in 1763.

of the Spitafields weavers, by the introduction of French silks (Langford 1989, 455).

Ricardo's analysis of the postwar transition, when compared with Smith's assessment of a similar event in 1763, lacks no "important empirical dimension." Ricardo's account of the relationship between disparate shocks and crises reflects what modern economists have discovered to be true: "business fluctuations differ from one another in their immediate causes, their subsequent courses, their duration, and in many other ways" so there is no reason to presume that one model fits all (Baumol 2003, 37–38). As to the initial postwar distress – Ricardo emphasized the transfer of capital from wartime to peacetime industries. This transition was accomplished within two years. His subsequent references to "misallocated capital" allude to misdirected investments in foreign trade and agriculture, which the historical chapters show to have occurred. Ricardo saw the instability of the paper pound as another factor in postwar crises, along with taxes, barriers to foreign trade, and a welfare system geared to produce unsupported children. His analysis is complex. It offers no neat, unified explanations. And, in light of postwar events, this is much to his credit as an empirical economist.

A comparison similar to that between Ricardo and Smith is made frequently between Ricardo and Malthus. For authors who associate Ricardo with Say's identity and the rigid quantity theory, it was the superficial appeal of his macroeconomic model that gave it such currency as to require "the whole force of the Keynesian revolution to overturn it" (Robinson 1978, 14). Keynes perhaps more than any other commentator popularized the negative view of Ricardo in contrast with Malthus (Keynes 1972, 87, 98, 100–101):[2]

It was Ricardo's more fascinating intellectual construction which was victorious, and Ricardo who, by turning his back so completely on Malthus's ideas, constrained the subject for a full hundred years in an artificial groove....

The almost total obliteration of Malthus's line of approach and the complete domination of Ricardo's for a period of a hundred years has been a disaster to the progress of economics....

If only Malthus instead of Ricardo had been the parent stem from which nineteenth-century economics proceeded, what a much wiser and richer place the world would be today! We have laboriously to re-discover and force through the obscuring envelopes of our misguided education what should never have ceased to be obvious.

---

[2] Keynes view was characteristic of the period. Dennis Robertson said that he never read Ricardo (Keynes 1973b, 504). John Hicks, similarly, mentioned that he "restrained his interest in the history of theory" to authors writing after 1870 (Keynes 1973c, 81).

Keynes' bias toward Malthus depended on the alleged superiority of Malthus' methodology, which centered on "handling practical economic problems," especially those related to postwar distress. He went so far as to describe Chapter 7 of Malthus' *Principles* as "the best economic analysis ever written of the events of 1815–20," in contrast with Ricardo, who failed "to see any significance in [Malthus'] line of thought" (Keynes 1972, 101–102). Keynes embraced his doctrinal forefather based on two presumptions: the post-Napoleonic era bore a striking resemblance to the decade following World War I;[3] and, in this milieu, Malthus made the "same fundamental critique of a market economy that Keynes was making" (Rutherford 1987, 187). That is to say, Malthus developed the doctrine of effective demand based on his "complete comprehension of the effects of excessive saving on output via its effects on profits" (Clarke 1988, 267; Keynes 1972, 99).

Neither presumption was correct. The post-Napoleonic era did not resemble the decade following World War I in the ways Keynes imagined. He thought that the 1820s and 1830s were characterized by monetary deflation and "twenty years of successive credit maladjustments" (Keynes 1981a, 339), accompanied by a drop in effectual demand caused by the diversion of wartime expenditures to private savings and by the return to gold (Keynes 1972, 101). The foregoing chapters have shown that in the postwar decade, there was no failure of consumers to "demand effectually"; monetary deflation was short-lived; and there was no prolonged depression.

Keynes also misread Malthus' analysis of postwar events. In *Essays on Biography*, he attributed to Malthus a sophisticated theory of demand that explained the role of excessive saving in the postwar depression (1972, 102, 101):

The whole problem of the balance between Saving and Investment had been posed in the Preface to the book [Malthus' *Principles*].
He [Malthus] points out that the trouble was due to the diversion of resources, previously devoted to war, to the accumulation of savings; that in such circumstances deficiency of savings could not possibly be the cause, and saving, though

---

[3] Testifying before the MacMillan Committee in February 1930, Keynes stated: "Throughout history I can only recall two occasions at all comparable to the present one. One was the highly analogous deflation which followed the Napoleonic Wars, the first period of which was similar to the deflation following 1920–1, and was carried through without very great difficulty. The second deflation, very much like the one we are going through now, was one which brought this country to the verge of revolution...the troubles of the [18]20s and [18]30s are largely traceable to that" (Keynes 1981b, 20:64).

a private virtue, had ceased to be a public duty; and that public works and expenditure by landlords and persons of property was the appropriate remedy.

It has already been shown that Malthus' explanation of postwar events involved more than a diversion of wartime expenditures to private savings. His main argument was that a fall in the incomes of landlords and farmers in 1813 set off a cascade of economic ruin that depressed domestic agriculture, manufacturing, and foreign trade for a decade. Additional causes were the cessation of wartime expenditures, the collapse of the country banks in 1815–1816, and the resumption of cash payments by the Bank of England in 1819. Malthus also allowed the theoretical possibility that excessive saving (in the sense of overinvestment) could lead to unemployment.

Some of Malthus' observations are consistent with a gap between *ex ante* saving and investment. The destruction of credit by country banks and by the Bank of England raised interest rates and caused planned savings to exceed investment. Periodic financial crises, marked by hoarding and high rates of interest, were also troublesome; but these were short-term phenomena. The point that interested Keynes – the possibility that planned saving could exceed investment as an ongoing state of affairs – was not part of Malthus' explanation of postwar conditions.

Malthus deserves credit for observing that aggregate demand affects output and employment, but it is wrong to assume that he articulated a viable theory of demand. Keynes himself began to appreciate this as he wrote the *General Theory*: "Since Malthus was unable to explain clearly (apart from an appeal to the facts of common observation) how and why effective demand could be deficient or excessive, he failed to furnish an alternative construction; and Ricardo conquered England as completely as the Holy Inquisition conquered Spain" (Keynes 1973a, 32). The barrier between Malthus' insight that demand is a strategic variable and an actual theory of demand lies in explaining how the elements of demand – in particular consumption and investment – fall short.

Keynes approached the problem by focusing on investment. In the model of the *General Theory*, investment continues until no capital-asset affords an expected yield greater than the market rate of interest. It follows that the decision to invest "depends partly on the investment demand-schedule and partly on the rate of interest" (Keynes 1973a, 137). There is a minimum market rate of interest; the rate exceeds zero[4] because

---

[4] In the *Essays in Biography*, Keynes noted how Malthus missed this point: "Malthus' defect lay in his overlooking entirely the part played by the rate of interest. . . . Malthus perceived, as often, what was true; but it is essential to a complete comprehension of why it is true,

of the risk premium attached to lending money (Laidler 1999, 263–265). According to Keynes, in undeveloped economies, planned saving equals investment at rates of interest above the minimum. As capital accumulates, investment opportunities dry up, causing a leftward shift of the investment demand schedule.[5] No corresponding shift occurs in the saving schedule. Over time, the market rate of interest falls to the minimum. From then on, and barring exogenous shocks to the investment and saving schedules, planned saving exceeds investment. Expressed geometrically, the saving schedule lies to the right of the investment demand schedule at all market rates of interest. Private consumption – in lieu of investment – might preserve investment opportunities: "In so far as millionaires find their satisfaction in building mighty mansions to contain their bodies when alive and pyramids to shelter them after death, or, repenting of their sins, erect cathedrals and endow monasteries or foreign missions, the day when abundance of capital will interfere with abundance of output may be postponed" (Keynes 1973a, 220). But individuals could not be relied on to spend unproductively. The solution, according to Keynes, was for government to spend, productively if possible, and allow the matching savings to be generated from the expanded output that resulted.

Nothing in Malthus' work anticipates Keynes' explanation of why demand becomes deficient. For Malthus, too little investment was never a problem: "it was essential to the Malthusian system that savings were automatically invested, not because of control via the rate of interest, but simply because parsimony was always with a view to active investment" (Corry 1962, 126). Investment became a concern only if it proceeded too rapidly, bringing unsaleable increments of consumer goods. To the extent that demand was deficient, Malthus thought the shortfall originated with private consumption. He may have been correct, but his theory of consumer behavior – that consumers spend too little because they are sated – obscured the merits of his insight. Ricardo considered the satiation argument untenable as an explanation of postwar conditions. It was especially untenable given that excise reports showed a rising consumption of basic articles.

---

to explain how an excess of frugality does not bring with it a decline to zero in the rate of interest" (Keynes 1972, 102).

[5] For Keynes, investment demand depended on the "marginal efficiency of capital," which he defined as "that rate of discount which would make the present value of the series of annuities given by the returns expected from the capital-asset during its life just equal to its supply price" (Keynes 1973a, 135). He aggregated marginal efficiency schedules across all types of capital to arrive at an "investment demand-schedule" (136).

In terms of his proposals for government policy, Malthus was fully orthodox: "in the final analysis, Malthus' remedy was *laissez-faire* as far as social control of the saving-investment mechanism was concerned" (Corry 1962, 128). He believed that public works subsidized the growth of population and, over time, might even depress wages (Corry 1962, 160). He also supported the gold standard and even recommended a return to convertibility in 1816, a year of general depression.

It is difficult to determine how Keynes' evaluation of Ricardo and Malthus might have changed had he been better informed about nineteenth-century economic history. But, he would not have penned the sweeping condemnation of Ricardo's alleged lack of empiricism nor so strongly lauded Malthus' "practical" analysis. Malthus resided closer than Keynes realized to the mainstream of classical economics in the concepts he used – especially the "saving is spending" idea – and in terms of proposals for government policy. The intellectual link with Keynes is "more apparent than real" (Corry 1962, 126) and relies on an exaggerated importance attached to Malthus' use of the term "effective demand."

The Predictive Power of the Ricardian Growth Model

Economic growth was a prominent theme in classical writings. Then, as now, no two economists shared an identical growth model, but they did share a number of concepts. Two have been identified by Professor Samuelson (1978): (1) in the absence of land-augmenting technical change, there will be diminishing returns in agriculture, and (2) *ceteris paribus*, the more rapid the rate of population growth, the lower the real wage. Whether classical economists made predictions about the actual path of economic variables based on these concepts or simply viewed the concepts as descriptions of general tendencies remains an open question.[6] Assuming the former, Wrigley and Schofield (1981) tested the predictive power of classical models as those models describe the inverse relationship between population and real wages and the positive correlation between population and the cost of subsistence. Their results are striking.

---

[6] In Ricardo's case, the model predicts that the cost of subsistence rises over time – barring technical advances in agriculture – because the margin of cultivation extends with every increase in population. At some point, the rise in the cost of subsistence translates into higher money wages; this slows the rate of capital accumulation and thus the rate of growth of the demand for labor. In the progressive state, there are periods of rising population and rising real wages. But Ricardo anticipated that as the economy approaches stationarity, a negative correlation develops between population and real wages.

For a period of 250 years, prior to 1800, there was a stable relationship between the rate of growth of population and the rate of change of the cost of subsistence. The data show that population and the cost of subsistence consistently fluctuated in a ratio of 1 to 1.5 – that is, a 10 percent rise (or fall) of population was associated with a 15 percent rise (or fall) in the cost of subsistence. For those 250 years, there was a similar negative correlation of about 1 to 1 between the rate of growth of population and the rate of change of real wages – that is, a 10 percent rise (or fall) in population translated into a 10 percent fall (or rise) in real wages (Wrigley and Schofield 1981, 402–412). Therefore, the classical model served well as a predictive engine for those events:

> There was no flaw in the general logic deployed by the classical economists. Their writings remain authoritative for the analysis of growth within the confines of a traditional economy, an economy bounded by the productivity of land. . . . The nature of the earlier system is depicted with great clarity in the writings of the classical economists. Their success in this regard is indeed the most notable of all the attempts to create an intellectual structure capable of giving insight into the functioning of the type of socio-economic system prevailing in early modern England (Wrigley 1988, 5, 17).

The predictive power of the classical model disappears when applied to the nineteenth century. The connection between population and the cost of subsistence breaks suddenly about 1811 as population, now rising rapidly, doubles over the next sixty years, while the cost of subsistence falls and then levels out. A similar break with respect to real wages occurs in 1806, from which point both population and real wages rise rapidly:

> The historic link between population growth and price rise was broken; an economic revolution had taken place. And by an ironic coincidence, Malthus had given pungent expression to an issue that haunted most pre-industrial societies at almost the last moment when it could still plausibly be represented as relevant to the country in which he was born (Wrigley and Schofield 1981, 403–404).

Classical economists did not foresee the transition that occurred. They did not anticipate the rapid gains in productivity – in agriculture no less than in other sectors – that overwhelmed the effects of diminishing returns to land. They did not expect the transition to free trade and the fall in transportation costs that made available to Britain distant agricultural regions where land scarcity was not so critical. And, perhaps most important, they failed to anticipate "that the food supply could greatly increase, but that the power of population could be checked before it fully adjusted to the available food supply, thereby allowing the average standard of living to rise" (Toye 2000, 92). The classical model assumes that a high real wage triggers a high rate of growth of population. This relationship continued to hold in the nineteenth century; population grew significantly faster than in earlier periods (Wrigley and Schofield 1981, 409–410). The rate of growth of population, however, was not sufficient to undermine the effects of productivity on real wages. Thus, the nineteenth century saw a rapid rise of both population and real wages.

The transformation of Britain's economy rendered the classical model obsolete as a predictive engine. Hutchison identifies the change as one reason for the abandonment of the classical theory:

> The 1850s and 1860s saw such a great increase in population accompanied by such a palpable rise in living standards that the classical population theory, and its law of 'natural' subsistence-wages, could only in some degree be saved by putting the main emphasis on those qualifications (already rather vaguely introduced by Malthus and Ricardo) which robbed the doctrine of almost all its sting and content (Hutchison 1953, 13).

The industrial revolution likely shifted the emphasis of economic study as well. In the late eighteenth and early nineteenth centuries, the presence of a turbulent underclass on the edge of subsistence provided a strong impetus for the study of economic growth. Classical economists responded to the concerns of their society, as shown by their powerful critique of the corn laws and the poor laws. With the prosperity of the industrial age, economic growth ceased to engage the popular imagination. Accordingly, the focus of economic inquiry turned elsewhere.

A Practical Monetary Policy

Doubts perhaps linger about the practicality of Ricardo's recommendations for public policy. Because of his role in Parliament, he has been described as "a prime specimen of that dangerous intellectual type, the extreme abstractionist-deductivist possessed by a passionate eagerness to apply the results of his unrealistic abstractions (models) to the real world" (Hutchison 1992, 104). The decision to revalue sterling according to the terms of the 1819 Resumption Act ranks first among the applications of his abstract models.

As a private institution from 1694 to 1946, the Bank of England suspended convertibility three times: early in the Napoleonic Wars, 1797; at the start of World War I, officially in 1919; and in 1931 after a failed attempt to return sterling to its prewar value. Convertibility had been often at risk,[7] but only under the weight of sustained, world-wide conflict did the gold standard break down. The two times the Bank returned to gold it faced the choice of either resuming cash payments at the prewar parity or devaluing sterling. In the first instance, the 1819 Resumption Act committed the Bank to deflation of 4 percent over two years. In the second instance, the 1925 Gold Standard Act attempted to regain the ancient par by immediately depressing all commodity and factor prices by about 10 percent. The Act of 1819 – which adhered to Ricardo's proposal – succeeded. The Act of 1925 did not. By comparing Ricardo's assessment of devaluation in 1819 with the policies chosen by Churchill's advisors in 1925 it becomes evident that Ricardo had a mature concern for the practical consequences of monetary policy. His position was, in fact, similar to Keynes' observations a century later.

Ricardo endorsed the ancient standard, but not at all costs. A significant revaluation of sterling would cause unacceptable losses to industry and high unemployment. The proximity of sterling to par in 1819 led him to believe that the real effects of deflation would be slight. At the same time, returning to par would keep faith with public creditors, while the alternative, devaluation, would set a bad precedent, possibly undermining the currency as a medium of investment.

Churchill faced a similar tradeoff between the output effects of returning to par and the damage to sterling as an international currency if failing to do so. The decision in 1925, however, was complicated by factors not known to Ricardo. Of upmost importance, the United States was now an economic power and it was on the gold standard. Thus, pegging sterling to gold meant fixing the sterling–dollar exchange rate.[8]

Officials at H. M. Treasury and the Bank of England looked to regain the palmy years before the war, when London was the hub of world trade and finance. In those years, Britain's strong current account,[9] the openness of the London gold market, and the success of the Bank of

---

[7] Cash payments were partially stopped in 1696 because of a lack of coinage from the Mint (Clapham 1945, 1:36). Reserves at the Bank were dangerously low at approximately ten-year intervals during the eighteenth century. In the nineteenth century, there were crises in 1825–1826 and 1838–1839; under the curious dichotomy of the 1844 Bank Charter Act the reserves of the Banking Department were again at risk in 1847, 1857, and 1866 (Andreades 1966).

[8] The prewar content of the pound had been 123.27 grains of fine gold, making it equivalent in value to $4.86. In the postwar period, sterling dropped to as low as $3.40 (Galbraith 1995, 167).

[9] In the century before 1913, Britain ran a current account surplus in all but two years. The tendency of sterling to rise on the foreign exchange because of its strong current account was offset by overseas lending (Moggridge 1972, 7). In the four decades leading up to the

England in maintaining convertibility made sterling the international standard. Forty percent of the world's foreign exchange reserves were held in sterling (Eichengreen 1996, 24). Perhaps 90 percent of world trade was settled through the London discount market (Broz 1997, 67). Britain was the premier supplier of capital, both in the volume of its exports and in the breadth of services offered by the City (Gallarotti 1995, 196–199). Moreover, the macroeconomic performance of leading nations was convergent – prices, interest rates, and business cycles tended to move in parallel – so that adjustments to the world's financial order could be accomplished by the subtle manipulation of the Bank rate that drew gold to London or sent it abroad as circumstances dictated (Gallarotti 1995, 202–203). The memory of that age faded slowly; in 1925, it remained too vivid for the governing class to realize all was undone.

Among the differences after the war, Britain's balance of payments had deteriorated. Exports were down[10] owing to a drop in world trade and, more importantly, to the collapse of cooperation among central banks. There arose instead competitive devaluations by all countries except the United States and Britain that deranged foreign exchange rates and trade flows: the French devalued the franc to one-fifth its prewar parity, the lira sunk to one-fourth, and the mark was worthless, though German exports were stimulated because the foreign exchange value of the mark fell more rapidly than prices rose internally. A similar devaluation occurred in the countries of Central and Eastern Europe (Feinstein, Temin, and Toniolo 1997, 46). Britain's capital position was also weak. The country found itself heavily indebted to the United States, with debts payable in an appreciating currency. At the same time, Britain was a creditor to France, Russia, and Italy, all of which were at various stages of default (Moggridge 1972, 30–31).

Officials hoped that a return to gold would restore London's preeminent place in trade and finance. They envisioned that convertibility would stabilize exchange rates and thereby stimulate foreign trade and boost the demand for Britain's manufactures. Stable exchanges would encourage foreign governments to hold balances in sterling. Perhaps sterling bills would again serve as the standard for settlement of international trade. Perhaps also the Bank of England could regain control of exchange rates.

---

war, 40 percent of British savings were invested abroad; returns on these investments accounted for a staggering 10 percent of national income (Gallarotti 1995, 196).

[10] Britain's trade deficit increased from £134 million in 1913 to £337 million in 1924 (Moggridge 1972, 30).

Doubts about the solidity of sterling in the postwar years had undermined the Bank's ability to manage capital movements. With confidence restored, adjustments to the discount rate might again draw short-term capital, enabling the Bank to control the exchanges within a range. If so, the transition to convertibility would be self-reinforcing, for convertibility would renew the willingness of international business to move financial assets through London; this, in turn, would enhance the security of sterling. By the same token, if Britain failed to resume gold payments, officials expected this would undermine the confidence of the international trading and financial communities.

The return to gold seemed feasible for a time. The U.S. Federal Reserve embarked on a mildly inflationary policy the summer of 1924, cutting interest rates 1.5 percent (Moggridge 1972, 51–53). The possible increase of American foreign lending also promised to depress the dollar (Moggridge 1972, 94). Speculation caused the sterling–dollar exchange rate to appreciate, nearing the prewar parity by late 1924.[11] It was hoped that the appreciation of sterling was sustainable. Some advisors thought it was, though the estimates of purchasing power parity upon which they relied were based on wholesale prices, which tended to underestimate the gap between the target rate of $4.86 and the rate sustainable under current conditions (Moggridge 1972, 89–90). Even if sterling was below par, the Federal Reserve and J. P. Morgan promised loans of up to $500 million to offset deficiencies in Britain's balance of payments while sterling was appreciating (Moggridge 1972, 60). The combination of these factors persuaded many officials that the negative effects of resumption would be brief.

There were risks, of course. No one knew whether the sterling–dollar exchange rate reflected permanent aspects of the current and capital accounts, or whether the rise of sterling was a short-term phenomenon based on speculation that the Bank would attempt to recover the ancient par. Heavy reliance also fell on the United States' willingness to pursue inflationary measures. But U.S. policy was – as it has always been – dominated by internal concerns. Thus there was a risk – and one eventually realized – that the Federal Reserve would raise interest rates, causing the transfer of capital to New York and undercutting Britain's balance of payments. There was also a possibility that the world relative price of gold would rise as twenty European countries resumed convertibility and

---

[11] Sterling moved from $4.49 in Oct. to $4.63 in Nov. and then to $4.72 on 31 Dec. 1924 (Moggridge 1972, 57n).

vied over a limited stock of bullion. Another factor about which little was known was how the home market would respond to deflation. If wages proved downwardly rigid, high interest rates were certain to create unemployment, especially in export industries which were already languishing (Sayers 1970, 89–90). Little consideration was given to the effects on British trade of pegging sterling at a high rate while other countries devalued their currencies. Officials, preoccupied with the capital account, somehow overlooked the fact that an exchange of \$4.86 might ruin exports and trigger an insoluble current account deficit (Moggridge 1972, 92–93).

Keynes personally cautioned Churchill against the return to gold. Economic conditions were already difficult: unemployment was high, sterling was overvalued, and export industries were struggling. The Chancellor's experts had erred in two respects, Keynes suggested, by underestimating the extent to which sterling was devalued and by failing to recognize that there was no mechanism to coordinate the fall of commodity and factor prices required by a move to the prewar parity:[12]

This meant unemployment and downward adjustments of wages and prolonged strikes in some of the heavy industries, at the end of which it would be found that these industries had undergone a permanent contraction. It was much better, therefore, to try to keep domestic prices and nominal wage rates stable and allow the exchanges to fluctuate.[13]

In the end, Churchill was won over by political considerations: "This isn't entirely an economic matter; it is a political decision, for it involves proclaiming that we cannot, for the time being at any rate, complete the undertaking which we all acclaimed as necessary in 1918, and introducing legislation accordingly."[14]

The decision to return to gold was announced in April 1925. The risks of that policy came home with a vengeance. From March 1925 to April 1927 the price level, as measured by the British Board of Trade index, fell 16 percent (Hawtrey 1931, 27). The Bank rate was put up to 5 percent, nominally, which meant that real interest rates were closer to 12 percent (Hawtrey 1931, 26). Wages were downwardly rigid; the attempt to cut

---

[12] Keynes (1925) *The Economic Consequences of Mr. Churchill*; reprinted in Keynes 1963, 246–250.

[13] Remarks by Keynes to Churchill, recorded by Churchill's private secretary, P. J. Grigg (Gilbert 1976, 100).

[14] Remarks by Churchill, recorded by his private secretary, P. J. Grigg (Gilbert 1976, 100).

wages brought widespread and violent strikes that were perhaps more costly than the savings anticipated from lower wages. The real burden of the national debt rose in proportion to the level of deflation; Keynes estimated that it was higher by £1 billion.[15] From January 1925 to December 1926, net exports fell by £125 million; the number of unemployed grew by one-fifth (Moggridge 1972, 118–119).

Conditions improved in 1927 and continued to mend through 1929: exports, GDP, and employment all rose; capital formation continued apace. In 1930, net exports fell slightly, and more important, invisible earnings from shipping and foreign investments declined by £110 million, pushing the current account into deficit (Moggridge 1972, 118). An influx of capital could have offset the deficit, but just the reverse happened. Overseas sterling countries, faced with a drop in demand for their exports and a decline in overseas lending, turned to London to meet their balance of payments deficits. At the same time, a liquidity crisis emerged on the Continent. The Bank of England managed the situation in 1930, but lost control in 1931 when the sudden exodus of nearly £300 million in short-term capital, combined with the current account deficit, made the defense of $4.86 impossible. The Bank and the Treasury lacked sufficient reserves of gold and foreign exchange. As doubts emerged about whether sterling would remain convertible, foreign lenders refused assistance that might otherwise have been forthcoming. The gold standard was suspended as a matter of necessity on 21 September 1931.[16]

One hundred and ten years earlier Ricardo testified before the Lords and Commons Committees on Resumption that the choice between devaluation and the prewar parity depended on a tradeoff. Devaluation brought the risk of "a great sacrifice of principle" and the injustice of redistributing wealth from creditors to debtors, whereas returning to the prewar parity required deflation and commercial distress. Because of his concern about deflation, Ricardo recommended that Parliament not return to the prewar parity if sterling was depreciated more than 5 percent. It is notable that in this choice he sided with the position later taken by Keynes. Given that, in 1925, sterling was depreciated by 10 percent, Ricardo would have advised the government to permanently devalue the currency, rather than incur the hardships of deflation.

---

[15] Keynes, Comments on the Speeches of the Bank Chairmen, Feb. 1927; reprinted in Keynes 1963, 239.

[16] Keynes (1931) *The End of the Gold Standard*; reprinted in Keynes 1963, 288.

Final Remarks

The Napoleonic conflict was depleting. That Britain prosecuted the war to victory and then returned to peacetime commerce without suffering economic collapse is a credit to the country's civilian and military leaders. Their success was no accident; it was the culmination of judicious policies steadfastly followed. In light of our present circumstances, it seemed good to me to remark on lessons of the British experience.

Of upmost importance, I hope my readers recognize that hard choices are inevitable for a government confronted by murderous enemies bent on global ascendance. In the best of situations, public officials select from less-than-ideal policy options. The difficulty with which Parliament financed the wars against revolutionary and Napoleonic France well illustrates the problem. Taxes were the government's preferred source of funds; but when revenues proved inadequate, the government ran up the national debt; and when the market could sustain no greater demand for funds, the government financed the campaign by having the Bank of England print paper money. Each source of funding was attended with problems: high taxes impeded economic growth, the national debt burdened future generations, and a surfeit of paper money led to inflation. And yet, weighed against the alternative of losing the war, high taxes, debts, and inflation became acceptable costs.

Public officials sometimes neglect the human tendency to respond to incentives. Here, the British experience cautions us against policies that rely on transcendent phenomena. John Bull, like ordinary people everywhere, was an unvarnished pragmatist. One Parliamentary committee after another observed that the demand for poor relief was greater in parishes where its distribution was more liberal. Then, as now, an entrenched system of public assistance fostered dependence. The reason is obvious: poor relief subsidized decisions that would otherwise have been too costly. The role of incentives applies equally to taxation. In the 1820s, thousands of wealthy Brits took their families and capital out of the country to avoid taxes. The mobility of capital was a fiscal constraint in Ricardo's lifetime. With that mobility now vastly increased, no government except one committed to its destruction will forget that the more parasitical a scheme of progressive taxation, the more artful are moneyed persons to fob the national treasury.

With respect to monetary policy, Britain's experience suggests that the central bank can legitimately pursue stable prices as its top priority. Parliament reinstated the gold standard in 1819, signaling a preference for stable prices over other objectives. In the century following, Britain enjoyed un-precedented economic growth. As for fiscal policy, events of the postwar years reinforce the view that management of the business cycle need not take precedence over policies that promote economic growth. Long-term and short-term policies do not necessarily conflict. But when an economy rapidly absorbs unemployed resources, as Britain's economy seemed to do, counter-cyclical fiscal measures can slow the rate of economic growth by diverting resources from private industry to less productive uses in the government sector.

The problems faced by classical economists – inflation, unemployment, wartime deficits, and the clamor for protection – are familiar by reason of our own experience. In part, Ricardo's thoughts about these problems have been integrated in modern economics. I noted several instances in the opening chapter. There is, however, no systematic accretion of economic knowledge; it follows that potentially generative ideas sometimes drop out of use. The study of classical texts is valuable because it preserves the content of economics and reinforces the lessons of recent experience. With this in view, I thank my readers for persevering to the end.

Abbreviations Used in the Appendices

JHC   *Journal of the House of Commons*
JHL   *Journal of the House of Lords*
PP   Great Britain, *Parliamentary Papers*
MF   Microfiche

The Bank of England

Appendix A.1   Bank of England Notes in Circulation, 1813 to 1824

Date	Circulation	Date Reported	Source
1813			
January	£24,390,140		
February	24,180,620		
March	23,294,790		
April	23,977,870		
May	24,471,880		
June	24,524,320		
July	23,908,500		
August	24,167,700		
September	23,964,310		
October	24,314,220		
November	24,172,710		
December	24,395,810		
1814			
January	23,671,420		
February	25,174,860		
March	24,976,750	30 Mar. 1814	PP 1813–1814, 12:119, MF 15.68
April	24,664,030		JHC 1813–1814, 69:825
May	26,172,760		
June	25,518,970		
July	25,901,880	21 July 1814	JHC 1813–1814, 69:826
August	29,483,480		
September	29,202,040		

(*continued*)

Appendix A.1   (*continued*)

Date	Circulation	Date Reported	Source
October	28,336,720		
November	27,857,290		
December	28,161,020		
1815			
January	27,549,120	13 Feb. 1815	PP 1814–1815, 10:223, MF 16.57
February	27,324,510		
March	26,969,580		
April	25,631,030		
May	27,568,310	30 May 1815	PP 1814–1815, 10:291, MF 16.58
June	27,232,310		
July	27,296,540		
August	27,673,070		
September	27,290,940		
October	27,388,370		
November	26,213,690		
December	25,750,550		
1816			
January	25,032,020		
February	26,816,240		
March	26,692,680		
April	26,401,820	29 Apr. 1816	PP 1816, 13:385, MF 17.77
May	26,931,680	20 June 1816	PP 1816, 13:421, MF 17.78
June	25,355,390		
July	25,600,740		
August	27,619,890		
September	26,366,010		
October	25,479,980		
November	26,663,990		
December	25,342,450	18 Feb. 1817	PP 1817, 17:25, 29, MF 18.83
1817			
January	24,959,690		
February	27,703,780		
March	27,182,580		
April	26,984,050		
May	28,351,000	1 July 1817	PP 1817, 17:43, MF 18.83
June	26,449,790		
July	25,800,260		
August	30,920,360		
September	28,938,560		
October	28,925,910		
November	29,658,950		
December	28,465,490		

Date	Circulation	Date Reported	Source
1818			
January	26,407,510	13 Feb. 1818	JHC 1818, 73:748
February	28,945,580		
March	28,248,120	9 Mar. 1818	JHC 1818, 73:748
April	26,989,740	15 Apr. 1818	JHC 1818, 73:748
May	28,466,690	2 June 1818	JHC 1818, 73:749
June	26,605,057		
July	26,034,980		
August	27,007,919		
September	26,091,967		
October	26,289,116		
November	26,279,878		
December	25,632,155		
1819			
January	25,338,830	1 Feb. 1819	JHC 1819, 74:1106
February	26,157,710		
March	25,048,220	3 Mar. 1819	JHC 1819, 74:1109
April	20,816,380	28 Apr. 1819	JHC 1819, 74:1109
May	26,178,080	24 May 1819	JHC 1819, 74:1110
June	24,951,040	6 July 1819	JHC 1819, 74:1110
July	23,280,770		
August	26,397,310		
September	24,684,450		
October	24,348,350		
November	24,547,470	3 Dec. 1819	JHC 1819–1820, 75:880
December	22,586,620	23 Dec. 1819	JHC 1819–1820, 75:880
1820			
January	23,177,920		
February	24,680,390		
March	23,011,480		
April	22,805,400		
May	24,317,730	4 May 1820	JHC 1819–1820, 75:880
June	22,655,190	3 July 1820	JHC 1819–1820, 75:880
July	23,417,910	15 July 1820	JHC 1819–1820, 75:880
August	25,066,740		
September	24,437,110		
October	22,736,120		
November	24,248,220		
December	22,771,180		
1821			
January	21,571,700		
February	24,914,280	12 Feb. 1821	JHC 1821, 76:1183
March	23,702,160		

(continued)

Appendix A

Appendix A.1 (*continued*)

Date	Circulation	Date Reported	Source
April	23,671,260		
May	24,346,050		
June	21,512,000	20 June 1821	JHC 1821, 76:1185
July	19,304,700		
August	21,770,490		
September	20,172,200		
October	18,742,220		
November	19,259,880		
December	17,635,910		
1822			
January	16,950,130		
February	19,211,830	15 Feb. 1822	JHC 1822, 77:1131
March	18,387,030		
April	17,149,290		
May	17,798,280	10 May 1822	JHC 1822, 77:1140
June	16,505,280	27 June 1822	JHC 1822, 77:1140
July	16,834,780	29 July 1822	JHC 1822, 77:1140
August	19,287,780		
September	17,149,130		
October	17,231,830		
November	17,753,060		
December	16,370,590		
1823			
January	16,379,510		
February	18,652,590	14 Feb. 1823	PP 1823, 14:139, MF 25.111
March	18,106,350		
April	16,845,830	3 May 1823	PP 1823, 14:149, MF 25.111
May	18,994,040		
June	17,602,970		
July	16,975,880		
August	20,221,900		
September	18,884,200		
October	17,879,250		
November	21,779,650		
December	18,664,200		
1824			
January	17,220,790		
February	20,309,170	16 Feb. 1824	PP 1824, 15:597, MF 26.98
March	19,301,020		
April	19,313,980		
May	20,514,120		
June	19,396,850		
July	18,804,980		

Date	Circulation	Date Reported	Source
August	21,312,110		
September	19,737,820		House of Commons
October	19,065,310		Bank Charter Committee
November	21,413,880		*Digest of Evidence* 1832, App. 13
December	20,352,080		

Sources: Each report is titled "Account of the Weekly Amount of Bank Notes in Circulation" and can be found in the *Journal of the House of Commons* (JHC) and in the *Parliamentary Papers* (PP).

Appendix A.2   Cash and Bullion Hoard of the Bank of England, 1814 to 1824

Date	Amount of Hoard	Bank of England's Index for the Hoard
1814		
January 29	£2,192,813	436
February		
March		
April 30	2,391,881	476
May		
June		
July 30	2,173,170	432
August		
September		
October 29	2,166,383	430
November 5	2,161,000	430
December		
1815		
January 28	2,049,679	408
February	2,009,000	
March 4	2,034,000	406
April 29	2,091,609	416
May		
June		
July 29	3,492,281	696
August		
September		
October 28	4,002,838	798
November		
December		

(*continued*)

Appendix A.2 *(continued)*

Date	Amount of Hoard	Bank of England's Index for the Hoard
1816		
January 27	4,474,028	892
February	4,566,000	
March 2	4,678,000	934
April 27	5,346,745	1066
May	5,816,300	
June		
July 27	6,645,973	1326
August	7,403,500	
September		
October 26	8,779,749	1752
November	9,626,100	
December		
1817		
January 25	9,922,034	1982
February 1	9,990,000	1998
March 1	9,674,000	1934
April 26	10,047,279	2006
May	10,770,900	
June		
July 26	11,483,701	2294
August	11,719,300	
September		
October 25	11,803,941	2358
November	11,449,100	
December 6		
1818		
January 31	10,848,808	2166
February	10,481,500	
March 7	10,078,000	2014
April 25	8,743,371	1746
May	8,348,000	
June		
July 25	7,159,998	1430
August	6,729,500	
September		
October 31	5,417,850	1080
November	5,078,900	
December		
1819		
January 30	4,562,946	910
February	4,354,000	
March		

Date	Amount of Hoard	Bank of England's Index for the Hoard
April 2	3,870,685	772
May	3,825,900	
June		
July		
August	3,685,300	
September	3,570,000	
October		
November	4,079,000	
December		
1820		
January		
February	4,907,000	
March	4,964,000	
April		
May	5,969,400	
June		
July		
August	7,979,200	
September		
October		
November	10,046,200	
December		
1821		
January		
February	11,639,000	
March		
April		
May	13,329,000	
June		
July		
August	11,149,400	
September		
October		
November	11,577,000	
December		
1822		
January		
February	10,958,000	
March	11,086,000	
April		
May	9,909,300	
June		
July		

(*continued*)

Appendix A.2 (*continued*)

Date	Amount of Hoard	Bank of England's Index for the Hoard
August	10,078,300	
September		
October		
November	9,855,000	
December		
1823		
January		
February	10,331,500	
March	10,372,000	
April		
May	11,857,100	
June		
July		
August	12,557,700	
September		
October		
November	13,761,700	
December	14,142,000	
1824		
January		
February	13,782,700	
March	13,945,000	
April		
May	13,007,700	
June		
July		
August	11,990,700	
September		
October		
November	11,448,000	
December	14,142,000	

Note: The hoard is measured by counting gold and silver bullion, foreign and British gold coin, foreign and British silver coin, as well as dollars and tokens at the Bank.

Sources: House of Commons. Committee of Secrecy on the Bank of England Charter 1832. *Digest of Evidence on the Bank Charter*, App. 1 and 2.

Bank of England. A Scale of Cash and Bullion in the Bank of England from March 1797 to February 1819, *Memorials, Contracts, Accounts for Parliament*, Vol. 1, 1819–1842, Bank of England Archive, Document C66/1, 15–16.

Bank of England. A Scale of the Gold and Silver in Possession of the Bank in January, April, July and October of Each Year from January 1814 to April 1819, *Memorials, Contracts, Accounts for Parliament*, Vol. 1, 1819–1843, Bank of England Archive, Document C66/1, 24–25.

Appendix A.3   British Gold Coin Issued by the Bank of England,
1815 to 1823

Date	British Gold Coin Issued	Foreign Gold Coin & Bar Gold Issued by the Bullion Office
1815		
January		£60,243
February		29,746
March		39,804
April		92,962
May		22,880
June		62,529
July		21,501
August		104,380
September		77,159
October		19,499
November		41,839
December		16,895
1816		
January		7,151
February		8,931
March		10,659
April		62,554
May		8,058
June		10,954
July	£15,355	22,935
August	7,184	6,785
September	0	8,731
October	0	5,635
November	0	8,781
December	0	5,224
1817		
January	32,585	62,371
February	5,435	29,754
March	0	17,570
April	0	47,501
May	0	48,076
June	0	64,330
July	120,158	65,530
August	78,821	35,962
September	44,921	86,499
October	432,921	59,196
November	289,234	48,706
December	274,367	54,947

(*continued*)

Appendix A.3   (*continued*)

Date	British Gold Coin Issued	Foreign Gold Coin & Bar Gold Issued by the Bullion Office
1818		
January	365,664	40,212
February	416,548	56,168
March	540,665	25,146
April	469,455	24,525
May	440,763	45,729
June	446,505	23,155
July	646,346	35,508
August	423,574	46,911
September	239,284	45,412
October	273,076	22,469
November	293,950	11,471
December	220,695	15,399
1819		
January	259,305	14,222
February	194,889	26,169
March	203,850	36,046
April	36,336	40,422
May	0	
June	0	
July	0	
August	0	
September	0	
October	0	
November	0	
December	0	
1820		
January	0	
February	0	
March	0	
April	0	
May	0	
June	0	
July	0	
August	0	
September	0	
October	0	
November	0	
December	0	
1821		
January	0	
February	0	

Date	British Gold Coin Issued	Foreign Gold Coin & Bar Gold Issued by the Bullion Office
March	0	
April	0	
May	1,968,871	
June	1,625,487	
July	1,138,609	
August	624,085	
September	456,557	
October	833,134	
November	253,022	
December	284,735	
1822		
January	1,154,976	
February	363,163	
March	415,747	
April	552,977	
May	199,383	
June	24,881	
July	740,586	
August	135,250	
September	82,075	
October	675,147	
November	0	
December	0	
1823		
January	712,380	
February	0	
March	133,391	
April	381,366	
May	12,341	
June	85,071	
July	495,522	
August	56,035	
September	0	
October	297,535	
November	0	
December	47,572	
1824		
January	684,763	
February	0	
March	112,432	
April	1,071,193	
May	568,468	

(*continued*)

Date	British Gold Coin Issued	Foreign Gold Coin & Bar Gold Issued by the Bullion Office
June	163,163	
July	1,190,848	
August	244,650	
September	60,250	
October	384,904	
November	260,059	
December	204,088	
1825		
January	908,875	
February	371,293	
March	295,546	
April	892,214	
May	418,477	
June	491,880	
July	966,352	
August	454,120	
September	231,024	
October	374,660	
November	287,824	
December	1,814,713	

Sources: Bank of England. Account of Sovereigns and Half-Sovereigns Issued in Each Month from March 1819, *Memorials, Contracts, Accounts for Parliament*, Vol. 1, 1819–1843, Bank of England Archive, Document C66/1, 58–59.

House of Commons. An Account of Sovereigns and Half-Sovereigns Issued by the Bank. *Journal of the House of Commons* 1818, 73:765.

House of Commons. Total Number of Sovereigns and Half-Sovereigns Issued from the Bank of England. *Journal of the House of Commons* 1819, 74:1117.

House of Commons. Amount of Monthly Sales of Gold and Silver in the Bullion Office of the Bank of England from April 1810 to April 1819. *Journal of the House of Commons* 1819, 74:1118.

House of Commons. Committee of Secrecy on the Bank of England Charter 1832. *Report*, App. 76.

House of Lords. Secret Committee to Enquire into the State of the Bank of England with Respect to the Expediency of the Resumption of Cash Payments 1819. *Second Report*, App. D. 3.

Appendix A.4 Public and Private Deposits in the Bank of England, 1810 to 1825

Year	Public Deposits	Private Deposits
1810	£11,093,648	£1,428,720
1811	11,950,047	1,567,920
1812	10,191,854	1,573,950
1813	10,390,130	1,771,310
1814	12,158,227	2,374,910
1815	11,737,436	1,690,490
1816	10,807,660	1,333,120
1817	8,699,133	1,672,800
1818	7,066,887	1,640,210
1819	4,538,373	1,790,860
1820	3,713,442	1,325,060
1821	3,920,157	1,326,020
1822	4,107,853	1,373,370
1823	5,526,635	2,321,920
1824	7,222,187	2,369,910
1825	5,347,314	2,607,900

Sources: House of Commons. Committee of Secrecy on the Bank of England Charter 1832. *Report*, App. 32 and 36.

J. Marshall 1833, Deposits in the Bank of England, *Digest of All the Accounts*, 2:172.

Appendix A.5

Part A. Commercial Discounts by the Bank of England Outstanding in January, 1800 to 1826

Year	Discounts to Merchants	Discounts to Manufacturers & Traders
1800	£3,356,627	£3,246,345
1801	3,511,216	3,839,185
1802	3,823,678	4,181,447
1803	5,185,006	5,118,810
1804	6,543,475	6,012,593
1805	5,133,531	4,790,911
1806	6,369,404	6,731,634
1807	6,551,592	7,183,379
1808	5,685,779	7,472,849
1809	5,992,696	8,594,615
1810	9,203,178	10,711,632
1811	8,189,784	9,675,698
1812	6,529,079	7,893,690
1813	6,505,614	7,360,324
1814	6,945,716	8,223,879
1815	7,398,521	7,951,238
1816	8,146,292	8,506,631
1817	3,723,748	3,880,597
1818	1,436,850	1,827,116
1819	5,002,226	4,607,039
1820	3,864,617	3,343,884
1821	2,257,908	1,871,376
1822	1,698,379	2,009,410
1823	2,796,073	2,729,833
1824	890,551	1,709,694
1825	1,045,785	1,939,749

Source: Bank of England. Outstanding Discounts to Merchants, Manufactures and Traders on January 1st, *Committee on Discounts: Analyses*, Vol. 20. Bank of England Archive, Document C36/20.

Part B. Advances by the Bank of England to the Government Outstanding in February and August, 1800 to 1826

Year	Advances out of Sums Issued to Pay Dividends	Advances Secured by Exchequer Bills	Exchequer Bills Purchased in the Market	Treasury Bills for Ireland & New Street Account	Total Advances to the Government
Feb. 1800	£376,739	£8,772,500	£4,052,400		£13,201,639
Aug. 1800	376,739	9,684,500	2,838,000		12,899,239
Feb. 1801	376,739	10,663,500	4,249,200		15,289,439
Aug. 1801	376,739	8,618,000	2,953,800		11,948,539
Feb. 1802	376,739	9,928,000	3,979,500		14,284,239
Aug. 1802	376,739	8,483,000	4,692,600		13,552,339
Feb. 1803	376,739	7,224,000	1,995,200		9,595,939
Aug. 1803	376,739	7,137,000	6,121,500		13,635,239
Feb. 1804	376,739	7,588,000	6,750,500		14,715,239
Aug. 1804	376,739	7,414,000	7,513,700		15,304,439
Feb. 1805	376,739	9,403,000	7,423,000		17,202,739
Aug. 1805	376,739	8,416,000	2,952,600		11,745,339
Feb. 1806	376,739	8,226,000	6,060,600		14,663,339
Aug. 1806	376,739	7,759,000	6,309,600		14,445,339
Feb. 1807	376,739	8,933,000	4,453,800		13,763,539
Aug. 1807	376,739	7,453,000	5,835,600		13,665,339
Feb. 1808	376,739	6,122,000	7,866,200		14,364,939
Aug. 1808	876,739	10,008,000	4,792,800		15,677,539
Feb. 1809	876,739	8,089,000	6,434,400		15,400,139
Aug. 1809	876,739	9,493,000	5,639,600		16,009,339
Feb. 1810	876,739	7,860,000	6,281,100		15,017,839
Aug. 1810	876,739	9,526,000	7,287,000		17,689,739
Feb. 1811	876,739	7,542,000	9,649,700		18,068,439
Aug. 1811	876,739	9,497,000	12,322,500		22,696,239
Feb. 1812	876,739	9,066,000	12,609,000		22,551,739
Aug. 1812	876,739	9,205,000	11,875,900		21,957,639
Feb. 1813	876,739	10,417,000	14,600,200		25,893,939
Aug. 1813	876,739	9,432,000	15,422,500		25,731,239
Feb. 1814	876,739	10,500,000	13,107,300		24,484,039
Aug. 1814	876,739	9,435,000	25,502,800		35,814,539
Feb. 1815	876,739	9,401,000	17,755,000		28,032,739
Aug. 1815	876,739	7,577,000	16,502,100		24,955,839
Feb. 1816	876,739	4,500,000	14,488,300		19,865,039
Aug. 1816	1,180,245	11,758,000	13,284,600	£1,000,000	27,222,845
Feb. 1817	974,070	9,000,000	13,319,500	3,080,000	26,373,570
Aug. 1817	979,482	10,217,218	13,723,500	3,380,000	28,300,200
Feb. 1818	1,033,523	9,000,000	14,952,000	3,050,000	28,035,523
Aug. 1818	1,026,965	11,030,000	13,080,900	2,950,000	28,087,865
Feb. 1819	1,098,820	5,900,000	13,080,900	2,950,000	23,029,720

Source: Bank of England. Account of the Advances made by the Bank to Government, *Memorials, Contracts, Accounts for Parliament*, Vol. 1. Bank of England Archive, Document C66/1, 4–8.

House of Commons. Secret Committee on the Expediency of the Bank Resuming Cash Payments 1819, *Second Report*, App. 3.

Appendix A.6 Annual Averages for Commercial Paper under Discount at the Bank of England, 1805 to 1825

Year	Discounted Commercial Paper
1805	£11,366,500
1806	12,380,100
1807	13,484,600
1808	12,950,100
1809	15,475,700
1810	20,070,600
1811	14,355,400
1812	14,291,600
1813	12,330,200
1814	13,285,800
1815	14,947,100
1816	11,416,400
1817	3,960,600
1818	4,325,200
1819	6,515,000
1820	3,883,600
1821	2,676,700
1822	3,366,700
1823	3,123,800
1824	2,369,800
1825	4,941,500

Sources: House of Commons. Committee of Secrecy on the Bank of England Charter 1832. *Report*, App. 56, 58 and 59.

J. Marshall 1833, *Digest of All the Accounts*, 2:171.

Appendix A.7   Forged Notes Presented to the Bank of England, 1798 to 1825

Year	Total Number of Forged Notes	Aggregate Value of Forged Notes
1798	1,102	£8,139
1799	2,075	4,417
1800	4,033	7,911
1801	7,794	15,549
1802	5,034	10,460
1803	3,233	6,798
1804	3,566	6,931
1805	3,791	7,451
1806	4,160	8,341
1807	5,830	9,234
1808	4,938	7,283
1809	6,622	9,595
1810	5,450	9,072
1811	8,803	15,729
1812	17,885	29,292
1813	15,315	22,206
1814	14,722	22,642
1815	17,765	24,258
1816	24,849	31,242
1817	31,180	37,040
1818	30,476	36,301
1819	23,035	28,050
1820	29,083	33,682
1821	18,126	21,068
1822	3,642	5,829
1823	1,648	2,962
1824	965	2,174
1825	770	1,396

Sources: For the years 1798 to 1818 the information is drawn from Bank of England. Account of the total number of notes of the Bank of England discovered to be forged, *Memorials, Contracts, Accounts for Parliament*, Vol. 1, 1819–1843. Bank of England Archive, Document C66/1, 10.

Data for 1819 to 1825 are drawn from a loose unnumbered sheet I found amid a pile of documents brought to me by the archivist at the Bank of England. The page is titled *An Account of the Number of Forged Notes of Each Denomination.*

Appendix A.8   Half-Yearly Average of the Bank of England's
Circulation, 1800 to 1817

Date	Average Value of Bank Notes in Circulation	Date	Average Value of Bank Notes in Circulation
1800		1809	
Jan.–June	£15,009,457	Jan.–June	18,214,026
July–Dec.	15,311,824	July–Dec.	19,641,640
1801		1810	
Jan.–June	16,134,249	Jan.–June	20,894,441
July–Dec.	15,487,555	July–Dec.	24,188,605
1802		1811	
Jan.–June	16,284,052	Jan.–June	23,471,297
July–Dec.	16,571,726	July–Dec.	23,094,046
1803		1812	
Jan.–June	15,967,094	Jan.–June	23,123,140
July–Dec.	17,043,450	July–Dec.	23,351,496
1804		1813	
Jan.–June	17,623,680	Jan.–June	23,939,693
July–Dec.	17,192,440	July–Dec.	24,107,445
1805		1814	
Jan.–June	17,272,429	Jan.–June	25,511,012
July–Dec.	16,480,713	July–Dec.	28,291,832
1806		1815	
Jan.–June	16,941,887	Jan.–June	27,155,824
July–Dec.	16,641,761	July–Dec.	26,618,210
1807		1816	
Jan.–June	16,724,368	Jan.–June	26,468,283
July–Dec.	16,687,438	July–Dec.	26,681,398
1808		1817	
Jan.–June	16,953,787	Jan.–June	27,339,768
July–Dec.	17,303,512	July–Dec.	29,210,305

Source: House of Commons. Account of the Average Amount of Bank Notes in Circulation, *Journal of the House of Commons* 1818, 73:748.

Country Banks, Coinage, and Instruments of Credit

Appendix B.1   Country Bank Circulation, 1810 to 1825

Year	Official Estimate (million sterling)	Bankers' Estimate (million sterling)	Burgess Index	Estimated Value of Country Bank Notes Stamped	Stamp Duties Paid On Country Notes
1810	21.8			£10,517,519	£99,633
1811	21.5			8,792,433	101,941
1812	19.9			10,577,134	119,562
1813	22.6			12,615,509	130,830
1814	22.7			10,773,375	103,314
1815	19.0			7,624,949	88,900
1816	15.1			6,423,466	83,213
1817	15.9			9,075,958	139,628
1818	20.5	20.5	100.0	12,316,868	148,320
1819	15.7	20.1	98.3	5,640,313	62,325
1820	10.6	19.3	94.2	3,574,894	53,654
1821	8.3	19.1	93.1	3,987,582	66,957
1822	8.4	18.1	88.3	4,217,341	62,178
1823	9.9	18.1	88.1	4,657,589	65,051
1824	12.8	19.6	95.4	6,093,367	93,274
1825	14.9	21.0	102.3	8,532,438	114,913

Note: The actual circulation of country-bank notes in 1818 is not known, but in the column "Bankers Estimate" I use the official estimate of 20.5 million. From 1819 onward I calculated changes in the circulation of country-bank notes based on the testimony of Henry Burgess.

Sources: House of Commons. Committee of Secrecy on the Bank of England Charter 1832. *Digest of Evidence on the Bank Charter*, App. 60 and 62.

House of Commons. Committee of Secrecy on the Bank of England Charter 1832. *Minutes of Evidence*, 412–416, by Henry Burgess, Secretary of the Country Bankers Committee.

House of Lords. Secret Committee to Enquire into the State of the Bank of England with Respect to the Expediency of the Resumption of Cash Payments 1819. *Second Report*, App. F.8, by I. Sedgwick, Chairman of the Stamp Board.

House of Lords. Country Bank Notes Stamped in Great Britain. *Journal of the House of Lords* 1826, 273.

House of Lords. Country Bank Notes Stamped in Great Britain. *Journal of the House of Lords* 1826, 277.

J. Marshall 1833, *Digest of all the Accounts*, 2:55.

Appendix B.2

Part A. Parliamentary Reports on the Circulation of Country Banks, 1814 to 1823

Report Date	Source	Period Covered
Mar. 23, 1814	JHC 1813–1814, 69:824	Oct. 1812–Oct. 1813
Feb. 17, 1815	JHL 1815, 52	Oct. 1813–Oct. 1814
Feb. 14, 1815	JHC 1814–1815, 70:890	Oct. 1813–Oct. 1814
May 3, 1816	JHL 1816, 577	Oct. 1813–Oct. 1815
Feb. 28, 1818	JHC 1818, 73:759–760	Oct. 1814–Feb. 1818
Jan. 25, 1819	JHL 1819, 22	Jan. 1815–Jan. 1819
Feb. 15, 1819	House of Commons. Secret Committee. *Second Report* App. 32; in PP 1819, 3:332–333, MF 20.29.	Jan. 1811–Jan. 1819
May 7, 1819	House of Lords. Secret Committee. *Second Report* App. F.1 & F.2; in PP 1819, 3:761–768, MF 20.33.	Oct. 1805–Oct. 1818
Mar. 15, 1821	JHC 1821, 76:939–941	Jan. 1819–Jan. 1821
Apr. 11, 1821	JHC 1821, 76:942	1805–Apr. 1821
Mar. 14, 1822	JHC 1822, 77:1143	Oct. 1818–Mar. 1822
Apr. 16, 1822	JHC 1822, 77:1143	Oct. 1818–Oct. 1821
Mar. 15, 1823	PP 1823, 14:311, MF 25.113	Oct. 1821–Jan. 1823

Appendix B.2

Part B. Parliamentary Reports on the Circulation of Scottish Banks

House of Commons. Secret Committee on the Expediency of the Bank Resuming Cash Payments 1819. *Second Report*, App. 31, Comparative Statement of the Notes of the British Linen Company, the Royal Bank of Scotland, and the Bank of Scotland.

House of Commons. Comparative Statement of the Notes of the British Linen Company in Circulation from 1810 to 1822. *Journal of the House of Commons* 1822, 77:1143.

House of Lords. Secret Committee to Enquire into the State of the Bank of England with Respect to the Expediency of the Resumption of Cash Payments 1819. *Second Report*, App. F.3, The Number and Value of Unstamped Small Notes Issued in Scotland by the Bank of Scotland, the Royal Bank, and the British Linen Company for the 10 years Preceding 5 January 1819.

House of Lords. Secret Committee to Enquire into the State of the Bank of England with Respect to the Expediency of the Resumption of Cash Payments 1819. *Second Report*, App. F.10, The Number of Banks in Scotland for which Licences to Issue Promissory Notes Have Been Taken Out in Each Year from 1808 to 1818.

Appendix B.3   Country Banks Committing Bankruptcy, 1812 to 1826

Date	Commissions of Bankruptcy by Country Bankers	Date	Commissions of Bankruptcy by Country Bankers
1812		1815	
January	3	January	3
February	3	February	0
March	0	March	1
April	1	April	1
May	0	May	3
June	0	June	4
July	0	July	3
August	3	August	5
September	1	September	0
October	2	October	0
November	3	November	3
December	1	December	2
TOTAL	17	TOTAL	25
1813		1816	
January	1	January	0
February	1	February	3
March	0	March	6
April	1	April	6
May	0	May	2
June	0	June	3
July	2	July	6
August	0	August	1
September	0	September	1
October	0	October	4
November	1	November	4
December	2	December	1
TOTAL	8	TOTAL	37
1814		1817	
January	0	January	1
February	0	February	0
March	0	March	0
April	0	April	2
May	2	May	0
June	0	June	0
July	9	July	0
August	2	August	0
September	6	September	0
October	0	October	0
November	6	November	0
December	2	December	0
TOTAL	27	TOTAL	3

Date	Commissions of Bankruptcy by Country Bankers	Date	Commissions of Bankruptcy by Country Bankers
1818		1821	
January	0	January	1
February	0	February	2
March	0	March	0
April	0	April	0
May	0	May	0
June	0	June	2
July	0	July	0
August	1	August	1
September	0	September	0
October	1	October	0
November	1	November	2
December	0	December	2
TOTAL	3	TOTAL	10
1819		1822	
January	0	January	1
February	0	February	3
March	2	March	1
April	1	April	1
May	2	May	3
June	0	June	0
July	2	July	0
August	0	August	0
September	1	September	0
October	1	October	0
November	1	November	0
December	3	December	0
TOTAL	13	TOTAL	9
1820		1823	
January	1	January	0
February	0	February	2
March	0	March	2
April	1	April	1
May	0	May	0
June	0	June	1
July	0	July	0
August	0	August	0
September	0	September	1
October	0	October	2
November	1	November	0
December	1	December	0
TOTAL	4	TOTAL	9

(*continued*)

Appendix B.3 *(continued)*

Date	Commissions of Bankruptcy by Country Bankers	Date	Commissions of Bankruptcy by Country Bankers
1824		July	0
January	2	August	0
February	1	September	1
March	0	October	5
April	0	November	0
May	1	December	30
June	3	TOTAL	37
July	0	1826	
August	0	January	12
September	2	February	10
October	0	March	11
November	0	April	3
December	1	May	5
TOTAL	10	June	0
1825		July	0
January	1	August	0
February	0	September	1
March	0	October	0
April	0	November	1
May	0	December	0
June	0	TOTAL	43

Sources: House of Commons. *Journal of the House of Commons* 1822, 77:1305.

House of Commons. Committee of Secrecy on the Bank of England Charter 1832. *Report*, App. 101, Numbers of Commissions of Bankruptcy issued against Country Banks.

Appendix B.4   Annual Data on British Coinage, 1810 to 1824

Year	Gold Coined at the Mint	Silver Coined at the Mint	British Silver Coin Issued by the Mint	Silver Tokens Issued by the Bank of England
1810	£316,935	£120		
1811	312,263	nil		
1812	nil	52		
1813	519,722	89		
1814	nil	161		£545,827
1815	nil	nil		322,139
1816	nil	1,806,181	nil	745,757
1817	4,275,337	2,439,894	£4,245,060	
1818	2,862,373	576,236	574,212	
1819	3,574	1,267,847	1,219,561	
1820	949,516	847,816	897,130	
1821	9,520,758	433,766	420,975	
1822	5,356,787	31,430		
1823	759,748	285,271		
1824	4,065,075	282,070		

Notes:
(1) From 1760 to 1820, the Mint produced only £64,271 in British silver coin.
(2) The new silver coinage, which the Mint began to produce in 1816, did not enter circulation till 1817, when a sufficient amount had been produced to replace the old silver coin. Old silver coin, much of it defaced or reduced in weight, was exchanged at its nominal value.
(3) The new silver coinage was completed on 12 Feb. 1817. The exchange of the new coin for the old was completed in two weeks.
(4) From 1804 through 1815, the Bank issued £4,457,649 in dollars and tokens. But with the success of the new silver coinage, dollars and tokens became unnecessary. The Bank stopped issuing tokens in 1817. The Bank stopped receiving both Bank dollars and tokens after 1819. Tokens were largely replaced by new silver coin.
(5) The "Sovereign," being valued at 20 shillings, was made current by proclamation on 1 July 1817. The half-sovereign was made current on 10 Oct. 1817.
(6) All copper coin, except that coined at the Mint after July 1797, was withdrawn from circulation in Dec. 1817.
(7) Of the gold coined in 1817, £4,261,320 was issued to the Bank. No gold coins were issued to private persons (JHC 1818, 73:765).
(8) Coins were struck of the following metals:

> Gold – guinea, half, and quarter guinea, seven shilling piece, the sovereign and half-sovereign.
> Silver – crown, half-crown, shilling, sixpence, fourpence, threepence, twopence, penny.
> Copper – twopence, penny, halfpenny, farthing.

Sources: The principal sources are listed in App. B.5, but another valuable source is Rogers Ruding 1840, *Annals of the Coinage of Great Britain*, Vol. 2.

Appendix B.5   Parliamentary Reports on Coinage, 1813 to 1823

I. Reports on Gold Coinage

House of Commons. Account of the Total Number of Sovereigns and Half
Sovereigns Issued by the Mint Otherwise than to the Bank of England, *Journal of the House of Commons* 1818, 73:765. The report indicates that the Mint
coined gold only for the Bank during 1817.

House of Commons. Account of the Gold Coin Issued from the Mint in the Course
of the Year 1818, *Journal of the House of Commons* 1819, 74:1119.

House of Commons. Account of the Quantity of Gold Imported into His Majesty's
Mint, and Gold Monies Coined, from 1st January 1815 to 1st January 1822,
Journal of the House of Commons 1822, 77:1148.

House of Commons. Account of the Quantity of Gold Imported into His Majesty's
Mint, and Gold Monies Coined, from 1st January 1822 to 1st January 1823,
Journal of the House of Commons 1823, 78:991.

House of Commons. An Account of All Sovereigns and Half Sovereigns Coined
at the Mint for Persons Other than the Bank of England from the 1st
January 1821...to the 1st May 1828, *Parliamentary Papers* 1830, 13:371,
MF 32.131.

House of Lords. Secret Committee to Enquire into the State of the Bank of
England with Respect to the Expediency of the Resumption of Cash Payments
1819. *Second Report*, App. D.2.

J. Marshall 1833, *Digest of All the Accounts*, 2:170.

II. Reports on Gold and Silver Coinage

House of Commons. Account of the Amount of Gold and Silver Coined at His
Majesty's Mint for the Two Years Preceding 1st January 1818, *Journal of the
House of Commons* 1818, 73:765.

House of Commons. *Parliamentary Papers* 1828, 16:493–497, MF 30.105.

III. Reports on Silver Coinage

House of Commons. Account of All Silver Coin Coined at the Mint, Since the
Last Regulation of the Silver Coinage, *Journal of the House of Commons* 1821,
76:1188.

House of Commons. Account of All Silver Coin Coined at the Mint, Since the
Last Regulation of the Silver Coinage, *Journal of the House of Commons* 1822,
77:1149.

House of Lords. Secret Committee to Enquire into the State of the Bank of
England with Respect to the Expediency of the Resumption of Cash Payments
1819. *Second Report*, App. D.1. The report indicates the amount of silver coined
in each year, 1760 through 1819.

House of Lords. Secret Committee to Enquire into the State of the Bank of
England with Respect to the Expediency of the Resumption of Cash Payments

1819. *Second Report*, App. D.10. The report explains the switch from the old to the new silver coinage in 1817.

IV. Reports on Gold Issued from the Bank of England

House of Commons. Account of the Total Number of Sovereigns and Half Sovereigns Issued from the Bank of England, *Journal of the House of Commons* 1818, 73:765.

House of Commons. Account of the Total Number of Sovereigns and Half Sovereigns Issued from the Bank of England to the Latest Period, *Journal of the House of Commons* 1819, 74:1117.

House of Commons. Committee of Secrecy on the Bank of England Charter 1832. *Report*, App. 76.

House of Lords. Secret Committee to Enquire into the State of the Bank of England with Respect to the Expediency of the Resumption of Cash Payments 1819. *Second Report*, App. D.3.

V. Reports on Silver Coins Issued by the Mint

House of Commons. Account of All Silver Monies Exchanged Throughout Great Britain, Guernsey, Jersey and the Isle of Man, *Journal of the House of Commons* 1817, 72:831.

House of Commons. Account of the Silver Coin Issued from the Mint in the Course of the Year 1817, *Journal of the House of Commons* 1818, 73:765.

House of Commons. Account of the Silver Coin Issued from the Mint in the Course of the Year 1818, *Journal of the House of Commons* 1819, 74:1119.

House of Commons. Account of All Silver Coin Coined at the Mint, Since the Last Regulation of the Silver Coinage, *Journal of the House of Commons* 1821, 76:1188.

House of Commons. Account of All Silver Coin Coined at the Mint, Since the Last Regulation of the Silver Coinage, *Journal of the House of Commons* 1822, 77:1149.

VI. Reports on Silver Tokens Issued by the Bank

House of Commons. Account of the Amount of All the Stamped Dollars and Silver Tokens Issued by the Bank of England from the 10th of December 1812 to the 1st of March 1814, *Journal of the House of Commons* 1813–1814, 69:823.

House of Commons. Account of the Amount of All the Stamped Dollars and Silver Tokens Issued by the Bank of England from the 1st of March 1814 to the 9th of February 1815, *Journal of the House of Commons* 1814–1815, 70:890.

House of Commons. Account of the Amount of All the Stamped Dollars and Silver Tokens Issued by the Bank of England from the 10th of February 1815 to the Date of the Return to the Order, *Journal of the House of Commons* 1816, 71:989.

House of Commons. Account of All Stamped Dollars and Silver Tokens Issued by the Bank of England from the 1st of January 1816 to the 1st of January 1817, *Journal of the House of Commons* 1817, 72:831.

VII. Reports on Copper Coin Issued from the Mint

House of Commons. Account of the Total Amount of Copper Coined and Issued from the Mint Since the Year 1790, *Journal of the House of Commons* 1819, 74:1123.

Appendix B.6   Aggregate of Notes and Coin in Circulation, 1818 to 1823

Year	B.E. Notes	Silver Coin	Gold Coin Issued at B.E.	Gold Coin Issued to Private Persons	Country-Bank Notes	Total Excluding Country Banks	Total Including Country Banks
1818	£26,005,240	£4,819,272	0	0	£20,500,000	£30,824,512	£51,324,512
1819	23,910,800	6,038,833	0	0	20,149,450	29,949,633	50,099,083
1820	23,278,030	6,935,963	0	0	19,302,800	30,213,993	49,516,793
1821	18,515,920	7,356,938	£7,184,500	£5,711	19,075,250	33,063,069	52,138,319
1822	17,165,940	7,388,368	11,528,685	9,164	18,109,700	36,092,157	54,201,857
1823	19,121,690	7,673,639	13,749,898	10,930	18,060,500	40,556,157	58,616,657

Notes: Figures for Bank of England notes represent fourth quarter averages, and do not include Bank post bills. All silver coin issued from 1817 onward remained in circulation owing to the seignorage on the coin. Almost all British gold coin issued before Aug. 1819 was exported. My figures for coin in circulation from 1820 onward do not reflect the amounts of British gold coin repatriated from the Continent. Trafficking in British coin was illegal, but several million sterling were exported in 1819 and repatriated later. I assume the Mint issued gold to private persons at a rate proportionate to the issues of gold from the Bank of England. The Stamp Office estimated that the circulation of country-bank notes in 1818 was £20.5 million. From 1819 onward, I estimate changes in the country circulation using Henry Burgess' estimates.

Sources: App. A.1, A.3, B.1, B.5, and House of Commons. Committee of Secrecy on the Bank of England Charter 1832. *Digest of Evidence*, App. 12.

Appendix B.7   Stamps Issued on Bills of Exchange, 1804 to 1825

Year	Amount of Stamps Issued on Bills of Exchange
1805	£384,449
1806	458,656
1807	464,417
1808	454,050
1809	541,804
1810	588,753
1811	530,520
1812	520,891
1813	537,239
1814	560,504
1815	673,116
1816	568,431
1817	552,965
1818	589,331
1819	575,782
1820	544,978
1821	527,877
1822	519,203
1823	535,847
1824	556,919
1825	597,080

Sources: House of Commons. Secret Committee on the Expediency of the Bank Resuming Cash Payments 1819. *Second Report*, App. 33, Account of the Produce of the Duties on Bills of Exchange and Promissory Notes, Not Re-issuable.

House of Commons. Account of the Number of Stamps on Bills of Exchange and Promissory Notes, Not Re-issuable, *Journal of the House of Commons* 1821, 76:940,941.

House of Commons. Statement of the Scale of Stamp Duties on Bills of Exchange ... for the Years 1793 to 1822 Inclusive, *Journal of the House of Commons* 1823, 78:844. The report was requested months before it appeared; see *JHC* 1823, 78:181,184.

House of Commons. An Account of the Amount of All Stamps on Bills of Exchange, *Parliamentary Papers* 1826, 22:17, MF 28.140.

Appendix B.8 Country Banks Licensed to Issue Promissory Notes

Year	Number of Country Banks in England and Wales	Licenses Granted for Country Banks
1808–09	755	573
1809–10	783	631
1810–11	741	654
1811–12	739	656
1812–13	761	646
1813–14	733	660
1814–15	699	657
1815–16	643	626
1816–17	585	575
1817–18	576	577
1818–19	587	596
1819–20	595	595
1820–21		606
1821–22	552	609
1822–23		623
1823–24		641
1824–25		660

Note: A list of the locations (by county) of country banks can be found in *the Journal of the House of Commons* 1822, 77:1144.

Sources: House of Commons. Account of the Number of Country Banks in England and Wales, Which Issue Promissory Notes Payable on Demand, *Journal of the House of Commons* 1822, 77:1143,1144.

House of Lords. Secret Committee to Enquire into the State of the Bank of England with Respect to the Expediency of the Resumption of Cash Payments 1819. *Second Report*, App. F.9, An Account of the Number of Country Banks in England and Wales for which Licences to Issue Promissory Notes Have Been Taken.

J. Marshall 1833, Number of Licenses Granted to Country Bankers, *Digest of All the Accounts*, 2:172.

Price Data

Appendix C.1   Prices of Wheat in Britain, 1813 to 1823

Date	Shillings/ Winchester Qtr.	Date	Shillings/ Winchester Qtr.
1813		November	70.4
January	122.7	December	69.6
February	127.5	1815	
March	126.5	January	59.4
April	127.4	February	59.6
May	122.7	March	70.2
June	120.1	April	69.4
July	117.9	May	67.1
August	113.8	June	65.4
September	91.1	July	64.0
October	91.9	August	67.9
November	83.7	September	59.1
December	66.7	October	63.1
1814		November	60.0
January	76.4	December	57.5
February	77.0	1816	
March	73.4	January	54.1
April	77.2	February	54.3
May	66.2	March	57.0
June	72.6	April	58.7
July	68.2	May	70.1
August	70.9	June	77.9
September	82.6	July	75.2
October	77.0	August	77.4

Date	Shillings/ Winchester Qtr.	Date	Shillings/ Winchester Qtr.
September	85.4	November	65.4
October	85.9	December	66.4
November	95.9	1820	
December	101.7	January	63.3
1817		February	63.5
January	103.4	March	66.7
February	100.9	April	70.3
March	97.5	May	70.2
April	102.1	June	71.0
May	102.8	July	70.7
June	107.0	August	73.8
July	108.4	September	72.2
August	86.9	October	61.1
September	81.5	November	57.5
October	74.8	December	55.5
November	78.7	1821	
December	85.6	January	54.8
1818		February	54.8
January	87.5	March	53.4
February	84.9	April	53.4
March	85.3	May	54.4
April	87.9	June	55.4
May	98.7	July	55.8
June	83.6	August	59.8
July	83.4	September	53.4
August	84.6	October	47.4
September	80.3	November	36.6
October	80.4	December	46.4
November	80.3	1822	
December	80.6	January	47.2
1819		February	43.0
January	77.1	March	40.0
February	77.5	April	42.2
March	78.7	May	46.2
April	76.9	June	47.4
May	73.1	July	44.6
June	68.6	August	42.9
July	70.7	September	38.7
August	76.2	October	40.4
September	72.9	November	38.9
October	66.8	December	38.5

(*continued*)

Appendix C.1 *(continued)*

Date	Shillings/ Winchester Qtr.	Date	Shillings/ Winchester Qtr.
1823		July	60.1
January	39.9	August	60.3
February	40.0	September	58.5
March	41.6	October	46.3
April	50.8	November	49.6
May	54.6	December	51.9
June	61.6		

Note on Measurements Used: Winchester quarter = 8 bushels or 2 barrels; hundredweight (cwt.) = 4 Winchester quarters.

Sources:

House of Commons. Account of the Weekly Average Prices of Barley, Oats, Rye and Wheat from 4 Jan. 1813 to 24 Feb. 1816, *Parliamentary Papers* 1816, 14:13, MF 17.83.

House of Commons. Select Committee to Whom the Several Petitions Complaining of the Depressed State of the Agriculture of the United Kingdom Were Referred 1821, *Report*, App. 1.

House of Commons. Average Price of Corn for the First Week in Every Month in the Years 1819 and 1820, *Journal of the House of Commons* 1821, 76:1033.

House of Commons. A Return of the Average Price of Corn per Barrel for the First Week in Every Month in the Year 1821 and up to the 5th July 1822, *Journal of the House of Commons* 1822, 77:983.

House of Commons. A Return of All Accounts that Have Been Received from His Majesty's Consuls Abroad, Relative to the Prices of Foreign Corn, During the Years 1822 and 1823, *Parliamentary Papers* 1824, 13:103–169, MF 26.113.

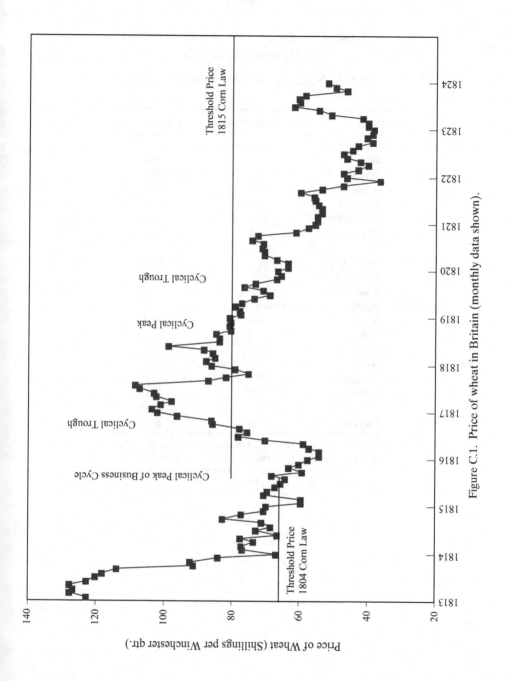

Figure C.1. Price of wheat in Britain (monthly data shown).

267

Appendix C.2　　Prices of Wheat in Amsterdam and Danzig, 1822 to 1823

(in British shillings per Winchester quarter)

Month	Price in Amsterdam	Price in Danzig
1822		
July		26.6
August	28.2	26.5
September	29.3	26.6
October	26.4	26.6
November	25.4	26.6
December	30.6	27.0
1823		
January		26.4
February		26.4
March	29.0	26.2
April	28.5	26.1
May	32.0	26.4
June	26.6	26.4
July	23.8	24.5
August	32.5	24.4
September	28.4	24.3
October	23.0	20.0
November	25.0	20.0
December	20.9	20.2

Source: House of Commons. A Return of All Accounts that Have Been Received from His Majesty's Consuls Abroad, Relative to the Prices of Foreign Corn, During the Years 1822 and 1823, *Parliamentary Papers* 1824, 18:103–169, MF 26.113.

Appendix C.3   Prices of Wheat and Other Grains in Russia, Prussia, Germany, and Holland, 1810 to 1825

(in British shillings per Winchester quarter)

Year	Archangel Wheat	St. Petersburg Wheat	Konigsberg, E. Prussia				Mecklenburgh-Schwerin			
			Wheat	Rye	Barley	Oats	Wheat	Rye	Barley	Oats
1810	27.5	30.9	25.6	11.7	10.7	7.0	31.1	13.7	9.5	8.7
1811	29.2	34.1	23.7	13.5	14.9	11.0	31.6	17.9	9.0	7.6
1812	40.1	52.4	33.5	26.1	24.2	22.0	32.1	23.2	16.3	23.3
1813	34.7	50.5	30.3	17.8	13.9	10.0	36.3	25.9	16.3	12.2
1814	29.0	36.3	29.3	19.5	13.5	10.0	36.9	27.4	16.3	12.8
1815	33.1	32.9	34.5	22.3	15.9	11.0	36.3	29.0	15.9	12.8
1816	26.7	42.6	39.5	25.1	15.3	12.0	36.9	23.7	15.3	12.2
1817	57.2	56.7	57.7	33.5	21.4	16.0	64.2	39.0	28.4	21.3
1818	40.2	44.4	51.1	29.3	22.7	17.0	58.5	33.8	29.5	19.9
1819	21.7	29.6	33.9	22.7	18.6	13.0	35.3	26.3	20.0	15.2
1820	20.1	25.8	27.0	16.8	11.2	8.0	28.4	17.4	11.6	11.2
1821	17.5	22.3	22.8	13.5	9.3	7.0	23.2	13.2	9.0	7.6
1822	14.2	29.9	22.8	13.0	10.2	8.0	21.1	12.7	9.0	8.7
1823	14.6		22.3	16.2	13.9	9.0	21.1	16.3	10.5	8.7
1824	14.3		17.7	8.9	6.5	5.0	17.9	10.0	7.9	5.6
1825	17.8	26.6	16.8	8.9	6.5	5.0	18.4	9.5	9.5	6.6

(continued)

Appendix C.3 *(continued)*

Year	Hamburg				Bremen				Rotterdam			
	Wheat	Rye	Barley	Oats	Wheat	Rye	Barley	Oats	Wheat	Rye	Barley	Oats
1810	33.9	20.1	17.5	14.5	36.4	26.7	18.3	13.3	55.1	29.2	20.9	14.2
1811	34.2	22.5	16.7	12.5	37.4	30.0	16.7	11.0	56.5	42.7	29.7	12.5
1812	52.5	40.2	26.5	21.8	60.1	40.0	23.3	15.0	81.8	68.3	34.9	19.6
1813	58.0	40.5	24.4	20.0	48.8	33.3	25.3	16.0	69.8	48.1	33.1	20.4
1814	49.0	35.0	19.6	16.7	47.2	30.0	23.3	15.3	49.1	32.6	21.4	19.9
1815	48.0	32.3	18.7	14.8	43.9	30.9	18.3	12.7	48.2	32.4	21.1	19.6
1816	56.5	35.7	23.2	16.0	60.9	40.0	25.9	14.3	65.4	44.3	31.6	21.1
1817	80.0	49.0	33.9	24.2	78.7	58.3	33.3	20.0	104.4	56.9	43.1	30.0
1818	62.7	41.7	36.5	24.7	61.8	38.3	37.5	21.0	70.1	43.9	37.0	29.0
1819	41.0	32.7	26.3	18.8	47.2	36.0	30.0	16.7	48.6	35.4	29.5	22.8
1820	35.5	23.5	17.0	13.0	34.2	25.0	18.3	10.7	43.9	27.5	19.8	17.2
1821	33.7	17.9	11.5	9.7	32.5	18.3	11.7	6.7	41.2	21.8	14.9	12.3
1822	27.5	15.4	13.0	9.3	29.2	18.3	11.7	6.3	35.0	21.1	14.9	10.2
1823	27.5	18.3	14.5	11.0	26.7	20.0	13.3	8.3	32.4	24.3	19.4	13.9
1824	24.0	13.0	12.5	8.5	24.4	11.7	11.7	5.7	26.4	15.8	14.0	10.1
1825	20.5	12.8	13.9	8.5	21.2	14.2	10.9	6.7	28.0	16.9	16.9	12.3

Notes: This document shows the prices of corn imported annually from leading Continental ports. My choice of ports can be explained by the fact that wheat, rye, and barley were primarily imported from Russia, Prussia, and Germany. Holland was an important supplier of oats. Castlereagh obtained and presented to Parliament reports similar to these on 9 Mar. 1820. The reports were updated in 1824; the updates are reprinted in *Parliamentary Papers* 1824, 18:103, MF 26.113.

Sources:

House of Commons. Account of the Grain of All Sorts, Imported into Great Britain from Foreign Parts, from 1800 to 1824, PP 1825, 20:233, MF 27.165.

House of Commons. Growth and Average Prices of Foreign Corn, 1700–1825, PP 1826–1827, 16:139–170, MF 29.129.

Appendix C.4   Monthly Prices of Gold, Silver, and the Foreign
Exchange, 1813 to 1824

Month	Price of Gold (British shillings/ounce)	Price of Silver (British shillings/ounce)	Hamburg Exchange (Flemish schillings/sterling)
1813			
January	86.50	5.75	32.40
February	89.00	5.90	32.00
March	94.00	5.90	32.30
April	107.00	6.75	28.20
May	106.00	6.75	28.50
June	102.00	6.75	26.50
July	106.00	6.80	26.50
August	110.00	7.00	26.00
September	108.00	6.90	26.50
October	108.00	6.90	26.50
November	110.00	7.00	26.50
December	110.00	7.00	28.00
1814			
January	108.00	6.95	29.00
February	108.00	6.95	29.00
March	108.00	6.90	29.00
April	105.00	6.90	29.00
May	103.00	6.90	28.00
June	100.00	6.50	28.50
July	91.00	5.90	30.00
August	84.00	5.50	33.00
September	86.00	5.50	33.00
October	85.00	5.70	32.70
November	88.00	5.90	32.00
December	86.50	5.75	32.33
1815			
January	86.50	5.75	32.30
February	89.00	5.90	32.10
March	94.00	6.00	30.00
April	107.00	6.75	28.20
May	106.00	6.80	28.40
June	104.00	6.50	28.00
July	92.00	5.75	32.00
August	89.00	5.50	32.50
September	88.00	5.75	32.75
October	83.00	5.30	34.20
November	83.00	5.40	34.00
December	82.00	5.30	34.30

(*continued*)

Appendix C.4 (*continued*)

Month	Price of Gold (British shillings/ounce)	Price of Silver (British shillings/ounce)	Hamburg Exchange (Flemish schillings/sterling)
1816			
January	82.00	5.40	34.40
February	82.00	5.33	34.50
March	82.00	5.33	35.10
April	81.00	5.20	35.40
May	80.00	5.10	35.70
June	80.00	5.10	36.10
July	79.00	5.00	36.90
August	79.00	5.00	36.80
September	79.00	4.90	36.90
October	78.50	5.00	37.80
November	78.50	5.00	37.00
December	78.50	4.95	36.80
1817			
January	79.50	5.00	36.00
February	78.50	5.10	36.20
March	78.50	5.10	36.50
April	78.50	5.20	36.10
May	79.00	5.20	35.50
June[a]	79.00	5.20	35.30
July	80.00	5.30	35.00
August	80.00	5.30	35.10
September	80.00	5.25	35.10
October	80.00	5.25	35.10
November	80.05	5.30	34.80
December	80.05	5.30	34.50
1818			
January	80.50	5.30	34.20
February	82.50	5.40	34.00
March	81.00	5.40	34.40
April	81.50	5.45	34.30
May	82.00	5.45	33.90
June	81.20	5.45	34.00
July	81.50	5.45	34.30
August	81.50	5.40	34.50
September	80.00	5.40	35.00
October	81.50	5.40	34.50
November	82.00	5.50	33.90
December	81.00	5.50	33.75
1819			
January	83.00	5.50	33.75
February	83.00	5.60	33.60
March	81.50	5.50	34.10
April	82.00	5.50	34.00

Month	Price of Gold (British shillings/ounce)	Price of Silver (British shillings/ounce)	Hamburg Exchange (Flemish schillings/sterling)
May	82.00	5.50	34.25
June[a]	79.00	5.20	35.33
July	78.00	5.17	35.75
August[b]	77.88	5.17	36.50
September	77.88	5.17	36.50
October	77.88	5.17	36.50
November	78.50	5.17	35.90
December	77.88	5.17	36.17
1820			
January	77.88	5.17	36.00
February	77.88	5.17	36.20
March	77.88	5.13	36.50
April[c]	77.88	5.08	36.60
May	77.88	5.04	36.90
June	77.88	5.00	37.00
July	77.88	5.00	37.40
August	77.88	5.00	37.50
September	77.88	4.96	37.60
October	77.88	4.96	37.67
November	77.88	4.96	37.50
December	77.88	4.96	37.70
1821			
January	77.88	4.96	38.20
February	77.88	4.96	38.20
March	77.88	4.96	38.40
April	77.88	4.90	38.65
May	77.88	4.90	38.65
June	77.88	4.85	38.80
July	77.88	4.90	38.80
August	77.88	4.90	38.20
September	77.88	4.90	38.20
October	77.88	4.90	38.00
November	77.88	4.90	37.80
December	77.88	4.95	37.50
1822			
January	77.88	5.00	37.40
February	77.88	4.95	37.40
March	77.88	4.95	37.30
April	77.88	4.95	37.30
May	77.88	4.95	37.50
June	77.50	4.95	37.80
July	77.50	4.95	38.00
August	77.50	4.95	37.80
September	77.50	4.95	38.00
October	77.50	4.95	37.90
November	77.50	4.95	37.70
December	77.50	4.95	37.70

(*continued*)

Appendix C.4   (*continued*)

Month	Price of Gold (British shillings/ounce)	Price of Silver (British shillings/ounce)	Hamburg Exchange (Flemish schillings/sterling)
1823			
January	77.50	4.95	37.70
February	77.50	4.95	37.90
March	77.50	4.95	38.40
April	77.50	4.90	38.20
May	77.50	4.95	38.40
June	77.50	4.95	38.10
July	77.50	4.95	38.20
August	77.50	4.95	38.20
September	77.50	4.95	38.20
October	77.50	4.95	38.00
November	77.50	4.95	37.80
December	77.50	4.95	37.70
1824			
January	77.50	4.95	37.60

Notes: The Mint Price of gold was £3 17s. 10 1/2 d. (or 77.88 shillings per ounce). By "par of the exchange" I mean the number of Flemish shillings needed to buy a quantity of silver that would in England exchange for gold worth £1 sterling. There was no true par of the exchange. Britain maintained a gold standard. Continental powers used silver. The par of the exchange fluctuated with the relative price of gold to silver. However, given a relative market price of gold to silver of 15 1/2 to 1 (the ratio fixed by the Bank of France) the par of the foreign exchange was 35 23/24 Flemish schillings per £ sterling. During the eighteenth century, the market ratio of gold to silver had been closer to 14 4/5 to 1, and thus the corresponding par of the foreign exchange had been 34 7/20 Flemish schillings per £ sterling (Morgan 1939, 214).

[a] Foreign exchange 2 percent below par.

[b] Gold at Mint price, 20 Aug. 1819.

[c] Foreign Exchange 2 percent above par.

Sources:

House of Commons. *Parliamentary Papers* 1813–1814, 12:119, 123, MF 15.68.

House of Commons. Account of the Market Prices of Standard Gold in Bars &c., *Journal of the House of Commons* 1814–1815, 70:890.

House of Commons. Account of the Market Prices of Standard Gold in Bars &c., *Journal of the House of Commons* 1816, 71:989.

House of Commons. Account of the Market Prices of Standard Gold in Bars &c., *Journal of the House of Commons* 1818, 73:767.

House of Commons. Account of the Market Prices of Standard Gold in Bars, Portugal Gold in Coin, Standard Silver in Bars, *Journal of the House of Commons* 1818, 73:765.

House of Commons. *Parliamentary Papers* 1819, 15:457, MF 20.137.

House of Commons. Committee of Secrecy on the Bank of England Charter 1832. *Report*, App. 96.

House of Lords. Secret Committee to Enquire into the State of the Bank of England with Respect to the Expediency of the Resumption of Cash Payments 1819. *Second Report*, App. C.

Appendix C.5 Commodity Prices in *Blackwood's* Commercial Report, 1818 to 1823

Commodity	Jan. 1818	Feb. 1819	Mar. 1819	Apr. 1819	July 1819	Mar. 1820	July 1820	Dec. 1820	Aug. 1821	Dec. 1821	May 1822	Dec. 1822	May 1823
Sugar (brown), s./cwt.	76.0	77.0	75.0	73.0	64.0	57.0	61.0	60.0	56.0	60.0	60.0	53.0	57.0
Molasses, s./cwt.	36.0	35.0	32.5	33.0	32.5	26.5	26.0	24.5	21.5	24.5	29.0	31.0	30.0
Coffee (Jamaica), s./cwt.	106.0	140.0	140.0	125.0	116.0	122.0	128.0	125.0	109.0	107.0	106.0	108.0	105.0
Portugal red wine – £/pipe	46.0	58.0	58.0	58.0	60.0	54.0	46.0	54.0	52.0	34.0	33.0	44.0	34.0
Spanish white wine – £/butt	55.0	65.0	65.0	65.0	68.0	55.0	55.0	55.0	55.0	55.0	55.0	55.0	55.0
Indigo, s./lb.	10.5	11.5	11.5	10.5	10.0	10.5	11.5	10.5	10.0	11.5	11.5	11.5	11.0
Pine timber (America), s./ft.	2.5	2.5	2.7	2.7	2.7	2.0	1.7	1.7	1.7	1.7	2.2	2.2	2.5
Tar (America), s./brl.	19.5	19.5	20.0	20.0	20.0	21.0	19.0	19.0	16.0	21.0	21.0	20.0	17.0
Hemp (Riga), £/ton	47.0	54.0	49.0	49.0	42.5	49.0	42.0	40.0	47.0	48.0	46.0	44.0	42.0
Flax (Riga), £/ton.	82.0	86.0	86.0	82.0	74.0	72.0	61.0	60.0	52.0	58.0	49.0	54.0	70.0
Whale oil, £/tun.	58.0	33.0	33.0	37.0	32.0	30.0	35.0	24.0	23.0	20.0	21.0	27.0	24.0
Tobacco (fine), s./lb.	0.67	1.15	0.67	0.67	0.50	0.75	0.75	0.70	0.50	0.63	0.63	0.63	0.63
Cotton (Sea Island), s./lb.	2.67	3.00	2.50	2.50	2.50	2.20	2.00	1.90	2.00	2.10	2.10	1.67	1.67

Note: London prices are shown (where available). The upper ends of price ranges are reported.

Appendix C.6   Contemporary Estimates of Inflation

Parliamentary committees estimated changes in price levels using rudimentary price indices. Here is a nonexhaustive list of the sources used by Parliament:

- Costs of provisions of the Military College at Chelsea
- Costs of clothing and provisions at the Royal Hospital in Greenwich
- Prices for articles of provision at the Royal Hospital in Chelsea
- Prices paid for provisions at Bethlehem Hospital
- Prices paid by the Commissariat for oats, bread, and meal, supplied to His Majesty's troops

The following is a price index based on costs at the Military College at Chelsea.

Year	Cost of Provision	Year	Cost of Provision
1810	12.0	1818	10.0
1811	12.8	1819	10.1
1812	12.8	1820	11.9
1813	13.1	1821	10.9
1814	13.1	1822	8.9
1815	12.0	1823	6.9
1816	10.0	1824	8.8
1817	11.5	1825	8.1

Sources:
House of Commons. Secret Committee on the Expediency of the Bank Resuming Cash Payments 1819. *Second Report*, App. 36.

House of Commons. Select Committee to Whom the Several Petitions Complaining of the Depressed State of the Agriculture of the United Kingdom Were Referred 1821. *Report*, App. 33, 34, 35, 36, 37.

House of Commons. Committee of Secrecy on the Bank of England Charter 1832. *Report*, App. 90, 91, 92 & 93.

House of Lords. Secret Committee to Enquire into the State of the Bank of England with Respect to the Expediency of the Resumption of Cash Payments 1819. *Second Report*, App. E.1, E.2, E.3, E.4 & E.5.

J. Marshall 1833, *Digest of All the Accounts*, 2:181.

Appendix C.7   Annual Average Prices of Wheat, Oats, Barley, Coal, Raw Cotton, and Iron in Britain, 1810 to 1825

Year	Wheat[a] (s./qtr.)	Oats[b] (s./qtr.)	Barley[b] (s./qtr.)	Coal[c] (s./chaldron)	Raw Cotton[d] (pence/lb.)	Bar Iron[e] (£/ton)
1810	106.4	28.6	48.1	51.7	15.3	14.6
1811	95.3	27.6	42.2	47.7	12.5	15.0
1812	126.5	44.5	66.7	44.9	16.8	14.0
1813	109.8	38.5	58.5	52.4	23.0	13.0
1814	74.3	25.7	37.3	59.1	29.5	13.0
1815	65.6	23.6	30.2	46.7	20.8	13.3
1816	78.5	27.2	33.9	41.7	18.3	11.6
1817	96.9	32.4	49.3	40.3	20.1	8.9
1818	86.3	32.4	53.9	39.9	20.0	13.0
1819	74.5	28.2	45.7	41.9	13.5	12.6
1820	67.9	24.2	33.9	41.8	11.5	11.0
1821	56.1	19.5	26.0	42.5	9.5	9.0
1822	44.6	18.1	21.9	41.9	8.3	8.0
1823	53.3	22.9	31.5	45.1	8.3	8.6
1824	63.9	24.9	36.3	40.5	8.5	8.9
1825	68.5	25.7	40.0	39.9	11.6	14.0

[a] Wheat is measured in imperial quarters. The standard measure in the early nineteenth century was the Winchester quarter, which is 31/32 of an imperial quarter. The prices shown are in shillings sterling per imperial quarter.

[b] The prices of oats and barley are stated in shillings sterling per imperial quarter.

[c] The price of coal is in shillings sterling per chaldron at London. The London chaldron weighed between 26 and 27 cwt.

[d] Cotton prices are for Upland or Middling American cotton. The prices are in (old) pence per lb.

[e] Iron prices are for bar iron at Liverpool in £ per ton.

Source: Mitchell 1988, 747, 756, 757, 760, 762.

APPENDIX D

Trade Statistics

Appendix D.1 Estimates of British Imports and Exports, 1807 to 1823

	Official Values[a]			Declared Values[b]		
		Domestic			Domestic	
Year	Imports	Exports	Re-exports	Imports	Exports	Re-exports
1807	26.7	23.4	7.7	53.8	37.2	8.3
1808	26.8	24.6	5.8	51.5	37.3	6.5
1809	31.8	33.5	12.8	73.7	47.4	14.3
1810	39.3	34.1	9.5	88.5	48.4	12.5
1811	26.5	22.7	6.2	50.7	32.9	6.7
1812	26.2	29.5	9.7	56.0	41.7	9.1
1813[c]						
1814	33.8	34.2	19.4	80.8	45.5	24.8
1815	33.0	42.9	15.7	71.3	51.6	16.8
1816	27.4	35.7	13.5	50.2	41.7	12.6
1817	30.8	40.1	10.3	61.0	41.8	10.1
1818	36.9	42.7	10.9	80.7	46.5	12.3
1819	30.8	33.5	9.9	56.0	35.2	10.2
1820	32.4	38.4	10.6	54.2	36.4	10.4
1821	30.8	40.9	10.6	45.6	36.7	9.5
1822	30.5	44.3	9.2	44.6	37.0	7.8
1823	35.8	43.8	8.6	52.0	35.4	7.2

[a] Official values reflect quantities traded.
[b] Declared values are the market values of the goods traded.
[c] Records destroyed by fire.
Source: Mitchell 1988, *British Historical Statistics*, App. External Trade 2.

Appendix D.2   Agricultural Commodities Imported into Britain, 1810 to 1824

	1810	1811	1812	1813	1814	1815	1816	1817	1818	1819	1820	1821	1822	1823	1824
Barley and barley meal, qtrs.	26,318	42,840	83,638	83,268	46,031	29,578	78,403	161,811	722,843	394,179	117,014	98,478	41,690	19,770	73,591
Beans and bean meal qtrs.	15,226	4,438	5,024	5,405	43,385	18,362	6,699	5,850	120,779	190,628	19,218	5,099	7,234	5,768	7,876
Raw cotton (million lbs.)															
Imported						101	95	126	179	151	152	133	143	191	149
Re-exported											6	15	18	9	13
Oats and oat meal, qtrs.	116,469	11,708	15,406	60,456	251,151	120,872	75,993	478,994	989,749	586,725	683,650	103,201	55,642	28,965	488,106
Rum, gal.															
Imported	5,582,805	6,998,853	6,469,226	9,200,285	8,569,067	6,817,134	2,887,102	6,355,230	5,482,571	6,386,514	7,035,909	7,127,131	4,246,096	4,864,741	4,782,837
Exported	1,145,728	1,667,700	2,171,539	2,254,325	3,933,280	3,589,032	2,777,863	3,146,233	3,157,303	2,397,747	3,731,771	3,158,050	1,855,898	1,863,639	1,950,004
Rye and rye meal, qtrs.	90,982	27,830	72,819	35,039	6,044	1,805	15,117	140,092	78,085	18,674	12,239	660	353	197	966
Raw silk, 1000 lb.															
Imported	1,341	602	1,312	no record	1,663	1,474	948	981	1,745	1,555	2,308	2,201	2,178	2,512	3,136
Re-exported	23	29	40		10	75	269	55	80	29	8	8	16	9	2
Thrown silk, 1000 lb.															
Imported	451	20	618		646	360	195	248	461	293	334	341	503	368	342
Re-exported	50	31	86		2	5	5	2	4	3	5			5	1
Sugar, cwt.															
Imported	4,808,663	3,917,543	3,763,423	4,000,000	4,035,323	3,984,782	3,760,548	3,795,550	3,965,947	4,077,009	4,063,541	4,200,856	3,643,122	4,012,144	4,195,970
Re-exported	1,319,349	690,869	1,158,192	1,615,500	2,002,105	1,906,711	1,663,617	1,671,740	1,695,627	1,302,179	1,659,556	1,579,919	1,048,297	1,204,329	1,190,914
Kept for home consumption	3,489,314	3,226,674	2,605,231	2,384,500	2,033,218	2,078,071	2,096,931	2,123,810	2,270,320	2,774,830	2,403,985	2,620,937	2,594,825	2,807,815	3,005,056

(continued)

Appendix D.2 (continued)

	1810	1811	1812	1813	1814	1815	1816	1817	1818	1819	1820	1821	1822	1823	1824
Tea, lb.															
Imported	19,791,356	21,231,849	23,318,153	30,383,504	26,110,550	25,602,214	36,234,380	31,467,073	20,065,728	23,750,413	30,147,994	30,731,105	27,362,766	29,046,887	31,682,007
Exported	3,346,542	4,093,560	4,004,143	3,977,713	8,576,508	5,303,078	3,654,596	3,924,980	4,378,607	4,201,873	3,504,677	4,342,396	4,093,450	3,993,306	4,037,395
Wheat and wheat flour (qtrs.)	1,439,615	188,564	129,867	341,846	626,745	194,931	210,860	1,030,829	1,586,030	471,607	591,731	137,684	47,598	23,951	85,182
Raw wool (million lb.)	4.7	7.0	no record	15.7	15.0	8.1	14.7	26.4	16.2	10.0	16.7	19.3	20.7	23.9	

Note: Imports of barley, oats, and wheat do not include those from Ireland.

Sources:

Barley, Beans, Oats, Rye, Wheat: House of Commons. Account of the Grain of All Sorts, Meal and Flour, Imported into Great Britain from Foreign Parts, *Parliamentary Papers* 1825, 20:233, MF 27.165; and House of Commons. Foreign Corn Imports and British Corn Exports, *Parliamentary Papers* 1826–1827, 16:487, MF 29.132.

Cotton, Silk, Wool: B. R. Mitchell 1988, *British Historical Statistics,* App. Textiles 3, 6, 8 and 9.

Rum: House of Commons. Account of the Quantity of Rum Annually Imported into and Exported from Great Britain, *Parliamentary Papers* 1826, 22:173, MF 28.141.

Sugar: J. Marshall 1833, *Digest of All the Accounts,* 2:79.

Tea: House of Commons. Account of the Quantity of Tea Annually Imported into and Exported from Great Britain, *Parliamentary Papers* 1826, 22:219, MF 28.142.

Appendix D.3 Wheat, Oats, and Barley Imported into Britain from Ireland, 1813 to 1824

Year	Wheat	Oats	Barley
1807	77,031	498,779	23,434
1808	55,178	815,143	33,408
1809	123,841	1,090,706	16,619
1810	456,269	662,526	9,882
1811	400,766	376,854	2,713
1812	494,716	575,206	44,742
1813	812,810	935,971	63,560
1814	759,079	722,107	16,779
1815	584,156	708,496	27,108
1816	426,172	795,585	62,252
1817	115,794	699,281	26,740
1818	228,709	1,429,535	25,334
1819	498,880	948,208	20,290
1820	1,073,371	1,040,917	87,944
1821	1,664,575	1,379,038	84,716
1822	1,598,167	673,755	22,531

Notes: Figures are in quarters and include corn, grain, meal, and flour. These figures differ from those in App. D.2 because the reports on which App. D.2 is based used a different measure for corn and grain. A Winchester quarter is 7 and 3/4 bushels.

Sources: House of Commons. Select Committee to Whom the Several Petitions Complaining of the Depressed State of the Agriculture of the United Kingdom Were Referred 1821. *Report*, App. 17, Irish Grain and Flour Imported into Great Britain, 1807–1820.

House of Commons. Imports from Ireland of All Types of Corn, Grain & Meal, *Journal of the House of Commons* 1823, 78:873.

Appendix D.4   Foreign Corn Warehoused at British Ports, 1820 to 1823

	5 Apr. 1820	5 Jan. 1821	5 Jan. 1822	5 Jan. 1823	16 Apr. 1823
Wheat	327,893	733,762	678,609	581,583	556,681
Wheat flour	129,964	715,004	534,608	308,772	275,296
Oats	58,721	13,369	100,196	140,126	138,636
Barley	8,333	31,422	35,955	48,906	48,461

Note: Quantities shown are in Winchester quarters.

Sources: House of Commons. Account of all Grain Warehoused Under the Act 55 Geo. III, c. 26, *Parliamentary Papers* 1820, 12:37, MF 22.73.

House of Commons. Account of all Grain Warehoused Under the Act 55 Geo. III, c. 26, *Parliamentary Papers* 1821, 17:39, MF 23.100.

House of Commons. Account of all Grain Warehoused Under the Act 55 Geo. III, c. 26, *Parliamentary Papers* 1822, 21:69, MF 24.157.

House of Commons. Account of all Grain Warehoused Under the Act 55 Geo. III, c. 26, *Parliamentary Papers* 1823, 16:535, MF 25.131.

House of Commons. Account of all Grain Warehoused Under the Act 55 Geo. III, c. 26, *Journal of the House of Commons* 1823, 78:871.

House of Commons. Select Committee to Whom the Several Petitions Complaining of the Depressed State of the Agriculture of the United Kingdom Were Referred 1821. *Report*, App. 20, Account of the Quantities of Grain, Meal and Flour Delivered from the Warehouses for Home Consumption in Each Year, 1815 to 1820.

Public Finance

Appendix E.1   Taxation Reports Presented to the House of
Commons, 1815 to 1823

Report Date	Data	Period Covered	Source
Feb. 10, 1815	quarterly	Jan. 1813–Jan. 1815	JHC 1814–1815, 70:721
Apr. 17, 1815	quarterly	Apr. 1813–Apr. 1815	p. 722
July 11, 1815	quarterly	July 1813–July 1815	p. 725
May 26, 1815	annual	1801–1814	p. 727
Feb. 13, 1816	quarterly	Jan. 1814–Jan. 1816	JHC 1816, 71:837
Apr. 11, 1816	quarterly	Apr. 1814–Apr. 1816	p. 839
Feb. 3, 1817	quarterly	Jan. 1815–Jan. 1817	JHC 1817, 72:687
May 21, 1817	quarterly	Apr. 1815–Apr. 1817	p. 689
Feb. 19, 1818	quarterly	Jan. 1816–Jan. 1818	JHC 1818, 73:630
Feb. 4, 1819	quarterly	Jan. 1817–Jan. 1819	JHC 1819, 74:852
Apr. 6, 1819	quarterly	Apr. 1817–Apr. 1819	p. 854
July 7, 1819	quarterly	July 1816–July 1819	p. 855
Dec. 30, 1819	quarterly	Jan. 1819–Oct. 1819	JHC 1819–1820, 75:690
Feb. 25, 1820	quarterly	Jan. 1818–Jan. 1820	JHC 1819–1820, 75:686
May 2, 1820	quarterly	Apr. 1818–Apr. 1820	p. 687
July 15, 1820	quarterly	July 1818–July 1820	p. 688
Oct. 17, 1820	quarterly	Oct. 1818–Oct. 1820	p. 689
Jan. 24, 1821	quarterly	Jan. 1819–Jan. 1821	JHC 1821, 76:910
Apr. 6, 1821	quarterly	Apr. 1819–Apr. 1821	p. 911
July 10, 1821	quarterly	July 1819–July 1821	p. 912
Feb. 7, 1822	quarterly	Jan. 1820–Jan. 1822	JHC 1822, 77:894
July 9, 1822	quarterly	July 1820–July 1822	p. 896
Feb. 10, 1823	quarterly	Jan. 1821–Jan. 1823	JHC 1823, 78:822
Apr. 10, 1823	quarterly	Apr. 1821–Apr. 1823	p. 824
July 9, 1823	quarterly	July 1821–July 1823	p. 824

Note: Each report is titled "Abstract of the Net Produce of the Revenue of Great Britain."

Appendix E.2 Quarterly Tax Receipts for Great Britain, 1813 to 1822

Part A. 1813–1815

	Apr. 1813	July 1813	Oct. 1813	Jan. 1814	Apr. 1814	July 1814	Oct. 1814	Jan. 1815	Apr. 1815
Consolidated fund									
Customs	£1,146,231	£866,694	£857,271	£837,473	£1,211,507	£576,590	£1,567,749	£1,582,453	£1,288,038
Excise	4,197,979	4,075,382	4,995,766	4,291,905	4,192,014	4,328,057	4,975,216	4,815,885	4,674,768
Stamps	1,280,092	1,316,934	1,395,061	1,348,624	1,321,867	1,410,320	1,459,855	1,406,531	1,278,576
Post office	352,000	335,000	361,000	358,000	335,000	355,000	405,000	355,000	411,000
Assessed taxes	665,508	2,402,812	624,086	2,594,406	717,926	2,533,972	577,008	2,582,765	614,861
Land taxes	150,921	438,640	146,694	407,026	119,817	432,805	145,368	431,233	104,949
Miscellaneous	82,601	144,254	92,515	103,748	83,590	126,503	69,169	137,984	58,160
Annual duties									
Customs	276,405	281,485	1,400,679	819,492	54,181	255,876	1,507,353	800,591	54,248
Excise	54,406	82,238	120,916	291,269	10,947	46,930	114,896	307,125	6,290
Pensions									
War taxes									
Customs	823,322	640,625	1,185,181	1,073,296	590,682	576,373	1,142,602	1,193,367	635,947
Excise	1,334,926	1,264,588	2,111,978	1,362,041	1,172,046	1,408,540	1,960,688	1,813,267	1,199,218
Property	4,570,491	2,147,318	5,240,071	2,007,923	5,009,901	2,059,232	5,112,081	2,037,119	4,869,912
Total net revenue	14,934,882	13,995,970	18,531,218	15,495,203	14,819,478	14,110,198	19,036,985	17,463,320	15,195,967
Total customs	2,245,958	1,788,804	3,443,131	2,730,261	1,856,370	1,408,839	4,217,704	3,576,411	1,978,233
Total excise	5,587,311	5,422,208	7,228,660	5,945,215	5,375,007	5,783,527	7,050,800	6,936,277	5,880,276

Sources: Listed in App. E.1.

Part B. 1815–1817

	July 1815	Oct. 1815	Jan. 1816	Apr. 1816	July 1816	Oct. 1816	Jan. 1817	Apr. 1817	July 1817
Consolidated fund									
Customs	£1,016,375	£1,458,946	£1,128,119	£1,394,639	£767,846	£1,499,288	£1,317,381	£1,719,314	£831,853
Excise	4,708,942	5,029,476	4,938,770	4,325,528	4,124,975	4,937,055	4,484,440	3,819,211	3,831,360
Stamps	1,388,944	1,686,515	1,516,378	1,520,536	1,500,414	1,487,447	1,461,324	1,492,611	1,589,615
Post office	396,000	387,000	354,000	378,000	353,000	365,000	330,000	342,000	323,000
Assessed taxes	2,514,392	564,391	2,521,343	726,909	2,207,659	714,270	2,134,484	868,104	2,216,806
Land taxes	447,548	143,891	383,605	133,227	426,503	180,067	388,132	154,550	464,664
Miscellaneous	80,139	78,506	150,065	72,712	70,554	41,848	56,085	98,595	62,160
Annual duties									
Customs	611,350	1,220,465	583,081	39,143	524,691	958,540	870,827	192,982	877,760
Excise	107,022	138,118	344,520	7,654	90,732	98,641	337,097	13,279	83,727
Pensions			16				4,016	0	0
War taxes									
Customs	793,695	927,789	769,469	517,659	490,151	31	525	0	0
Excise	1,493,091	2,098,917	1,823,300	1,067,266	1,354,616	1,259,533	780,659	809,565	779,647
Property	2,155,021	5,196,955	2,096,684	4,861,027	2,071,776	2,960,576	1,292,205	0	472,338
Total net revenue	15,712,519	18,930,969	16,609,350	15,044,300	13,982,917	14,502,296	13,457,175	9,510,211	11,532,930
Total customs	2,421,420	3,607,200	2,480,669	1,951,441	1,782,688	2,457,859	2,188,733	1,912,296	1,709,613
Total excise	6,309,055	7,266,511	7,106,590	5,400,448	5,570,323	6,295,229	5,602,196	4,642,055	4,694,734

Sources: Listed in App. E.1.

Part C. 1817–1819

	Oct. 1817	Jan. 1818	Apr. 1818	July 1818	Oct. 1818	Jan. 1819	Apr. 1819	July 1819	Oct. 1819
Consolidated fund									
Customs	£1,880,180	£2,458,628	£1,991,718	£1,568,030	£2,795,889	£1,530,779	£1,658,340	£1,335,073	£1,346,138
Excise	4,025,209	4,695,074	4,248,082	4,658,989	4,927,456	5,113,923	4,358,557	4,704,195	4,959,207
Stamps	1,688,663	1,566,532	1,588,759	1,599,814	1,672,165	1,530,532	1,570,757	1,534,723	1,575,437
Post office	354,000	319,000	336,000	324,000	360,000	319,000	355,000	367,000	375,000
Assessed taxes	782,602	2,260,017	917,414	2,208,976	787,426	2,303,778	835,246	2,257,960	781,448
Land taxes	190,502	353,604	178,295	441,220	181,801	408,366	148,440	444,753	198,177
Miscellaneous	76,799	255,318	73,270	112,282	49,150	133,381	75,245	62,785	77,628
Annual duties									
Customs	1,241,770	558,993	11,946	289,114	873,865	934,885	434,010	909,566	1,407,029
Excise	124,684	36,441	6,520	106,316	134,124	299,780	82,827	118,101	127,204
Pensions	0	0	0	0	0	16	0	0	0
War taxes									
Customs	0	0	0	0	0	0	0	0	0
Excise	739,943	768,157	897,203	872,496	805,224	824,337	936,494	869,974	588,276
Property	407,072	389,048	254,190	154,439	72,249	661	0	0	0
Total net revenue	11,511,424	13,660,812	10,503,397	12,335,676	12,659,349	13,399,438	10,454,916	12,604,130	11,435,544
Total customs	3,121,950	3,017,621	2,003,664	1,857,144	3,669,754	2,465,664	2,092,350	2,244,639	2,753,167
Total excise	4,889,836	5,499,672	5,151,805	5,637,801	5,866,804	6,238,040	5,377,878	5,692,270	5,674,687

Sources: Listed in App. E.1.

286

Part D. 1820–1822

	Jan. 1820	Apr. 1820	July 1820	Oct. 1820	Jan. 1821	Apr. 1821	July 1821	Oct. 1821	Jan. 1822
Consolidated fund									
Customs	£1,958,855	£1,878,412	£844,772	£1,107,921	£1,885,415	£1,792,576	£801,934	£1,251,781	£1,515,105
Excise	5,746,359	5,165,663	6,003,687	6,852,987	5,656,602	5,090,931	5,694,226	7,039,890	5,368,664
Stamps	1,499,609	1,453,224	1,581,445	1,581,204	1,535,474	1,467,799	1,518,493	1,625,220	1,497,128
Post office	378,000	302,186	352,000	375,000	321,000	350,000	318,000	342,000	308,000
Assessed taxes	2,301,875	873,716	2,343,380	760,576	2,333,674	842,531	2,328,040	793,532	2,292,708
Land taxes	442,955	149,409	440,744	174,522	427,582	137,427	445,366	207,481	473,000
Miscellaneous	180,787	48,860	59,249	71,642	114,187	57,573	64,972	61,222	119,696
Annual duties									
Customs	273,018	82,291	1,038,074	1,562,762	232,244	112,700	1,096,765	1,269,327	971,791
Excise	72,379	0	0	112,770	15,448	0	0	293,082	298,119
Pensions	0	0	0	0	0	0	0	0	0
War taxes									
Customs	0	0	0	0	0	0	0	323,123	0
Excise	620,805	671,350	616,922	586,264	643,687	616,659	604,584	816,254	724,006
Property	0	0	0	0	0	0	0	0	0
Total net revenue	13,474,642	10,625,111	13,280,273	13,185,648	13,165,313	10,468,196	12,872,380	14,022,912	13,568,217
Total customs	2,231,873	1,960,703	1,882,846	2,670,683	2,117,659	1,905,276	1,898,699	2,844,231	2,486,896
Total excise	6,439,543	5,837,013	6,620,609	7,552,021	6,315,737	5,707,590	6,298,810	8,149,226	6,390,789

Sources: Listed in App. E.1.

287

Part E. 1822–1823

	Apr. 1822	July 1822	Oct. 1822*	Jan. 1823	Apr. 1823	July 1823
Consolidated fund						
Customs	£1,983,208	£1,119,496	£7,329,997	£6,291,908	£5,656,279	£5,618,938
Excise	5,856,798	6,268,738	1,674,503	1,450,987	1,573,854	1,620,011
Stamps	1,582,346	1,500,716	360,000	324,000	330,000	333,000
Post office	320,000	355,000				
Assessed taxes	832,672	2,192,521				
Land taxes	152,999	474,749				
Miscellaneous	56,463	99,451				
Annual duties						
Customs	112,670	826,612				
Excise	0	0				
Pensions	0	0				
War taxes						
Customs	0	0				
Excise	0	0				
Property	0	0				
Total net revenue	10,897,156	12,837,283				
Total customs	2,095,878	1,946,108				
Total excise	5,856,798	6,268,738				

* An accounting change took place after July 1822.
Sources: Listed in App. E.1.

288

Appendix E.3   Public Income and Expenditure of the United Kingdom, 1806 to 1823

	1806	1807	1808	1809	1810	1811	1812	1813	1814	1815	1816	1817	1818	1819	1820	1821	1822	1823
Customs & excise	34.90	39.30	40.20	39.40	41.80	40.90	39.90	41.80	44.30	43.80	38.80	36.60	40.20	39.50	41.50	42.60	42.00	41.00
Income & property tax	6.20	10.20	11.40	12.40	13.50	13.20	13.10	14.30	14.50	14.60	11.80	2.30	0.60	0.20	0.00	0.00	0.00	0.00
Other revenue	19.00	15.30	16.60	17.40	17.70	16.90	17.30	18.60	19.10	20.70	18.70	18.70	18.70	18.40	18.40	19.00	17.90	17.60
Total receipts	60.10	64.80	68.20	69.20	73.00	71.00	70.30	74.70	77.90	79.10	69.30	57.60	59.50	58.10	59.90	61.60	59.90	58.60
Debt charges	23.20	23.80	23.10	24.20	24.20	24.60	26.40	27.30	30.10	32.20	32.90	31.40	31.30	31.00	32.00	31.90	31.40	30.00
Civil government	7.50	8.50	8.20	8.80	9.00	9.10	9.50	9.50	10.40	10.80	10.30	9.60	10.60	9.80	9.70	9.90	9.90	9.90
Fighting services	41.10	40.90	44.80	48.30	48.00	53.40	57.30	74.20	72.50	56.50	28.20	17.70	15.70	16.70	16.60	16.60	15.20	14.40
Total expenditure	71.80	73.20	76.10	81.30	81.20	87.10	93.20	111.00	113.00	99.50	71.40	58.70	57.60	57.50	58.40	58.40	56.50	54.30
Budget surplus	(11.70)	(8.40)	(7.90)	(12.10)	(8.20)	(16.10)	(22.90)	(36.30)	(35.10)	(20.40)	(2.10)	(1.10)	1.90	0.60	1.50	3.20	3.40	4.30

Note: Figures are in million pounds sterling. When this report appeared in the 1860s, national income accounting procedures were not the same as when the revenue reports shown in App. E.2 were presented.

Sources: House of Commons. Gross Public Income and Expenditure of the United Kingdom.
Parliamentary Papers 1868–1869, 35:516–535, MF 75.292.

Mitchell 1988, App. Public Finance 3 and Public Finance 4.

Appendix E.4   Level of the National Debt, 1800 to 1825

Year	National Debt (£ million)	Debt Charges (£ million)
1800	456.1	
1801	498.6	
1802	516.4	
1803	523.8	
1804	539.6	
1805	564.4	
1806	583.1	
1807	591.3	
1808	599.0	
1809	607.4	
1810	607.4	
1811	609.6	
1812	626.9	
1813	652.3	27.3
1814	725.5	30.1
1815	744.9	32.2
1816	788.3	32.9
1817	766.1	31.4
1818	843.3	31.3
1819	844.3	31.0
1820	840.1	32.0
1821	838.3	31.9
1822	831.1	31.4
1823	836.1	30.0
1824	828.6	
1825	820.2	

Sources: For the total debt, see Mitchell 1988, 601; for debt charges, see App. E3.

Economic Articles in Periodicals Read by Ricardo, 1810 to 1823

The articles are arranged by topic, journal, and date of publication. An asterisk by an article indicates Ricardo was reading that periodical when the article appeared.

Bank of England and the Money Supply

*	*Blackwood's*	July	1817	Grenfell's Speech
*	*Blackwood's*	Nov.	1817	New Gold Coinage
	British Critic	Jan.	1812	William Pitt – The Bullion Debate
	Edinburgh Magazine	July	1819	Principal Banking Companies of Europe
	Edinburgh Magazine	Jan.	1819	Repeal of Bank Restriction Act
*	*Edinburgh Review*	Aug.	1811	Pamphlets on the Bullion Question
*	*Edinburgh Review*	Feb.	1811	Depreciation of Paper Money
*	*Edinburgh Review*	Dec.	1818	Increase of Forgeries
*	*Edinburgh Review*	July	1821	Pernicious Effects of Degrading the Standard
	Quarterly Review	Nov.	1810	Huskisson on Depreciation of the Currency
	Quarterly Review	Feb.	1810	Ricardo on Bullion
	Quarterly Review	Nov.	1810	Sinclair's Observations on the Bullion Committee
	Quarterly Review	Feb.	1811	Sinclair's Remarks
	Quarterly Review	Feb.	1811	Tracts on the Bullion Report
*	*Quarterly Review*	Apr.	1822	State of the Currency
*	*Scots Magazine*	Mar.	1818	On the State of the Currency
*	*Scotsman*		1820	Reduction of the Standard
*	*Scotsman*		1822	Money
*	*Scotsman*		1822	Peel's Bill

National Finance: Debt, Expenditure, and Taxes

*	*Blackwood's*	May	1818	Thoughts Concerning Tythes
	Blackwood's	Jan.	1820	Heathfield's Plan for Liquidation of National Debt
	British Critic	Sept.	1814	Hamilton on the National Debt
	British Critic	Feb.	1815	Commutation of Tythes
	British Critic	Feb.	1815	Property Tax
	British Critic	Jan.	1815	Boyd – Financial System of Great Britain
	British Review	Oct.	1813	Review of Hamilton's National Debt of Great Britain
	British Review	Nov.	1816	The Tythes System
*	*British Review*	Feb.	1817	McCulloch's Interest on the National Debt
*	*Edinburgh Magazine*	Oct.	1818	Effects of War and Taxes
*	*Edinburgh Magazine*	Dec.	1818	Other Remarks on War and Taxes
*	*Edinburgh Review*	Feb.	1815	Hamilton on the National Debt
*	*Edinburgh Review*	Oct.	1815	Boyd on the Financial System of Great Britain
*	*Edinburgh Review*	Jan.	1820	Finance
*	*Edinburgh Review*	Jan.	1820	Taxation and the Corn Laws
*	*Edinburgh Review*		1821	Mushet on Gains and Losses of Fundholders
*	*Edinburgh Review*	Feb.	1822	Comparative Productiveness of High and Low Taxes
*	*Edinburgh Review*	Oct.	1823	The Funding System, British Finances
	Scots Magazine	Sept.	1815	Revenue of England & Scotland – 1801 to 1814 (part 1)
	Scots Magazine	Nov.	1815	Revenue of England & Scotland – 1802 to 1814 (part 2)
	Scots Magazine	Feb.	1816	Expediency of Continuing the Income Tax
	Scots Magazine	Oct.	1816	Revenue of England & Scotland – 1815
	Scots Magazine	Apr.	1817	Report from the Select Committee of Finance
	Scots Magazine	May	1817	Account of Produce of Assessed Taxes – 1815 to 1817
	Scots Magazine	Jan.	1817	Financial Statements for 1816 and 1817
*	*Scotsman*		1820	Ricardo's Plan to Repay National Debt
*	*Scotsman*		1821	High and Low Taxation

Poor Laws and Relief of the Poor

*	*Blackwood's*	June	1817	Relief of the Poor
*	*Blackwood's*	Apr.	1818	On the Poor Laws in England
*	*Blackwood's*	June	1818	Management of Poor in Scotland
	Blackwood's	May	1819	Poor Rates
	British Critic	Apr.	1815	Education of the Poor

British Critic	June	1815	Review: Weyland on the Poor Laws
* *British Review*	Feb.	1817	Commons Report on Education of Lower Orders
* *British Review*	Nov.	1817	Committee Reports on the Poor Laws
* *Edinburgh Review*	Oct.	1813	Guarinos on Poor Laws
* *Edinburgh Review*	Mar.	1817	Causes and Cures of Pauperism – I
* *Edinburgh Review*	Feb.	1818	Causes and Cures of Pauperism – II
* *Edinburgh Review*	Feb.	1818	Reports on the State of the Poor
* *Edinburgh Review*	Mar.	1819	Pamphlets on Education and Abuse of Charities
* *Edinburgh Review*	Jan.	1820	Pamphlets on the Poor Laws
* *Edinburgh Review*	Jan.	1820	Abuses of Charities
* *Edinburgh Review*	Oct.	1821	Mr. Scarlett's Poor Bill
Quarterly Review	Dec.	1812	Inquiry Respecting the Poor Laws
Quarterly Review	Oct.	1814	On Improving the Condition of the Poor
Quarterly Review	Oct.	1815	Mendicity
* *Quarterly Review*	Apr.	1816	The Poor
* *Quarterly Review*	Jan.	1818	On the Poor Laws
Quarterly Review	Jan.	1823	The Poor Laws
Scots Magazine	Jan.	1814	Loan Fund for the Poor
Scots Magazine	Dec.	1815	Edinburgh Charity Workhouse
Scots Magazine	Feb.	1816	Report of Society for the Suppression of Begging
Scots Magazine	Sept.	1816	Annuity Fund for the Poor
Scots Magazine	Sept.	1816	Extension of the Society for the Suppression of Begging
Scots Magazine	Nov.	1816	Commons Report: Education of Lower Orders
Scots Magazine	Jan.	1817	Relief of Labouring Classes in Edinburgh
Scots Magazine	Jan.	1817	Edinburgh Charity Workhouse
Scots Magazine	Mar.	1817	The Poor in London
Scots Magazine	July	1817	Committee to Afford Relief to the Labouring Classes
Scots Magazine	Aug.	1817	Principles of the Poor Laws
* *Scots Magazine*	June	1818	Management of the Poor in Scotland
* *Scots Magazine*	July	1818	On the Poor Laws of England
* *Scots Magazine*	Sept.	1818	Management of the Poor

Corn Laws

British Critic	Aug.	1814	Corn Laws – Lauderdale, Rose, Malthus
British Critic	Jan.	1815	Corn Laws
British Critic	Mar.	1815	Corn Laws
British Critic	Mar.	1815	Review: Malthus' Grounds of an Opinion
British Critic	Apr.	1815	Review: Malthus' Nature of Rent
* *Edinburgh Review*	Feb.	1815	Malthus on the Corn Laws

* *Edinburgh Review*	Jan.	1820	Taxation and the Corn Laws
Scots Magazine	Nov.	1814	Evidence before Houses of Parliament on the Corn Trade
* *Scotsman*		1820	The Corn Laws

Usury Laws

* *British Review*	May	1817	Bentham's Defense of Usury
* *Edinburgh Review*	Dec.	1816	Bentham's Defense of Usury
* *Scots Magazine*	Aug.	1818	Principles of the Usury Laws
Scots Magazine	Mar.	1819	Proposed Repeal of Usury Laws

Theory of Population

* *Blackwood's*	Nov.	1818	Reflections on the Theory of Population
British Review	Nov.	1816	Principles of Population and Production
Edinburgh Magazine	Jan.	1819	Principle of Population – Source of Vice and Misery
* *Edinburgh Review*	July	1821	Godwin on Malthus
* *Quarterly Review*	July	1817	Malthus on Population
* *Quarterly Review*	Oct.	1821	Godwin and Malthus on Population

State of the Nation

British Critic	Oct.	1815	Colquhoun's Treatise
British Critic	Sept.	1815	Colquhoun's Treatise – Wealth of the British Empire
British Critic	May	1821	Review: Craig's Commercial State of Britain since 1815
* *British Review*	Aug.	1817	Letter on Distresses of the Country
* *Edinburgh Magazine*	Oct.	1818	Commerce of United Kingdom: Public Accounts
Edinburgh Magazine	Apr.	1819	Commercial Embarrassments of the Country
* *Edinburgh Review*	June	1816	Distresses of the Country
* *Edinburgh Review*	Dec.	1816	Commercial Distresses of the Country
* *Edinburgh Review*	Oct.	1819	Comparative Skill and Industry of France and England
* *Edinburgh Review*	Oct.	1819	Owen's Plans for Relieving National Distress
* *Edinburgh Review*	Jan.	1820	Speeches on the Distress of the Country
* *Edinburgh Review*	May	1820	State and Prospects of Manufacturers
* *Edinburgh Review*	Feb.	1822	State of the Nation
Quarterly Review	Jan.	1815	Wealth, Power and Resources of the British Empire
Quarterly Review	Jan.	1820	State of Public Affairs
Quarterly Review	Apr.	1823	Tooke – On High and Low Prices
Scots Magazine	Oct.	1815	Causes of our Domestic Embarrassments
Scots Magazine	Dec.	1816	General View of British Commerce – 1814 to 1815
Scots Magazine	Aug.	1817	General View of Credit and Commerce of the Country

State of Agriculture

Blackwood's	Oct. 1822	On the Agricultural Distress
Blackwood's	Oct. 1822	Hints to Country Gentlemen – I
Blackwood's	Nov. 1822	Hints to Country Gentlemen – II
British Critic	Jan. 1816	Agricultural Distress and the Prices of Corn and Bullion
British Review	Aug. 1816	On the State of Agriculture
* *Edinburgh Review*	Nov. 1814	Sinclair on the Agriculture of Scotland
* *Edinburgh Review*	Feb. 1816	Wilson on Corn and Money
* *Edinburgh Review*	Feb. 1822	Agricultural Distress, Causes and Remedies
* *Quarterly Review*	July 1821	Report on the State of Agriculture
Scots Magazine	Jan. 1814	Sinclair – Husbandry of Scotland
Scots Magazine	Dec. 1815	Distress of the Landed Interest
Scots Magazine	June 1816	Abstract: Board of Agriculture Queries and Responses
* *Scotsman*	1819	Importation of Foreign Corn
* *Scotsman*	1821	Report of Agricultural Committee
* *Scotsman*	1822	Review of Ricardo's Protection to Agriculture

Foreign Trade

* *Blackwood's*	Aug. 1817	Exportation of Cotton Yarn
* *Edinburgh Review*	July 1812	Orders in Council
* *Edinburgh Review*	July 1819	Commercial Embarrassments and Trade with France
* *Edinburgh Review*	May 1820	Restrictions on Foreign Commerce
* *Edinburgh Review*	May 1823	The Navigation Laws
Quarterly Review	Mar. 1812	America – Orders in Council
Scots Magazine	Feb. 1814	Commercial Intelligence
Scots Magazine	Mar. 1815	Commercial Intelligence – Trade Data
Scots Magazine	Mar. 1817	Table of British Exports – 1792 to 1817
Scots Magazine	July 1817	Official Value of British Exports – 1815 and 1816
* *Scotsman*	1820	Merchant's Petition

Reviews of Ricardo's Publications

* *Blackwood's*	May 1817	Ricardo on Political Economy
* *Blackwood's*	Oct. 1818	Ricardo and the Edinburgh Review
British Review	May 1816	Review of Secure Currency
* *British Review*	Nov. 1817	Review of Ricardo's Principles & Say's Traite
* *Edinburgh Magazine*	Oct. 1818	Ricardo's Doctrine of Exchangeable Value
* *Edinburgh Magazine*	Nov. 1818	Vindication of Ricardo on Exchangeable Value
* *Edinburgh Review*	Dec. 1818	Economical and Secure Currency
* *Edinburgh Review*	June 1818	Ricardo's Political Economy
Monthly Review	Sept. 1820	Ricardo's Principles
* *Scotsman*	1818	Review of Ricardo's Principles

General Gluts

British Critic	Sept.	1820	Malthus' Principles – General Gluts
British Critic	Dec.	1820	Say's Letters to Malthus – General Gluts
British Critic	Feb.	1822	Mill's Political Economy – General Gluts
Monthly Review	May	1821	Malthus and Say – General Gluts
Monthly Review	May	1822	Mill's Political Economy – General Gluts
* Scotsman		1823	Blake's Observations on Expenditure

Miscellaneous

* Blackwood's	Apr.	1818	Banks for Saving in Scotland
British Critic	Apr.	1811	Three Replies to Calumnies of the Edinburgh Rev.
British Critic	June	1811	Dugald Stewart – Philosophical Essays I
British Critic	Aug.	1811	Dugald Stewart – Philosophical Essays II
British Critic	Dec.	1811	Interest and Annuities
British Critic	Jan.	1812	Parliamentary Reform
British Critic	May	1813	Sinclair's Scottish Husbandry
British Critic	Feb.	1814	Malthus' Letter to Lord Grenville (Hertford Coll.)
British Critic	Sept.	1814	Apprentice Laws
British Critic	Nov.	1814	Craig's Elements of Political Economy
British Critic	Feb.	1815	Buchanan's Edition of the Wealth of Nations
British Critic	Apr.	1816	Say's Catechism of Political Economy
* British Review	May	1818	Parliamentary Reform
* Edinburgh Review	June	1815	Savings Banks
* Edinburgh Review	Mar.	1821	Effects of Machinery and Accumulation
* Quarterly Review	Oct.	1816	Tracts on Savings Banks
Scots Magazine	Jan.	1814	Society for the Suppression of Begging, Report
Scots Magazine	Nov.	1814	Society for the Suppression of Begging, Savings Banks
Scots Magazine	Sept.	1816	Juvenile Delinquency in the Metropolis
Scots Magazine	Mar.	1817	Characters of the Late Francis Horner
* Scotsman		1823	Combination Laws

Ricardo was known to have used the periodicals listed above in these years:

British Review	1817–1818	See Ricardo, 7:222, 7:248–9
Edinburgh Review	1802–1823	See Sraffa's Index, 27–28
Edinburgh Magazine	1818	
Blackwood's	1817–1818	See Ricardo, 7:219
Quarterly Review	1816–1819, 1821–1822	See Ricardo, 7:247, 8:44, 9:109, 122, 147, 154, 249
Scotsman	1817–1823	See Sraffa's Index, 51, 92
Morning Chronicle	1815, 1817, 1822	
Times	1817, 1819	

Bibliography

Bibliography – Government Documents

Bank of England. *Committee on Discounts: Analyses*, Vol. 20. Bank of England Archive C36/20.

Bank of England. *Committee on Discounts: Minutes*, Vol. 1. Bank of England Archive C35/1.

Bank of England. *Memorials, Contracts, Accounts for Parliament*, Vol. 1. Bank of England Archive C66/1.

Bank of England. *Minutes of the Court of Directors*, Vols. 30–34. Bank of England Archive G4/30–G4/34.

Cobbett's Parliamentary Debates. London.

Great Britain. House of Commons. Select Committee Appointed to Take into Consideration the Present State of Commercial Credit. *Report*. 1793. Reprinted in *Parliamentary Papers*, 1826, Vol. 3. MF 28.15.

Great Britain. House of Commons. Select Committee on the High Price of Gold Bullion. *Report*. 1810. Reprinted in *Monetary Policy – General*, Vol. 1. Series of British Parliamentary Papers. Shannon: Irish University Press, 1969.

Great Britain. House of Commons. Select Committee on Petitions Relating to the Corn Laws of This Kingdom. *Report* and *Minutes of Evidence* and *Appendix*. 1814. Reprinted in *Parliamentary Papers*, Vol. 3. MF 15.15.

Great Britain. House of Commons. Committee on the State of Mendicity in the Metropolis. *Report* and *Minutes of Evidence*. 1815. Reprinted in *Parliamentary Papers*, Vol. 3. MF 16.14.

Great Britain. House of Commons. Select Committee on Laws Respecting Roman Catholic Subjects. *Report*. 1816. Reprinted in *Parliamentary Papers*, Vol. 7. MF 17.33.

Great Britain. House of Commons. Select Committee on the Education of the Lower Orders in the Metropolis. *Report*. 1816. Reprinted in *Parliamentary Papers*, Vol. 4. MF 17.17.

Great Britain. House of Commons. Select Committee on the State of Children Employed in the Manufactories of the United Kingdom. *Report* and *Minutes of Evidence*. 1816. Reprinted in *Parliamentary Papers*, Vol. 3. MF 17.12.

Great Britain. House of Commons. Select Committee on the State of Mendicity in the Metropolis. *Report* and *Minutes of Evidence*. 1816. Reprinted in *Parliamentary Papers*, Vol. 5. MF 17.27.

Great Britain. House of Commons. Committee on the State of the Police of the Metropolis. *Report*. 1816. Reprinted in *Parliamentary Papers*, Vol. 5. MF 17.23.

Great Britain. House of Commons. Committee of Secrecy to Whom the Several Papers which Were Presented (Sealed up) to the House. *Report* and *Second Report*. 1817. Reprinted in *Parliamentary Papers*, Vol. 4. MF 18.20.

Great Britain. House of Commons. Committee on Employment of Boys in Sweeping of Chimnies. *Report* and *Minutes of Evidence*. 1817. Reprinted in *Parliamentary Papers*, Vol. 6. MF 18.29.

Great Britain. House of Commons. Select Committee on Finance. *Fourth Report*. 1817. Reprinted in *Parliamentary Papers*, Vol. 4. MF 18.20.

Great Britain. House of Commons. Select Committee on the Poor Laws. *Report* and *Minutes of Evidence* and *Appendix*. 1817. Reprinted in *Parliamentary Papers*, Vol. 6. MF 18.28.

Great Britain. House of Commons. Select Committee Appointed to Consider of the Several Petitions Relating to Ribbon Weavers. *Report* and *Minutes of Evidence*. 1818. Reprinted in *Parliamentary Papers*, Vol. 9. MF 19.46.

Great Britain. House of Commons. Select Committee on Finance. *Eleventh Report*. 1818. Reprinted in *Parliamentary Papers*, Vol. 3. MF 19.16.

Great Britain. House of Commons. Select Committee on the Poor Laws. *Report*. 1818. Reprinted in *Parliamentary Papers*, Vol. 5. MF 19.24.

Great Britain. House of Commons. Select Committee on the Usury Laws. *Report*. 1818. Reprinted in *Parliamentary Papers*, Vol. 6. MF 19.31.

Great Britain. House of Commons. Select Committee on the Poor Laws. *Report* and *Minutes of Evidence*. 1819. Reprinted in *Parliamentary Papers*, Vol. 2.

Great Britain. House of Commons. Secret Committee on the Expediency of the Bank Resuming Cash Payments. *Report* and *Second Report*. 1819. Reprinted in *Monetary Policy – General*, Vol. 2. Series of British Parliamentary Papers. Shannon: Irish University Press, 1968.

Great Britain. House of Commons. Select Committee on Finance. *First Report*. 1819. Reprinted in *Parliamentary Papers*, Vol. 2. MF 20.19.

Great Britain. House of Commons. Select Committee on Framework Knitters Petition. *Report* and *Minutes of Evidence*. London, 1819. Reprinted in *Parliamentary Papers*, Vol. 5. MF 20.47.

Great Britain. House of Commons. Select Committee to Whom the Several Petitions Complaining of the Depressed State of the Agriculture of the United Kingdom Were Referred. *Report* and *Minutes of Evidence*. 1821. Reprinted in *Parliamentary Papers*, Vol. 9.

Great Britain. House of Commons. Select Committee Appointed to Inquire into the Allegations of the Several Petitions Complaining of the Distressed State of the Agriculture of the United Kingdom. *Report* and *Second Report*. 1822. Reprinted in *Parliamentary Papers*, Vol. 5. MF 24.32.

Great Britain. House of Commons. Select Committee on the Public Accounts of the United Kingdom. *Report*. 1822. Reprinted in *Parliamentary Papers*, Vol. 4.

Great Britain. House of Commons. Select Committee on Labourers Wages. *Report*. 1824. Reprinted in *Parliamentary Papers*, Vol. 6.

Great Britain. House of Commons. Committee of Secrecy on the Bank of England Charter. *Digest of Evidence on the Bank Charter*. 1832.

Great Britain. House of Commons. Committee of Secrecy on the Bank of England Charter. *Report* and *Minutes of Evidence*. London, 1832. Reprinted in *Monetary Policy – General*, Vol. 4. Series of British Parliamentary Papers. Shannon: Irish University Press, 1968.

Great Britain. House of Commons. Select Committee on Bank Acts. *Report, Part II: Appendix and Index*. London, 1857. Reprinted in *Monetary Policy – General*, Vol. 8. Series of British Parliamentary Papers. Shannon: Irish University Press, 1969.

Great Britain. House of Lords. Lords Committees Appointed to Enquire into the State of the Growth, Commerce and Consumption of Grain. *Reports Respecting Grain and the Corn Laws*. London, 1814. Reprinted in *Parliamentary Papers*, Vol. 5. MF 16.24.

Great Britain. House of Lords. Lords Committees on the Poor Laws. *Report*. London, 1817. Reprinted in *Parliamentary Papers*, Vol. 5. MF 19.25.

Great Britain. House of Lords. Secret Committee of the House of Lords Appointed to Take into Consideration the Several Papers Sealed up in a Bag. *Report*. London, 1817. Reprinted in *Parliamentary Papers*, Vol. 4. MF 18.20.

Great Britain. House of Lords. Secret Committee to Enquire into the State of the Bank of England with Respect to the Expediency of the Resumption of Cash Payments. *First Report* and *Second Report* and *Minutes of Evidence*. London, 1819. Reprinted in *Parliamentary Papers*, Vol. 3. MF 20.29.

Great Britain. *House of Commons Parliamentary Papers*. Published in microfiche by Chadwick-Healey.

Great Britain. *Index to the Journals of the House of Lords, 1780–1819*.

Great Britain. *Journals of the House of Commons*.

Great Britain. *Journals of the House of Lords*.

Great Britain. Parliament. Abstracts of Population Returns for 1811, *Parliamentary Papers*, 1812, Vol. 11.

Great Britain. Parliament. Enumeration and Parish Registers of Great Britain According to the Census of 1821, *Parliamentary Papers*, 1822, Vol. 15.

Great Britain. Parliament. *Hansard's Parliamentary Debates*, 1st–3rd series, 1803–1891.

Great Britain. Parliament. *The Parliamentary History of England, 1066–1803*. London.

Lords Commissioners. Speech of the Lords Commissioners to both Houses of Parliament, on Thursday the 21st day of January 1819. *London Gazette*, January 23, 1819; reprinted in *Bulletins of State Intelligence*, 1819, page 15.

Marshall, J. (1833) *A Digest of All the Accounts . . . Diffused through More than 600 Volumes of Journals, Reports, and Papers, Presented to Parliament during the Last Thirty-Five Years*. London: W. Robson.

Bibliography – Contemporary Periodicals

Annual Register, London.
Blackwood's Edinburgh Magazine.
Cobbett's Weekly Political Register.
Critical Review.
Edinburgh Magazine.
Edinburgh Review.
Farmer's Magazine.
London Magazine.
Morning Chronicle.
New Monthly Magazine.
Quarterly Review.
Scots Magazine.
Times, London.

Bibliography – Primary Authors

Anderson, Adam. (1801) *The Origin of Commerce*, Vol. 4. Reprinted with Introduction by Joseph Dorfman. New York: A. M. Kelley, 1967.

Bacon, Francis. (1824) Of Goodness and Goodness of Nature. *The Works of Francis Bacon*, Vol. 2. London: W. Baynes.

Baring, Sir Francis. (1797) *Observations on the Establishment of the Bank of England and on the Paper Circulation*. London: Minerva Press.

Barton, John. (1817) *Observations on the Circumstances which Influence the Condition of the Labouring Classes of Society*. Reprint, Baltimore: Johns Hopkins Press, 1934.

Blake, William. (1823) *Observations on the Effects Produced by the Expenditure of Government during the Restriction of Cash Payments*. Reprint, New York: Franklin, 1969.

Colquhoun, Patrick. (1814) *A Treatise on the Wealth, Power and Resources of the British Empire*. London: J. Mawman.

Grund, Francis. (1834) *The Merchant's Assistant*. Boston: Hilliard Gray.

Horner, Francis. (1802) Review of *Paper Credit* by Henry Thornton. *Edinburgh Review*, **1**: 172–201.

Hume, David. (1752) Of the Balance of Trade. In *The Philosophical Works*, Vol. 3. Edited by Thomas Green and Thomas Grose. London: Longmans, Green, 1874–1875. Reprint, Aalen: Scientia Verlag, 1964.

King, Lord Peter. (1804) *Thoughts on the Effects of the Bank Restrictions*. 2nd edition. London: Cadell and Davies.

Liverpool, Lord. (1819) Letter to Canning dated 23 September 1819. Reprinted in *English Historical Documents, 1783–1832*. Edited by A. Aspinall and E. Smith. New York: Oxford University Press, 1959.

Lowe, Joseph. (1822) *The Present State of England*. London: Longman.

Malthus, T. R. (1814) *Observations on the Effects of the Corn Laws and of a Rise or Fall in the Price of Corn on the Agriculture and General Wealth of the Country*. Reprint, New York: A. M. Kelley, 1970.

Malthus, T. R. (1815a) *The Grounds of an Opinion on the Policy of Restricting the Importation of Foreign Corn*. Reprinted in *The Works of Thomas*

Robert Malthus, Vol. 7. Edited by E. A. Wrigley and David Souden. London: Pickering & Chatto, 1986.

Malthus, T. R. (1815b) *The Grounds of an Opinion on the Policy of Restricting the Importation of Foreign Corn; Intended as an Appendix to 'Observations on the Corn Laws.'* Reprint, New York: A.M. Kelley, 1970.

Malthus, T. R. (1815c) *An Inquiry into the Nature and Progress of Rent.* Reprint, New York: A.M. Kelley, 1970.

Malthus, T. R. (1820) *The Principles of Political Economy.* London: Murray.

Malthus, T. R. (1824) Political Economy. *Quarterly Review*, **30**: 297–334. Reprinted in *The Works of Thomas Robert Malthus*, Vol. 7. Edited by E. A. Wrigley and David Souden. London: Pickering & Chatto, 1986.

Malthus, T. R. (1826) *Essay on Population.* Reprinted in *The Works of Thomas Robert Malthus*, Vol. 3. Edited by E. A. Wrigley and David Souden. London: Pickering & Chatto, 1986.

Malthus, T. R. (1836) *The Principles of Political Economy.* 2nd edition. Reprint, New York: A.M. Kelley, 1964.

Malthus, T. R. (1963) *Occasional Papers of T. R. Malthus on Ireland, Population, and Political Economy.* Edited by Bernard Semmel. New York: Franklin.

Porter, G. R. (1836) *The Progress of the Nation.* Vol. 1. London.

Ricardo, David. (1951–1973) *The Works and Correspondence of David Ricardo.* 11 Vols. Edited by Piero Sraffa. Cambridge: Cambridge University Press.

Ruding, Rogers. (1840) *Annals of the Coinage of Great Britain*, Vol. 2. 3rd edition. London: J. Hearne.

Say, J. B. (1821) *Letters to Thomas Robert Malthus on Political Economy.* Reprint, London: George Harding's Bookshop, 1936.

Say, J. B. (1821) *A Treatise on Political Economy.* 1st American edition. Reprint, New York: A.M. Kelley, 1964.

Smith, Adam. (1776) *The Wealth of Nations.* 5th edition. Edited by Edwin Cannan. 1904. Reprint, New York: The Modern Library, 1994.

Spence, William. (1815) *Objections Against the Corn Bill Refuted.* London: Longman.

Thornton, Henry. (1802) *The Paper Credit of Great Britain.* Edited by F. A. Hayek, 1939. Reprint, Fairfield, N.J.: A.M. Kelley, 1991.

Tooke, Thomas. (1823) *High and Low Prices.* 2 Vols. London: J. Murray.

Tooke, Thomas. (1829) *A Letter to Lord Grenville.* London: J. Murray.

Tooke, Thomas and Newmarch, William. (1838–1857) *A History of Prices.* 6 Vols. London: Longman.

Torrens, Robert. (1815) *An Essay on the External Corn Trade.* Reprinted in the *Collected Works of Robert Torrens*, Vol. 2. Edited by G. de Vivo. Bristol: Thoemmes, 2000.

Bibliography – Secondary Authors

Abel, Andrew. (1987) Ricardian Equivalence Theorem. In *The New Palgrave*, Vol. 4. Pages 174–179. Edited by J. Eatwell, M. Milgate and P. Newman. London: Macmillan.

Acworth, A. W. (1925) *Financial Reconstruction in England.* London: King.

Ahiakpor, James. (1985) Ricardo on Money: The Operational Significance of the Non-neutrality of Money in the Short Run. *History of Political Economy*, **17**(1): 17–30.

Ahiakpor, James and Carr, Jack. (1982) Ricardo on the Non-neutrality of Money in a World with Taxes. *History of Political Economy*, **14**(2): 147–165.

Andreades, Michael. (1966) *History of the Bank of England 1640 to 1903*. 4th English edition. London: F. Cass.

Arnon, Arie. (1987) Banking between the Invisible and Visible Hands. *Oxford Economic Papers*, **39**(2): 268–281.

Arnon, Arie. (1989) The Early Tooke and Ricardo: A Political Alliance and First Signs of Theoretical Disagreements. *History of Political Economy*, **21**(1): 1–14.

Arnon, Arie. (1991) *Thomas Tooke: Pioneer of Monetary Theory*. Ann Arbor: Elgar.

Arnon, Arie. (1999) Free and Not So Free Banking Theories among the Classicals. *History of Political Economy*, **31**(1): 79–107.

Ashton, T. S. (1959) *Economic Fluctuations in England, 1700–1800*. Oxford: Clarendon Press.

Aspinall, A. (1926) English Party Organization in the Early Nineteenth Century. *The English Historical Review*, **41**(163): 389–411.

Aspinall, A. and Smith, E., eds. (1959) *English Historical Documents, 1783–1832*, Vol. 11. London: Eyre & Spottiswoode.

Barnes, Donald. (1930) *A History of the English Corn Laws*. Reprint, New York: A.M. Kelley, 1965.

Baumol, William. (1977) Say's (at Least) Eight Laws, or What Say and James Mill May Really Have Meant. *Economica*, **44**(174): 145–162.

Baumol, William. (1997) J. B. Say on Unemployment and Public Works. *Eastern Economic Journal*, **23**(2): 219–230.

Baumol, William. (2003) Say's Law and More Recent Macro Literature. In *Two Hundred Years of Say's Law*, pages 34–38. Edited by Steven Kates. Northampton: Edward Elgar.

Berg, Maxine. (1980) *The Machinery Question and the Making of Political Economy*. New York: Cambridge University Press.

Bladen, Vincent. (1974) *From Adam Smith to Maynard Keynes*. Toronto: University of Toronto Press.

Blaug, Mark. (1956) The Empirical Content of Ricardian Economics. *Journal of Political Economy*, **64**: 41–58. Reprinted in *David Ricardo: Critical Assessments* (1985) Vol. 1, pages 157–177.

Blaug, Mark. (1958) *Ricardian Economics*. New Haven: Yale University Press.

Blaug, Mark. (1963) The Myth of the Old Poor Law and the Making of the New. *Journal of Economic History*, **23**(2): 151–184.

Blaug, Mark. (1964) The Poor Law Report Reexamined. *Journal of Economic History*, **24**(2): 229–245.

Blaug, Mark. (1980) Marx's Bourgeois Mentor. *Times Literary Supplement*, April 11, 1980: 421.

Bonar, James. (1885) *Malthus and His Work*. London: Macmillan.

Bowley, A. L. (1898–1899) The Statistics of Wages in the United Kingdom during the Last Hundred Years. Parts 1–5. *Journal of the Royal Statistical Society,* December 1898, March, June, September, and December 1899.

Boyer, George. (1990) *An Economic History of the English Poor Law, 1750–1850.* New York: Cambridge University Press.

Broz, J. (1997) The Domestic Politics of International Monetary Order: The Gold Standard. In *Contested Social Orders and International Politics: A Critical Reader,* pages 53–91. Edited by David Skidmore. Nashville: Vanderbilt University Press.

Buchanan, James. (1976) Barro on the Ricardian Equivalence Theorem. *Journal of Political Economy,* **84**(2): 337–342.

Buer, M. C. (1921) The Trade Depression Following the Napoleonic Wars. *Economica,* **1**(2): 159–79.

Churchman, Nancy. (1999) Public Debt Policy and Public Extravagance. *History of Political Economy,* **31**(1): 653–673.

Claphan, John. (1945) The Bank of England: a History. 2 Vols. New York: Macmillan.

Clarke, Peter. (1988) *The Keynesian Revolution in the Making, 1924–1936.* Oxford: Clarendon Press.

Coleman, William. (1996) How Theory Came to English Classical Economics. *Scottish Journal of Political Economy,* **43**(2): 207–228.

Corry, B. A. (1958) The Theory of the Economic Effects of Government Expenditure in English Classical Political Economy. *Economica,* **24**: 34–48.

Corry, B. A. (1962) *Money, Saving and Investment in English Economics.* London: Macmillan.

David Ricardo: Critical Assessments. (1985–1994) 7 Vols. Edited by John Wood. London: Croom Helm.

Davis, T. (1999) Ricardo's Use of Say's Law: The Case of the Post-Napoleonic War Depression, Chapter 16 in *Reflections on the Classical Cannon in Economics.* 1st edition. Edited by Evelyn Forget. New York: Routledge.

Davis, T. (2002) David Ricardo, Financier and Empirical Economist. *European Journal of the History of Economic Thought,* **9**(1): 1–16.

Davis, T. (2003) The Historical Context of the General Glut Controversy, Chapter 8 in *Two Hundred Years of Say's Law: Essays on Economic Theory's Most Controversial Principle.* Edited by Steven Kates. Cheltenham, UK, and Northampton, Mass.: Edward Elgar.

Dean, P. and Cole, W. A. (1967) *British Economic Growth, 1688–1959.* 2nd edition. Cambridge: Cambridge University Press.

De Marchi, N. B. (1970) The Empirical Content and Longevity of Ricardian Economics. *Economica,* **37**: 257–276.

De Vivo, G. (1987) David Ricardo. In *The New Palgrave,* pages 183–198. Edited by J. Eatwell, M. Milgate, and P. Newman. London: Macmillan.

Dictionary of National Biography (DNB). (1949–1950) 22 Vols. New York: Oxford University Press.

Duffy, I. P. (1982) Discount Policy of the Bank of England during the Suspension of Cash Payments. *Economic History Review,* 2nd ser., **35**(1): 67–81.

Eagly, Robert and Smith, Kerry. (1976) Domestic and International Integration of the London Money Market, 1731–1789. *Journal of Economic History*, **36**(1): 198–212.

Eichengreen, Barry. (1996) *Globalizing Capital: A History of the International Monetary System*. Princeton: Princeton University Press.

Feinstein, C., Temin, P., and Toniolo, G. (1997) *The European Economy between the Wars*. New York: Oxford University Press.

Ferguson, C. (1973) The Specialization Gap: Barton, Ricardo and Hollander. *History of Political Economy*, **5**(1): 1–13. Reprinted in *David Ricardo: Critical Assessments* (1985) Vol. 4, pages 90–99.

Fetter, Frank. (1953) Authorship of Economic Articles in the *Edinburgh Review*. *Journal of Political Economy*, **61**(3): 232–259.

Fetter, Frank. (1958) The Economic Articles in the *Quarterly Review* and Their Authors. *Journal of Political Economy*, **66**(1): 47–64; **66**(2): 154–170.

Fetter, Frank. (1960) Economic Articles in *Blackwood's*. *Scottish Journal of Political Economy*, **7**: 85–107; 213–31.

Fetter, Frank. (1962) Economic Articles in the *Westminster Review* and Their Authors. *Journal of Political Economy*, **70**(6): 570–596.

Fetter, Frank. (1964) *Selected Economic Writings of Thomas Attwood*. London: LSE.

Fetter, Frank. (1965) *The Development of British Monetary Orthodoxy, 1797–1875*. Cambridge, Mass.: Harvard University Press.

Fetter, Frank. (1969) The Rise and Decline of Ricardian Economics. *History of Political Economy*, **1**: 67–84. Reprinted in *David Ricardo: Critical Assessments* (1994) Vol. 5, pages 15–30.

Fetter, Frank. (1980) *The Economist in Parliament: 1780–1868*. Durham, N.C.: Duke University Press.

Flinn, M. W. (1961) The Poor Employment Act of 1817. *Economic History Review*, 2nd series, **1**(1): 82–92.

Friedman, Milton. (1987) The Quantity Theory of Money. In *The New Palgrave*, Vol. 4. Edited by J. Eatwell, M. Milgate, and P. Newman. London: Macmillan.

Fussell, G. and Compton, M. (1939) Agricultural Adjustments after the Napoleonic Wars. *Economic History*, **3**(14): 184–204.

Galbraith, J. K. (1995) *Money: Whence It Came, Where It Went*. New York: Houghton Mifflin.

Gallarotti, Giulio. (1995) *The Anatomy of an International Monetary Regime: The Classical Gold Standard, 1880–1914*. New York: Oxford University Press.

Gayer, A. D., Rostow, W. W., and Schwartz, A. J. (1953) *The Growth and Fluctuation of the British Economy*, Vol. 1. Oxford: Clarendon Press.

Gilbert, Martin. (1976) *Winston S. Churchill, 1922–1939*, Vol. 5. Reprint, London: Heinemann, 1990.

Haberler, Gottfried. (1960) *Prosperity and Depression*. Cambridge: Harvard University Press.

Hamilton, Henry. (1956) The Failure of the Ayr Bank, 1772. *Economic History Review*, **8**: 405–17.

Hawtrey, R. G. (1923) *Currency and Credit*. 2nd edition. London: Longmans.

Hawtrey, R. G. (1931) *Trade Depression and the Way Out*. New York: Longmans.

Hawtrey, R. G. (1932) *The Art of Central Banking*. Reprint, New York: F. Cass, 1970.

Hawtrey, R. G. (1934) *Currency and Credit*. London: Longmans.

Hayek, F. A. (1942) The Ricardo Effect. *Economica*, **5**: 127–152.

Heckscher, Eli. (1922) *The Continental System: An Economic Interpretation*. Edited by Harald Westergaard. Reprint, Gloucester, Mass.: Peter Smith, 1964.

Heertje, Arnold. (1991) Three Unpublished Letters by David Ricardo. *History of Political Economy*, **23**(3): 519–526.

Heertje, A. and Weatherall, D. (1978) An Unpublished Letter of David Ricardo to Thomas Smith of Easton Grey. *Economic Journal*, **88**(351): 569–71. Reprinted in *David Ricardo: Critical Assessments* (1985) Vol. 4, pages 152–155.

Heertje, A., Polak, R. and Weatherall, D. (1985) An Unpublished Letter of David Ricardo to Francis Finch. *Economic Journal*, **95**(380): 1091–1092. Reprinted in *David Ricardo: Critical Assessments* (1994) Vol. 6, pages 282–284.

Hicks, J. R. (1967) *Critical Essays in Monetary Theory*. Oxford: Clarendon Press.

Hicks, J. R. (1969) *A Theory of Economic History*. Oxford: Oxford University Press.

Hicks, J. R. and Hollander, S. (1977) Mr. Ricardo and the Moderns. *Quarterly Journal of Economics*, **91**(3): 351–369.

Hilton, Boyd. (1977) *Corn, Cash, Commerce*. Oxford: Oxford University Press.

Hollander, Jacob. (1911a) The Work and Influence of Ricardo. *American Economic Review*, **1**: 71–84. Reprinted in *David Ricardo: Critical Assessments* (1985) Vol. 1, pages 42–51.

Hollander, Jacob. (1911b) The Development of the Theory of Money from Adam Smith to David Ricardo. *Quarterly Journal of Economics*, **25**(May): 429–470.

Hollander, Samuel. (1969) Malthus and the Post-Napoleonic Depression. *History of Political Economy*, **1**: 306–335.

Hollander, Samuel. (1971) The Development of Ricardo's Position on Machinery. *History of Political Economy*, **3**: 105–135.

Hollander, Samuel. (1973) *The Economics of Adam Smith*. Toronto: University of Toronto Press.

Hollander, Samuel. (1977) Ricardo and the Corn Laws: A Revision. *History of Political Economy*, **9**: 1–47.

Hollander, Samuel. (1979) *The Economics of David Ricardo*. Toronto: University of Toronto Press.

Hollander, Samuel. (1982) The Economics of David Ricardo: A Response to Professor O'Brien. *Oxford Economic Papers*, **34**(1): 224–246.

Hollander, Samuel. (1984) The Wage Path in Classical Growth Models: Ricardo, Malthus and Mill. *Oxford Economic Papers*, **36**(2): 200–212. Reprinted in S. Hollander (1995), *Ricardo: The New View, Collected Essays*, Vol. 1, pages 195–201. New York: Routledge.

Hollander, Samuel. (1987) *Classical Economics*. New York: Basil Blackwell.

Hollander, Samuel. (1989a) On Composition of Demand and Income Distribution in Classical Economics. *History of Economics Society Bulletin*, **11**(2): 216–221. Reprinted in S. Hollander (1995), *Ricardo: The New View, Collected Essays*, Vol. 1, pages 195–201. New York: Routledge.

Hollander, Samuel. (1989b) Review of *History and the Economic Past* by D. C. Coleman. *Albion*, **21**(Fall): 525–27. Reprinted in S. Hollander (1995), *The Literature of Political Economy, Collected Essays*, Vol. 2, pages 393–396. New York: Routledge.

Hollander, Samuel. (1992) On Malthus' Abandonment of Agricultural Protection. *American Economic Review*, **82**: 650–659.

Hollander, Samuel. (1995a) Review of *Thomas Tooke: Pioneer of Monetary Theory* by Arie Arnon. *Research in the History of Economic Thought and Methodology*, **13**: 271–76. Reprinted in S. Hollander (1995), *The Literature of Political Economy, Collected Essays*, Vol. 2, pages 187–192. New York: Routledge.

Hollander, Samuel. (1995b) Sraffa's Rational Reconstruction of Ricardo: On Three Contributions to the *Cambridge Journal of Economics*. In *Ricardo – The New View, Collected Essays*, Vol. 1, pages 79–88. New York: Routledge.

Hollander, Samuel. (1997) *The Economics of Thomas Robert Malthus*. Toronto: University of Toronto Press.

Hollander, Samuel. (2001) Classical Economics: A Reification Wrapped in an Anachronism? In the festschrift *Reflections on the Classical Canon in Economics*, pages 7–26. Edited by E. L. Forget and S. Peart. New York: Routledge.

Homer, Sidney and Sylla, Richard. (1991) *A History of Interest Rates*. 3rd edition. New Brunswick, N.J.: Rutgers University Press.

Horsefield, J. K. (1944) Origins of the Bank Charter Act of 1844. *Economica*, **11**(44): 180–189.

Horsefield, J. K. (1949) The Bankers and the Bullionists in 1819. *Journal of Political Economy*, **57**(5): 442–448.

Hutchison, T. W. (1952) Some Questions about Ricardo. *Economica*, **19**: 415–432. Reprinted in *David Ricardo: Critical Assessments* (1985) Vol. 1, pages 72–85.

Hutchison, T. W. (1953) Ricardo's Correspondence. *Economica*, **20**: 263–273. Reprinted in *David Ricardo: Critical Assessments* (1985) Vol. 1, pages 86–95.

Hutchison, T. W. (1992) *Changing Aims in Economics*. Oxford: Blackwell.

Huzel, James. (1980) The Demographic Impact of the Old Poor Law: More Reflexions on Malthus. *Economic History Review*, 2nd series, **33**: 367–381.

Jenks, Leland. (1927) *The Migration of British Capital to 1875*. Reprint, London: T. Nelson, 1963.

Jonsson, P. O. (1997) On Gluts, Effective Demand and the True Meaning of Say's Law. *Eastern Economic Journal*, **23**(2): 203–218.

Kates, Steven. (1997) On the True Meaning of Say's Law. *Eastern Economic Journal*, **23**(2): 191–202.

Keynes, J. M. (1933) *Essays in Biography*. London: Macmillan.

Keynes, J. M. (1963) *Essays in Persuasion*. New York: W.W. Norton.

Keynes, J. M. (1971) *A Tract on Monetary Reform*. Vol. 4 of *The Collected Writings of John Maynard Keynes*. Edited by Donald Moggridge. London: Macmillan.

Keynes, J. M. (1972) *Essays in Biography*. Vol. 10 of *The Collected Writings of John Maynard Keynes*. Edited by Donald Moggridge. London: Macmillan.

Keynes, J. M. (1973a) *The General Theory of Employment, Interest and Money*. Vol. 7 of *The Collected Writings of John Maynard Keynes*. Edited by Donald Moggridge. London: Macmillan.

Keynes, J. M. (1973b) *The General Theory and After: Preparation*. Vol. 13 of *The Collected Writings of John Maynard Keynes*. Edited by Donald Moggridge. London: Macmillan.

Keynes, J. M. (1973c) *The General Theory and After: Defense and Development*. Vol. 14 of *The Collected Writings of John Maynard Keynes*. Edited by Donald Moggridge. London: Macmillan.

Keynes, J. M. (1981a) *Activities 1922–1929: The Return of Gold and Industrial Policy*. Vol. 19 of *The Collected Writings of John Manyard Keynes*. Edited by Donald Moggridge. London: Macmillan.

Keynes, J. M. (1981b) *Activities 1929–1931: Rethinking Employment and Unemployment Policies*. Vol. 20 of *The Collected Writings of John Maynard Keynes*. Edited by Donald Moggridge. London: Macmillan.

Klein, Judy. (1997) *Statistical Visions in Time*. New York: Cambridge University Press.

Klein, Lawrence. (1961) *The Keynesian Revolution*. New York: Macmillan.

Klein, Lawrence. (1966) *The Keynesian Revolution*. 2nd edition. New York: Macmillan.

Laidler, David. (1987) Henry Thornton. In *The New Palgrave*, Vol. 4. Edited by J. Eatwell, M. Milgate, and P. Newman. London: Macmillan.

Laidler, David. (1989) The Bullionist Controversy. In *The New Palgrave: Money*, pages 60–71. Edited by J. Eatwell, M. Milgate, and P. Newman. London: Norton.

Laidler, David. (1991a) *Golden Age of the Quantity Theory*. Princeton, N.J.: Princeton University Press.

Laidler, David. (1991b) The Quantity Theory Is Always and Everywhere Controversial – Why? *The Economic Record*, **67**: 289–306.

Laidler, David. (1999) *Fabricating the Keynesian Revolution: Studies of the Inter-War Literature on Money, the Cycle, and Unemployment*. New York: Cambridge University Press.

Lange, Oscar. (1942) Say's Law: A Restatement and Criticism. In *Studies in Mathematical Economics and Econometrics*. Edited by O. Lange, M. McIntyre, and T. Yntema. Reprint, Freeport, N.Y.: Books for Libraries Press, 1968.

Langford, Paul. (1989) *A Polite and Commercial People: England, 1727–1783*. New York: Oxford University Press.

Link, Robert. (1959) *English Theories of Economic Fluctuations, 1815–1898*. New York: Columbia University Press.

Macleod, Henry. (1855–1856) *The Theory and Practice of Banking*. 2 Vols. 1st edition. London: Longmans.

Macleod, Henry. (1902–1906) *The Theory and Practice of Banking*. 2 Vols. 6th edition. London: Longmans.

Maital, S. and Haswell, P. (1977) Why Did Ricardo (Not) Change His Mind? On Money and Machinery. *Economica*, **44**(176): 359–368.

Marcuzzo, M. and Rosselli, A. (1994) Ricardo's Theory of Money Matters. *Revue Economique*, **45**(5): 1251–1267.

Mitchell, Brian. (1988) *British Historical Statistics*. Cambridge: Cambridge University Press.

Mitchell, B. R. and Deane, P. (1962) *Abstract of British Historical Statistics*. Reprint, Cambridge: Cambridge University Press, 1971.

Mitchell, W. (1949) *Lecture Notes on Types of Economic Theory*. New York: A.M. Kelley.

Mitchison, Rosalind. (1959) The Old Board of Agriculture, 1793–1822. *The English Historical Review*, **74**(290): 41–69.

Moggridge, D. E. (1972) *British Monetary Policy 1924–1931: The Norman Conquest of $4.86*. Cambridge: Cambridge University Press.

Morgan, Victor. (1939) Some Aspects of the Bank Restriction Period, 1797–1821. *Economic History*, **3**(14): 205–221.

Morgan, Victor (1943) *The Theory and Practice of Central Banking, 1797–1913*. Cambridge: Cambridge University Press.

Neal, Larry. (1987) The Integration and Efficiency of the London and Amsterdam Stock Markets in the Eighteenth Century. *Journal of Economic History*, **47**(1): 97–115.

Niehans, Jurg. (1987) Classical Monetary Theory, New and Old. *Journal of Money, Credit and Banking*, **19**(4): 409–424.

Niehans, Jurg. (1990) *A History of Economic Theory*. Baltimore: Johns Hopkins University Press.

O'Brien, D. P. (1975) *The Classical Economists*. Oxford: Clarendon Press.

O'Brien, D. P. (1981) Ricardian Economics and the Economics of David Ricardo. *Oxford Economic Papers*, **33**(1): 1–35.

O'Brien, D. P. (1982) Ricardian Economics. *Oxford Economic Papers*, **34**(2): 247–252.

Patinkin, Don. (1948) Relative Prices, Say's Law and the Demand for Money. *Econometrica*, **16**(2): 135–154.

Patinkin, Don. (1949) The Indeterminacy of Absolute Prices in Classical Economic Theory. *Econometrica*, **17**(1): 1–27.

Patinkin, Don. (1951) The Invalidity of Classical Monetary Theory. *Econometrica*, **19**(2): 134–151.

Peach, Terry. (1993) *Interpreting Ricardo*. Cambridge: Cambridge University Press.

Peach, Terry. (1995) Unemployment in Post-Napoleonic Britain: The Ricardo–Malthus Debate Revisited. *History of Economic Thought Newsletter*, **54**: 6–8.

Peake, Charles. (1978) Henry Thornton and the Development of Ricardo's Economic Thought. *History of Political Economy*, **10**(2): 193–212.

Pullen, J. M. (1995) Malthus on Agricultural Protection: An Alternative View. *History of Political Economy*, **27**(3): 517–529.

Redford, Arthur. (1976) *Labour Migration in England, 1800–1850*. 3rd edition. Edited by W. H. Chaloner. Manchester: Manchester University Press.

Robbins, Lionel. (1967) Malthus as an Economist. *The Economic Journal*, **77**: 256–261.

Robbins, Lionel. (1968) *The Theory of Economic Development in the History of Economic Thought*. London: Macmillan.

Robbins, Lionel. (1970) *The Evolution of Modern Economic Theory*. London: Macmillan.

Robbins, Lionel. (1976) *Political Economy: Past and Present*. London: Macmillan.

Roberts, R. O. (1942) Ricardo's Theory of Public Debts. *Economica*, 9(35): 257–266.

Roberts, R. and Kynaston, D. (1995) *The Bank of England*. New York: Oxford University Press.

Robinson, Joan. (1978) Keynes and Ricardo. *Journal of Post Keynesian Economics*, 1(1): 12–18. Reprinted in *David Ricardo: Critical Assessments* (1985) Vol. 4, pages 146–151.

Rose, Michael. (1971) *The English Poor Law, 1780–1930*. Newton Abbott: David and Charles.

Rostow, W. W. (1942) Adjustments and Maladjustments after the Napoleonic Wars. *American Economic Review*, 32(1): Suppl. Part 2: 13–23.

Rousseaux, P. (1938) *Les Mouvements de Fond de l'economie Anglaise, 1800–1913*. Louvain.

Ruffin, Roy. (2002) David Ricardo's Discovery of Comparative Advantage. *History of Political Economy*, 34(4): 727–748.

Rutherford, R. P. (1987) Malthus and Keynes. *Oxford Economic Papers*, 39(1): 175–189.

Ryan, Franklin. (1924) *Usury and Usury Laws*. Boston: Houghton Mifflin.

Samuelson, Paul. (1978) The Canonical Classical Model of Political Economy. *Journal of Economic Literature*, 16(4): 1415–1434.

Samuelson, Paul. (1989) Ricardo was Right! *Scandinavian Journal of Economics*, 91(1): 47–62.

Sayers, R. S. (1953) Ricardo's Views on Monetary Questions. *Quarterly Journal of Economics*, 67: 30–49. Reprinted in *David Ricardo: Critical Assessments* (1985) Vol. 4, pages 53–68.

Sayers, R. S. (1970) The Return to Gold, 1925. In *The Gold Standard and Employment Policies Between the Wars*. Edited by Sidney Pollard. London: Methuen & Co.

Schumpeter, J. A. (1954) *History of Economic Analysis*. New York: Oxford University Press.

Schwartz, Anna. (1989) Banking School, Currency School, Free Banking School. In *The New Palgrave: Money*, pages 41–49. Edited by J. Eatwell, M. Milgate, and P. Newman. London: Norton.

Schumpeter, Elizabeth. (1938) English Prices and Public Finance, 1660–1822. *Review of Economic Statistics*, 20: 21–37.

Silberling, N. J. (1923) British Prices and Business Cycles, 1779–1850. *Review of Economic Statistics*, 5: 223–247. Silberling's price index is reprinted in Morgan (1939).

Skinner, A. S. (1967) Say's Law: Origins and Content. *Economica*, 34(134): 153–166.

Skinner, A. S. (1969) Of Malthus, Lauderdale and Say's Law. *Scottish Journal of Political Economy*, 16: 177–195.

Smart, William. (1910–1917) *Economic Annals of the Nineteenth Century*. 2 Vols. Reprint, New York: A.M. Kelley, 1964.

Sowell, T. (1963) The General Glut Controversy Reconsidered. *Oxford Economic Papers*, **15**: 193–203.

Sowell, T. (1972) *Say's Law: An Historical Analysis*. Princeton, N.J.: Princeton University Press.

Sowell, T. (1974) *Classical Economics Reconsidered*. Princeton, N.J.: Princeton University Press.

Sraffa, Piero. (1951) Introduction to *The Works and Correspondence of David Ricardo*, Vol. 1, pages xxx–xxxiii. Cambridge: Cambridge University Press.

Stigler, G. J. (1953) Sraffa's Ricardo. *American Economic Review*, **43**: 586–599.

Toye, John. (2000) *Keynes on Population*. New York: Oxford University Press.

Trebilcock, Clive. (1969) "Spin-Off" in British Economic History: Armaments and Industry, 1760–1914. *Economic History Review*, 2nd ser, **22**: 474–490.

Tucker, G. S. L. (1960) *Progress and Profits in British Economic Thought*. Cambridge: Cambridge University Press.

Viner, J. (1924) *Canada's Balance of International Indebtedness*. Reprint, Toronto: McClelland and Stewart, 1975.

Viner, J. (1937) *Studies in the Theory of International Trade*. Reprint, New York: A.M. Kelley, 1965.

Winch, Donald. (1987) *Malthus*. Oxford: Oxford University Press.

Wrigley, E. A. (1988) *Continuity, Chance and Change*. Cambridge: Cambridge University Press.

Wrigley, E. A. and Schofield, R. S. (1981) *The Population History of England, 1541–1871*. London: Edward Arnold.

Index